Kim Kaye-Small
248-889-5144

Thou Shall Not Steal

Alfred
Delp, sj

:)

D0062630

MODERN SPIRITUAL MASTERS
Robert Ellsberg, Series Editor

This series introduces the writing and vision of some of the great spiritual masters of the twentieth century. Along with selections from their writings, each volume includes a comprehensive introduction, presenting the author's life and writings in context and drawing attention to points of special relevance to contemporary spirituality.

Some of these authors found a wide audience in their lifetimes. In other cases recognition has come long after their deaths. Some are rooted in long-established traditions of spirituality. Others charted new, untested paths. In each case, however, the authors in this series have engaged in a spiritual journey shaped by the influences and concerns of our age. Such concerns include the challenges of modern science, religious pluralism, secularism, and the quest for social justice.

At the dawn of a new millennium this series commends these modern spiritual masters, along with the saints and witnesses of previous centuries, as guides and companions to a new generation of seekers.

Already published:
Dietrich Bonhoeffer (edited by Robert Coles)
Simone Weil (edited by Eric O. Springsted)
Henri Nouwen (edited by Robert A. Jonas)
Pierre Teilhard de Chardin (edited by Ursula King)
Anthony de Mello (edited by William Dych, S.J.)
Charles de Foucauld (edited by Robert Ellsberg)
Oscar Romero (by Marie Dennis, Rennie Golden,
    and Scott Wright)
Eberhard Arnold (edited by Johann Christoph Arnold)
Thomas Merton (edited by Christine M. Bochen)
Thich Nhat Hanh (edited by Robert Ellsberg)
Rufus Jones (edited by Kerry Walters)
Mother Teresa (edited by Jean Maalouf)
Edith Stein (edited by John Sullivan, O.C.D.)
John Main (edited by Laurence Freeman)
Mohandas Gandhi (edited by John Dear)
Mother Maria Skobtsova (introduction by Jim Forest)
Evelyn Underhill (edited by Emilie Griffin)
St. Thérèse of Lisieux (edited by Mary Frohlich)
Flannery O'Connor (edited by Robert Ellsberg)
Clarence Jordan (edited by Joyce Hollyday)

ALFRED DELP, SJ

Prison Writings

With an Introduction by
THOMAS MERTON

ORBIS BOOKS

Maryknoll, New York 10545

Founded in 1970, Orbis Books endeavors to publish works that enlighten the mind, nourish the spirit, and challenge the conscience. The publishing arm of the Maryknoll Fathers and Brothers, Orbis seeks to explore the global dimensions of the Christian faith and mission, to invite dialogue with diverse cultures and religious traditions, and to serve the cause of reconciliation and peace. The books published reflect the views of their authors and do not represent the official position of the Maryknoll Society. To learn more about Maryknoll and Orbis Books, please visit our website at www.maryknoll.org.

Copyright © 2004 by Orbis Books

Published by Orbis Books, Maryknoll, NY 10545-0308.

First published in German as *Im Angesicht des Todes* by Verlag Josef Knecht, Carolusdruckerei, Frankfurt am Main, 1958.

First English edition, published as *The Prison Meditations of Father Alfred Delp,* copyright © 1962 by Bloomsbury Publishing Co. Ltd. (New York: Herder and Herder, 1963).

Introduction by Thomas Merton, © Copyright 1963 by The Abbey of Gethsemani. Reprinted in *Faith and Violence* by Thomas Merton. Copyright 1968, 1994 by University of Notre Dame Press, Notre Dame, Indiana 46556.

Queries regarding rights and permissions should be addressed to:
Orbis Books, P.O. Box 308, Maryknoll, NY 10545-0308.

Manufactured in the United States of America.

Library of Congress Cataloging-in-Publication Data

Delp, Alfred.
   [Im Angesicht des Todes. English]
   Alfred Delp, SJ : prison writings / with an introduction by Thomas Merton.
     p. cm.
   ISBN 1-57075-524-8 (pbk.)
   1. Delp, Alfred. 2. Jesuits – Germany – Biography. 3. Meditations. Title: Prison writings. II. Merton, Thomas, 1915-1968. III. Title.

BX4705.D422A53 2004
242 – dc22

                                    2003066163

Contents

Biographical Preface
by Alan C. Mitchell

In 1947, a volume of selected writings of Fr. Alfred Delp, SJ, was published in Germany under the title, *Im Angesicht des Todes* ("In the Face of Death").[1] Paul Bolkovac, SJ, Delp's friend and confrere, edited the work. It was a selection of letters and meditations, which Delp had written between August 1944 and January 1945, while he was in prison in Berlin, awaiting trial and execution. He had been charged with high treason and the betrayal of his country for participating in anti-Nazi discussions and for preaching against National Socialism. That book was so widely read that by 1981 it appeared in its 11th edition.

The first English edition of any of Delp's writings was, in fact, a translation of Bolkovac's book, published in 1963 by Herder and Herder, under the title *The Prison Meditations of Fr. Alfred Delp*. Thomas Merton wrote an Introduction for that volume, in which he called attention to Delp's Christian witness in the face of a godless totalitarian regime. Some fifty-eight years after his death, Delp's words still capture the imagination and draw attention to what is of lasting value and true in the human heart. Delp's story is as dramatic and compelling today as it was in 1944–45. The present volume reprints the Herder edition.

Alfred Delp was born on September 15, 1907, in Mannheim, Germany, the second of six children of Johann Adam Friedrich Delp, a Lutheran, and Maria Bernauer, a Roman Catholic. His childhood was happy and uneventful, except for the fact that he experienced an early conflict of faith. Although he had been baptized a Catholic, he was, for his first fourteen years, raised as a Lutheran. After a falling out with the Lutheran pastor, he went to the local Catholic parish in Lampertheim, where his family lived, and followed in the religion of his mother.

Delp was a playful and mischievous child; in his own judgment, a rascal.[2] He was also bright and energetic. He began his elementary education in the local Lutheran school, but transferred to a diocesan-run Catholic school in Dieberg to finish it. Upon finishing his elementary education, he remained in that town, attending the Goethe School, a classical German gymnasium. One month after he completed his secondary education he entered the Jesuit Novitiate in Feldkirch, Austria, on August 22, 1926.

At the end of his two-year noviceship, Delp pronounced his first perpetual vows on April 27, 1928. Shortly after that, he moved to the Berchmanskolleg in Pullach, just outside of Munich, to begin the next phase of his Jesuit formation, the study of philosophy. While at Pullach, Delp excelled in his studies, mastering the scholastic philosophy that was the staple of Jesuit formation, and delving into more contemporary philosophical thinkers. In these years, he worked diligently on a book manuscript, a critical study of Martin Heidegger's philosophy, which was published under the title of *Tragic Existence* in 1935.

In April 1931 Delp received Minor Orders, and at the end of June he completed his philosophy exams. Three months later, he moved back to Feldkirch to begin the next phase of his Jesuit formation, regency, as he assumed the position of a Prefect at the Jesuit gymnasium, Stella Matutina.

As with many a Jesuit regent, Delp was immensely popular with his students. He himself found the work demanding. Perhaps his most notable achievement during this time was the writing and production of a Christmas play entitled "The

Eternal Advent." The play was performed on December 21, 1933, after which the school newspaper reported: "The well performed piece so rightly aroused the yearning for Christmas."[3] This play was also Delp's first public foray into social commentary, touching on current issues in German society, as it featured three scenes: the first, dead soldiers, the second, miners cut off from the outside world because of a tunnel collapse, and the third, a worker-priest. The three scenes presented Delp's understanding of a humanity beset by its own desperate circumstances. The meaning of Christmas is developed throughout the play as the hope humans have for being liberated from the extremes of the human condition.[4]

After Hitler came to power, Stella Matutina was forced to close its doors. In the summer of 1933, the Jesuits purchased an old Benedictine monastery in St. Blasien in the Black Forest. It needed a lot of work, and so it could not open for classes until April 1934. Delp moved with the school, as did about 190 boarders from the former Stella Matutina. There he completed his last months of regency.

Delp undertook his theological studies in Valkenburg, Holland, at Ignatiuskolleg in the fall of 1934. During this time, he threw himself into his work. This was a time of intense literary activity for him. Not only did his book *Tragic Existence* appear in 1935, but he also planned a collaborative book with several of his Jesuit confreres, who included Hans Urs von Balthasar and Karl Rahner. This book would engage National Socialism and propose an alternate society to the one being built by the Nazis. It was to be entitled *The Reconstruction*. The project broke down, and the book was never written. Among his *Collected Works,* it remains in outline form only.[5]

In October 1936, Delp moved to Frankfurt to the Jesuit theologate of Sankt Georgen to finish his theological studies. In March 1937 he was ordained sub-deacon and deacon. His ordination to priesthood took place in the Jesuit church of St. Michael in Munich on June 24, 1937, the 400th anniversary of the ordination of Ignatius of Loyola, the Jesuit founder. On July 4, 1937, Delp celebrated his First Mass in his home town of Lampertheim. From July until October, he ministered as a priest at St. Michael's in Munich. He began his tertianship, the last formal phase of a Jesuit's spiritual training in Rottmannshöhe on Lake Starnberg on September 16, 1938. He stayed there, however, only five days, as the tertianship was moved to Feldkirch/Vorarlberg, where he had done his noviceship and part of his regency.

With the permission of his Provincial, Delp had planned to attend the University of Munich to pursue a doctorate in social philosophy. The long-term goal was for him to help begin an institute for social thought. To his disappointment, the Nazi administrator of the University denied him the opportunity to matriculate. Ten days before that, on the basis of his exams at Pullach, he had been awarded a doctorate in Philosophy from the Gregorian University in Rome.[6]

Delp remained in Munich and in July 1939 joined the staff of the Jesuit opinion journal, *Stimmen der Zeit*. He was the editor for social and political matters, and he wrote on a wide range of topics, some that directly challenged National Socialism. Perhaps his most important piece was on "The Christian at the Present Moment" (1939), in which he reflected again on the situation of humans in history, and in particular the place and obligation of the Christian in the world.

The Gestapo shut down the publication of *Stimmen der Zeit* on April 18, 1941. Delp and the other Jesuits working there were forced to go elsewhere. In June, he became the pastor of St. George's church in Munich-Bogenhausen. He offered excellent pastoral care for his people, and even helped them clean up after bombing raids, which damaged their houses. Another important part of Delp's work at this time was to help Jews, by collecting food and money for them and by aiding their escape to Switzerland.

While he was pastor at St. George's, Delp became an instrumental member of a resistance group that had been established by Helmuth James von Moltke and Peter Yorck von Wartenberg. The group met in Kreisau in Silesia, and would later, in 1944, be designated the Kreisau Circle by the Gestapo.[7] The group's purpose was to prepare for the day that National Socialism fell apart, so that it could reconstruct a just society in its place. Von Moltke asked Delp's Provincial, Augustin Rösch, if he could supply the group with a social scientist who might advise them on labor issues affecting German workers and help to design a re-Christianized environment for workers in a post-Nazi Germany.

Rösch, too, was a member of the group, as was another Jesuit, Lothar König. Those participating in the discussions were both Catholics and non-Catholics. They held three weekend meetings in Kreisau in 1942–43, two of which were attended by Delp. Apart from those gatherings they usually met in Berlin, but occasionally they met in Munich, in Delp's rectory. He did not participate in those meetings, but merely offered them a place to meet, and at least on one occasion provided them with a meal. Delp's contribution to the discussions drew a lot on Catholic social teaching, particularly Pius XI's encyclical, *Quadragesimo Anno,* which had been issued in 1931. He also incorporated into his thought ideas he had learned from the Jesuit Oswald von Nell-Breuning and Prof. Adolf Weber, an economist from the University of Munich, whose lectures he audited after he was denied matriculation as a graduate student.[8]

The day he was arrested, July 28, 1944, two Gestapo agents waited outside of St. George's for a while and at some time during the Mass came into the back of the Church, waiting for him to finish. One of them was an old schoolmate of his. It was the feast of Sts. Nazarius, Celsus, Innocent and Victor, two martyrs and two popes. Perhaps the assigned Gospel from Luke 21:9–19, about being handed over to kings and magistrates, cut too close to the bone for a man who must have known his arrest was imminent. He chose instead to say the votive Mass of the Holy Spirit, whose Gospel, John 14:12–23, offered peace in the words, "Do not let your hearts be troubled and do not let them be afraid. You have heard me say I am going away and then I will return."[9] Was he seeking to console himself, signaling to his congregation not to interfere with his arrest, or both?

A rather dramatic moment occurred when his good friend Dr. Ernst Kessler went to the sacristy with a note for Delp, informing him that a secret meeting he had hoped for with the resistance wing of the Social Democrats was rejected, out of concern for security. Kessler gave the note to the sacristan, to place on the altar for Delp to see. He was already at the Offertory of the Mass, so she gave it to him in the sacristy afterward. After he read the note, Delp ate it.[10]

After the Mass, Delp was arrested. As he left his house with the two Gestapo agents he said to those waiting outside, "I've been arrested. God protect you and good-bye."[11] Things became quite hectic as Delp was taken to a Gestapo prison in Munich. His friends tried to locate him. His Provincial went from one prison or Gestapo office to another trying to find him, without success.

During the night of August 6/7 Delp was taken to Berlin by train. As he got off the train, under guard at the Anhalter train station, an old friend of his, Dr. Fritz Valjavec, spotted him and got within earshot to hear Delp say two words under his breath,

"Hapig" and "suitcase." Valjavec understood that Delp wanted him to get a message to Marianne Hapig, a social worker in Berlin, who was active in the resistance. Upon receiving the message she thought that he wanted her to bring him a suitcase with fresh clothing, but then in a telephone conversation with Marianne Pünder, they both remembered that Delp kept a suitcase at home, in which he stored important documents.[12] He may have wanted them to get someone to secure that suitcase. Were there incriminating documents within it?

Delp's Berlin imprisonment has three phases. First, on August 8, 1944, he was placed in a Gestapo prison on Lehrter Street. It was a harsh and hard place, and doubtless he was beaten there, as the blood stains on one of the shirts collected with his laundry would indicate. Again, it took some time for his friends to locate him, but Marianne Hapig did, on August 15. Second, on September 27, he was moved to a prison in the Tegel section of Berlin. The conditions were somewhat better there, and his friends could receive more news about him, since the Lutheran chaplain, Harald Polechau, was a member of the Kreisau Circle. He actually saw to it that Delp had hosts and wine with which to offer Mass. Delp remained there through his trial. Third, on January 31, 1945, he was transferred to the execution site in the prison at Berlin-Plötzensee.

The present volume of writings comes from those months in prison, as he reflected on the Advent season, and wrote letters to his friends, as well as other meditations and reflections. Remarkably, through the agency of the "two Mariannes" (Hapig and Pünder) these writings have survived. They smuggled them all out in his laundry and passed information to him in the same way. In addition to the letters and writings, there are a series of "order slips" that were also used for communication.[13] One of them, dated December 8, 1944, brought Delp the good news that he would be able to pronounce his final vows as a Jesuit. It reported that his dear friend Franz von Tattenbach would visit him and that he had full authority to receive Delp's vows, which were supposed to have been pronounced on August 15.[14]

The story is even more poignant. Delp should have taken the vows in August 1943, but for some reason they were postponed. Since all the information regarding the process of his promotion to final vows is highly confidential, no one knows why they were postponed, and it is pointless to speculate. It is known that the postponement hurt Delp dearly and caused him deep sorrow.[15]

Tattenbach did come, and in a brief but emotional ceremony, Delp pronounced his final vows as a Jesuit on the Feast of the Immaculate Conception. The event was not without its stressful moments. Since the vows had to be recited in Latin, Tattenbach informed the guard that he and Delp would be praying in Latin, and offered him a German translation, so he could follow along. The guard, however, remained suspicious, as he was concerned that they might be passing secret information. When Tattenbach gave Delp the vow formula to read, he was so overcome with emotion that Delp sank in his chair. Worried about the validity of the vows, Tattenbach got Delp to sign the formula and then reminded him that he had to speak it aloud and could not just read it. Delp managed to get the words out in a moving, broken voice.[16]

The next day Delp wrote a letter to Tattenbach apologizing for being so emotional and told him that he was so happy that the Lord considered him worthy enough to wear the chains of love (a reference to the vows) that the actual irons he had to wear daily were now of little importance to him. He also advised that the vow formula be kept safe from a bomb attack. Having suffered so much over the postponement, and not knowing whether he would have pronounced the vows before his death, he wasn't taking any chances on the actual document getting destroyed. He joked that the formula would be a fitting substitute for the letter he would have written asking to leave the Jesuits, had he followed the advice of the Gestapo. They had offered him a deal that he could go free in exchange for his exit from the Society of Jesus.[17]

Delp's daily life was rote during these months of imprisonment. Some days were more stressful than others. At times, he writes of great peace and confidence in God, at others of sleepless nights. He took pleasure in small things, like the communication the two Mariannes perilously conveyed to and from the outside, or when the chains that bound his hands were so loose that he could slip them off freely to celebrate Mass. In his letters he refers to these chains, and they have deep significance in his life. He had thought much and written often on the human condition, particularly on human freedom. Now his final writings were penned "with bound hands." This image must have reminded him of the one he kept on his desk in the rectory of St. George's, the detail of the bound hands of St. Sebastian from the wood-carved statue of Tilman Riemenschneider. One can still purchase a postcard of this detail, entitled "Die gefesselten Hände," "the bound hands."

On December 16, Delp found out from his lawyer what the actual charges were that he faced: (1) his role in the Kreisau resistance group; (2) his participation in resistance discussions in Munich, some of which took place at his rectory; (3) the confession of Nicolaus Gross, that Delp told him that Carl Goerdler and Helmuth von Moltke sought the undoing of National Socialism; (4) the fact that he had met with Claus von Stauffenberg, who was instrumental in placing the bomb in the July 20 attempt on Hitler's life; (5) the statement of Franz Sperr that Delp had confided to him that he had known about von Stauffenberg's plan to kill Hitler; (6) his general attitude towards National Socialism. Sperr's statement was incorrect, as his conversation with Delp took place several days after July 20. In the end, there was very little to proceed on, and Delp was hopeful that he would be acquitted. The Sperr matter concerned him greatly, and he focused his energies and those of his lawyer on getting Sperr to set the record straight. Sperr, however, never recanted.[18]

The trial was high theater, running from January 9 to 11, 1945. The chief judge, Roland Freisler, notorious for his hatred of priests, especially Jesuits, was ruthless and mean-spirited. At one moment he expressed his contempt for Jesuits in an outburst of venom, claiming that he disliked them so much that, if he came to a town or a city and discovered a Jesuit Provincial were there, he would leave it immediately.[19] In the end, Delp was not found to have known of or to have participated in the July 20 assassination attempt. What it all came down to was his association with von Moltke and the fact the he was a Jesuit. All other charges were of no interest to Freisler. Freisler's mind had already been made up about Delp, so that Sperr's claim didn't really play much of a role in his decision. Freisler condemned Delp to death. The day after Delp's execution, Freisler himself was killed in a bombing raid.

The weeks after the trial were especially stressful for Delp, and he could not understand why the usual custom of a quick execution was not being followed. He had hoped against hope that the Russians would reach Berlin and liberate the Nazi prisoners. Delp tried to bring himself to peace and wrote his farewell letters, perhaps the most touching of which are to his mother and to his fellow Jesuits. To them he apologized for his shortcomings, thanked them for their support, and stated clearly what he believed to be the reason for his impending execution: "The actual basis for the judgment is that I am a Jesuit and I have remained one.... The atmosphere of the trial was so infused with hatred and enmity. Its fundamental thesis: a Jesuit is *a priori* an enemy and an opponent of the Reich. Even Moltke was badly mishandled because of his connection to us, especially to Rösch. The whole thing was, on the one hand, a farce and, on the other, it became the defining motif of my life" (*GS*, 4:103).

It is that defining theme that Delp came to appreciate so deeply during his imprisonment. He grasped clearly the irony of his life. A man committed to others and concerned for their true freedom in God now lived deprived of freedom. Someone who dedicated himself completely to justice was so unjustly condemned. A person full of life, who wished life's fullness for his fellow humans beings would now go to his death. A philosopher obsessed with the place of humans in history, and who believed that the humans created their own history, was now a victim of a history he was desperately trying to change. A man of God, whose whole life was given in service to others, was now at the mercy of a godless regime. The months in prison had given him plenty of opportunity to reflect on these and other contradictions of sense. Thus, he came to understand more fully the human condition that he had written about so extensively. With this understanding he stood in the face of death and accepted his fate.

On February 2, 1945, the feast of the Purification of Mary, one of the two days on which a Jesuit could pronounce his final vows, around 10 a.m., Delp made an offering more final than the one he made on the previous December 8.[20] As the Catholic chaplain, Peter Bucholz, bid him farewell, Delp turned to him and said, "May God protect you. In half an hour I will know more than you do."[21] Even in this most extreme situation his sense of humor could not be suppressed. Perhaps he recalled what he wrote in his tertianship retreat journal, "How great is a heart that manifests itself in its ability to make sacrifices. The greatest victory is where the greatest sacrifices have been made" (*GS*, 1:255). Thus he ended his life in victory, as he was hanged in the prison at Berlin-Plötzensee. Delp's corpse was cremated, and his ashes were strewn over a part of Berlin.

On February 15, 1945, his mother, Maria, received an official letter stating: "The religious priest Alfred Delp was condemned to death for high treason and the betrayal of his country by the People's Court of the Great German Reich. The sentence was carried out on February 2, 1945. Any public notice of his death is improper."[22]

Whoever meets Delp in the writings of his last months of life will find a devoted son and brother, a dedicated Jesuit, a patriotic German whose whole life was directed to a better future for his country and his church. There will they meet a man who understood the price of engagement with history, and when they read his story they will understand one of the most profound things he ever wrote: "Whoever does not have the courage to make history, becomes its poor object. Let's do it."[23]

Notes

1. The following sources were used in the writing of this preface: *Alfred Delp S.J.: Kämpfer, Beter, Zeuge,* ed. Marianne Hapig (Berlin: Morus Verlag, 1955); Roman Bleistein, *Alfred Delp: Geschichte eines Zeugen* (Frankfurt: Verlag Josef Knecht, 1989); idem, *Begegnung mit Alfred Delp* (Frankfurt: Verlag Josef Knecht, 1994); idem, "Die Christusnachfolge des P. Alfred Delp: Zu seinem 50. Todestag am 2. Februar," *Geist und Leben* 68 (1995) 24–37; Alfred Delp, *Gesammelte Schriften I–V,* 2nd ed., ed. Roman Bleistein (Frankfurt: Verlag Josef Knecht, 1985); Victor von Gostomski, "Der Todeskandidat in Zelle 317: Erinnerung an Pater Delp im Gefängnis Berlin-Plötzensee," *Regensburger Kirchenzeitung* 51 (1982): 7 and 11; *Glaube als Widerstandskraft: Edith Stein, Alfred Delp, Dietrich Bonhoeffer,* ed. Gotthard Fuchs (Frankfurt: Verlag Josef Knecht, 1986); Benedicta Maria Kempner, *Priester vor Hitlers Tribunalen*

(Munich: Rütten/Loening Verlag, 1966); Petro Müller, *Sozialethik für ein neues Deutschland: Die "Dritte Idee" Alfred Delps* — *ethische Impulse zur Reform der Gesellschaft* (Munich: Lit Verlag, 1994); Oskar Simel, "Alfred Delp SJ † 2.2.1945," *Stimmen der Zeit* 175 (1965): 321–28; Ger van Roon, *Neuordnung im Widerstand: Der Kreisauer Kreis innerhalb der deutschen Widerstandsbewegung* (Munich: R. Oldenbourg Verlag, 1967); Freya von Moltke, *Erinnerungen an Kreisau 1930–1945* (Munich: C. H. Beck Verlag, 1997); Franz von Tattenbach, S.J., "Das entscheidende Gespräch: Zum 10. Todestag P. Alfred Delps, S.J.," *Stimmen der Zeit* 155 (1955) 321–29; idem, "Pater Alfred Delp SJ," in *Bavaria Sancta: Zeugen christlichen Glaubens in Bayern*, vol. 2, ed. Georg Schwaiger (Regensburg: Verlag Friedrich Pustet, 1971), 417–38. Quotations from Delp's writings are indicated in the notes by *GS*, followed by the volume and page numbers. All translations are mine.

2. *GS*, 4:115.
3. Bleistein, *Alfred Delp*, 69.
4. *GS*, 1:51–68.
5. *GS*, 1:195–99.
6. Bleistein, *Alfred Delp*, 442.
7. Ibid., 255.
8. Ibid., 242.
9. Hapig, *Alfred Delp S.J.*, 30.
10. Bleistein, *Alfred Delp*, 296–97.
11. Ibid., 297.
12. Hapig, *Alfred Delp S.J.*, 32.
13. Bleistein, *Alfred Delp*, 321–26.
14. *GS*, 4:38–39.
15. Tattenbach, "Pater Alfred Delp SJ," 426.
16. Bleistein, *Alfred Delp*, 331–34.
17. *GS*, 4:39–41.
18. Bleistein, *Alfred Delp*, 364–70.
19. H. von Moltke quoted by M. Hapig, *Alfred Delp S.J.*, 77.
20. Gostomski, "Der Todeskandidat in Zelle 317," 11.
21. Tattenbach, "Das entscheidende Gespräch," 326.
22. Bleistein, *Alfred Delp*, 411.
23. Ibid., 289.

Father Alfred Delp during his trial.
Photo courtesy of Archivum Monacense SJ, Abt. 80 Nr. 611 © AMSJ München.

Introduction
by Thomas Merton

Those who are used to the normal run of spiritual books and meditations will have to adjust themselves, here, to a new and perhaps disturbing outlook. Written by a man literally in chains, condemned to be executed as a traitor to his country in time of war, these pages are completely free from the myopic platitudes, and the insensitive complacencies of routine piety. Set in the familiar framework of seasonal meditations on the Church year, these are new and often shocking insights into realities which we sometimes discuss academically but which are here experienced in their naked, uncompromising truth. These are the thoughts of a man who, caught in a well-laid trap of political lies, clung desperately to a truth that was revealed to him in solitude, helplessness, emptiness and desperation. Face to face with inescapable physical death, he reached out in anguish for the truth without which his spirit could not breathe and survive. The truth was granted him, and we share it in this book, awed by the realization that it was given him not for himself alone, but for us, who need it just as desperately, perhaps more desperately, than he did.

One of the most sobering aspects of this book is the conviction it imparts that we may one day be in the same desperate situation as the writer. Though we may perhaps still seem to be living in a world where, in spite of wars and rumors of wars, business goes on as usual, and Christianity is what it has always been, Fr. Delp reminds us that somewhere in the last fifty years we have crossed a mysterious limit set by Providence and have entered a new era. We have, in some sense, passed a point of no return, and it is both useless and tragic to continue to live as if we were still in the nineteenth century. Whatever we may think of the new era, whether we imagine it as the millennium, the noosphere, or as the beginning of the end, there has been a violent disruption of society and a radical overthrow of that modern world which goes back to Charlemagne.

In this new era the social structures into which Christianity had fitted so comfortably and naturally, have all but collapsed. The secularist thought patterns which began to assert themselves in the Renaissance, and which assumed control at the French Revolution, have now so deeply affected and corrupted modern man that even where he preserves certain traditional beliefs, they tend to be emptied of their sacred inner reality, and to mask instead the common pseudo-spirituality or the outright nihilism of mass-man. The meditations of Father Delp were written not only in the face of his own death, but in the terrifying presence of this specter of a faceless being that was once the image of God, and toward which the Church nevertheless retains an unchanging responsibility.

The first pages were written in Advent of 1944, when the armies of the Third Reich launched their last, hopeless offensive in the Ardennes. Defeat was already certain. The Nazis alone refused to see it. Hitler was still receiving lucky answers from the stars. Fr. Delp had long since refused to accept the collective delusion. In 1943 at the request of Count Von Moltke and with the permission of his religious Superiors, he had joined in the secret discussions of the "Kreisau Circle," an anti-Nazi group that was planning a new social order to be built on Christian lines after the war. That was all. But since it implied a complete repudiation of the compulsive myths and preposterous fictions of Nazism, it constituted high treason. Since it implied that

Germany might not win it was "defeatism" — a crime worthy of death.

The trial itself was a show, staged by a specialist in such matters. It was handled with ruthless expertise and melodramatic arrogance before an obedient jury and public of SS men and Gestapo agents. The scenario did not provide for a serious defense of the prisoners. Such efforts as they made to protest their innocence were turned against them and only made matters worse. Count Von Moltke and Fr. Delp were singled out as the chief villains, and in Delp's case the prosecution smeared not only the prisoner but the Jesuit Order and the Catholic Church as well. Moltke came under special censure because he had had the temerity to consult bishops and theologians with sinister "re-Christianizing intentions." The prosecution also tried to incriminate Moltke and Delp in the attempted assassination of Hitler the previous July, but this was obviously out of the question and the charge was dropped. This was plainly a religious trial. The crime was heresy against Nazism. As Fr. Delp summed it up in his last letter: "The actual reason for my condemnation was that I happened to be and chose to remain a Jesuit."

Nearly twenty years have passed since Fr. Delp was executed in the Plotzensee prison on February 2, 1945. During these twenty years the world has been supposedly "at peace." But in actual fact, the same chaotic, inexhaustible struggle of armed nations has continued in a different form. A new weaponry, unknown to Fr. Delp, now guarantees that the next total war will be one of titanic destructiveness, when a single nuclear weapon contains more explosive force than all the bombs in World War I put together. In the atmosphere of violent tension that now prevails, there is no less cynicism, no less desperation, no less confusion than Fr. Delp saw around him. Totalitarian fanaticisms have not disappeared from the face of the earth: on the contrary, armed with nuclear weapons, they threaten to possess it entirely. Fascism has not vanished: the state socialism of the Communist countries can justly be rated as a variety of fascism. In the democratic countries of the west, armed to the teeth in defense of freedom, fascism is not unknown. In France, a secret terrorist organization seeks power by intimidation, violence, torture, blackmail, murder. The principles of this organization of military men are explicitly fascist principles. Curiously enough, neo-Nazism recognizes its affinities with the French terrorists and proclaims its solidarity with them. Yet among the French cryptofascists are many who appeal paradoxically to Christian principles, in justification of their ends!

What in fact is the position of Christians? It is ambiguous and confused. Though the Holy See has repeatedly affirmed the traditional classical ethic of social and international justice, and though these pronouncements are greeted with a certain amount of respectful interest, it is increasingly clear that their actual influence is often negligible. Christians themselves are confused and passive, looking this way and that for indications of what to do or think next. The dominating factor in the political life of the average Christian today is fear of Communism. But, as Fr. Delp shows, the domination of fear completely distorts the true perspectives of Christianity and it may well happen that those whose religious activity reduces itself in the long run to a mere negation, will find that their faith has lost all content.

In effect, the temptation to negativism and irrationality, the urge to succumb to pure pragmatism and the massive use of power, is almost overwhelming in our day. Two huge blocs, each armed with a quasi-absolute, irresistible offensive force capable of totally annihilating the other, stand face to face. Each one insists that it is armed in defense of a better world, and for the salvation of mankind. But each tends more and more explicitly to assert that this end cannot be achieved until the enemy is wiped out.

A book like this forces us to stand back and reexamine these oversimplified claims. We are compelled to recall that in the Germany of Fr. Delp's time, Christians were confronted with more or less the same kind of temptation. First there must be a war. After that a new and better world. This was nothing new. It was by now a familiar pattern, not only in Germany but in Russia, England, France, America and Japan.

Was there another choice? Is there another choice today? The western tradition of liberalism has always hoped to attain a more equable world order by peaceful collaboration among nations. This is also the doctrine of the Church. Fr. Delp and Count Von Moltke hoped to build a new Germany on Christian principles. Pope John XXIII in his encyclical *Mater et Magistra* clarified and exposed these principles. If there remains a choice confronting man today, it is the crucial one between global destruction or global order. Those who imagine that in the nuclear age it may be possible to clear the way for a new order with nuclear weapons are even more deluded than the people who followed Hitler, and their error will be a thousand times more tragic, above all if they commit it in the hope of defending their religion.

Fr. Delp had no hesitation in evaluating the choice of those who, in the name of religion, followed the Nazi government in its policy of conquest first and a new world later. He said: "The most pious prayer can become a blasphemy if he who offers it tolerates or helps to further conditions which are fatal to mankind, which render him unacceptable to God, or weaken his spiritual, moral or religious sense."

This certainly applies to cooperation with militant atheism first of all, but it applies equally well to any current equivalent of Nazism or militaristic Fascism.

•

What did Fr. Delp mean by "conditions fatal to mankind?"

His prison meditations are a penetrating diagnosis of a devastated, gutted, faithless society in which man is rapidly losing his humanity because he has become practically incapable of belief. Man's only hope, in this wilderness which he has become, is to respond to his inner need for truth, with a struggle to recover his spiritual freedom. But this he is unable to do unless he first recovers his ability to hear the voice that cries to him in the wilderness: in other words, he must become aware of his devastated and desperate condition before it is too late. There is no question of the supreme urgency of this revival. For Fr. Delp it seems clear that the time is running out.

In these pages we meet a stern, recurrent foreboding that the "voice in the wilderness" is growing fainter and fainter, and that it will soon no longer be heard at all. The world may then sink into godless despair.

Yet the "wilderness" of man's spirit is not yet totally hostile to all spiritual life. On the contrary, its silence is still a healing silence. He who tries to evade solitude and confrontation with the unknown God may eventually be destroyed in the meaningless chaotic atomized solitariness of mass society. But meanwhile it is still possible to face one's inner solitude and to recover mysterious sources of hope and strength. This is still possible. But fewer and fewer men are aware of the possibility. On the contrary: "Our lives today have become godless to the point of complete vacuity."

This is not a cliche of pulpit rhetoric. It is not a comforting slogan to remind the believer that he is right and that the unbeliever is wrong. It is a far more radical assertion, which questions even the faith of the faithful and the piety of the pious. Far from being comforting, this is an alarming declaration of almost Nietzschean scandalousness. "Of all messages this is the most *difficult* to accept — *we find it hard to believe that the man of active faith no longer exists."* An extreme statement, but he follows it with another: "Modern man is not even *capable* of knowing God." In order to understand these harsh assertions by Fr. Delp we must remember they were written by a man in prison, surrounded by Nazi guards. When he speaks of "modern man," he is in fact speaking of the Nazis or of their accomplices and counterparts. Fortunately not all modern men are Nazis. And even in reference to Nazis, when stated thus bluntly and out of context, these statements are still too extreme to be true. They are not meant to be taken absolutely, for if they were simply true, there would be no hope left for anyone, and Fr. Delp's message is in fact a message of hope. He believes that "the great task in the education of present and future generations is to *restore man to a state of fitness for God."* The Church's mission in the world today is a desperate one of helping create conditions in which man can return to himself, recover something of his lost humanity, as a necessary preparation for his ultimate return to God. But as he now is, alienated, void, internally dead, modern man has in effect no capacity for God.

Fr. Delp is not saying that human nature is vitiated in its essence, that we have been abandoned by God or become radically incapable of grace. But the dishonesty and injustice of our world are such, Fr. Delp believes, that we are blind to spiritual things even when we think we are seeing them: and indeed perhaps most blind when we are convinced that we see. "Today's bondage," he says, speaking of Germany in 1944, "is the sign of our untruth and deception."

The untruth of man, from which comes his faithlessness, is basically a matter of arrogance, or of fear. These two are only the two sides of one coin — attachment to material things for their own sake, love of wealth and power. Alienation results in the arrogance of those who have power or in the servility of the functionary who, unable to have wealth and power himself, participates in a power structure which employs him as a utensil. Modern man has surrendered himself to be used more and more as an instrument, as a means, and in consequence his spiritual creativity has dried up at its source. No longer alive with passionate convictions, but centered on his own empty and alienated self, man becomes destructive, negative, violent. He loses all insight, all compassion, and his instinctual life is cruelly perverse. Or else his soul, shocked into insensitivity by suffering and alienation, remains simply numb, inert and hopeless. In such varying conditions, man continues in "blind conflict with reality" and hence his life is a repeated perpetration of a basic untruth. Either he still hopes in matter and in the power he acquires by its manipulation, and then his heart is one to which "God himself cannot find access, it is so hedged around with insurance." Or else, in abject self-contempt, alienated man "believes more in his own unworthiness than in the creative power of God."

Both these conditions are characteristic of materialist man, but they also appear in a pseudo-Christian guise. This is particularly true of the negative, lachrymose and "resigned" Christianity of those who manage to blend the cult of the status quo with a habit of verbalizing on suffering and submission. For such as these, indifference to real evil has become a virtue, and preoccupation with petty or imaginary problems of piety substitutes for the creative unrest of the truly spiritual man. A few phrases about the Cross and a few formal practices of piety concord, in such religion, with a profound apathy, a bloodless lassitude, and perhaps an almost total incapacity to love. It is the indifference of a man who, having surrendered his humanity, imagines that he is therefore pleasing to God. Unfortunately Fr. Delp suggests that such a one is already faithless, already prepared for any one of the modern pseudo religions, the worship of the Class, Race or State.

What can be done to save such resigned and negative Christians from becoming crypto-fascists? Certainly no amount of "baroque glamorizing" of the mysteries of faith, no dramatic banalities, no false glitter of new apologetic techniques. Seen from the silence of Fr. Delp's prison cell, the much publicized movements dedicated to so many worthy ends, take on a pitiable air of insignificance. Too often, he says, these efforts represent a failure to meet the genuine needs of man. Sometimes they do not imply even an elementary awareness of man's real desperation. Instead of being aimed at those whom the Church most needs to seek, these movements seem to him in many cases to concern themselves with the hunger of pious souls for their own satisfaction: they produce an illusion of holiness and a gratifying sense that one is accomplishing something.

Instead of the difficult exploratory and diagnostic work of seeking modern man in his spiritual wilderness with all its baffling problems, these movements are scarcely aware of anything new in the world — except new means of communication. For them, *our problems are still the same ones* the Church has been confronting and solving for two thousand years. It is assumed that we know what is wrong, and that all we lack is zeal and opportunity to fix it: then everything will be all right. It is not a question of truth or insight but of power and will, we imagine: all we need is the capacity to do what we already know. Hence we concentrate on ways and means of gaining influence so that we can obtain a hearing for our familiar answers and solutions. But in actual fact we are, with everybody else, in a new world, unexplored. It is as though we were already on the moon or on Saturn. The walking is not the same as it was on earth.

Too much religious action today, says Fr. Delp, concentrates on the relatively minor problems of the religious minded

minority and ignores the great issues which compromise the
very survival of the human race. Man has gradually had the
life of the spirit and the capacity for God crushed out of him by
an inhuman way of life of which he is both the "product and
the slave." Instead of striving to change these conditions, and
to build an order in which man can gradually return to himself,
regain his natural and supernatural health, and find room to
grow and respond to God, we are rather busying ourselves with
relatively insignificant details of ritual, organization, ecclesiastical bureaucracy, the niceties of law and ascetical psychology.
Those who teach religion and preach the truths of faith to an
unbelieving world are perhaps more concerned with proving
themselves right than with really discovering and satisfying the
spiritual hunger of those to whom they speak. Again, we are
too ready to assume that we know, better than the unbeliever,
what ails him. We take it for granted that the only answer he
needs is contained in formulas so familiar to us that we utter
them without thinking. We do not realize that he is listening
not for words but for the evidence of thought and love behind
the words. Yet if he is not instantly converted by our sermons
we console ourselves with the thought that this is due to his
fundamental perversity.

Fr. Delp says: "None of the contemporary religious movements take for their starting point the position of mankind as
human beings...they do not help man in the depths of his need
but merely skim the surface.... They concentrate on the difficulties of the religious minded man who still has religious leanings.
They do not succeed in coordinating the forms of religion with
a state of existence that no longer accepts its values." Before we
can interest non-Christians in the problems of cult and of conduct that seem important and absorbing to us, we must first try
to find out what they need, and perhaps also we might devote

a little more thought to the question whether it is not possible that, in a dialogue with them, *they* might have something to give us. Indeed, if we do not approach the dialogue as a genuine dialogue, if it is simply a benign monologue in which they listen to us in abashed and grateful awe, we cannot give them the one thing they most need: the love which is our own deepest need also. "Man," says Father Delp, "must be educated to resume his proper status of manhood, and religion must be taught intensively by truly religious teachers. The profession has fallen into disrepute and it will have to be reestablished." What is needed, he says, is not simply good will and piety, but "truly religious men *ready to cooperate in all efforts for the betterment of mankind and human order.*"

However, these efforts must not be a matter of an interested and manipulative religious politic. The world has become disillusioned with religious politics devoid of genuine human and spiritual concern, interested only in preparing the way for peremptory doctrinal and moral demands. Fr. Delp makes it clear that we are in no position to make such demands on modern man in his confusion and despair. The following paragraph is one of the most sobering and perhaps shocking in the book, but it contains profound truths for those who know how to listen:

> A Church that makes demands in the name of a peremptory God no longer carries weight in a world of changing values. The new generation is separated from the clear conclusions of traditional theology by a great mountain of boredom and disillusion thrown up by past experience. We have destroyed man's confidence in us by the way we live. We cannot expect two thousand years of history to be an unmixed blessing and recommendation. History can be a handicap too. But recently a man turning to the Church for enlightenment has all too often found only a tired man

to receive him — a man who then had the dishonesty to hide his fatigue under pious words and fervent gestures. At some future date the honest historian will have some bitter things to say about the contribution of the Churches to the creation of the mass mind, of collectivism, dictatorships and so on.

More than this, Fr. Delp realizes the profound responsibility of the Christian to his persecutors themselves "lest those who are our executioners today may at some future time be our accusers for the suppression of truth."

In such statements as these, Fr. Delp makes no attempt to gloss over what he believes to be the truth, and he speaks with all the authority of a confessor of the faith who knows that he must not waste words. He himself adds, in all frankness: "Whoever has fulfilled his duty of obedience has a right to cast a critical eye over the realities of the Church and where the Church fails the shortcomings should not be glossed over." It is impossible to dismiss these criticisms as the words of an embittered rebel, disloyal to the Church. Fr. Delp *died* for the Church. The words of one who has been obedient unto death cannot be dismissed or gainsaid. These meditations "in face of death" have a sustained, formidable seriousness unequalled in any spiritual book of our time. This imposes upon us the duty to listen to what he has said with something of the same seriousness, the same humility and the same courage.

Nevertheless it must be recognized that since 1945 other voices have joined themselves to Fr. Delp's and have reiterated the same criticisms. Perhaps they have done so in milder or more general terms, but there is a widespread recognition of the fact that the Church is seriously out of contact with modern man, and can in some sense be said to have failed in her duty to him. This awareness, though stated in general terms, can be discerned in statements of certain bishops, even of the Pope himself. Certainly the convocation of the Second Vatican Council was intended, in the mind of John XXIII, to meet precisely the situation which Fr. Delp described with an almost brutal forthrightness.

Archbishop Hurley of Durban has recommended a radical reform in seminary education to enable priests to meet the new needs that confront the Church. Though stated with less urgency than the strictures of Fr. Delp, these recommendations of the South African Archbishop reflect something of the same sense of crisis.

> Unless the change of methods is systematically pursued a first class crisis will result, for there is no better way of promoting a crisis than by allowing a situation to drift into change without adjusting the approach of those most directly involved in the situation. Priests engaged in the pastoral ministry are the persons most directly involved in the Church's day-to-day life and activity. There is therefore no more urgent task confronting us than a reconsideration of the methods by which our priests are trained for their ministry. If we fail to face up to it the developing crisis may strain to a breaking point the relations between a laity in desperate need of a new approach and to some extent led to expect it, and a clergy incapable of supplying the need. (Pastoral Emphasis in Seminary Studies, Maynooth, 1962)

The diagnosis of our modern sickness has been given to us by Fr. Delp in the most serious unambiguous terms. What of the prognosis?

First of all, he asks us to face the situation squarely, but warns that it is not enough to take a perverse pleasure in contemplating our own ruin. "Pious horror at the state of the world will not help us in any way." An apocalyptic mood of general disgust and contempt for the hopes of our struggling fellow-Christians would only further aggravate the negativism and despair which he has so lucidly pointed out to us. Yet at the same time there can be no question that we must start from where we are: we must begin with the fact that in the midst of a twisted and shattered humanity we too are leading an "existence that has become a reproach." Yet here he lays open to us the paradox on which our salvation depends: the truth that even in our blindness and apparent incapacity for God, God is still with us, and that an encounter with him is still possible. Indeed, it is our only hope.

Impatience, willfulness, self-assertion, and arrogance will not help us. There is no use in Promethean self-dramatization. Things have gone too far for that. The encounter with God is not something we can produce at will. It is not something we can conjure up by some made effort of psychological and spiritual force. Indeed, these are the temptations of the secular false prophets: the masters of autonomy, for whom "untrammeled subjectivity is the ultimate secret of being," the artists of Faustian self-assertion whose efforts "have silenced the messengers of God" and reduced the world to a spiritual waste land.

The Advent discovery which Fr. Delp made, pacing up and down his cell in chains, was that in the very midst of his desolation the messengers of God were present. This discovery was in no way due to his own spiritual efforts, his own will to believe, his own purity of heart. The "blessed messages" were pure gifts from God, which could never have been anticipated, never foreseen, never planned by a human consciousness. Unaccountably, while he saw with a terrible and naked clarity the horror of his world gutted by bombs, he saw at the same time the meaning and the possibilities of man's condition. In the darkness of defeat and degradation, the seeds of light were being sown.

What use are all the lessons learned through our suffering and misery if no bridge can be thrown from one side to the other shore? What is the point of our revulsion from error and fear if it brings no enlightenment and does not penetrate the darkness and dispel it? What use is it shuddering at the world's coldness which all the time grows more intense, if we cannot discover the grace to conjure up better conditions?

In his Advent meditations, with all the simplicity of traditional Christian faith, and in images that are seldom remarkable for any special originality, Fr. Delp proceeds to describe the ruin of Germany and of the western world as an "advent" in which the messengers of God are preparing for the future. But this golden future is not a foregone conclusion. It is not a certainty. It is an object of hope. But it is contingent upon the spiritual alertness of man. And man, as Fr. Delp has already repeated so often, is totally sunk in darkness.

Man must begin by recognizing and accepting his desolation, in all its bitterness.

"Unless a man has been shocked to his depths at himself and the things he is capable of, as well as the failings of humanity as a whole, he cannot understand the full import of Advent."

The tragedy of the concentration camps, of Eichmann and of countless others like him, is not only that such crimes were possible, but that the men involved could do what they did *without being in the least shocked and surprised at themselves.* Eichmann to the very last considered himself an obedient and God-fearing man! It was this dehumanized bureaucratic conscientiousness that especially appalled Fr. Delp: the absurd and monumental deception that practices the greatest evil with ritual solemnity as if it were somehow noble, intelligent, and important. The inhuman complacency that is *totally incapable* of seeing in itself either sin, or falsity, or absurdity, or even the slightest impropriety.

Two things then are necessary to man. Everything depends on these.

First he must accept without reserve the truth "that life . . . by itself has neither purpose nor fulfillment. It is both powerless and futile within its own range of existence and also as a consequence of sin. To this must be added the rider that life demands both purpose and fulfillment."

"Secondly it must be recognized that it is God's alliance with man, his being on our side, ranging himself with us, that corrects this state of meaningless futility. *It is necessary to be conscious of God's decision to enlarge the boundaries of his own supreme existence by condescending to share ours, for the overcoming of sin.*"

In other words, Fr. Delp is reiterating the basic truth of Christian faith and Christian experience, St. Paul's realization of the paradox of man's helplessness and God's grace, not as somehow opposed, fighting for primacy in man's life, but as a single existential unity — sinful man redeemed in Christ.

Acceptance does not guarantee a sudden illumination which dispels all darkness forever. On the contrary it means seeing life as a long journey in the wilderness, but a journey with an invisible Companion, toward a secure and promised fulfillment not for the individual believer alone but for the community of man to whom salvation has been promised in Jesus Christ. But as soon as these familiar words are uttered, we imagine that it is now once again a question of lulling ourselves to sleep in devout psychological peace. "Everything will be all right. Reality is not as terrible as it seems."

On the contrary, Fr. Delp will have us turn back to the real contemporary world in all its shocking and inhuman destructiveness. We have no other option. This is the prime necessity.

The urgent need for courage to face the truth of untruth, the cataclysmic presence of an apocalyptic lie that is at work not only in this or that nation, this or that class and party, this or that race, but in all of us, everywhere. "These are not matters that can be postponed to suit our convenience. They call for immediate action because untruth is both dangerous and destructive. It has already rent our souls, destroyed our people, laid waste our land and our cities; it has already caused our generation to bleed to death."

Yet at the same time, truth is hidden in the very heart of untruth. "Our fate no matter how much it may be entwined with the inescapable logic of circumstance, is still nothing more than the way to God, the way the Lord has chosen for the ultimate consummation of his purpose."

The light and truth which are hidden in the suffocating cloud of evil are not to be found only in a stoical and isolated individual here and there who has surmounted the horror of his fate. They must appear somehow in a renewal of our entire social order. "Moments of grace both historical and personal are inevitably linked with an awakening and restoration of genuine order and truth." This is most important. It situates the profound and mystical intuitions of Fr. Delp in a securely objective frame of reference. His vision has meaning not for himself alone but for our society, our Church and for the human race.

In other words, Fr. Delp prescribes not only acceptance of our "fate" but much more, acceptance of a divinely appointed task in history. It is, note clearly, not simply the decision to accept one's personal salvation from the hands of God, in suffering and tribulation, but the decision to become *totally engaged in the historical task of the Mystical Body of Christ* for the redemption of man and his world.

It is then not only a question of accepting suffering, but much more, of accepting *happiness*. This in its turn implies much

more than a stoical willingness to put up with the blows of fortune, even though they may be conceived as "sent by God." It
means a total and complete *openness to God*. Such openness
is impossible without a full reorientation of man's existence according to exact and objective order which God has placed in
his creation and to which the Church bears infallible witness.

If we surrender completely to God, considered not only as
an inscrutable and mysterious Guest within ourselves, but as
the Creator and Ruler of the world, the Lord of history and
the Conqueror of evil and of death, then we can recover the
meaning of existence, we rediscover our sense of direction. "We
regain faith in our own dignity, our mission and our purpose in
life precisely to the extent that we grasp the idea of our own life
flowing forth within us from the mystery of God."

Perfect openness, total receptivity, born of complete self-
surrender, bring us into uninhibited contact with God. In
finding him we find our true selves. We return to the true order
he has willed for us.

Such texts show that Fr. Delp was at the same time profoundly mystical and wide open to the broadest ideals of
Christian humanism. It was by the gift of mystical intuition
that he not only found himself in God but also situated himself
perfectly in God's order and man's society, even though paradoxically his place was to be a condemned man in the prison
of an unjust and absurd government. Yet it was here that, as
this book so eloquently proves to us, he fulfilled all that God
asked of him. It was here that he could write, without exaggeration, "To restore divine order and to proclaim God's presence —
these have been my vocation."

Fr. Delp's exact obedience to God, his perfect acceptance of
God's order in the midst of disorder, was what gave him a
sublime authority in denouncing the cowardice of Christians

who seek refuge from reality in trifling concerns, petty sectarian opinions, futile ritualism or religious technicalities which they alone can understand. Christians must not be afraid to be people, and to enter into a genuine dialogue with other men, precisely perhaps with those men they most fear or stand most ready to condemn.

"The genuine dialogue no longer exists," says Fr. Delp, "because there are no genuine partners to engage in it. People are frightened. They are scared to stride out firmly and honestly to the boundaries of their potential powers because they are afraid of what they will find at the borderline."

In his impassioned plea for Christian liberty and personal dignity, Fr. Delp stands out as an advocate of true Christian humanism. This is exactly the opposite of the Promethean pseudo-humanism of anti-Christian culture since the Renaissance.

The supposed "creativity" claimed by the untrammeled subjectivism of men who seek complete autonomy defeats itself, because man centered on himself inevitably becomes destructive.

The humanism of Fr. Delp, which is also the humanism of the Church, recognizes that man has to be rescued precisely from this spurious autonomy which can only ruin him. He must be liberated from fixation upon his own subjective needs and compulsions, and recognize that he cannot fully become himself until he knows his need for the world and his duty of serving it.

In bare outline, man's service of the world consists not in brandishing weapons to destroy other men and hostile societies, but in creating an order based on God's plan for his creation, beginning with a minimum standard for a truly human existence for all men. Living space, law and order, nourishment for *all,* are basic needs without which there can be no peace and no stability on earth. "No faith, no education, no government, no science, no art, no wisdom will help mankind if the unfailing certainty of the minimum is lacking."

There is also an ethical minimum: honesty in every field, self-respect and mutual respect for all men, human solidarity among all races and nations. There must finally be a "minimum of transcendence," in other words the cultural and spiritual needs of man must be met. In the words of Pope John XXIII, in *Mater et Magistra:* "Today the Church is confronted with *the immense task of giving a human and Christian note to modern civilization:* a note that is almost asked by that civilization itself for its further development *and even for its continued existence.*" It is no easy task to meet these minimal standards. At the present moment the fury and compulsions of the Cold War seem to be the chief obstacle to our progress. Yet we too are in the same "advent" as Fr. Delp, and its laws are the same for us. If we pay attention, rouse ourselves from our despairing sleep, open our hearts without reserve to the God who speaks to us in the very wilderness where we now are, we can begin the work he asks of us: the work of restoring order to society, and bringing peace to the world, so that eventually man may begin to be healed of his mortal sickness, and that one day a sane society may emerge from our present confusion.

Is this impossible? When Fr. Delp died, he surrendered his life into the hands of God with the full conviction that it was not only possible, but that the work would one day be done.

But he also believed that the only hope for the world was this return to order and the emergence of the "new man," who knows that "adoration of God is the road that leads man to himself."

Unless man is made new, in the new order for which Fr. Delp laid down his life, there is no hope for our society, there is no hope for the human race. For man, in his present condition, has been reduced to helplessness. All his efforts to save himself by his own ingenuity are futile. They bring him closer and closer to his own destruction.

Such then is the deeply disturbing yet hopeful message of these pages. It is the message not of a politician, but of a mystic. Yet this mystic recognized his inescapable responsibility to be involved in politics. And because he followed messengers of God into the midst of a fanatical and absurd political crisis, he was put to death for his pains.

What remains now is to understand this final most important lesson. The place of the mystic and the prophet in the twentieth century is not totally outside of society, not utterly remote from the world. Spirituality, religion, mysticism are not an unequivocal rejection of the human race in order to seek one's own individual salvation without concern for the rest of men. Nor is true worship a matter of standing aside and praying for the world, without any concept of its problems and its desperation.

The mystic and the spiritual man who in our day remain indifferent to the problems of their fellow men, who are not fully capable of facing those problems, will find themselves inevitably involved in the same ruin. They will suffer the same deceptions, be implicated in the same crimes. They will go down to ruin with the same blindness and the same insensitivity to the presence of evil. They will be deaf to the voice crying in the wilderness, for they will have listened to some other, more comforting voice, of their own making. This is the penalty of evasion and complacency.

Even contemplative and cloistered religious, perhaps especially these, need to be attuned to the deepest problems of the contemporary world. This does not mean that they must leave their solitude and engage in the struggle and confusion in which they can only be less useful than they would be in their cloister. They must preserve their unique perspective, which solitude alone can give them, and from their vantage point they must understand the world's anguish and share it in their own way, which may, in fact, be very like the experience of Fr. Delp.

No one has a more solemn obligation to understand the true nature of man's predicament than he who is called to a life of special holiness and dedication. The priest, the religious, the lay-leader must, whether he likes it or not, fulfill in the world the role of a prophet. If he does not face the anguish of being a true prophet, he must enjoy the carrion comfort of acceptance in the society of the deluded by becoming a false prophet and participating in their delusions.

October 1962

1

Extracts from
Fr. Delp's Diary

1944

December 28

In the course of these last long weeks life has become suddenly much less rigid. A great deal that was once quite simple and ordinary seems to have taken on a new dimension. Things seem clearer and at the same time more profound; one sees all sorts of unexpected angles. And above all God has become almost tangible. Things I have always known and believed now seem so concrete; I believe them but I also live them.

For instance how I used to mouth the words "hope" and "trust." I know now that I used them uncomprehending, like a child. And in doing so I deprived my life of much fruitfulness and achievement and I also cheated my fellow men and women of many substantial blessings because I was incapable of taking really seriously God's command that we should trust them absolutely and whole-heartedly. Only someone who really believes and hopes and trusts can form any idea of humanity's real status or catch a glimpse of the divine perspective.

December 29

Far more than a civilization or a rich heritage was lost when the universal order went the way of medieval and ancient civilizations. Western humanity today is spiritually homeless, naked and exposed. The moment we start to be anything beyond "one of the masses" we become terribly aware of that isolation which has always encompassed the great. We realize our homelessness and our exposure. So we set to work to build ourselves some sort of house and shelter. Our ancestors, those among them who were really great, could have left us a legacy much more helpful for our progress. We can only account for the contorted thought of men like Paracelsus or Bohme on the grounds that life's insufferable loneliness and lack of design forced them to build a shelter for themselves. And although it is such a self-willed and distorted and angular structure it still has the marks of painstaking care and trouble and in that must command our respect. Goethe had rather more success; his instinct was surer and it led him to guess at some of nature's more important designs. Moreover he had a good — though not in all respects dependable — master whose ideas he copied to a very large extent.

Every now and then someone comes along and tries to impose his own plan on the rest of the world, either because he knows he has stumbled on a universal need or because he thinks he has and overestimates his own infallibility. Such people will never lack followers since so many people long for a well-founded communal home to which they can feel they "belong." Time after time in the end they come to realize that the shelter offered is not all it purports to be — it cannot keep out the wind and the weather. And time and time again the deluded seekers conclude they have been taken in by a mountebank; the man probably had no intention of deliberately deceiving but he was nevertheless a charlatan misleading himself and others.

•

It is quite remarkable. Since Midnight Mass on Christmas Eve I have become almost light-heartedly confident although nothing outwardly has changed. Somewhere within me ice has been melted by the prayers for love and life — I cannot tell on what plane. There is nothing tangible to show for it and yet I am in good heart and my thoughts soar. Of course the pendulum will swing back and there will be other moods — the sort that made St. Peter tremble at the wind and the waves.

•

I have a great yearning to talk to a few well-loved friends... when?

December 30

Everything is still in the balance. Yesterday news filtered through by the grapevine that Bolz has been condemned. No one knows whether sentence has already been carried out or not. For endurance one has to rely on resources outside oneself. I find three great supports: *show forth thy mercy — we have trusted in thee — in patience you shall possess your souls.* Steadfastness really is a *virtue;* it is not merely temperament.

December 31

The experience we are all passing through must surely at least produce one thing — a passionate love of God and desire for his glory. As far as I am concerned I find I have to approach him in a new and quite personal way. I must remove all the barriers that still stand between him and me, I must break down all the hidden reserve that keeps me from him. The prayer of van de Flue* must become a living reality. Divine life within me as faith, hope and love. All this must combine with my temperament, abilities, faults, limitations, together with external circumstance to form a new mission, a pattern to whose realization I am now pledged.

In a quiet hour tonight I will pass in review the year now ending, recollecting my personal acts in a prayer of repentance, of gratitude, of resignation, in short of trust and love.

I have to keep reminding myself what is happening and wonder whether I am suffering from hallucinations or self-deception. There can be no over-stating the seriousness of the situation and yet it all seems like a bad dream, quite unreal. Our Lord himself demanded that we should have the kind of faith that moves mountains, the trust that never fails. To him these were part of an infallible law which we can and must take seriously. Apart from the occasion when he drove the merchants from the temple we know of only one occasion on which he was really angry and that was when the apostles failed to heal the boy sick with the palsy because they had no confidence in their power. Surely we can remove by faith and prayer the one obstacle on which all this mistrust rests. When I think of the grace and the guidance vouchsafed to me in the past in spite of all that I have done....

•

It is difficult to sum up the year now ending in a few words. So much has happened during this year and yet I cannot see what its real message is for me, or its real achievement. Generally speaking it has not produced anything really effective. Hardship and hunger and violence have intensified and are all now more shattering than anyone could have imagined. The world

---

*St. Nicholas of Flue, the patron saint of Switzerland.

lies in ruins round us. It is full of hatred and enmity. Everyone clings to their few miserable possessions because these are the last remaining things that they can really call their own.

Spiritually we seem to be in an enormous vacuum. Humanly speaking there is the same burning question — what is the point of it all? And in the end even that question sticks in one's throat. Scarcely anyone can see, or even guess at, the connection between the corpse-strewn battlefields, the heaps of rubble we live in and the collapse of the spiritual cosmos of our views and principles, the tattered residue of our moral and religious convictions as revealed by our behavior. And even if the connection were fully understood it would be only a matter for academic interest, data to be noted and listed. No one would be shocked or deduce from the facts a need for reformation. We have already travelled so far in our progress toward anarchy and nihilism. Luckily powerful interests still oppose the hordes from across the Steppes for the world could not survive an alliance with them.

How can one assess the nations of today? Portugal is in a kind of sleeping beauty trance — foreigners will eventually decide her future. Spain will go into the melting pot again because she did not meet her last challenge squarely but solved the problem by cheating. Nowadays there is no room for feudalism even when it masquerades as people's tribunals. The only solutions are social ones. Spain has missed her chance to her eternal shame — and the shame of the Church too who stood by and made no protest. Italy has become purely objective. The transition from historical subject to historical object has hardly ever been made more quickly. Past guilt and ruptured loyalties make her suspect as a friend; no ally trusts her — quite apart from her people's inability to make history and the country's lack of historical genius from the modern point of view. Nothing was ever achieved in Italy without war and violence — and after all,

all that's left is a few fine rather strained attitudes. Poland is paying a bitter penalty for her conceited pretensions and offenses against other nations, particularly in the east. The Poles have never had much sense of reality though individually they are fine people. The Balkans lie at present in Russia's shadow. If as a result of all this suffering they should be at last welded into unity that would at least be one gain. For Hungary I fear a severer judgment. Many mistakes have been made there, particularly social ones. The Scandinavians are just waiting to see who will take them or force them to submit to foreign influence.

Russia is inscrutable. One really ought to visit Russia. Communism is nothing more than a donkey for an imperialism of limitless proportions. When Russia dreams she dreams magnificently and her fantasies are of unparalleled splendor. Possibly Communism needs the balance provided by Russia's interests. In any case a Russian-dominated Europe could not last long. Russia still has a great deal to learn — she is too indisciplined herself to rule others. The Slavs have not yet been absorbed by the west and are like a foreign body in the working of the machine. They can destroy and annihilate and carry away enormous quantities of booty but they cannot yet lead or build up. France is as disunited as ever, the moment western tension relaxes. Unless she joins hands with Germany she will go the way of Russia and fly to extremes. That England is on the down grade even I am beginning to believe. The English have lost their keenness and their spiritual gifts; the philosophy of materialism has eaten into England's bones and paralyzed the muscles of her heart. The English still have great traditions and imposing forms and gestures; but what kind of people are they? The social problem has been overlooked in England — and also the problem of youth and the problem of America and of spiritual questions which can all too easily masquerade as cultural or political questions.

Germany on every plane is still struggling for its very existence. One thing is certain — there can be no Europe without Germany. And a Germany in which the original currents — Christianity, Germanism (*not* Teutonism) and classicism — no longer flow is not Germany at all and can be no help to the west. But here, quite apart from the outcome of the war, the more vital problem of bare subsistence plays a profoundly important part. In other words our problem too is a social one.

The picture of the west for the moment is decidedly grim. Foreign and arbitrary powers — Russia and America — are thrusting irresponsible hands into our lives from all directions.

Finally there are the Vatican and the Church to be considered. So far as concrete and visible influence goes the attitude of the Vatican is not what it was. It is not merely that it seems so because we get no information. Of course it will be shown eventually that the Pope did his duty and more, that he offered peace, that he explored all possibilities to bring about peace negotiations, that he proclaimed the spiritual conditions on which a just peace could be based, that he dispensed alms and was tireless in his work on behalf of prisoners of war, displaced persons, tracing missing relatives and so on — all this we know and posterity will have documentary evidence in plenty to show the full extent of the papal effort. But to a large extent all this good work may be taken for granted and also to a large extent it leads nowhere and has no real hope of achieving anything. That is the real root of the trouble — among all the protagonists in the tragic drama of the modern world there is not one who fundamentally cares in the least what the Church says or does. We overrated the Church's political machine and let it run on long after its essential driving power had ceased to function. It makes absolutely no difference so far as the beneficial influence of the Church is concerned whether a state maintains diplomatic relations with the Vatican or not. The only thing that really matters is the inherent power of the Church as a religious force in the countries concerned.

This is where the mistake started; religion died, from various diseases, and humanity died with it. Or perhaps it is truer to say that humanity died of great possessions, of modern development, of the pace of modern life and so on — and religion died as humanity succumbed. In any case the west became a void so far as religion, as humanity and its spirit are concerned. In these circumstances how can any word or act on the part of the Church awaken the slightest echo in world affairs? The Church faces the same tasks that nations and states and the western world in general have to face — the problem of human beings, how they are to be housed and fed and how they can be employed in order to support themselves. In other words we need social and economic regeneration. And then humans also must be made aware of their true nature — in other words we need intellectual and religious regeneration. These are problems for the world, for individual states and nations, and they are also problems for the Church — far more so, for instance, than the question of liturgical forms. If these problems are solved without us, or to our disadvantage, then the whole of Europe will be lost to the Church, even if every altar faces the people and Gregorian chant is the rule in every parish. The supernatural demands a certain amount of expert action in regard to daily life, a degree of natural capacity for living without which life cannot survive. And the Church as an institution, an authority, requires a minimum of religious practice. Otherwise it can only have an idealistic value.

Therefore this year now ending leaves behind it a rich legacy of tasks and we must seriously consider how to tackle them. Above all else one thing is necessary — religious minded people must become more devout; their dedication must be extended and intensified.

And that brings me to my own affairs. Have I grown in stature in the past year? Have I increased my value to the community? How do things stand with me?

Outwardly they have never been worse. This is the first New Year I have ever approached without so much as a crust of bread to my name. I have absolutely nothing I can call my own. The only gesture of goodwill I have encountered is that the jailor has fastened my handcuffs so loosely that I can slip my left hand out entirely. The handcuffs hang from my right wrist so at least I am able to write. But I have to keep alert with one ear as it were glued to the door — heaven help me if they should catch me at work!

And undeniably I find myself in the very shadow of the scaffold. Unless I can disprove the accusations on every point I shall most certainly hang. The chances of this happening have never really seriously occupied my thoughts for long although naturally there have been moments of deep depression — handcuffs after all are a symbol of candidacy for execution. I am in the power of the law which, in times like the present, is not a thing to be taken lightly.

An honest examination of conscience reveals much vanity, arrogance and self-esteem; and in the past also a certain amount of dishonesty. That was brought home to me when they called me a liar while I was being beaten up. They accused me of lying when they found I mentioned no names except those I knew they knew already. I prayed hard, asking God why he permitted me to be so brutally handled and then I saw that there was in my nature a tendency to pretend and deceive.

On this altar much has been consumed by fire and much has been melted and become pliable. It has been one of God's blessings, and one of the signs of his indwelling grace, that I have been so wonderfully helped in keeping my vows. He will, I am confident, extend his blessing to my outward existence as soon as I am ready for the next task with which he wishes to entrust me. From this outward activity and intensified inner light new passion will be born to give witness for the living God, for I have truly learned to know him in these days of trial and to feel his healing presence. *God alone suffices* is literally and absolutely true. And I must have a passionate belief in my mission to humankind, showing the way to a fuller life and encouraging the willing capacity for it. These things I will do wholeheartedly — *in opine Domine.*

1945

January 1

Jesus. The name of our Lord and of my Order shall be the first word I write in the New Year. The name stands for all the things I desire when I pray, believe and hope; for inner and outer redemption; for relaxation of all the selfish tensions and limitations I place in the way of the free dialogue with God, all the barriers to voluntary partnership and surrender without reserve: and for a speedy release from these horrible fetters. The whole situation is so palpably unjust; things I have neither done nor even known about are keeping me here in prison.

The name Jesus stands also for all that I intended to do in the world, and still hope to do among humankind. To save, to stand by ready to give immediate help, to have goodwill toward all people, and to serve them, I still owe much to so many.

And in conclusion the Order, too, is embraced in my invocation of this name — the Order which has admitted me to its membership. May it be personified in me. I have pledged myself to Jesus as his loving comrade and blood-brother.

The Name stands for passionate faith, submission, selfless effort and service.

January 2

Next week, it seems, my fate will be finally decided. I am full of confidence; God lit an inner light in my soul at Christmas and it has revived my hope. I am already dreaming of my journey home, as excited as any schoolboy. If nothing unexpected happens I shall be celebrating my last Mass before the trial on Friday, the feast of Epiphany.

My sister is very brave; I depend a lot on her prayers and her loyalty. I had not expected her to come until the end of the week.

Things still look very grim but I hope and pray. I have learned a great deal in the past year. God seems much nearer and more real.

Recently I was reading Langbehn. He made it pretty difficult for people to see the truth he was proclaiming among all his general remarks. We used to rave about his work as students. My recent return to it was in many respects a farewell. The outstanding passages really ought to be extracted and collected in an anthology....

We are to be here two days more, then we go before the Gestapo. I shall keep the Sacrament with me until then so that I can go on celebrating Mass but I dare not take it with me then as I don't know how thoroughly we shall be searched there and the risk of desecration is too great.

To add to all the rest I have just learned that the presiding judge is anti-Catholic and a priest hater; yet another reason for leaving everything confidently in God's hands. It always comes back to this — only he can handle this situation.

During the daytime I read a little Eckhart, the only one of my books I have managed to retain. The whole Eckhart question would be simpler if people remembered that he was a mystic and his mind and soul and spirit were always soaring into higher spheres. He did his best to follow their flight in word and expression — but how can any ordinary mortal succeed in an undertaking that defied even St. Paul? Eckhart failed as, in his own way, every one must fail when it is a matter of analyzing and passing on an intimate personal experience: *individuum est ineffabile.* Once we have got back to the point where the ordinary person can have inexpressible secrets then a favored few will emerge and God will find them sufficiently advanced to draw them into the creative dialogue as he drew Eckhart. With this in mind reading him becomes more rewarding and more comforting. It gives the reader a glimpse of the divine secret in every human heart.

Tomorrow morning I shall pass on this sheet and there may not be any more before our fate is decided. To be quite honest if there were any way of escaping that day's ordeal I should seize it gladly, cowardly as that may sound. That's what it is to be weak! And everything depends on such trifles. The whole business really has no central theme — it just doesn't make sense. If N. sticks to his deposition — which is false — there is no hope at all. But what is the use of thinking about it — far better to kneel and pray placing everything in God's hands. *Ad majorem Dei gloriam.*

January 6, the Epiphany

Thank God my fetters were so loosely fastened that tonight I could slip them off again. So I could celebrate Mass exactly as on Christmas Eve with my hands quite free. And this is the last night before the final stage and I am taking the Lord with me after all.

The new hiding place the Mariannes have supplied me with is easily disposed of, so God will be with me during the proceedings.

Today the lawyer came to see me again. If all is to go well three things must happen. I have great confidence and my friends will not let me down. This is a moment in which the whole of existence is focused at one point and with it the sum total of reality. I must make my choice and take my stand. The reality of my faith, of God, of the world, of things and their interconnection, of responsibility and the willingness to be answerable for words and actions, as well as the inward urge to fight for existence: all these must be engaged in a single gigantic effort. I have prayed earnestly to God for both kinds of freedom and I shall do so again. After that I will read a little, or perhaps write a little more, till the night warder comes on his round. Then I have to pretend to be asleep.

Sometimes my own reactions puzzle me and I hardly recognize myself. How is it that I can live through these endless hours and days as if the whole wretched misery did not exist? It all seems so unreal. Very often I am not even conscious of it. Then suddenly it all comes back to me. Sometimes I feel like going raving mad and I have to pull myself together. I have to remind myself of the courage of my friends.

To be honest I am actually more afraid of the actual trial than its possible outcome. Although literally everything is in the balance I have complete confidence in life; and inwardly too I feel not the slightest temptation to despair.

January 7

The only opportunity to pass anything on occurs just after exercise — hence just a few more lines.

Yesterday I was more absorbed in contemplating Leonardo da Vinci than the accusations brought against me. I really must study this many-sided and contradictory personality more closely. Many of the puzzling features of modern humans seem to be encountered in him for the first time — but there are also a few clues for possible solutions.

•

The warder will soon be here. And tomorrow we are off to the "house of silence."* I wish my mother the joy of today's gospel and that speedily. She has borne enough of sorrow and sacrifice by now. *In the name of the Lord.* I have not written any farewell letters; my innermost feelings are beyond utterance.

---

*I.e., the Gestapo headquarters.

2

Meditations

THE PEOPLE OF ADVENT

Advent is the time for rousing. Humanity is shaken to the very depths, so that we may wake up to the truth of ourselves. The primary condition for a fruitful and rewarding Advent is renunciation, surrender. Humans must let go of all their mistaken dreams, their conceited poses and arrogant gestures, all the pretenses with which they hope to deceive themselves and others. If they fail to do this stark reality may take hold of them and rouse them forcibly in a way that will entail both anxiety and suffering.

The kind of awakening that literally shocks a person's whole being is part and parcel of the Advent idea. A deep emotional experience like this is necessary to kindle the inner light which confirms the blessing and the promise of the Lord. A shattering awakening; that is the necessary preliminary. Life only begins when the whole framework is shaken. There can be no proper preparation without this. It is precisely in the shock of rousing while he is still deep in the helpless, semi-conscious state, in the pitiable weakness of that borderland between sleep and waking, that a person finds the golden thread which binds earth to heaven and gives the benighted soul some inkling of the fullness it is capable of realizing and is called upon to realize.

We ought not to ignore Advent meditations such as these. We have to listen, to keep watch, to let our heart quicken under the impulse of the indwelling Spirit. Only in this quiescent state can the true blessing of Advent be experienced and then we shall also recognize it in other ways. Once awakened to an inner awareness we are constantly surprised by symbols bearing the Advent message, figures of tried and proved personalities that bring out in a most forceful way the inner meaning of the feast and emphasize its blessing.

I am thinking of three in particular — the man crying in the wilderness, the herald angel, and our blessed Lady.

•

The man crying in the wilderness. We live in an age that has every right to consider itself no wilderness. But woe to any age in which the voice crying in the wilderness can no longer be heard because the noises of everyday life drown it — or restrictions forbid it — or it is lost in the hurry and turmoil of "progress" — or simply stifled by authority, misled by fear and cowardice. Then the destructive weeds will spread so suddenly and rapidly that the word "wilderness" will recur to our minds willy-nilly. I believe we are no strangers to this discovery.

Yet for all this, where are the voices that should ring out in protest and accusation? There should never be any lack of prophets like John the Baptist in the kaleidoscope of life at any period; brave men and women inspired by the dynamic compulsion of the mission to which they are dedicated, true witnesses following the lead of their hearts and endowed with clear vision and unerring judgment. Such persons do not cry out for the sake of making a noise or the pleasure of hearing their own voices, or because they envy other people the good things which have not come their way on account of their singular attitude toward life. They are above envy and have a solace known only to those who have crossed both the inner and outer borders of existence. Such persons proclaim the message of healing and salvation. They warn us of our chance, because they can already feel the ground heaving beneath their feet, feel the beams cracking and the great mountains shuddering inwardly and the stars swinging in space. They cry out to us, urging us to save ourselves by a change of heart before the coming of the catastrophes threatening to overwhelm us.

Oh God, surely enough people nowadays know what it means to clear away bomb dust and rubble of destruction, making the rough places smooth again. They will know it for many years to come with this labor weighing on them. Oh may the arresting voices of the wilderness ring out warning humankind in good time that ruin and devastation actually spread from within. May the Advent figure of St. John the Baptist, the incorruptible herald and teacher in God's name, be no longer a stranger in our own wilderness. Much depends on such symbolic figures in our lives. For how shall we hear if there are none to cry out, none whose voice can rise above the tumult of violence and destruction, the false clamor that deafens us to reality?

•

The herald angel. Never have I entered on Advent so vitally and intensely alert as I am now. When I pace my cell, up and down, three paces one way and three the other, my hands manacled, an unknown fate in front of me, then the tidings of our Lord's coming to redeem the world and deliver it have quite a different and much more vivid meaning. And my mind keeps going back to the angel someone gave me as a present during Advent two or three years ago. It bore the inscription: "Be of good

cheer. The Lord is near." A bomb destroyed it. The same bomb
killed the donor and I often have the feeling that he is rendering me some heavenly aid. It would be impossible to endure
the horror of these times — like the horror of life itself, could
we only see it clearly enough — if there were not this other
knowledge which constantly buoys us up and gives us strength:
the knowledge of the promises that have been given and fulfilled. And the awareness of the angels of good tidings, uttering
their blessed messages in the midst of all this trouble and sow-
ing the seed of blessing where it will sprout in the middle of
the night. The angels of Advent are not the bright jubilant beings who trumpet the tidings of fulfillment to a waiting world.
Quiet and unseen they enter our shabby rooms and our hearts
as they did of old. In the silence of night they pose God's questions and proclaim the wonders of him with whom all things
are possible.

Advent, even when things are going wrong, is a period from
which a message can be drawn. May the time never come when
men and women forget about the good tidings and promises,
when, so immured within the four walls of their prison that
their very eyes are dimmed, they see nothing but grey days
through barred windows placed too high to see out of. May
the time never come when humankind no longer hears the soft
footsteps of the herald angel, or his cheering words that penetrate the soul. Should such a time come all will be lost. Then
indeed we shall be living in bankruptcy and hope will die in our
hearts. For the first thing we must do if we want to raise ourselves out of this sterile life is to open our hearts to the golden
seed which God's angels are waiting to sow. And one other
thing; we must ourselves throughout these grey days go forth
as a bringer of glad tidings. There is so much despair that cries
out for comfort; there is so much faint courage that needs to be

reinforced; there is so much perplexity that yearns for reasons and meanings. God's messengers, who have themselves reaped the fruits of divine seeds sown even in the darkest hours, know how to wait for the fullness of harvest. Patience and faith are needed, not because we believe in the earth, or in our stars, or our temperament or our good disposition, but because we have received the message of God's herald angel and have ourselves encountered him.

•

Our blessed Lady. She is the most comforting of all the Advent figures. The fact that the angel's annunciation found a motherly heart ready to receive the Word, and that it grew beyond its earthly environment to the very heights of heaven, is the holiest of all Advent consolations. What use are all the lessons learned through our suffering and misery if no bridge can be thrown from our side to the other shore? What is the point of our revulsion from error and fear if it brings no enlightenment, does not penetrate the darkness and dispel it? What use is it shuddering at the world's coldness, which all the time grows more intense, if we cannot discover the grace to conjure up visions of better conditions?

Authors of legends and fairy tales have always used mothers as a favorite theme for rousing the strongest human feelings. Often these authors use motherhood as the symbol of the earth's fertility. They have even glamorized the hidden brood chambers of the eel in stream beds, identifying them with the mysterious upsurging of new life. Behind this symbolism lies a universal hunger and yearning, a premonition of the Advent-like expectation of our blessed Lady. That God should have condescended to become a human mother's son; that one woman whose womb was sanctified as the holy temple and tabernacle of the living God should have been permitted to walk the earth — these wonders make up the sum-total of the earth's actual purpose and they are the fulfillment of all its expectations.

Our eyes rest on the veiled form of the blessed, expectant Mary, and so many different kinds of consolation radiate from her. How great a gift this was to be bestowed on the earth that it might bring forth such fruit. What a miracle that the world should have been permitted to present itself before God in the shape of this laden warmth, the trustful security of a mother's heart.

On the grey horizon eventually light will dawn. The foreground is very obtrusive; it asserts itself so firmly with its noise and bustle but it does not really amount to much. The things that really matter are farther off — there conditions are different. The woman has conceived a child, has carried it in her womb and has brought forth a son and thereby the world has passed under a new law. You see this is not just a sequence of historical events that stand out in isolation. It is a symbol of the new order of things that affects the whole of our life and every phase of our being.

Today we must have the courage to look on our Lady as a symbolic figure. At their core these times through which we are living also carry the blessing and the mystery of God. It is only a matter of waiting and of knowing how to wait until the hour has struck.

Advent in three holy and symbolic forms. It is not meant as a flight of fancy but as a message addressed to me and to you, reader, if ever these pages find you. Its purpose is not good prose but an exposition of truth which we must refer to again and again as a standard and a source of encouragement when the burden of these dreadful days becomes too heavy and confusing.

Let us pray for receptive and willing hearts that the warnings God sends us may penetrate our minds and help us to overcome the wilderness of this life. Let us have the courage to take the words of the Messenger to heart and not ignore them, lest those who are our executioners today may at some future time be our accusers for the suppression of truth.

And let us kneel and pray for clear vision, that we may recognize God's messenger when he comes, and willing hearts to understand the words of warning. The world is greater than the burden it bears, and life is more than the sum-total of its grey days. The golden threads of reality are already shining through; if we look we can see them everywhere. Let us never forget this; we must be our own comforters. Those who promote hope are themselves people of promise, of whom much may be expected.

And once again let us pray for faith in the maternal blessing of life as symbolized by our Lady of Nazareth. Life has to hold its own against ruthless and tyrannical forces, not only today but at all times. Let us have patience and wait in the spirit of Advent for that hour in which it shall please God to reveal himself anew. It may be in the very darkest hour — as the fruit and the mystery of these terrible times.

The air still vibrates with the noise of violence and destruction, of impudence and conceit, of weeping and despair. But silently the eternal values are gathering on the horizon. They are like the first pale rays of light as the promise of radiant fulfillment creeps upward accompanied by the first tentative notes of jubilation. It is not yet a full chorus but only an indication, a hint, far away. But it is drawing nearer. That is all for today; but for tomorrow the angels will joyfully proclaim the event and we shall be happy if we have believed and faithfully trusted in the Advent.

THE SUNDAYS OF ADVENT

First Sunday

Unless we have been shocked to our depths at ourselves and the things we are capable of, as well as at the failings of humanity as a whole, we cannot possibly understand the full import of Advent.

If the whole message of the coming of God, of the day of salvation, of approaching redemption, is to seem more than a divinely inspired legend or a bit of poetic fiction two things must be accepted unreservedly.

First, that life is both powerless and futile in so far as by itself it has neither purpose nor fulfillment. It is powerless and futile within its own range of existence and also as a consequence of sin. To this must be added the rider that life clearly demands both purpose and fulfillment.

Secondly it must be recognized that it is God's alliance with humanity, his being on our side, ranging himself with us, that corrects this state of meaningless futility. It is necessary to be conscious of God's decision to enlarge the boundaries of his own supreme existence by condescending to share ours for the overcoming of sin.

It follows that life, fundamentally, is a continuous Advent; hunger and thirst and awareness of lack involve movement toward fulfillment. But this also means that in this progress toward fulfillment humanity is vulnerable; we are perpetually moving toward, and are capable of receiving, the ultimate revelation with all the pain inseparable from that achievement.

While time lasts there can be no end to it all and to try to bring the quest to an ultimate conclusion is one of the illusory temptations to which human nature is exposed. In fact hunger and thirst and wandering in the wilderness and perpetual rescue by a sort of life-line are all part of the ordinary hazards of human existence.

God's promises are given to meet and deal with all these contingencies — not merely to satisfy human arrogance and conceit. All we have to rely on is the fact that these promises have been given and that they will be kept. We are bound to depend on them — "the truth shall set you free." That is the ultimate theme of life. All else is mere explanation, compromise, application, continuation, proof, practice. God helps us to find ourselves and then to get away from ourselves, back to him. Any attempt to live by other principles is bound to fail — it is a living lie. This is the mistake we have made as a race and as a nation and are now paying for so bitterly. We have committed an unpardonable sin against our own being and the only way to correct it is through an existential reverse — back again to truth.

But this reverse, this return, must be made *now. The threatening dangers of our sins.* Recognizing the truth of existence and loosening the stranglehold of this error are not matters that can be postponed to suit our convenience. They call for immediate action because untruth is both dangerous and destructive. It has already rent our souls, destroyed our people, laid waste our land and our cities; it has already caused another generation to bleed to death.

None that wait on thee shall be confounded. We must recognize and acknowledge the hunger and thirst for satisfaction outside ourselves. After all it is not a case of waiting for something that may not happen. We have the comforting assurance of all those who wait knowing that the one they expect is already on the way.

If we are terrified by the dawning realization of our true condition, that terror is completely calmed by the certain knowledge that God is on the way and actually approaching. Our fate, no matter how much it may be entwined with the inescapable logic of circumstance, is still nothing more than the way to God, the way the Lord has chosen for the ultimate consummation of his purpose, for his permanent ends. *Lift up your heads because Your redemption is at hand.*

Just as falsehood entered the world through the heart and destroyed it, so truth begins its healing work there.

Light the candles quietly, such candles as you possess, wherever you are. They are the appropriate symbol for all that must happen in Advent if we are to live.

Second Sunday: Rise and Stand on High

The value or worthlessness of human life, its profundity or shallowness, depends very much on the conditions of our existence. Life ought to preserve its real stature and not dissipate itself in superficial interests or empty sterility. Western civilization is responsible for much misconception, foreshortening of views, distortion and so on both in public and personal life. We are the products of that faulty outlook. Distortion is a danger inherent in human nature to which we as a generation seem to have been more than ordinarily prone.

Moments of grace, both historical and personal, are invariably linked with an awakening and restoration of genuine order and truth. That, too, is part of the meaning of Advent. Not merely a promise, but conversion, change. Plato would have said preparation for the reception of truth. St. John more simply called it a change of heart. The prayers and the message of Advent shake us out of our complacency and make us more vividly aware of all that is transmutable and dramatic in our lives.

The first Sunday in Advent has the shock of awakening as its theme; it is concerned with underlining our helplessness (the gospel), our turning toward God, the pivot of our life (introit, epistle, gradual, offertory), our appeal for divine freedom which will recompense our helpless movement of surrender (the collect: *stir up thy might...*).

The second Sunday carries these thoughts a stage further, making them more concrete through the exercise of personal will. The message of this second Sunday can be divided into three parts: first, affirmation, emphasizing God's reaching out toward humanity. God is always the one who approaches. Not just occasionally but all the time (introit, epistle, gospel, secret). Affirming that he comes for our healing and salvation (introit, epistle, the first half); the injunction to take God seriously; those who trust in God will be steadfast and equal to whatever is demanded of them.

Second — all this is not a simplification or a neutralization of life. God's blessing while giving us the pleasure of freedom does not relieve us of responsibility. The encounter with God is not of our choosing either in regard to the place or the manner of it. Therefore the central portion of the message runs: "Blessed is he that shall not be scandalized in me." That is to say God is approaching but in his own way. Those who insist that their salvation shall depend on their own ideas of what is right and proper are lost. It means further that the starting point of the movement toward salvation is the point at which contact is made with Christ. The way to salvation in the world is the way of the Savior. There is no other way. We have to see this clearly and constantly affirm it.

Third, the keynote of this Sunday is the *decision*, the deliberate choice of salvation in Christ. Decision regarding the after-life (post communion); this love of heavenly things is a difficult and weighty matter. Decision in favor of freedom from minor entanglements and points of view — arise and stand on high (communion); the heights determine the range of vision

and the air a soul may breathe. Decision as to character and behavior (gospel, the figure of the man, John). Decision regarding
one's duty as a Christian; our salvation depends upon our leading a Christian life which cannot be separated from personal
obligation to the figure and the mission of Christ (gospel, collect). Decision to let the grace of God work in us (collect: *stir
up our hearts,* the companion piece to *stir up thy might* on the
previous Sunday), that God may dissolve our opposition and
render us worthy to receive him and to execute his mission.

So this Sunday we must again fold our hands and kneel
humbly before God in order that his salvation may be active
in us and that we may be worthy to call upon him and be
touched by his presence. The arrogance so typical of modern
men and women is deflated here; at the same time the icy loneliness and helplessness in which we are frozen melts under the
divine warmth that fills and blesses us.

Third Sunday: True Happiness

What actually is happiness, true happiness? Philosophers have
defined it as contentment with one's lot. That definition may
fit certain aspects of the happy state but it certainly does not
describe true happiness. If it did how could I possibly be happy
in my present circumstances?

As a matter of fact we may ask ourselves whether it is worth-
while wasting time on an analysis of happiness. Is happiness not
one of the luxuries of life for which no room can be found in
the narrow strip of privacy which is all we have left when war
occupies almost the whole of our attention? Certainly it would
seem to be so in a prison cell, a space covered by three paces
in each direction, one's hands fettered, one's heart filled with
longings, one's head full of problems and worries.

Yet it does happen, even under these circumstances, that every now and then my whole being is flooded with pulsating life and my heart can scarcely contain the delirious joy there is in it. Suddenly, without any cause that I can perceive, without knowing why or by what right, my spirits soar again and there is not a doubt in my mind that all the promises hold good. This may sometimes be merely a reaction my defense mechanism sets up to counter depression. But not always. Sometimes it is due to a premonition of good tidings. It happened now and then in our community during a period of hardship and nearly always it was followed by an unexpected gift due to the resourceful ness of some kind soul at a time when such gifts were not customary.

But this happiness I am speaking of is something quite different. There are times when one is curiously uplifted by a sense of inner exaltation and comfort. Outwardly nothing is changed. The hopelessness of the situation remains only too obvious; yet one can face it undismayed. One is content to leave everything in God's hands. And that is the whole point. Happiness in this life is inextricably mixed with God. Fellow creatures can be the means of giving us much pleasure and of creating conditions which are comfortable and delightful, but the success of this depends upon the extent to which the recipient is capable of recognizing the good and accepting it. And even this capacity is dependent on our relationship with God.

Only in God are we capable of living fully. Without God we are permanently sick. Our sickness affects both our happiness and our capacity for happiness. That is why, when they still had time for leisure people made so much noise about their happiness. And in the end even that was forbidden. Their world became a prison which claimed them so completely that even happiness was made an excuse for further encroachment on their liberty.

In order to be capable of leading a full life a person must stand in a certain relationship to God and obey certain rules. And the capacity for true happiness and joyful living is also dependent on certain conditions of human life, on a serious attitude toward God. Where life does not unfold in communion with God it becomes grey and sordid, calculating and joyless.

How must we live in order to be, or to become, capable of happiness? The question is one which ought to occupy us nowadays more than ever before. Humans should take their happiness as seriously as they take themselves. And they ought to believe God and their own hearts when, even in distress and trouble, they have an intuitive feeling that they were created for happiness. But this entails certain clear convictions. For a full and satisfying life we must know what it is all about. We must have no doubts about being on the right road with all the saints to back us up, and divine strength to support us. Such a life is a dedicated one, conscious of being blessed and touched by God himself.

How must we live in order that happiness may overflow our hearts and shine from our eyes, making our countenance radiant? How must we live to ensure that the work of our hands, conscientiously competent, will be crowned with success?

The liturgy for today, the third Sunday in Advent, gives us five conditions for the achievement of happiness and the capacity to enjoy it. In weighing up these conditions we have to examine our conscience and at the same time meditate on some of the historical causes for joylessness in modern life. We have to ask ourselves how it comes about that humanity has been fobbed off with a substitute so blatant that, were they not soul-sick, right-thinking people would never have been taken in by it. Perhaps too this will give us an inkling of how matters stood with great people of the past who were really capable of happiness — whose eyes were so clear that they detected happiness everywhere. The sun song of St. Francis is not a lyrical dream but a creative expression of that inner freedom which made it possible for him to extract the last ounce of pleasure from every experience and to perceive it in the successful issue of everything he undertook.

The conditions of happiness have nothing whatever to do with outward existence. They are exclusively dependent on our inner attitude and steadfastness, which enable us, even in the most trying circumstances, to form at least a notion of what life is about.

•

For the first essential condition for true happiness today's liturgy turns to St. Paul: *Rejoice. Rejoice in the Lord...the Lord is nigh.* Piety and happiness are closely interwoven. The question of piety and joyous fulfillment (or a joyless waste and void) both in personal life and in cultural tradition seem to the thoughtful mind so closely interwoven as to be inextricable.

They are linked in a double sense. To begin with, in the sense of the first commandment. Life comes under the control, and must conform to the order of, eternal laws. It is bound up with eternal values and meanings. *The Lord is nigh.* This is not merely one of the things we should memorize, part of the repository of truth we need to be constantly reminded of from the pulpit. It should be so completely absorbed as to become part of our consciousness. Thus absorbed it forms part of the tension which substantiates one's existence as an eternal being. Truth is not a haphazard collection of discoveries one makes in the course of manifold experiences; it is an order ratified by the Church. False values never cease importuning to wean us from this order, but by steadfastness in our belief we defeat the snares that beset us. Or at least we secure a firm foothold from which to defend ourselves.

A Godless life is one delivered up to a vast army of kill-joys. When we lose touch with the eternal truths we get submerged in the weeds that sprout all over the garden of our life. They are senseless trivialities that assume an air of real importance. Though they pretend to have a purpose they are quite futile, and merely add obscurity and confusion to a life which is gradually engulfed in a sort of eternal twilight without light or direction. Torn between the claims of inconsistent and conflicting values we lose our taste for the exact standards set up by the Church and, deprived of guidance, sink into a barbarism which proclaims the loudest attractions as being most worthy of approval, even though they are quite worthless. Hunted and driven and bewitched we are no longer masters of our own fate, no longer free. It is hard enough to meet the ordinary hazards incidental to every existence; but the Godless person has no defenses and is delivered up, bound and disarmed. Left to cope with them in this defenseless fashion he falls back on the excuse that fate is against him and the world is all wrong. He is a failure and it takes very little to keep him bogged down in depression and despair. The world becomes a cheerless place, not worth living in, although there seems to be no way out of it. Or, on the other hand, he may persuade himself that a flippant attitude is the right one to adopt, and he seeks a cheap way out of his troubles by various forms of escapism. The great illusion begins, the age of noise and mass mentality and organized animation — "circuses" — for crowds. Till at last the earth begins to quake and underground rumblings, which have been more or less effectively drowned by the surface uproar, imperatively assert themselves. Thunder crashes proclaiming the day of judgment.

That is the way a race, a nation, an individual, wandering in the wilderness, can go to hell in a life without happiness. One terrifying factor about such a state of affairs is that it gets progressively worse. People grow to hate one another, all creation is disrupted and the harmony of the spheres is shattered by an orgy of violence and destruction.

There is only one remedy for such a state; each person must return to God, listen to his inner voice, consciously make contact with him. The great conversion will invariably win a blessing, one which will make our wilderness blossom. It will open up new perspectives and unseal forgotten springs. We should aspire to true good and not seek to fill our life with mere sensual gratification. Aspiration involves renunciation; but no sooner have we shed the trappings of selfish desire than freedom and mastery are within our possession. A surrender without reserve is essential; then "these things" are given back to us. Our eyes are opened and acquire a new perception. His earth regains its fruitfulness under the healing streams, which strengthen us for our appointed tasks and give us mastery as they carry the ship of our life on its way.

That is the meaning of *rejoice in the Lord*. Separated from God we are cut off from the eternal current of life and everything withers. This cannot be too firmly impressed upon us; it is the most important message of today. Above all we who proclaim that message must know it ourselves, and give our hearts to it, setting an example.

And that brings me to the second sense in which piety and happiness are interwoven. *In the Lord*. It is not only because of divine law and order that God will, and must, perpetually rekindle the light of illumination for us. *The Lord is nigh:* God is personally here in our midst. The theological truths concerning providence and divine guidance, concerning his actual presence in us through divine grace must be correctly understood and must become a living reality. Only thus can we live through the

hazards and mischances of workday and holiday, through sun-
shine and shadow, probing every eventuality to that inner core
in which God reveals their mystery and true significance. His
interrogation, his guidance, his leading, his chastisement, his
judgment, his comfort, his help. This is the hidden and holy burden of all the experiences we undergo. Not only where churches
remain standing will there be temples of God; they will rise
wherever human hearts beat high in adoration, wherever knees
are bent in prayer, wherever the spirit is receptive to divine inspiration, wherever human beings, loving and worshipping, find
and fulfill their true selves. And they will discover that they are
living God's life within themselves, in their very hearts' core,
proving the truth of the words of great and intuitive men like
Eckhart, St. Augustine and the rest. They will arrive at a state
of perception in which they realize that the Supreme Being actually resides within them. They will find themselves and regain
faith in their own dignity, their mission and their purpose in
life precisely to the extent that they grasp the idea of their own
life flowing forth within them from the mystery of God. In this
realization any disasters that may threaten and all despairing
moods are overcome, completely disarmed from within. Evil is
unmasked and deprived of all its seeming power.

Only when we arrive at that state of mastery and freedom
can we breathe freely. The world and life itself then owe us
nothing for we live with every fiber of our being. Life gives us
all it has to offer because nothing less can match the prodigal
abundance of divine love which is poured out to meet our receptive heart the moment we open it unreservedly. We regain
the clear vision which enables us to perceive eternal glory in all
things. It moves us to awe, thanksgiving and praise. Everything
is endowed with an inner radiance because our hearts and the
work of our hands are touched by creative truth. Such people

cannot help being happy and extending happiness to others. *Rejoice.*

•

Humans cannot attain a state of happiness without conversion, a complete reorientation of their entire existence. It cannot be achieved by their own effort, it can only result from the supreme freedom which God bestows as soon as we cease to hedge ourselves round with self-sufficiency, isolation and arrogance. The question is: how can human beings cross the borderline of human limitation to that divine intimacy which calls for complete surrender, and in return gives us all the resources of the infinite. To find the answer we must turn to St. John the Baptist, the man of Advent: *he confessed and did not deny. . . . It is not I.* We must know the truth about ourselves without equivocation; we must be brought to the point of absolute honesty before ourselves and before others. Again and again we will be tempted to stand on the pedestal of our own self-esteem and this temptation must be overcome at all costs. We may cavort for a time on our high horse of vanity and self-deception but sooner or later the animal will throw us and make off leaving us stranded in the wilderness. We must abandon the fictions we have labored to polish so as to increase their plausibility.

An honest self-appraisal combined with a sober summing-up of one's own capacities and potentialities is the first step toward truth in life. *The truth shall set you free* — and freedom, in every part of life, is all that matters.

Humans have a great tendency to lapse into dreams; we rarely stop dreaming. There are genuine creative dreams that entice us on and drive us out of the rut of routine. Woe to youth if it should ever lose its capacity to conjure up glorious visions

and to feel the breath of the Holy Spirit. But there are also misleading and foolish dreams that bemuse the dreamer, weakening
one's judgment so that one cannot distinguish the false from the
true. They prevent one progressing by one's own effort; they
tempt one to have too good an opinion of one's own powers —
and on the level of absolute being such errors are fatal.

There are two tests by which we can tell whether the impulse
moving us is genuine or not — the test of service and the test of
proclamation of truth. St. John is the guide again.

First, the warning voice. It reminds us of what we owe to our
own integrity and helps us avoid becoming puffed up with pride
and self-sufficiency. It reminds us constantly that we are on this
earth for a purpose. To discover that purpose and to fulfill it
is our mission in life. The idea of service and a true sense of
duty cannot be separated from a fruitful human existence; they
are its very essence. Anyone who fails in these essentials makes
a fundamental mistake and will never find the road to self-
knowledge. Duty and service may take many different concrete
forms — but the emphasis must always remain constant.

The second test — *he it is*. Affirmation, testimony, praise of
the Lord. In this supreme state of reverence we shed our limitations; in this frame of mind we can arrive at complete honesty
and absolute clarity of vision. It is not a thing that comes easily — it needs much practice. But it is the only state in which
a person is receptive to divine grace and it cannot be attained
without considerable personal effort. We can only comprehend
the great realities we are meant to comprehend by making a
supreme effort.

•

Absolute honesty in regard to oneself is essential because it
keeps a person from sinking into a dream-like Nirvana in which
he views his life with detachment and disinterest. Instead of

dreaming he must be wide awake to prepare the way for progress in an active and upward direction. For this a receptive and
selfless state of mind is necessary — a state in which precisely
because it is selfless he finds a greater personal freedom than he
had ever imagined possible. The attitude can best be summed up
as one of obedient receptivity, selfless service, exultant gratitude.
Personal limitations are shed like worn out garments and with
them the anxiety that accompanies them. The world and its affairs are viewed with a new and far more penetrating insight.
A long road must be traveled before one arrives at uninhibited
contact with God, but it is the road — and the only road —
to one's own fulfillment. What one must recognize is that the
whole process is entirely a personal one, can only be worked
out in one's individual existence, cannot be measured by outward events at all even though the trials one meets every day
play their part in opening one's eyes to the connection and significance of the happenings of life. To aspire to a higher state is
an inborn attribute of human nature. The person who is completely satisfied with things as they are and has no desire to
rise above his limitations can only be described as spiritually
mediocre, self-centered, obtuse, pompous and narrow-minded.

So for all the humility of self-surrender we must still try
to rise above ourselves — we must still have ambition. But a
very different kind of ambition — not the usual arrogant, self-
seeking kind. This is a genuine effort to meet human nature's
inherent need to fulfill itself. Such dynamic principles under-
lie human nature that its driving power must find an outlet.
When the individual falls into the most dangerous of human
errors, attempting to pose as a superman and so on, he reveals
the mainspring of his nature just as clearly as if he were genuinely seeking to fulfill himself. In order to become more of a
human he finds he has to be a human and so he is back at his

starting point. Unless a person reaches out, letting his imagination soar, striving toward a high ideal, the only alternative is to vegetate — and a person who vegetates ends by becoming less than human. This is the psychological explanation of the great human tragedy through which we are passing today.

Here again — we must be honest with ourselves. The great freedom cannot be won without drastic action, certainly, but our approach must be co-operative, never defiant, challenging or demanding. The fire of Prometheus is a fable: the divine fire is strong enough and efficient enough in its action to command our respect without any theatrical gestures of violence and vengeance to deck out its power and effectiveness. The Lord is not a vengeful God; he is himself and anyone who fails to recognize this is preparing for himself a burden under whose weight he is eventually bound to collapse. Humanity's contribution to the attainment of the great freedom consists of an honest personal assessment, an open and receptive heart, willing obedience combined with readiness to serve and genuine acknowledgment of God — that is to say thanksgiving and praise. The person who approaches Advent in this frame of mind will experience the supreme encounter and the resultant liberation, for God gives freedom to those who make his coming their own personal experience, with all the comfort and support that experience conveys.

Thou hast blessed thy land ... and turned away the captivity: stir up thy might and come ... (introit, collect, offertory, post communion). All these are pointers to God's intervention in the affairs of humankind and thus to the benefits that result. But the fundamental attitude on humanity's part is essential — we must fulfill this condition before the benefits can be received.

The attitude is one of complete surrender even to the point of ignoring all outward distractions. The liturgy calls this state *captivitas* — captivity — and *iniquitas* — guilt. Humanity is only

capable of ultimately realizing its true self by the direct intervention of God, who breaks the fetters, absolves the guilt and
bestows the inevitable blessing. For the moment I am not in
the least concerned with how a person arrives at this state. But
what I am concerned with, what concerns us all, most urgently,
is the resigned, shoulder shrugging indifference of modern men
and women to these vital issues — and the fact that this attitude
seems to be accepted by the Church. Because this indifference
only increases the material problems and makes them appear
ever more insoluble, it ought to make us stop and think and try
to produce some constructive results. One has the impression
almost of being lost in a vast forest with every step leading farther and farther into the depths however hard one looks for
the way out. Sooner or later we all make the discovery that
human beings are subject to prohibitions and restraints that are
even harsher, more irksome and more inexorable than the limitations of nature. The liturgy calls this imprisonment — a word
we often use very glibly, for only those who have actually suffered it can have any idea of the effect it has on one's inner
nature. The person who has had a taste of prison life knows
what it means to be shut up in a narrow cell, his wrists fettered,
his mind occupied with a thousand depressing thoughts as he
visualizes the flag of freedom drooping forgotten in some obscure corner. Again and again his hopes rise only to fall back
into despair when the steps of the warder approach or the key
grates harshly in the lock. Then dreams fade into reality and
it all seems hopeless. Again and again you come back to the
same point — you have no key, and even if you had there is
no keyhole on the inside of a prison door. And the window
is barred and it is so high up you can't even look out. Unless
someone from the outside comes to set you free there can be no
end to your misery — all the will power in the world makes no
difference. The facts clamor for recognition.

And when you think about it this is precisely the state humankind as a whole is in today. We have become incapable of living
fully because we have not found divine freedom. I know perfectly
well that only God can unlock the handcuffs and open that door
and that his creative power could make me free again in the eyes
of the world. Humanity's condition in general is just like mine.
What we need is a new awareness of the gospel, the good tidings
so that we may *really* hear and understand. We need an open, receptive mind — God will not force any person to accept salvation.
We must keep on reminding modern people that God stands at
the door, ready and waiting, but that they themselves must open
the door. The grim happenings round us — the devastation and
violence — are not exaggerated rumor but solid fact. And God's
knock at the door of our spirit, his invitation to surrender to him
and accept in return his freedom, is a thing that should be taken
just as seriously.

On one point let there be no misunderstanding — left to ourselves with only our own strength to rely on, we shall never find
freedom. The text about human beings not being able to call a
foot of earth their own is an exact picture of our helplessness on
a purely human level. Where divine freedom is concerned there
is no question of bargaining, of exchanging one set of chains
for another as is the case in human affairs. With God the only
way to complete freedom is complete surrender — there is no
alternative. But his summons is always creative.

The indispensable preparation on our part is a change of
heart. We must reorder our lives. And it is desperately urgent
that we do it *now* and do not try to put it off. We must make
a complete surrender of ourselves, not in a sudden rush of emotion which is likely to be as transitory as it is violent, but wholly
and continually until placing ourselves in God's hands has become habitual and permanent. Only then can God's will for our
own liberation and salvation be done in us. And for western

men and women particularly this change of heart is something very urgently needed — it has become a question of life and death not only for their eternal well-being but for their very existence here on earth. The whole future of history — whose sole purpose really is the glory of God — depends on their regaining their freedom, on battling their way through the wilderness to the open sea.

And it is all so intimately linked with human desire and the capacity for happiness. Only the person capable of seeing ultimate truth and being saved by it can experience real joy. Freedom is truly the breath of life. We sit in damp dug-outs and shelters and cells, gasping in the foul air and reeling under fate's devastating blows. It is time we stopped attributing false values to things, glamorizing them. We should see things as they really are. Our present life is bankrupt. And if we really admit this then already there is a faint foreshadowing of change — a slight lessening of tension, a gradual calming of the beating of our hearts. The clank of chains loses its grating harshness in response to prayer. *Drop dew ye heavens...* we really need to go into things deeply, to see the connecting link between them, to call on God our Savior for deliverance from the evil that is oppressing us. Then we shall discover freedom, though at first it may only be elbow room; the walls of our cell will open out and we shall breathe more easily; the horizon will beckon with promise. The weeping and wailing may still go on but a new undertone of yearning, of understanding, of joy, seems to filter through the broken voices of the sorrowing multitude.

Once a person has attained inner knowledge and freedom ordinary annoyances and unexpected happenings lose their power to disturb. He or she can stand back and look at things dispassionately, with detachment, not in cold, calculating appraisal but with the kindly glance of the person who is in control of the situation. And such a person is not easily disturbed, whatever

happens. *Be in nothing solicitous* — the epistle applies this to
the freedom we achieve when we forsake the hectic rush of bur-
dened days, tight schedules and feverish haste. Decisions can be
made without hesitation because we have clearer insight. Situations can be assessed correctly because all the implications are
at once clear. In this state of freedom the healing, creative power
of God and the restless, adventurous impulse of humanity meet
and bear fruit. The need is still there but the anguish has gone;
the burden still has to be carried but the shoulders are stronger;
the struggle for existence continues but without the constant
anxiety. St. Paul reminds us that humans have certain charac-
teristics and that certain conditions are most natural to them —
to love, for instance, is one; to adore is another. And St. Paul
lists others including gratitude, reverence, prayerful hope. The
person who, in his inner being, has entered into the perfect relationship with God fulfills the real purpose of his existence;
from that point on the dialogue can begin. Such a person discovers his real self because he has first put his mind in order.
Long-forgotten talents, and some that have atrophied for want
of use, are brought to life again. His whole being grows — his
eyes are clearer and keener and he feels more sure of himself in
spite of constant lapses and moods of depression. He is still at
the testing stage but he is beginning to get over the worst. His
soul begins to sing and he has a vague awareness of the stirring
of deep fountains... until eventually he comes to the full realization of the truth *in the Lord*. And the day will come when the
singing soul will be ready to join in the ultimate alleluia.

All this is true — provided a person takes the essential first
step of relinquishing his personal self of his own free will. Only
thus can he come to the necessary state of receptivity. It is an
attitude conditioned by the relationship of the creature to the
Creator, and the only attitude in which a person can bear the
reality and the overwhelming bliss of God's presence. For the

fully awakened consciousness that knows and believes, this bliss is sufficient reward in itself. But it is really only a foretaste; it allows a person to get his breath back ready for the next step, and the constantly increasing wonder of the experience keeps the soul alert.

Thus life goes on to reach to its furthest horizons and supreme hour. Never do the promises cease to beckon. Isaiah's wonderful words, in the communion prayer, are addressed to everyone: "Say to the faint hearted — take courage and fear not." They heal the deepest wounds and bring comfort and solace to the most cheerless situations. Woe to the world and to all humanity if it ever ceases to believe in the promises. Without them there can be no life; all splendor, all courage and all joy will be at an end. If belief in them dies, happiness dies also.

God's promises are always before us; they are more constant than the stars, more effective than the sun; they heal us and set us free. They transform us and widen the compass of our existence to infinity. In the face of the promises even grief loses its bitterness; trouble discloses inner courage and in loneliness is sown the seed of trust.

And what about the "good cheer" we are told of and which we so much want to share? I have said nothing about the exciting kinds of happiness that can flood one's whole being with nothing to stimulate it except the simple everyday gifts God in his goodness bestows upon us. Warm sun; the glint of light on moving water; the prodigal exuberance of spring flowers; meeting another human being who is sincere and with whom we have an immediate understanding. Nor have I dwelt on the emotional impulse that expresses itself in true love or true sorrow, the way in which both heaven and earth can give us cause for great and profound happiness. I have not mentioned these — I know very well that happiness can come from so many sources and that all of them can suddenly dry up. But

I am not concerned with these things. I am only concerned with
what has become now a familiar theme in my own life, the nearness of God and the divine order which alone can heal one's
mortal ills. It is this — and only this — that can both fit us for
happiness and give us the means to be happy. To restore divine order and proclaim God's presence — these have been my
vocation, the task to which my life is dedicated.

Fourth Sunday: Binding and Loosing

What is true of the Advent prayers applies also to Advent in
life. Before the curtain rises and the scene is disclosed, stretching
into infinity, expectation mounts in a crescendo of excitement.
Our confidence is well founded and so is the suspense of waiting
because the promise is already fulfilled and its truth demonstrated. Day triumphs and the darkness shrinks back into
nothingness — like the shadows in the wings when the stage
is set as a temple of light. On the fourth Sunday in Advent the
acute awareness of shrouded mystery is deepening for the final
hour of darkness that heralds the dawn. There is an intense
awareness of captivity, of crippling disability and despair, but
it is already shot through with a premonition of divine grace —
the premonition that will so soon become certainty.

The Three Laws of Bondage

The law of guilt: "Grace which is hindered by our sins"
(collect).

All the jargon about "fate," "bad luck," having a life of misfortune and so on is dealt with in this one sentence. As we move
from night to day we are beset with decisions the heart has to
make and we ought to think about them very seriously for the
whole outcome will depend on the choices we make. And this

is true not only of individual personal lives but also of generations, races, epochs. Good and evil come from the same source; a false decision, a wrong inclination of our will and all that follows is doomed; the vision is clouded, the hands grow clumsy and the work *they* produce is malformed if not harmful. Or the complete opposite — a change of heart, illumination, repentance and a blessing that results in fruitful and productive work.

This is true of all our personal life. The events which affect us are doubly interwoven. In one way they are accidents that result from a logical sequence of causes which apparently we cannot escape. But their deeper significance as opportunities for the healing and cleansing of our soul is even more important. The whole art of assessing the value or worthlessness of our experiences and of events lies in knowing their existential significance and being willing to admit it. It gives us power to deal with anything fate may have in store. It allows us to penetrate to the inner meaning of things and the moment the meaning of anything is clear it ceases to be mysterious — it "makes sense." And with this weapon we can strike the hardest, coldest, most unyielding rocks and draw living water from them.

Today more than ever it is vital that this should be universally known and recognized. Life in our age has become so degenerate and unhealthy that even the natural obstacles are multiplied by widespread evil hampering and delaying the good. And there can be no escape from it except through a great conversion, a change of heart which like most true conversions will take place in silence growing until it is strong enough to break through the ice that clings to modern life and crushes it like a curse.

The law of history. No life is ever outside the scope of history or insignificant for it. But there is no such thing as holy, or unholy, history. History is creative being in action. Development, unfolding, are processes of "becoming" whether they are the result of an internal motive force or an external intervention, and they make up the sum-total of existence. Any attempt to escape history, to live outside it as it were, to run away from reality, only leads to illusion. Escapism and reaction have no place in real life.

The gospel for the fourth Sunday in Advent evokes history. It refers to the mighty who determine the structure of the small room in which the Light of the World will come into being, bringing salvation. In order to recognize that a moment of historical crisis is implied here, we have to clothe these names with the memory of the part they played in history. From the imperial throne to the holy of holies the outlook was hopeless; even the priesthood had been corrupted by power politics, family egoism and narrow-minded bigotry.

Hopeless — that is the iron with which history often seeks to fetter healing hands, breaking the hearts of the enlightened few and reducing them to trembling hesitancy or cheap silence or tired resignation. As Christians we ought to recognize these shackles of history for what they are; indeed to ignore them is sinful evasion. History does not have the last word but it is only through history that the decisive word can be carried into effect. If we fail to recognize this we are performing a masque before a graven image which deceives us, or with which we are trying to deceive ourselves, into a false sense of security.

The law of mysteries. Goethe says: if you want the eternal make the most of the temporal. The grand old man of Weimar spoke from a good deal of experience but he had no real personal metaphysical background. Borrowing freely from Spinoza's pantheistic logic he translated it into lyric form and made it sound like his own discovery. It would be hard to find a more sympathetic guide, or a more dogmatic one, than Goethe as far as essential conduct and values are concerned — despite the pleasure he took in accumulating experience and the liberty he boasted of. Schiller is different in that the tension springs mainly from his inability to reconcile Kant's ideas with Spinoza's.

But this is not really relevant. Reaching out to "infinity in all directions" contributes nothing ultimately to human knowledge except in conjunction with an already established *a priori,* or the recognition that there are limits to human perception and beyond them all is veiled and silent in unutterable mystery. It is precisely the road leading to the *finite* in all directions — which most great men and women have a talent for exploring — that makes one aware of the mystery surrounding us on every hand. Ultimately we have to concede that there are many questions to which we can find no answer and that there are countless things in heaven and earth for which we possess no explanation whatsoever.

Humanity would give a great deal to get rid of this thorn in its flesh, this great question mark which seems a reproach to its idea of a properly ordered existence. We may try to ignore it, to blunt our senses to the mysteries surrounding us and bury ourselves in the round of everyday reality; then one day an avalanche overwhelms us and we are driven from our secure little home and well-kept garden on to the highway of displaced persons, seeking a destination somewhere, somehow, and finding life very hard indeed. Or we may try to think up new categories from which we might possibly be able to wring an answer — categories of logic or emotion, of sense or nonsense. But whether we tackle the problem skeptically or with heroic optimism, whether we attack it little by little or by main force, it always comes to the same thing in the end. We always have to plunge into more and more thought — the only respite from facing the seriousness of the situation and the hopelessness of ever finding adequate solutions to all the problems that remain unsolved.

The threads of which life is made up are too intricately interwoven for us to be able to separate them. Its burdens and its rewards are such that human beings, left to our own resources, can neither bear nor understand. When, after untold labor, we think we have reached the ultimate it always proves to be the penultimate; and so it goes on, always new signs, new missions, new information, new questions, new tasks. Hence despite the most vigilant care and all human endeavor, despite alertness and willingness, life remains an inscrutable mystery and often a disquieting one at that.

The Three Laws of Freedom

We only find our true self when we rise above ourselves. Beyond our own natural resources we find the strength and power to realize our potentialities and the freedom we need to draw the breath of life — in other words we come to self-realization. Yet the ability to tap this source of strength and power depends on decisions which rest entirely with our own personal will and can only be made by us.

Overcoming the law of guilt. The power that will overcome the law of sin is not to be found within the heart of the sinner who seeks it. And he must first fulfill the necessary condition of a change of heart before he can even receive that redemptive power which lies beyond his reach. He must first call upon it and then make himself ready so that he may go to meet it. Advent does not offer freedom to the person who is convinced he is already converted. *Stir up thy power: by the help of thy grace.* It is a case of God against sin. Sin is very like a handcuff — only the person with the key can unlock it. It doesn't matter how fervently I desire it, I cannot rid myself of my handcuffs because I have no key. And sin is like the door of my cell — even if I had a key I could not unlock the door because it has no keyhole on this side. It can only be opened from outside. And opposed to sin is God, as accuser and judge if we are obstinate in error, as liberator and savior if we will turn to our Redeemer and ally ourselves with our Creator against sin. But the recognition of this entails something else. We have come to a time when devout souls are much needed, souls who will pray for us all, lifting up our plight to God and ensuring by the inclination of their own hearts that others will be moved to do the same. The plea must swell to a clamor and must go on ceaselessly. We have to take God at his word — the laws of prayer are his own — cf. Matt. 21:18; Luke 17:5 and many other texts. The outcome of so many things, the occurrence of so many miracles depends on the wholeheartedness of our plea to God. He will not always provide sensational miracles — though they will occur now and again, witnessing to his divine power. But with truly regal bounty he will reveal himself in a thousand little everyday adjustments proving by innumerable apparently casual events that his will prevails in the end. Persons of real faith have no doubt about the outcome — they leave the means to God. And when God repays, and more than repays, our trust, we can only stand speechless in amazement and awe.

Now particularly is the time for prayers that will storm heaven. This is no Quietist dispensation from responsibility and action. On the contrary — there is a very stringent law regarding deeds and the time has come for that deed which is inherently blessed. We should remember St. Ignatius's rule — it is the intention that matters. That is the rule for today. Intervention, action and achievement must come from devout prayer — that is perhaps truer today than it has ever been.

There is no cause for depression, resignation or despair in all this — rather it should give us greater confidence and spur us on to unrelenting effort. We must make a covenant with God against the evils that surround us: *show mercy on us for we have hoped in thee.* It is essential and is the measure of the demand that God makes of us. He is as near to us as our desire for him is sincere; his mercy is as great as the wholeheartedness of our appeal for it; his freedom is as real and imminent as our belief in him and in his coming is unshaken and unshakable. That is the truth.

Freedom from the law of history. The Holy Spirit, Almighty God, the Lord of all history is alone outside history, above it. But we must not delude ourselves that we can find freedom by running away from history. We have to find this freedom within the framework of history in alliance with God for the fulfillment of his purpose.

This is obvious if we look at the gospel. In the time when the historic situation was hopeless, even within the holy of holies, God's word went forth to John. We can picture what happened: the voice rang out and people were greatly disturbed. They flocked to Jordan where baptism promised the way to freedom. They heard the warning and prophecy of the great upheaval that was to prepare the way for the Messiah and a new life. Shutters were pulled down and windows thrown open — the whole horizon widened and John's mission was a success.

And history was fulfilled both by the withdrawal to the wilderness and the return to the highways to proclaim the message. The wilderness — John's wilderness — is not a place of escape, adding to the armor of our self-esteem; it is a place of preparation, a place for gathering our strength and collecting our thoughts, for rearming ourselves, for listening expectantly for the word of command. Bodily preparation, immediate response to God's message, confidence and courage in passing it on — these are the things that safeguard history. They will culminate at the right historic hour — not just any hour one might wish or dream of — and when history unfolds in this way it is drawn back into the original order of creation which exists for the glory of God.

The word of God cannot be embraced in fetters, cannot be heard when all human values are chained in fear and frustration and fatigue and weighed down with the escapist urge to compromise. Prepare the way is the task that lies at the heart of history. Again and again history will surrender to the Word because history too knows its Master and cannot exist away from its true source.

Freedom from the law of mystery. This shackle too is loosened by the message of the fourth Sunday of Advent, and in three ways. First we are obliged to acknowledge the truth, that our life is full of mysteries. The ability to realize that there are mysteries and to endure them is a test to which humans must submit. It is part of the act of adoration to acknowledge God, above and beyond, and to take him seriously even in the stress and strain of everyday life.

Then the message conveys the Christmas blessing reminding us that things are sanctified; that thanks to the presence of God and his immanence in creation particular mysteries do exist and that certain times and certain things transmit his blessing. The whole character of the feast has a grace-bestowing quality which is peculiarly typical.

Hold on and speak out: again a command, a mission. The night we are enduring is bound to yield to light; the chosen moment of history is bound to hear the tidings of the Redeemer.

Until he come: everything is concentrated in expectation, waiting and watching for the coming of the Lord. *He is the Lord* — the awareness of God in the midst of our life. The infinite value of steadfastness is stressed here — unremitting watchfulness touched by God and, because of that divine touch, capable of renewing itself time and time Again, of remaining wakeful. *Until he come:* to keep on, to be forever on the way. That is the law that governs a truly free life.

God is day and night, bondage and freedom, prison cell and the whole world. The great encounter is only explicable thus. But we have to go on seeking for that explanation, putting question after question until they are all answered. God is the source of both question and answer and each answer must be followed up. The eve of Christmas is both a proclamation and a mission; a holy night and a night pregnant with promise. The wise, the watchers and those who bring tidings, persons who know God and his order, those who watch expectantly and pray ceaselessly are those who will transform our fetters into a sacrament of freedom.

THE VIGIL OF CHRISTMAS

Concerning the Blessed Burden of God

There has always been a lot of misunderstanding about the feast of the nativity. Superficial familiarity, sentimental crib-making and so on have to some extent distorted our view of the stupendous event the feast commemorates.

This year (1944) the temptation to make an idyllic myth of Christmas will no doubt be less in evidence than usual. The harsh realities of life have been brought home to us as never before. Many who spend Christmas in dug-outs and shelters that would make the stable at Bethlehem seem cozy by comparison will have little inclination to glamorize the ox and the ass. They may even stumble on the idea of asking themselves what really happened that holy night — was the world made a better, a more beautiful place? Did life acquire a blessing because the angels sang *Gloria in excelsis,* because the shepherds were astounded and hurried to pay homage, because a king lost his nerve and ordered the innocents to be massacred? Yet at this point the questions have already started to run wild — for this crime took place simply and solely because it was the holy night.

Yet Christians probably never pray more fervently than when they offer up the *respirare* at the conclusion of the vigil Mass. We breathe again because the birth of the Only-Begotten will, we trust, ease our burdens. A load has been lifted from our hearts. Life takes on a new meaning because a new perspective is disclosed, because the decisive moment has been reached again, because the relative security we normally count on has not yet been swallowed up by the uncertainties of this abnormal time.

To breathe again. To be honest I too long to be able to breathe again, to be relieved of my troubles. How earnestly I prayed the prayer for speedy deliverance in yesterday's Mass. Each day I have to steel myself for the hours of daylight and each night for the hours of darkness. In between I often kneel or sit before my silent Host and talk over with him the circumstances in which I am. Without this constant contact with him I should have despaired long ago.

The question that applies to the whole world applies to me personally and concretely on this feast of the nativity. Is there anything different about celebrating Mass here in this narrow cell where prayers are said and tears are shed and God is known, believed in and called on? At stated hours the key grates in the lock and my wrists are put back into handcuffs; at stated hours they are taken off — that goes on day after day, monotonously, without variation. Where does the breathing again which God makes possible come in? And the waiting and waiting for relief — how long? And to what end?

It is necessary to celebrate the feast of the nativity with great realism, otherwise one's imagination will conjure up magical happenings for which one's sober reason can discover no justification nor prospect. And as a result of that the celebration of the feast could easily lead to bitter disappointment and deep depression. The vigil Mass leads to the necessary restrained, expectant and realistic frame of mind in three ways.

God whose coming we celebrate is and remains the God of promises. At the introit we pray: *This day you shall know — and in the morning you shall see,* clearly referring to the coming feast day and the connection between it and the vigil. But it also refers to a perpetual state, to the fundamental condition of our life. It is one of the most tragic and disturbing factors of our existence that we may know a great deal and have vast experience behind us and yet fail to find a place of shelter, a secure refuge. Humanity would so much like to regard its acquired knowledge as final, to make itself at home here and feel secure. But every now and then we grow uncomfortably aware of the fact that our wanderings are not yet over. Again and again the truth we believe we have grasped proves to be merely a prelude, an overture to something that lies beyond, beckoning and leading us onward. And we must go on, must continue our journey if we are to obtain life's reward. To call a halt before the end is reached means death, metaphysical and religious ruin.

This "in the morning you shall see" absorbs the wholesome, creative unrest to which we owe all that is genuinely alive in our own make-up. But at what a price. The Lord calls it hunger and thirst after righteousness and one needs to have experienced the agony of counting the hours until the next ration of bread is due really to understand what this means and how much is expected of us in this eternal quest.

And the alternative? Indifference, resignation, insensitivity, loss of appetite, the atrophying of the organs, the loss of our spiritual nerve, over-strain and deadly fatigue — in short one of those fatal wounds through which the life-blood of so many human beings nowadays is ebbing away. A person may think he can escape the curve of tension into which the law has forced him but in the end he comes to the realization that burdens are part and parcel of the condition of life.

So now, on the threshold of Christmas which we like to approach as if it were a kind of earthly paradise, we come on the same motif: *you shall know* — *you* have received tidings: *you shall see* — *you* must be on your way to find real fulfillment in real encounter. Here again we have real tension, the theme of the bow which can only be stretched when the arrow is applied to it.

We ought to remember we are approaching the feast of God-made-man, not of man rendered divine. The divine mystery takes place on earth and follows the natural course of earthly events. As the epistle so emphatically states: *according to the flesh — from the seed of David.* It cannot be interpreted any other way. It is an indisputable but incomprehensible fact that God enters our homes, our existence, not only like us but actually as one of us. That is the unfathomable mystery. From this point on the Son is absorbed by history, his fate becomes part of history and history's fate is his fate. In the darkest cells and the loneliest prisons we can meet him; he is continually on the high roads and in the lanes. And this is the first blessing of the burden — that he is there to help us bear it. And the second blessing of it is that all we who have to bear it know at once when the strong shoulder is pushed under to relieve the weight. And the third blessing is that since that holy night when divine life and the original pattern of existence was born on earth, strength enabling us to master life has grown from that upsurge of divine vitality in human existence and is reflected in the existence of the community, to which he revealed himself.

We shall be better able to cope with life's demands if we remain constantly aware of the directions this night provides. Let us continue our journey along the highway of life without allowing ourselves to be deterred or frightened by occasional desolate stretches. A new spirit has entered into us and we will not waver in our belief in the star of the promises or weary of acknowledging the angels' *Gloria* even if we sometimes have tears in our eyes as we join in. Many disasters have been turned into blessings because people have risen above them.

God in the Christmas encounter is still the challenging God. The greatest misconceptions all center round the typical Christmas picture of God. Here too humanity is so wrapped up in appearances that the breath-taking terrible reality of the birth of God as a human child scarcely enters our mind and the soul doesn't grasp its significance. The truth is too tremendous to be appreciated unless one concentrates on it fully. Of course the externals — the sweetly sentimental pictures, the carols, the cribs and so on are a comfort both to humanity as a whole and to the individual. But there is a great deal more to the nativity than that. The comfort we derive from the externals is only the symbol of the far greater gifts this event, and the feast commemorating it, bestowed and continue to bestow on humankind. Since the birth of our Lord we have been confirmed in the hope with which we turn to God's throne for grace: God is on our side. But as I have said before this does not mean that God has dethroned himself any more than it means that human life has been turned into a primrose path by that stupendous event.

We need to look critically at this tendency to sentimentalize the divine attributes by personifying them in the person of an innocent child or by over-beautifying the figure of the adult Jesus. The glamorizing of the nativity story, the lowering of the whole tone of Christ's life to the level of a baroque sermon full of portentous warnings and grave moralizings has contributed quite a lot to the west's present helplessness in the face of conditions that keep us fettered and restrained. Certainly God became man, a man among others; but nevertheless God, master of all creation. Therefore human beings must approach this God-made-man with reverence and adoration, subjugating themselves in order to find themselves — it is the only way.

The vigil points out how we ought to approach this feast. St. Paul, in his epistle to the Romans, says this about his relationship to Christ: *for obedience to the faith in all nations.* Even allowing for the Pauline tendency to overemphasize, it is clear that every contact with God means prayer and response to a command. Whoever enters into the divine way of life automatically comes under the divine law. That, as far as the worshipper is concerned, means that the nearer one gets to God the more one yearns to return there for it is essentially a homecoming. God's nearness has dynamic power. Worshippers may know by the state of unrest into which they are thrown by this attraction just how much we have grasped of the secret relationship between God and humanity.

And the vigil further prevents our becoming bemused by the over-glamorized picture of the divine Child by pointing out another fundamental relationship between God and humanity. Suddenly and unexpectedly the collect reminds us that the Child, whose coming we so joyfully await, will be our future judge — in fact is already sitting in judgment over our lives. That someday the laughing eyes of the Child will harden with adult sternness, questioning and judging. The increased capacity for life which comes from heeding this warning, the awakened sense of responsibility, remains with us long after Christmas is over — provided we have entered the vigil in the proper spirit. And if we remember that the divine Child of Christmas is already engaged in the serious business of judging the world, how many of the people who represent the human race today can

honestly approach the crib? Most of them don't even want to.
The small and narrow door will not admit those who come riding on a high horse. But simple shepherds have no difficulty
in getting through. The star leads the regal wise men to it but
the arrogance of Jerusalem is thrown into a panic by the Child.
How much there is in all our lives today that cannot face the
Child. How different our individual lives would be if only we
realized that the world's supreme hour struck that midnight
when Almighty God condescended to come among us as a little
child. We should not behave so greedily, so arrogantly, so high-
handedly to one another if we did. Children do not strike to
wound. But we pretend to be grown up and responsible; we are
so proud and self-assured — and look at the result. The world
lies in bomb dust and ruins around us.

Every hour of our Lord's life from the crib to the Cross by
which we were redeemed is a judgment on some part of our
existence. That is why we are so defeated and in such trouble.
But his last hour was his resurrection, his glorious homecoming.
We ought to take the Christ Child very seriously.

God whose coming we joyfully await is still the God of judgment. It is no easy or light matter to face the scrutiny of the
divine Judge. The commandments alone make quite severe demands on us. And unwavering obedience to the Word which
has to be the basis of our lives increases our responsibility. But
even that is not the end. The laws are for the general ordering of
life. Over and above them there are the entirely personal twists
and turns of fate through which God intervenes in the lives of
individuals. And so often he seems to leave us alone with our
burden to cope with our troubles as best we can.

Let us reread the gospel of the vigil from a human angle —
looking at the episode in our Lady's life from a purely human
point of view. We know how it all ended so it doesn't disturb us, but at the time there must have been a great deal of

heartache. Joseph's belief in a trusted human being had been shattered — but what must Mary herself have gone through? She had dedicated herself to God — her submission was complete and unreserved. She had received the Word in a way no other human being would ever share. And then God became silent. She must have felt her husband's questioning eyes following her; she must have known the torment he was going through and the blow his sense of justice had received. And God left her alone in this hour with all the weight of her trouble pressing on her. From a purely human point of view what a terrible position to be in.

And what about our own fate? We have heard the promises and believed in the messages and accepted the prophecies. And then something unexpected happens and our life is twisted out of shape — human life is subject to that sort of thing, even the life of Christians. Ought it to be different in their case? — it isn't. And it is precisely when we come up against occurrences like these that our faith is put to the real test. To adhere steadfastly to the Word even when we strike our foot against a stone, even when we feel we are beaten, even when we are fastened in chains and handcuffs — that is the answer. And that is the answer that will be expected when each person is questioned at the seat of judgment; no one can escape it. God is posing that very question to us today in a hundred different ways and we have to see to it that we give the right answer. Steadfastness is not an easy virtue to acquire but it makes us fit to face our Maker and it opens our eyes to the actual reality of God.

Once a person honestly tries to acquire it the face of the whole world is changed. The stark features of unavoidable accident, of logical consequence and necessity are softened. The world, and life, take on a more friendly look — they seem to assume an almost parental compassion. The thousand and one small blessings which God takes delight in showering on humankind begin to reveal his nearness to us. Outwardly things are just as before and yet something has happened — there is a new consciousness of God's fatherly care in those who have stood the test of his questions. Suddenly one discovers that events are not impersonal and universal but that they have more than one meaning. In the personal dialogue between God and humanity which is the whole point of life, achievements have meanings quite different from those commonly attributed to them. And what one person regards as trivial everyday occurrences are to another blessed signs of God's mercy and guidance.

To breathe again. That brings us back to *respirare,* the deep breath of relief which can and should bring ease. Nothing has happened to the world but it is now the ark of God which no storm can overturn, no flood can wreck. Life has not shaken off its laws or lost its tension but the Lord has subdued it, made sense of it all. The very tensions are harnessed now to increase the strength and the power of humankind.

And there is one other thing — humanity is no longer on its own. Monologue has never been able to make our life happy and healthy; we are only genuinely alive when we are engaged in a dialogue. All mono-tendencies are evil. But by bringing the God-imposed tensions and burdens into the dialogue the most terrible of all human maladies — loneliness — is overcome. From that point there are no more starless nights, no more days of solitary confinement, no more lonely paths or pitfalls without companionship or guidance. God with us. That was the promise, that was what we prayed for and cried out for. In his own way, in the natural course of things, far more simply but also far more effectively than we could ever have imagined, God came to us as our ally.

We must not try to shirk the burdens he imposes on us. They are his way of communicating with us and they are his blessing.

Whoever is true to life, however hard and barren it may be, will discover in himself fountains of very real refreshment. The world will give him more than he ever imagined possible. The silver threads of God's mystery will begin to sparkle visibly in everything around him and there will be a song in his heart. His burdens will turn to blessings because he recognizes them as coming from God and welcomes them as such.

God becomes man but humankind does not become divine. The human order remains unchanged with the same obligations. But it has acquired a blessing and humanity has grown in stature, has become stronger, mightier. Let us trust in life because this night will pass and a new day will dawn. Let us trust in life because we do not have to live through it alone. God is with us.

THE PEOPLE OF CHRISTMAS

What Is It That Separates People from God?

Life with God and in God has its own laws and we cannot discover what they are from a reference book. Yet the conditions for their fulfillment are very straightforward and clear cut — less obscure indeed than those of the ten commandments. All the same the thin thread on which they depend, the thread which unites the personal Thou of God with the personal I of the created being, can only be spun when they are being fulfilled.

The bridge linking the human with the divine has a very definite architecture. Its foundations are God's affair. In his all-embracing omnipotence he reaches out to humanity in a thousand different ways. To penetrate his mysteries, prayerfully and reverently to become aware of him, is one of the highest exercises of the human mind and we are most likely to find the key to his perpetual, relentless, compassionate, gracious reaching-out toward us in the lives of those whom we call saints. But the pattern which he has set for his relationship with humanity is not really my present concern. If that were my only preoccupation I should simply be satisfying a pious but very ordinary curiosity in spite of the exalted subject. But in order to get anywhere I must probe much more deeply, as indeed I am trying to do. It is a question of the fundamental conditions a person must achieve in his own personal life — what he has to do to draw the bow-string taut and release the arrow so that the creative dialogue may begin.

I am not here casting the least doubt on the dogmatic teaching of the divine omnipotence and its good-will toward humankind. There is no hint of doubt of the operation of grace, of God's goodness or of the merit of good deeds and decisions by which we confirm our attitude toward our Maker. But within this framework humans have certain liberties and responsibilities and these are the crux of the matter. It is here that mere curiosity is converted into existential thought about the mystery of the success — or failure — of one's life.

To take an example, how is it that the most eloquent, logical, well-prepared sermon may produce response in some and leave others unmoved? How is it that whole generations and periods can exist in complete ignorance of, or without response to, the idea of God's creative immanence as if they were incapable of receiving the divine impulse? How is it that there are people in all periods of history who remain unmoved by the greatest miracles, by the most convincing proofs of providential guidance, by the severest penances or the most inexorable strokes of divine justice?

Obviously this is more than merely an interesting theological or philosophical question — it is very pertinent to our fate today. It sums up everything and on the attitude we adopt to it depends whether we are going to place ourselves once again under the law of God's grace or whether, on the contrary, we are going to continue this miserable dance of death to the bitter end. It comes down to this — and there is no escape — to which order will we give our allegiance? Are we prepared to promote conditions in which the living contact with God can be reestablished? For our lives today have become Godless to the point of complete vacuity. God is no longer with us in the conscious sense of the word. He is denied, ignored, excluded from every claim to have a part in our daily life. We have ceased to admit him to our lives, we behave as if we no longer need him and, what is worse, we have actually become incapable of being God-conscious. It is a terrible thing to say about this modern world but as far as I can see it is true. We don't even have to look very far for proof of it — there is sufficient evidence in the things that are happening every day and pious horror at the state of the world will not help us in any way. The law to which our lives are subject which has brought about this state of affairs has already made our existence a reproach, reduced the world to rubble and ashes, to carnage and destruction. Now our most urgent concern is how to overcome the inner misery and seal off the source of this external chaos.

Christmas is the mystery of contact with God, fundamentally and actually. Those who are part of the approach to it can show us the human requirements which will make it possible for humanity once more to converse with God, and the conditions necessary if we are to reestablish contact with him.

Three different kinds of approach are suggested by the Christmas mystery. First there is the historical sequence of events recalled by the feast; secondly there is the liturgical reconstruction of the mystery; and thirdly there is the silent, yet eloquent, participation of all present. Even the empty places have speech of their own and a message for us.

Those Round the Crib

We are familiar with the crib figures inside the stable or making their way to it. And on that journey to the stable they all have something significant to say to us about the mystery of life and the everyday world. Mary, Joseph, the angels, the shepherds, the wise men; these are the people gathered round the Child. Let us seek their message and learn their judgment on our own lives.

Mary. Let us put aside, for the moment, the venerated figure of the Blessed Virgin as such. It would be impossible to discuss that holy figure in one short paragraph; as our Lady she is a theme with an endless and perpetual message. But let us here think of her simply as the young girl, Mary, kneeling humbly before the manger in which lies the child she has just given us. She has her own message, a few words to offer us in the turmoil to which the estrangement between our benighted generation and the divine mystery has thrown us.

The fact that this night of nights brought forth the Light, that Mary kneels before the Child, that motherhood and the grace of compassion have become a law of our life, that the ice of our inner solitude can be broken and melted by healing warmth — all this became possible only because the maid Mary yielded of her own free choice to the inner prompting of God's voice. Her secret is self-surrender and willing acceptance, offering herself to the point of complete obliteration of her personal will.

That is both her message and her judgment of us. As a generation we are completely wrapped up in ourselves; we are always concerned with *our* self-fulfillment, *our* self-realization, *our* living conditions and so on. Everything is organized for our self-gratification. And precisely because of this we are getting progressively poorer and more miserable. Mary's decision was complete surrender to God and it is the only thing that can lead to human fulfillment. Hers is the decision that obeys the law of life.

Joseph. He is the man on the outskirts, standing in the shadows, silently waiting, there when wanted and always ready to help. He is the man in whose life God is constantly intervening with warnings and visions. Without complaint he allows his own plans to be set aside. His life is a succession of prophecies and dream-messages, of packing up and moving on. He is the man who dreams of setting up a quiet household, simply leading a decent home life and going about his everyday affairs, attending to his business and worshipping God and who, instead, is condemned to a life of wandering. Beset with doubts, heavy hearted and uneasy in his mind, his whole life disrupted, he has to take to the open road, to make his way through an unfriendly country finding no shelter but a miserable stable for those he holds most dear. He is the man who sets aside all thought of self and shoulders his responsibilities bravely — and obeys.

His message is willing obedience. He is the man who serves. It never enters his head to question God's commands; he makes all the necessary preparations and is ready when God's call comes. Willing, unquestioning service is the secret of his life. It is his message for us and his judgment of us. How proud and presumptuous and self-sufficient we are. We have crabbed and confined God within the pitiable limits of our obstinacy, our complacency, our opportunism, our mania for "self-expression." We have given God — and with him everything that is noble and spiritual and holy — only the minimum of recognition, just as much as would serve to flatter our self-esteem and further our self-will. Just how wrong this is life itself has shown us since in consequence of our attitude we have come to abject bondage dominated by ruthless states which force the individual to sink his identity in the common mass and give his service whether he wishes or not. The prayer of St. Paul — *do with me what thou wilt* — the quiet and willing readiness to serve of the man Joseph, could lead us to a truer and more genuine freedom.

The angels. Not the plaster images we have made of them but spirits of a higher order of existence identified with freedom, loyalty, wisdom and love. We meet them in the opening scene on the plain of Bethlehem singing hymns of joy and praise. But that is not the mystery or the law they represent — that is its fruit and reward. They bring tidings; they announce God's mystery and summon the listeners to the adoration from which they themselves have risen. Their mystery is that they represent the afterglow of the divine reality they proclaim.

That is their message and their judgment of us. For a long time now there have been no great spirits among us. They have dwindled and died out because gifted men and women have themselves broken the laws of the spirit. For the last hundred years intellectualism has been obsessed by the glorification of self, as if truth and reality ought to consider it an honor to be perceived and recognized by such marvelous individuals. Spirit is no longer regarded as the living reflection of a higher life. Perception and awareness now pose as spirit itself. Dozens of prophets kindle new lights, each with his own message, his own ideas but with no notion of mission or dedication — that would be an offense against the autocracy and autonomy of genius. That is why for a very long time there have been no communications worth listening to. We have had no messengers of glad tidings singing paeans of praise. Whenever such a voice has been raised it has seemed illusory or has come from agonies of suffering — an indication of the depths of our soul sickness.

Adoration, perception, proclamation; this is the cycle that represents the life of the spirit. Adoration prepares the soul for perception since it loosens the tensions and dispels obstacles.

The message once perceived enriches the soul, fulfilling its innermost needs and desires. But the proof is in the unfolding of life itself.

Let us return to praising God, to proclaiming him joyfully and then we shall find words that are significant and valuable. We shall see visions again and penetrate mysteries. Insight and decision and the message of the spirit will again become matters of importance, pushing aside the empty show and the bombast of "presentation" which have so much influence nowadays.

The shepherds. They are symbolic of a type. That they happened to be shepherds is unimportant — they might equally have been farmers or hedge-crawling tramps who spent their nights in the open. But they had to be men capable of registering wonder so I very much doubt whether they could have been products of this mechanical age. They had to be men whose hearts still warmed to the recollection of the old promises. Men, therefore, whose lives still had wide horizons from which the light of intuition and a thousand forebodings of spiritual realities were not excluded. Men still able to believe in miracles. Men upright and healthy enough to accept facts as facts even when their mathematical calculations and the results of their experiments pointed to the contrary. Their secret lay in their modest purity of heart, their lively wakefulness of soul, their instant readiness to respond to the call. And underneath all this lay the fact that their lives still held desire and expectation; they longed for the fulfillment of the promises they remembered and implicitly believed.

That is their message for us and the standard they judge us by. As a type, men like these simple shepherds no longer exist. I am not referring to the profession or occupation but simply to the character of these men, to that wakeful readiness to accept miracles, that genuine inner prompting which altogether overshadowed self. The astonishing instinctive confidence which expects a miracle springs from the inner relationship between the yearning of humankind and the promises of God. This type is no longer with us. The world is full of miracles but no one perceives them; our eyes have lost the power to see. God's messengers would take a hand in our affairs more frequently if only our hearts could recapture the rhythm that calls them forth. Of all messages this is the most difficult to accept — we find it hard to believe that the person of active faith no longer exists. If we can revive faith in all its strength the whole world will change.

The wise men. Whether they were really kings or just local eastern chieftains or learned astronomers is not the least important. Their hearts were filled with wisdom and the aspirations of their race and that is what really concerns us. Only men of the highest type could have undertaken such a journey for such a purpose. They brought all the longing of their people with them to the place of the encounter for its fulfillment. Through the desert, by way of royal palaces, the libraries of the learned and the counsel chambers of the priests — and they ended their journey at last at a manger in a poor stable.

Here again we have a distinct type. The secret of these people is as plain as in the case of the shepherds. They are the men with clear eyes that probe things to their very depths. They have a real hunger and thirst for knowledge.

I know what that means now. They are capable of arriving at right decisions. They subordinate their lives to the end in view and they willingly journey to the ends of the earth in quest of knowledge, following a star, a sign, obeying an inner voice that would never have made itself heard but for their hunger and the intense alertness hunger produces. They believed in that voice more implicitly than they believed in the tangible realities of the mortal existence. Such men are regal in every impulse; they can rise above every situation even when it involves great suffering.

The compelling earnestness of their quest, the unshakable persistence of their search, the royal grandeur of their dedication — these are their secrets.

And it is their message for us and their judgment of us. Why do so few ever see the star? Only because so few are looking for it. People often resolve to do things and then trivial, more pressing preoccupations get in the way. At the time of the nativity the world had already been under firm control for a thousand years. Everything was well organized and things were getting better every day! We have been saying this for so long nowadays that our middle-class complacency has become sated with banal truisms and at last is forcing us to ask a few questions. But we are still at the perplexed and puzzled and frustrated stage; we have not yet reached the point where these questions set up a sense of inner compulsion and urgency. The star which could light the way is still invisible to our half-closed eyes.

What are we looking for anyway? And where will we find a genuine yearning so strong that neither fatigue, nor distance nor fear of the unknown nor loneliness nor ridicule will deter us? Only such a passionate desire can prompt the persistence which is content to kneel even when the ultimate goal turns out to be a simple stable. Those capable of such dedication penetrate to the heart of things and understand why that should be the outcome. A thousand secret longings of the spirit and the heart have paved the way for faith and sanctified them for the act of adoration.

Figures Linked with the Feast

So many figures come to mind when we are thinking about the feast of Christmas. All of them have a very special message for us. The innocents of Bethlehem even have a place in history. The others are so intimately associated with the mystery of contact which is the essence of this feast that they throw a penetrating light on our question and supply a valid answer. It is still the same question — how is the human soul prepared and fitted for this great encounter — and further, how can we help make it ready? What are the essential decisions of the heart for establishing a real and living contact with God?

St. Stephen. His secret is easy to discern. He saw clearly that humankind had been lifted to a new plane through the miracle of the holy night and the encounter with Christ; that human beings now had new strength and the new responsibility of bearing witness. What had been enough before was enough no longer. Hence the expressions full of grace and strength — signs and wonders. But these things have not been given to us merely for us to master ourselves. Since Christmas God is with us and injustice and even murder are sanctified and transformed into signs of grace and strength and salvation. St. Stephen's law is that of extraordinary self-surrender and extraordinary witness.

This is his message and his judgment. He challenges us to get out of our rut. As we draw near to God the old and familiar become useless. God will transform us into faithful witnesses if we earnestly and with complete surrender turn to him for help.

St. John. The very mention of that figure of glowing light conjures up many mysteries. We need only select three words which express the whole range of divine reality and at the same time sum up the character of the evangelist himself — light, truth and love.

These three words suffice both for the message and the judgment. Where today are those radiant souls whose light extends to eternity? Where are those whose ways are the ways of truth? "The truth shall set you free," St. John said. Today's bondage is the sign of our untruth and deception. So in these conditions let us take as our example those who have dedicated themselves to love. Seeking the light, living the truth and practicing love will cure all our ills.

The holy innocents. The children of Bethlehem. They too have their place here. They share the scene with our Lord. And the mystery of the words "all this happened — *because the Lord came,*" applies particularly to them. They were not martyred because of the power of a frightened and insane tyrant — that is made quite clear. And we see how completely all life is in the possession of our Lord. It is not mere pious sentiment to call the Child *kyrios.* Our concept of God must retain its grandeur and become firmer. Then the love we profess will also be strong, effective, reliable.

The mystery of the innocents is that they are the victims. The divine eagle gathered them as booty to himself. The blow aimed by the tyrant at our Lord fell on them instead. They serve as a kind of guard of honor to the divine Child — and the militant dialogue between God and anti-God in which they are caught up earns them heaven. But we have lost our awareness of that ceaseless duel — we so little realize that we have a share in the struggle that we ignore it completely. Yet no one can escape responsibility and at any moment God, exercising his sovereign power, may draw us into the thick of it. So far as an adult is concerned, this can lead to salvation only if the victim voluntarily accepts the combat and enters it on God's side. But in the case of the innocents the manger sealed their fate and was sacrifice enough. That is their mystery.

And it is also their message and judgment. We have become insensitive to the sovereignty of God. Even where awareness of it still exists a clear-cut concept of the relationship and of the order to which it belongs is lacking. The God under whose inexorable law we exist has been dissolved in a mist of psychological outpourings, subjective living conditions or collective existential needs. This is one of the worst evils of our time.

St. Thomas of Canterbury. He too fits into the nativity picture. Here we have a man with a two-sided personality. He was chancellor and later archbishop — that is a man of authority living in the sphere of power, of palaces, of renown, a man of the purple. The mystery of St. Thomas is on two different planes. When the chancellor became archbishop he was expected to subordinate the Church to the state. And the man who had been chancellor would probably have done so. But the office changed the man. He took the conditions of his new rank seriously. And this matter of the inherent order of things is vitally important. And it involves a second condition. Because of this inherent order Thomas sacrificed his life for God. He died for the greatest Christian mystery, yielding his life for the sanctity of the Church.

His message and judgment are supremely important. The laws of order that govern this life are in no way inferior to the divine laws. Only those who submit to them with complete resignation can face judgment calmly. That is a message that should be taken to heart by a generation that has lost all sense of reverence and at the same time it is a measuring rod by which that generation must be judged. Untrammeled subjectivity is not the ultimate secret of being. A genuine contact must be established in which the partner, whether a thing or a person, is under no sort of compulsion either idealistic or material. The partner must have freedom to respond and speak for himself according to his nature, even to the point of being helped to speak his mind and express what he feels so that the dialogue may be truly reciprocal.

St. Thomas's second message and judgment are closely linked with the first. The mystery of contact on the night of the nativity is not a subjective and lyrical romance. It embraces very clear ordinances of the Church. Oh I know well the Church often stands in its own light as well as in God's. But this is precisely where loyalty and steadfastness are called for. When all is said and done Bethlehem was no palace but a common stable. God lives in his laws. Since the clear duty of the Church is to conform and obey there can be no hope of finding God in disobedience. Whoever has fulfilled the duty of obedience has a right to cast a critical eye over the realities of the Church, and where the Church fails the short-comings should not be glossed over. This is a matter of vital concern to intelligent and capable men and women who have truth and its fruitfulness at heart.

The People Who Are Not at the Crib

Even those who are not there have a message for us and a judgment to give if only to make us realize what it is that keeps us separated from God. After all as a race today we are not at the crib either. Yet the emotions aroused by all that we are living through ought certainly to make us want to be there.

Those who were not there include the powerful, the wealthy and the learned leaders of the synagogue, that is, the heads of the established church.

The powerful. Neither the Roman procurator nor the recognized native rulers made their appearance at the crib to receive ratification of their power. Power can only be genuine and good when it is rooted in the divine. These people possessed power in their own right and used it only to further their own ends. Theirs is the mystery of power. Those who possess power have the implicit duty — and the opportunity — to serve as God's deputies. The French, more realistic than we are, have two different words, *force* and *puissance*. *Puissance* conveys the awe-inspiring impression of inner power. Power in itself and as the sum-total of all the means of enforcing it becomes destructive in the hands of arrogant totalitarian authority and ruins both the one who wields it and the subjects on whom he exercises it. The tyrant in possession of such power is no longer capable of spiritual sensitivity. He is suspicious of everything that does not fit into the narrow limits of permitted and regimented expression. There was no paragraph in the rules at Jerusalem covering the birth of the Child at Bethlehem. Hence the reaction of perplexity and fear and the prompt recourse to the sword. In circumstances like these the subject beings grow timid and cowardly; they accept that their claim to life is cut to the basic minimum of official permission.

Dare we ignore this message and judgment? The history of power in the western world is one long story of ruthless force. There is no room in it for the glory of God which is neither safeguarded nor respected. The great are concerned only with their own importance and spend their lives jockeying for position. And the consequences, as far as they concern humankind as a whole, are only too obvious. Fear has become a cardinal virtue. This is not said in a spirit of anarchy. But power must regain its proper dimension, allying itself with eternal purpose and genuine mission. Otherwise it will merely evoke counteraction and the ghastly struggle for survival will never end. And as a subordinate being, a human being must waken to the inherent sovereignty of his spirit, believing in conscience and in his relationship with God.

The wealthy. There is nothing wrong in a person's having great possessions. But when his possessions rob him of his freedom and make him a slave then they become evil. It was like this at the time of the nativity and the palaces and fine houses were not destined to shelter the Lord. Great possessions can and should be a blessing. But the owners of treasure are also people who are afraid of any order of things not covered by the official records. It is so now and it was so then — our Lord's words on the subject are well known.

A great many hasty judgments have been made in this connection and much prejudice has been based on them — Marxist
socialism, the condemnation of private ownership, and so on.
We must keep a sense of proportion. All the same it is clear that
the unsolved problem of wealth, of unearned income and so
on is one of the themes of our time. In the last century control
passed from the hands of great men and these burning questions
no longer came up against the moderating influence of toler-
ance, wisdom and a sense of duty. Evils that were dealt with
by the materialistic society of the nineteenth century were at
the mercy of self-interest, expediency, indignation. The highest
ideals were lacking and there was palpably no trace of that spiritual attitude based on the divine nature that makes all persons
free. So it is not surprising that the ordinary person's spiritual
mechanism has rusted and become practically useless. Therefore
those endowed with great possessions cannot be found in the
devout circle round the crib. Some are absent because their possessions have robbed them of proper insight, others because the
things they covet have made them incapable of any other interest. It is undeniable that every human being is entitled to living
space, daily bread and the protection of the law as a common
birthright; these are fundamentals and should not be handed
out as an act of charity.

The learned. Learning and prayer have little in common. It
was so then and it is still so today. Learning is besotted and
bemused by the brilliance of its own ideas and has an over-
weeningly high opinion of its own interpretation of the world's
affairs. And whenever the world takes a course not laid down
in the books it is immediately suspect.

Western thought is inordinately proud of having "grown up"
in the last century. It considers itself completely adult and self-
possessed. Meanwhile in obedience to its own law it is no
longer spreading its wings like an eagle, no longer adventuring

to the horizon. It has become a mere appendage to earth-bound utility blind and blunted to certain aspects of the truth. But human nature is so constituted that even in its most debased and blinded state it still needs to ape God and set itself on a pedestal as if it were divine. Unconsciously it is reaching out toward a state it might be capable of achieving if it were not so in love with itself and forever leading itself and its world into the icy mire of materialism.

No, the learned are certainly not found among those devout souls kneeling round the crib in the stable. They are the types whom later, when he had grown to manhood, the Child was to embrace in the lament "Woe, woe"; but then they did not understand that either. The wise men, those whose prescience came from the heart, knew where they were going and the goal they were looking for. *They* were capable of adoration.

The learned today cannot be bothered with prayer. Should their thoughts ever wander in the direction of the crib they would surround it with signs and symbols, propaganda slogans, culture jargon and so on. They overlook the simple, unquestionable truths God has laid down. Clearly the whole destiny of the west is tied up with this problem. A glance into our schools and universities should suffice to prove that the problem of destiny is unsolved.

The established church. The synagogue had no part in the adoration at the manger. The synagogue in fact was one-track minded; it had an expectation and had no time or attention for anything except that clear-cut idea and its hoped-for realization. The books had even foretold that Bethlehem was the place where that realization would come to pass, yet so completely were the priests shrouded in their own shriveled ideas that their senses had become numbed and that numbness prevented their recognizing the signs of their time. No star pointed the way for them, no gleam of intuition lightened their darkness. They were bemused by their own self-sufficiency and heard nothing of the angels' song.

If only this were merely a tale to point a moral. But it is the plain truth; it really happened. The new spirit of Creation flows without interruption through the new Church — but how much force it requires to achieve its purpose. The officers of the Church have the inner guidance of the Spirit — but what about the executive departments? And the bureaucratic officials? And the mechanical "believers" who "believe" in everything, in every ceremony, every ritual — but know nothing whatever about the living God? One has to be very careful in formulating this thought, not from cowardice but because the subject is so awe-inspiring. One thinks of all the meaningless attitudes and gestures — in the name of God? No, in the name of habit, of tradition, custom, convenience, safety and even — let us be honest — in the name of middle-class respectability which is perhaps the very least suitable vehicle for the coming of the Holy Spirit.

The Spirit will go on pouring forth and bringing about its work of renewal but things might have worked more smoothly if there had been no rift, no quarrels, no secession, defamation and suspicion, if the Spirit had found living organs to work through instead of withered officials. And the obstacles are still there. Creative theology, spiritually conscious worshippers, active, effective love have yet to be achieved. Let us go back to the genuine contact and learn its laws once more; let us regain the capacity to see visions and know intuitively, moved by the Spirit. Let us give free rein to the divine instinct with which we are endowed and climb out of this morass in which we are bogged, emerge from this trance of false security. Then we shall discover the real efficacy of prayer and its power to bless and to heal.

The Crux of the Matter

Now I ought to sum all this up in a pattern of behavior toward which we could be educated so that we can be capable of knowing God once more. But I am desperately short of time. I can hear the jailer already coming down the passage and besides I have no more paper. So the friend for whom these lines are intended, and any others who may one day chance to read them, will have to gather up the ends for themselves.

But one thing must be said. I shall be accused of being concerned only with the "natural" life of human beings. I will not attempt to deny or disguise the fact. But *his kindness appeared* in one of the Christmas messages. Without a minimum of sound humanity, genuine human dignity and human culture, no one is capable of making contact with God. One is not even capable of ordinary understanding and behavior.

I am perfectly aware that only extraordinary grace can reawaken us and heal us; I also know that the divine impulse is forever prompting us, yearning to be allowed to do its healing work. To proclaim this is the task of those among us who still have perception and know it for the truth.

For God will not deny his mercy is the law of our salvation. But the main task is to render human beings capable and willing for the Spirit to do its work. This is even more urgent than the proclamation of the central mystery for no one can understand this anyway until he has surrendered and opened his heart to the will of God within him. So it may be that even this shambles in which we now live, this devastation swept by bitter winds of fate, is the destined place and hour of a new holy night, a new birth for humanity seeking God, a new nativity. Darkness shall not frighten us or distress wear us out; we will go on waiting, watching and praying until the star rises.

EPIPHANY 1945

It may be possible to find an hour to think today. How many things there are to think about and what contrasts they present. The feast itself with its rich symbolism; the emergence of God from the quiet corner of Bethlehem into the wider world; the guiding star; the men who have braved the wilderness; the joy of the encounter; the terror-stricken king; the indifferent clergy; the wonderful providence of God. And besides all this, all the other things the feast commemorates — the baptism in Jordan, the hearing of the Father's voice, the marriage feast of Cana. So very much to turn over in one's mind.

Then the personal aspect. The many years I have spent in preparation and the day for renewing my holy vows. This year, in this time when men and women are yearning for a star to guide them and not a glimmer of a star appears because their eyes are blind and cannot see, the message of the feast is more than usually urgent. We must pass it on and stir people's understanding.

But to come back to my own personal predicament; in two more days my case will come up for trial. Just two days in which I can *rely* only upon God for there is no other help I can turn to. How I have prayed for a Christmas star, for light on this problem. But God has left it unanswered; he is asking me to make the "step to freedom" — the decisive stride which will carry me from myself to lose myself completely in him. Here also is a wilderness to be crossed and a terrified ruler only too eager to use the sword.

How can I best sum this up, make a mental picture which will unravel my perplexity? Situated as I am I should so love to be able to give my friends (and myself) one word whose genuineness would be unquestionable because it had been won from God himself. But up to now I have not found that word.

Will the last hour eventually produce it for me? I realize now as never before that a life is wasted if it cannot be summed up in one word, one direction, one ruling passion. Only a human being who has this secret can rise to his full stature; everything else is mass-produced, subject to any conditions others choose to impose. And the hall-marked individuals are rarely met with nowadays — that is why life lacks purpose and makes so little sense. The genuine dialogue no longer exists because there are no genuine partners to engage in it. People are frightened, they are scared to stride out firmly and honestly to the boundaries of their potential powers because they are afraid of what they will find at the border line. The person who aims at fulfillment only within the framework of his own limitations must always be afraid of the unknown. The existence of the limitless, the eternal that is beyond our comprehension and yet vaguely draws us as being within our capacity for experience is the real source of our uneasiness. It is precisely here that human judgment and assessment of values comes in.

For those who desire to develop their highest potentialities today's feast gives the laws and conditions which should regulate their lives. It shows them the way by which they can achieve a real proved individuality.

The Law of Freedom

Humans need freedom. As slaves, fettered and confined, they are bound to deteriorate. We have spent a great deal of thought and time on external freedom; we have made serious efforts to secure our personal liberty and yet we have lost it again and again. The worst thing is that eventually humans come to accept the state of bondage — it becomes habitual and they hardly notice it. The most abject slaves can be made to believe that the condition in which they are held is actually freedom.

During these long weeks of confinement I have learned by personal experience that a person is truly lost, is the victim of circumstances and oppression only when he is incapable of a great inner sense of depth and freedom. Anyone whose natural element is not an atmosphere of freedom, unassailable and unshakable whatever force may be put on it, is already lost; but such a person is not really a human being any more; he is merely an object, a number, a voting paper. And the inner freedom can only be attained if we have discovered the means of widening our own horizons. We must progress and grow, we must mount above our own limitations. It can be done; the driving force is the inner urge to conquer whose very existence shows that human nature is fundamentally designed for this expansion. A rebel, after all, can be trained to be a decent citizen, but an idler and a dreamer is a hopeless proposition.

Human freedom is born in the moment of our contact with God. It is really unimportant whether God forces us out of our limits by the sheer distress of much suffering, coaxes us with visions of beauty and truth, or pricks us into action by the endless hunger and thirst for righteousness that possess our soul. What really matters is the fact that we are called and we must be sufficiently awake to hear the call.

The law of freedom is an appropriate theme for today. When those worshippers knelt in homage on the floor of the humble stable with everything else put behind them — their homes, the wilderness, the guiding star, the agony of the silent star, the palace of the king and the grandeur of the city — when all these had lost their value and their impressiveness and the worshippers' whole being was concentrated in the single act of adoration, the symbolic gesture of laying gifts before the manger signified the achievement of liberty. Then they were free.

We must leave ourselves behind if we hope to have even a glimpse of our true potentialities. But this surrender of self is the thing we find most difficult to accomplish and so rarely succeed in. To the modern mind it makes no sense because we have lost any concept of the boundless glory, the shimmering, unlimited wonder of the divine to which we gain access by yielding up our own limited personality. Only when we trim our sails to the eternal winds do we begin to understand the sort of journey we are capable of undertaking. Only by voluntary unreserved surrender to God can we find our home. Any other sort of refuge is only a temporary shelter, a poor hovel on shifting sand destined eventually to fall in ruins. Adoration in a stable is preferable to terror before a throne. There is much wisdom in the ancient teaching about the passing of the soul because it embodies the idea that human beings can become themselves only by stepping outside themselves. Pray and praise are the two key words to human liberty. The kneeling attitude with outstretched hands is the correct attitude for a free person.

Our age, like those before us, has tried many other ways. But the life-urge is very strong in any person of genuine feeling and it keeps forcing us back to our own potentialities. We found it very hard to let go of beautiful things. But in the end we had to. We came to the stable by a road which was laborious, terrifying and bloodsoaked and this miserable dwelling was at the end of it. Our hands are empty — more than empty. They are torn and bleeding because things literally had to be wrenched from their grasp. But if in spite of everything we can hear and recognize the call, if we can discover the inner meaning of the grim experience through which we are passing and if in the midst of this frightfulness we can learn to pray, then this hell will bring forth a new human being and a blessed hour will strike for the troubled earth in the middle of the night — as it has so often before.

The fate of humankind, my own fate, the verdict awaiting me, the significance of the feast, can all be summed up in the sentence *surrender thyself to God and thou shalt find thyself again*. Others have you in their power now; they torture and frighten you, hound you from pillar to post. But the inner law of freedom sings that no death can kill us; life is eternal. *Pray and praise* — the fundamental words of life, the steep roads to God, the doors that lead to fulfillment, the ways that lead a person to his true self.

The Law of the Wilderness

Those for whom the hour of freedom struck in the stable at Bethlehem had faced and overcome the wilderness, both the external wilderness of isolation, forsaken homeland, lost relationships and friendships of a momentous and strenuous pilgrimage, and the inner wilderness of uncertainty, doubt, fear and anxiety. It had been a long and a weary journey and their faces still bore the marks of the hours of strain even in the glow of the blissful encounter. The wilderness has its proper place in the drama. Human freedom is the fruit of liberation, of the persistent and tireless scaling of the enemy fortifications.

When children kneel before the crib lisping *adoro* and *suscipe* their prayer is valid — but more is expected of an adult. He must master the real meaning of the words and gestures or go back and learn his lessons over again. Human freedom is the result of a tough and painful liberation; healing and happiness are not imposed on humankind and life is not a lottery with colossal prizes.

The wilderness is part of it all, the wilderness of the soul as well as the body. One could write a whole history about wildernesses. All really great men and women have had to fight against loneliness and isolation and the great fundamental questions that occur to a person in such circumstances. The fact that our Lord retired into the wilderness shows how genuinely he took to heart the laws and problems of humanity. And then, after the trial of the wilderness had been withstood there will still be the temptations to be met. Great issues affecting humankind always have to be decided in the wilderness, in uninterrupted isolation and unbroken silence. They hold a meaning and a blessing, these great, silent, empty spaces that bring a person face to face with reality.

There are no more profitable places in history than wildernesses — vast areas — the sea, high mountains, trackless forests, plain and pampas and steppe, barren land as well as fruitful, all exercise their own peculiar influence, not only on the physical being but even more on the dispositions and characters of the human beings affected by them. They all leave their mark on history. And of all wildernesses the streets of great cities — deserts of stone — are unique in that again and again they have ended up as the graveyard of history. The wilderness concerns all humanity, all its actions and decisions, in a very special way.

Any life that cannot measure up to the wilderness, or seeks to evade it, is not worth much. There must be periods of withdrawal alternating with periods of activity and companionship or the horizons will shrink and life lose its savor. Unless a person consciously retires within himself to that quiet place where he may think out great problems he cannot hope to solve them and if he denies himself this healing effort an evil fate will certainly overtake him. God, who loves him, will chain him in loneliness, perhaps to his own undoing.

And the world too will be in a bad way if ever it happens that there are no more wildernesses, no more silent unspoiled places to which a person can retire and think, if every corner of the earth is filled with noise and underground tunnels and soaring airplanes and communication networks, if cables and sewers scar the surface and undermine the crust. Humanity needs to keep a few quiet corners for those who seek a respite and feel the urge to retreat for a while from over-civilization to creative silence. For those who occasionally feel the hermit instinct there should at least be a chance to try it out. The law of absolute utility, of total functionalism, is not a law of life. There is an extraordinarily close connection between the wilderness and fruitful, satisfying life. Where all the secluded places ring with tumult, where the silent muses have been degraded to pack-horses and all the sources of inspiration forced into the service of official mills grinding out propaganda, the wilderness has indeed been conquered — but at what a price. Even greater devastation has taken its place.

The wilderness has a necessary function in life. "Abandonment" one of my friends called it and the word is very apt. Abandonment to wind and weather and day and night and all the intervening hours. And abandonment to the silence of God, the greatest abandonment of all. The virtue that thrives most on it — patience — is the most necessary of all virtues that spring from the heart — and the Spirit.

Please don't think I am trying to write an ode to the wilderness. Anyone who has ever had to encounter and withstand a wilderness must have a healthy respect for it — and must speak of it with the reserve that prompts us to hide our wounds and our weaknesses. It is a great place for thinking things out, for recognizing facts, for getting new light on problems and for reaching decisions. A heavy load brings the ship low in the water but it also keeps her steady. The wilderness represents the law of endurance, the firmness that makes a person. It is the quiet corner reserved for tears, prayers for help, humiliations, terror. But it is a part of life and to try to avoid it only postpones the trial.

The Law of Grace

However the wilderness is neither the beginning nor the end. In our perilous climb to the heights of freedom we are not entirely dependent on our own resources. The more we have to over-come, the greater the distance we have to travel, to transcend ourselves and find our true self, the less we can depend on our own unaided power. Both as a race and as individuals we have experienced and discovered how miserably inadequate our own feeble efforts are. Please God it may be a long time before we again overrate our personal powers in so devastating a fashion.

Freedom is born in the hour of contact. And it is not as if God simply stood there, waiting for the weary traveller to ar-rive. Both God and humanity are travelling toward one another. God shows in hundreds of ways his willingness to meet us more than half-way — to put out his hand when we tend to stumble. And this is not the full extent of our divine aid — this is merely the preliminary. The summit is reached when we hear his voice; then we can no longer doubt that his destiny is to rise above ourselves to our fulfillment.

Today's feast uses three symbols for the divine attraction that draws humanity with gifts of grace — the star, the sacred river, and the water changed into wine. But they are only symbols, not the truth itself. For the star signifies the Child, the river sig-nifies the Lord and the divine remission and forgiveness of sin, and the wedding feast signifies the coming of the Spirit for our salvation. Humanity is made to see that it is not only under the law that demands grace but it is also under the law of genuine and effective grace. Precisely where we most need help we find it because God has placed himself on an equal footing with us. We are not alone — we can face anything that befalls us. And more than that, we are capable of living effectively when every-thing in our world seems to be against us. Remember St. Paul said: "My grace is sufficient" — and it was sufficient to such an extent that to this day the world still admits it. Another great man said: "God alone suffices" — and he did suffice for a life whose fruits the world is still reaping.

At the present time we are still wandering in the wilderness. The cry for help still rises from our hearts. It is true as far as we are all concerned and it is true for me personally. In this situation the wilderness has lost its peaceful appeal and assumed its more threatening aspect hinting at unknown dangers. This is no figure of speech but actual fact. We nine are acutely aware of the great community, the world of men ranged against us, and we are the "lost ones" who tomorrow have to start on an unknown journey to meet our fate.

But the wilderness will not lead us to final doom but to a great freedom. The wilderness exists to be overcome. And I know that I am not alone. The law of truth and love and prayer still holds good. I must let the healing current run its course so that the waters of bitterness will be turned into the wine of divine blessing; *pray and praise.*

3

The Tasks in Front of Us

THE FUTURE OF HUMANITY

God-Conscious Humanism

Every meditation on humanism is historically handicapped at the outset. There has already been a humanism — in fact there have been several. And unless the humanism of the future succeeds in cutting itself off completely from its predecessors it is hardly likely to inspire confidence. And quite rightly. But it is not easy to establish that we are dealing with true humanism and at the same time overcome, or rather transform, the versions that have gone before.

The essential requirement is that humanity must wake up to the truth about itself. We must rouse our consciousness of our own worth and dignity, of the divine and human potentialities within ourselves and at the same time we must master the undisciplined passions and forces which, in our name and by bemusing us with delight in our own ego, have made us what we are. This is not a disparagement of passions. Woe to the person who tries to live without any — that is the way to disintegration. Humanity must take itself as it is with all the undercurrents and the fire of its nature. But the destructive element in passions, the element which knows neither limit nor restraint, must be brought under control or it will tear us to pieces and destroy us. Our passionate preoccupation with self must be subordinated; we must retain all the strength and fire of devoted human love but without the blindness, the irresponsibility, the lack of instinct that makes it destructive.

Humans want to be happy and it is right that they should. But by thinking only in terms of self we destroy ourselves for it is a limited concept and has no room for anything stronger than the human order. Left entirely to themselves humans are unhappy and intrinsically insincere. We need other people to give us a sense of completeness; we need the community. We need the world and the duty of serving it. We need eternity, or rather we need the eternal, the infinite. And there we come to the new, God-conscious humanism.

The Lessons of History

In my study of history I have been constantly filled with regret that we only hear of things after they have already happened. We ought to be able to arrange matters so that we could shape our own history. That would save humankind much distress and suffering. As things are, the road through history is often a way of the cross.

Those who make history are swayed by conditions as they find them, by the dynamics of situations and by the rhythm of their own individual characters. These can affect trivial and unimportant matters and they can also affect whole states, bringing decisions as to the fate of nations down to the narrowest personal level.

Such decisions which condition the actual pattern of any given period are dictated sometimes by intuition, by mood, by fancy or by wishful thinking; sometimes too by expediency, by necessary defense measures which force many detours and false starts on the historical subjects before they can arrive at their predestined consummation.

Every age and nation has its mission in history. And the sooner they realize this, and set about fulfilling their role the quicker they will escape from history's ruthlessness to a state of comparative peace. But the problem is always to discover the right theme for a given nation and a given period. A great many people — the majority in fact — never get beyond the stage of viewing life from the historical standpoint as a perpetual struggle for the bare necessities of existence. Life to them is a workroom for the exploitation of subjective passions or for labor in the service of the great "I." So it is important that every nation should have a few individuals capable of perceiving universal tendencies and of making them known again and again. Even Plato wished that philosophers were kings. We are in just such a situation today. My own opinion is that it offers possibilities and responsibilities for Christians. It is not a major task but it is still a function that Christians are capable of performing if they take their purpose in life seriously because they know of the supernatural influence on history.

The bitter lessons humanity has learned from experience in the past hundred years ought not to be erased by chaotic events or a way of life that has again become primitive. These things should be thought out and the results handed on to act as a guide in future trials. It is impossible for me at this moment to arrange the experiences and results in either hierarchic or logical order. I can only put down a few points that seem important to me. The tasks in front of us are:

1. An "existence minimum," consisting of sufficient living space, stable law and order and adequate nourishment, is indispensable. The "socialism of the minimum" is not the last word on the subject but the essential first word, the start. No faith,

no education, no government, no science, no art, no wisdom will help humankind if the unfailing certainty of the minimum is lacking.

2. A minimum of honesty in every field is equally necessary.

3. A minimum of personal standards and human solidarity is necessary.

4. There must be a minimum of worldwide dedication and sense of service. Any idea or ideal the age calls forth, even if it is only the shadow of absolute truth, is preferable to mass-minded thoughtlessness since it keeps alive in humankind a certain feeling for spiritual values without which our receiving apparatus for the spark of truth ceases to function.

5. A minimum of transcendence is essential — we must have something to look up to, to reach for, some kind of aspiration, if we are to be human at all.

6. In addition to these minimum essentials there must be qualities to which one's desire can be wakened, which one can feel oneself capable of attaining.

All this is the "existence minimum" that I would like to sum up in the words respect, awe, devotion, love, freedom, law — the words which, in my opinion, represent genuine fulfillment.

And in conclusion the "existence minimum" will only work if all the essentials are coordinated to work in harmony with each other. Individually this adds up to character; collectively it means the family, the community, the economy....

THE EDUCATION OF HUMANITY

To return to my familiar theme, that humanity today is profoundly Godless. This is a basic fact affecting both its judgment and its decisions. But it also goes even deeper than that for modern people are no longer *capable* of knowing God. The great task in the education of the present and future generations is to restore humanity to a state of fitness for God and religion.

What actually does the present state of things amount to? It means that certain human organs have become atrophied and no longer function normally. And also that the structure and the constitution of human life today put such a strain on humanity that people are no longer able to express their true nature. This applies on the technical-sociological plane as well as on the moral plane. Hence humans have built up in their own mind a picture of themselves as a sensitive animal with mind, reason, temperament depending on circumstance.

We have to ask ourselves very seriously what has brought this state of affairs about. We cannot, for instance, lay all the blame on the last few decades. They are the harvest but the seed was sown much earlier. Reading Goethe — particularly *Dichting & Wahrheit* and *Wilhelm Meister* — one cannot help noticing signs that modern humanity was even then well on the way. The center of gravity had already begun to slip. He indicated the different processes of development of which present-day humanity is the end-product. There is the inner development resulting from this shifting of the human center of gravity which has its own inescapable logic and consequences. And there is the external development represented by the technical, sociological, scientific and industrial world. These developments have influenced and furthered each other. Present-day humans are in the strictest sense both the product and the slave of the world in which they live. But that world has become what it is because of the breakdown of the inner standard which should have controlled our choices and safeguarded our ability to master the conditions in which we live.

And what now? Three possibilities suggest themselves. First we must preach the divine order and center our hopes on it. Secondly we must restore human order and await a general improvement as a result. And thirdly we must bring order to the chaos of human living conditions and then trust to the emergence of a new human being.

But if I preach till I am black in the face, trying with whatever skill I may possess to persuade humans to resume their proper status yet as long as human beings have to exist in inhuman and unworthy conditions the majority will succumb to them and nothing will make them either pray or think. Nothing short of a complete change of the conditions of life will have the least effect. The revolution of the twentieth century has need of an ultimate aim; it ought to be to guarantee every human being space to grow in.

But even if this happens under a democratic constitution, if things are left in the charge of present-day humans then sooner or later they will degenerate into chaos again. For present-day humanity is sick and incapable of handling its affairs — it can no longer cope with life. So a new approach is necessary, a more intensive method. Humans must be shown how to help themselves; they must be spiritually and physically strengthened in order to rise to full stature. This involves education toward self-reliance, responsibility, judgment, conscience; education that will instill good-neighborliness and eliminate the countless forms of superficial thinking and mass-mindedness; education toward transcendence, purposeful education toward perfect adulthood, education toward God. All these things are intimately connected and you cannot have one without the others. Only a person with a certain spiritual awareness, however small, is fit to accept the word of God and fulfill the divine order in his everyday life. For no order can be achieved except in accordance with God's law. The new order of the world must be based on the historical fulfillment of the order of God, otherwise it will be just another edifice on shifting sand doomed to destruction like the rest. Human regeneration must come from

within according to the pattern which defines us as being created in God's image. Otherwise history will repeat itself and we
shall be faced with further madness and confusion.

But how are we to set about it? It is obvious that all these
things are important and linked — but where are we to begin?
What is the first requirement, the essential foundation?

There will always be a few persons who see things as a
whole, aware of all the connections and implications, who can
trace the truth in every outward manifestation to its roots, to
that source where all things are linked by God and sustained by
him. Such persons must immerse themselves in two aspects of
being — in the recognition and acknowledgment of God, that
is to say in religion, and in the recognition and acknowledgment of the laws that apply to human existence, that is to say
in humanity itself. Actually these two requirements need not be
bracketed together. The person of great holiness is not necessarily an adept in worldly affairs. But if a saint should by chance be
mixed up in worldly affairs they would inevitably start moving
in the right direction for the mission of the saint, to render exceptional homage to God, is by no means opposed to the ideal
order of things in this world.

All the same specialization is fashionable nowadays and absolute thoroughness in both spheres is necessary. Religion in
the past has often occupied itself so little with the practical
problems of everyday life that it has been discredited, and
worldly wisdom has so often overreached itself that it has lost
confidence in its own power.

Re-education and re-inspiration of the people will help to restore religion to its proper state of prestige and for that reason
both are necessary. Anything that can help to heal our spiritual
ills or improve the conditions of our life should be encouraged
even if it cannot solve the whole problem. Humanity must be
induced to take itself seriously as being created with a divine

purpose to a divine pattern. We must be taught to recognize that pattern and to understand that it is our duty to realize it (existential humanism). Then through a sense of responsibility this humanism must be nursed and broadened into a new humanism, a God-conscious humanism.

But can this be described as the education of the individual to God? Let us start with the basic necessities. First the need to bring about conditions which will no longer require an almost superhuman effort on our part to turn our attention to God. Then the need for conditions in which the human heart is healed, even as far as its desires are concerned, quickened by that holy yearning which only finds true satisfaction in God and therefore turns to God again. And most important of all, conditions which encourage a human being who is God-like, filled with divine power to address and challenge others.

In my opinion all the direct religious effort of the present time falls short as far as any permanent effects are concerned. As long as a person lies bleeding, beaten and robbed by the wayside, the person who tends and helps him will be the one who wins his heart — not the one who passes by on the other side on the way to his holy offices because the person doesn't concern him. Therefore fuller and deeper religious teaching is needed for those who already have the genuine kernel of religious knowledge in them. They must be equipped so that they can go to the rescue of the rest of humanity and cope with the task of healing them. Humanity must be educated to resume its proper human status and religion must be taught intensively by truly religious teachers. The profession has fallen into disrepute and it will have to be reestablished. For the next few years those chosen to teach should be truly religious and ready to co-operate in all efforts for the betterment of humankind and human order. They should insist authoritatively on these efforts and not be satisfied with the mediocre.

In insisting on these I feel I am condemning present-day religious endeavors as sterile because they do not help humanity in the depths of need but merely skim the surface. But it is how I see it — for instance none of the contemporary religious movements take as their starting point the position of humankind as human beings. They really concentrate on the difficulties of the religious minded person who still has religious leanings. They do not succeed in coordinating the forms of religion with a state of existence that no longer accepts its values.

Equally efforts directed toward bettering humanity's physical or spiritual existence ought not be made in order to acquire power. For the next few centuries Europe is hardly likely to tolerate alliances between altars and any kind of throne. The effort must be brought down to the level of the outcast lying by the wayside; he is the one who must be restored to human dignity by the release of his latent virtues and all the inherent good in his nature. Our concern must be with a person's reverence, devotion, love; only when he is using these capacities is he a human being at all. We must direct our efforts toward reawakening love. When this has been achieved humans will begin to feel at home for a while and then the restless Spirit will lead them on to further progress.

THE FATE OF THE CHURCHES

In future years the fate of the churches will not be decided by whatever their prelates and leaders can produce in the way of skill, wisdom, diplomatic talent and so on. Nor will it depend on the important positions their members attain. That kind of achievement belongs to the past. For the sake of their very existence the churches must somehow break away from their sentimentalism and outmoded liberalism. They must get back to fundamentals. Hierarchy is essential for genuine order and direction; the Church at least should know this by its own origin. But order and direction are not to be confused with formalism and feudalism. The hierarchy must make it plain not only that it is aware of the errors and foolishness of individuals but also that it is also conscious of the despair and yearning of the age, of the unrest of contemporary trends and that it can hear and answer the bewildered, frightened seekers who cannot find their way. Humanity must feel that the concerns of the modern age and the problems of the new generations are not simply filed away as records but are matters of active and urgent concern to those who have assumed the task of dealing with them.

A Church that makes demands in the name of a peremptory God no longer carries weight in a world of changing values. The new generation is separated from the clear conclusions of our traditional theology by a great mountain of boredom and disillusion thrown up by past experience. We have destroyed people's confidence in us by the way we live. We cannot expect two thousand years of history to be unmixed blessing and recommendation — history can be a handicap too. But recently the person turning to the Church for enlightenment has all too often found only a tired man to receive him — a man who then had the dishonesty to hide his fatigue under pious words and fervent gestures. At some future date the honest historian will have some bitter things to say about the contribution made by the churches to the creation of the mass-mind, of collectivism, dictatorships and so on.

Whether the Church once again finds its own way to the heart of modern humanity depends on two things. The first is so obvious that it can hardly need elaborating. If the churches persist in presenting humanity with the spectacle of a Christendom at logger-heads with itself they might as well give up. It is no use saying we should resign ourselves to the rift as a historical legacy, a thing we must bear like a cross. That impresses nobody nowadays. It is to *our* eternal reproach that we were not capable of preserving the heritage of Christ intact.

The second essential is the return of the Church to the service of humanity in a way that conforms to human needs, not to private tastes or to the code of a privileged clergy. The Son of Man came to serve. . . . By this standard the realities of many religious institutions would be found wanting. No one will believe our message of salvation unless we work ourselves to the bone, physically, socially, economically or otherwise, in the service of ailing humanity. Modern humanity is sick; perhaps I shall be able in the next few days to write down some thoughts on this sickness. Modern humanity has become an expert in many departments of life — our range of power is enormous. But we are intoxicated by our own cleverness and we have not yet realized all the sacrifices that have had to be made, how much has had to be given in exchange for this power. These things have not yet forced themselves on our attention — and it is pointless to try to keep reminding us of them. A wise guide keeps an account but tactfully refrains from producing it until the proper moment comes. Modern humans, those worldly wise persons who think they know all the answers, are extremely sensitive to any form of presumption, real or imagined. And the precision which the scientific age imposes on many people makes them highly critical of the superficial way in which we clergy often perform our duty in the wider sense of the word.

I said we must get back to the ideal of service. By that I mean meeting the man in the street on his own ground, in all circumstances, with a view to helping him to master them. That means walking by his side, accompanying him even into the depths of degradation and misery. "Go forth," our Lord said — not "sit and wait for someone to come to you." There is no sense in preparing a fine sermon while we are losing contact with the listeners and leaving them to their fate. I look on the spiritual encounter as a dialogue, not a monologue or an address, a monotonous drone of words.

But all this will only be understood and desired when the Church again produces men and women who are in themselves properly fulfilled. Fullness; the word had a special attraction for St. Paul. It applies today even more forcibly than it did then. Fulfilled men and women — not pious caricatures. People who are genuinely impregnated with the spirit of their calling, people who have prayed with all sincerity: *make my heart like thine*. Whether the Church will again produce such fulfilled, creative people we do not know. But only if she does so will those she sends forth feel sufficiently secure to dispense with insistence on rights, sufficiently self-reliant to relax the perpetual preoccupation with traditions and so on. Only then will they see God's requirements with clear eyes even in the darkest hours. Only then will their willing hearts beat with a compassion that sweeps aside as negligible the old stubborn attachment to being "right after all." Their hearts will beat with one desire — to help and heal in God's name.

But how can we get to that stage? Churchmen seem to stand in their own light because of the habits they have acquired, historically speaking. Personally I believe that unless we voluntarily stride out across new ground, leaving the well-worn paths, history-in-the-making will destroy us with a thunderbolt of judgment. And that applies both to the personal destiny of the individual churchman and to religious institutions as a whole. Despite all right thinking and orthodox belief we have arrived at a dead end. The Christian idea is no longer one of the leading and formative ideas today. The plundered human victim lies bleeding by the wayside — must it be a stranger that comes to the rescue? It seems to me we ought to think about this very seriously. The burden that is pressing on the Church at the present time and disturbing it so much is humans themselves — those outside whom we cannot find a way to reach because they have no longer any belief, and those inside who no longer believe in themselves because they have experienced and given too little love. All this should make us see that it is no use making fine speeches about reform or drawing up reform programs. We ought to devote our energies to the development of the Christian character, preparing ourselves to *deal* with the needs of humankind, helping and healing in this age of unfathomable distress.

Most of the ordained in the official Church must realize for themselves that at present the Church is a misunderstood — and incomprehensible — reality to contemporary people and must be aware how disturbing, threatening and dangerous a state of affairs this is. We are going along two parallel roads and no bridge links them. Further we have both encouraged the belief that each is constantly sitting in judgment on the other. So far as the Church is concerned she has much to answer for. We ought to start with an honest examination as to how this state of affairs came about. And this probe must be free from any tendency to blame our opponents. And at this point of course up crops the old question — what good could such an examination achieve? Well first in importance is the recognition of the need for promoting respect for others. We must abandon our arrogant pretensions to reverence as a right. The Church must come to look upon herself far more as a sacrament, as a way and a means, not as a goal and an end in itself. Nowadays personal regeneration and revitalization is far more important than even the most comprehensive factual knowledge. In sober honesty we must face the fact that the Church today is no longer one of the controlling powers in human affairs. And that it cannot be made comparable with any other powerful historical factor (alliance of throne and altar in any form) but its influence must be centered in the integration of inner life with human potentialities (*puissance,* not *force*). And the impact made by the Church's message on this plane depends upon the sincerity of its transcendental surrender and devotion. Arrogance anywhere near the Church is objectionable — and never more so when it occurs in the name of the Church, or worse, actually as part of the Church herself.

4

Making Ready

THE OUR FATHER

On this ultimate peak of existence at which I have arrived many ordinary words seem to have lost the meaning they used to have for me and I have now come to see them in quite a different sense. Some I don't even care to use at all any more; they belong to the past which already is far away. Here I am, on the edge of my cliff, waiting for the thrust that will send me over. In this solitude time has grown wings — angels' wings; I can almost sense the soft current as they cleave the air, keeping their distance because of the immense height. And the noises from below are softened and quietened — I hear them rather as the distant murmur of a stream tossing and tumbling in a narrow gorge. And the cliff edge is too narrow, movement is too constricted for real assessment and analysis. All along intuitively I have had the impression of frustration through restraint. Up here the only words that keep their validity and take on even deeper meaning are the words of the old prayers and particularly the prayer our Lord himself taught us.

Father

The word Father sounds strange in these surroundings. But it is constantly in my mind. Even in that ugly little room filled with hatred where men were making a travesty of justice, it never left me. In the past few months I have met nothing but hatred, enmity, pride and presumption from the people with whom I have been thrown into contact; nothing but ruthless force intoxicated with its own autocratic power and usurped dominion. It would be a terrible thing if the grace-less life, to which today we are all subjected in one form or another, were the final revelation of reality. All we can do is to remember faithfully that God does call himself our Father, that we are bidden to call on him by that name and to know him as such — and that this pompous, self-important world in which we live is only the foreground to the center of reality which so many scarcely notice in the noise and tumult surrounding them. The fundamental motif of our life is compassion and paternal guidance. Humanity has produced so many mad ideas to account for our condition — fate, environment, heredity, the world as the ultimate end of everything. Up here in this rarefied atmosphere it all sounds like the bleating of a lot of silly sheep pretending to be men — the words are not worthy of human beings.

God as Father, as source, as guide, as comforter; these are the inner resources with which a person can withstand the mass assault of the world. And this is no mere figure of speech — it is actual fact. The person of faith is aware of the solicitude, the compassion, the deep-seated support of providence in innumerable silent ways even when he is attacked from all sides and the outlook seems hopeless. God offers words full of wonderful comfort and encouragement; he has ways of dealing with the most desperate situations. All things have a purpose and they help again and again to bring us back to our Father.

Our *Father*

One of the most terrifying weapons in the hands of ruthless authority is enforced solitary confinement. It is still so even now
we are all condemned to the same sentence and only await its
execution. We never see each other — the whispered words of
fellow-sufferers and friends are denied us on this last painful
journey. We have come to the end of all things where we are utterly on our own. And the old truism, it is not good for man to
be alone, applies especially to this situation and this dark hour. I
would so love to shout across to another cliff where a friend sits
equally isolated. But the words do not carry — they are caught
up in this thin air where sounds do not travel. But then — *our*
Father — and all at once the chasm is spanned. Suddenly we see
the truth that in God, through God, we have always possessed
the shortest route to reach our neighbor. Humanity knows itself to be at one with all who pray and believe and love. The
common center, the personal God who speaks to us, and to
whom we speak, makes humankind human and the community
a genuine whole.

Who *Art in Heaven*

The reality that lies beyond our earthly experience is often distorted and obscured. In this age we have almost ceased to think
about it. Thus we have obliged God to make us very painfully
aware of the temporal and impermanent nature of existence.
The realization often comes as a brutal shock. Even those of us
who believe in the future life share the worldly view of the rest
to some extent. Yet a person is only human in so far as he respects the laws of his being in relation to his *whole* existence.
Only such a person is capable of the true attitude, the proper

approach, the reverence, the devoted love, the absolute obedience due to the Creator. We can only arrive at our true nature by lifting our eyes to the hills. It is because we have failed to do this that we are such mass-products, so "typed," so incapable of coping with life — really incapable of recognizing the fundamental principles and intuitions that belong to the person created in God's image.

Nor is it enough to have ideas or an ideal — much more is needed. The idealist is certainly more of a human than the purely earth-bound, materialist individual who has no time for anything except "facts." But complete fulfillment and realization can never come from idealism alone. The inner crust is unbroken — untouched and sterile. A person only becomes human in the inner fastness of his own personal *I am*. And unless the dialogue takes place this inner identity slowly congeals and freezes to death. Humans cannot dispense with the dialogue; they need it so that they may grow and fulfill themselves. And the dialogue with the Absolute is of paramount importance, something far beyond a mere idea or ideal. The God of life is a personal God and only when humans enter into the dialogue with him do they begin to realize their dreams. In this conversation they learn the fundamental principles of their being — adoration, veneration, love, trust. Anything undertaken on a plane lower than this dialogue, no matter how much zeal and sincerity and devotion go into it, is in the end incomplete. Adoration is the road that leads us to ourselves.

The realm of the personal God is heaven, that is to say it is the sum-total of all that we consider to be our life's greatest happiness. Fulfillment and more. It is not primarily a place or a period in time or anything like that. It is fundamentally God himself — a conscious union with him. Anyone who has achieved that union is in heaven. It is a union that uproots all our limitations and destroys our previous habits if we are fortunate enough to begin to experience it here on earth. The records of the world's great mystics that have come down to us witness this. But for most of us the breaking up of our present form of our existence, that is our death, is the usual gateway to God. On that plane things merge into each other; the things a person loves or longs for, happiness, joy, heaven, and the things he reverently praises, God and his fullness are brought to one focus.

Love of heavenly things is something the Church often prays for as the summit of grace and fulfillment. It is important to throw a bridge across to fulfillment, to the future, to that which is hoped for not only as far as the desires of our nature go but also as far as our attitude and conscious effort are concerned. We must aim at heaven with all our strength. Humanity will have to relearn, much more positively and intensively than before, that life leads from the personal dialogue with God to the actual personal encounter and the experience of unity with God. We will have to learn that this is our heaven and our real, our only, home. Then we will learn to pray, not merely as a duty and in obedience, but with intense vitality and with all the driving force of our own free will.

Hallowed Be Thy Name

The images evoked by the Lord's prayer vividly illustrate our life. Humanity stands or falls by the things that are mentioned in it. If this is realized we can begin to make progress. If it is not realized, or not taken seriously, we sink and decline. That is the real key to the grim picture of life today. And this phrase, *hallowed be thy name,* teaches us to pray for the worthy ideal, for the unassailable, holy, venerated standard. Unless they have something of supreme value, something at the center of their being which they can venerate, human beings gradually deteriorate. Human nature is so constituted that it must have something holy that it can worship, otherwise it becomes cramped and distorted and instead of a holy object of veneration something else will take its place. I ought to know for I have just emerged from a murderous dialogue with such a self-appointed object of veneration. These substitute values are far more autocratic and demanding than the living God himself. They have no idea of courtesy or of waiting for their turn, or of the blissful encounter, of voluntary persuasion, of gracious appeal. All they know is demand, compulsion, force, threats and liquidation. And woe to anyone who does not conform.

The word of God should evoke and receive the great veneration this phrase suggests, praise, reverence, awe. This effects the realization of those fundamental categories of life I referred to just now. The name of God is the holy of holies, the central silence, the thing that above all others calls for humble approach. We not only ought to believe in the truth at the center of our being, in the purpose of our existence, but we should also bear testimony to this belief by the proper fulfillment of our life's purpose. We should subjugate everything to this law of holiness and reject everything that does not harmonize with it. God, the great object of human veneration, will then also be our whole life. "There is no healing in any other name." How little there is to say once we have said this. And how much that is said is mere cant. We have so many pious phrases that are utterly without genuine reverence for God. Religious chastity and silence go well together.

Let us resume the practice of giving names to life and to things. I have been a mere number long enough to know what it means to be nameless and what effect it has on life. As long as life itself has no name, or at least none that it honors, people and things will continue to lose their identity in the dreadful regimentation and anonymity into which we have sunk.

Life has a sensitive nervous system through which everything is connected. Since the name of God is no longer the first and foremost of all names in the land and the voice of the people, then everything else that was once precious and prized has lost its name and been subjected to false and falsifying labels. The cliche, the label, the uniform, the slogan, the "dominant trend of the masses" — these are our rulers. And pity the one who dares to differ, to proclaim his own thoughts or use his own name.

Prayer is our way to freedom and education in the method of prayer is the most valuable service that can be given to humankind. It makes it possible for the temple and the altar to occupy again their rightful place and for humanity to humble itself and measure its responsibilities in the name of God.

Thy Kingdom Come

Humanity has permanent need of supernatural power and strength. If our communication with the divine is stopped we begin to have strange dreams and set up false gods — success, people, new orders and so on. I know this only too well. I have dreamed and yearned and loved and labored and it has all added up to a hymn of longing for something final and permanent. No one can get much further with his dreams and ideals — he keeps coming up against his own limitations and the insufficiency of his creative efforts. This, too, I have proved for myself. I know how often one discovers one is playing with shards while dreaming of shapely vessels full to the brim, and how the heroic song we set out to sing so often dwindles into a plaintive whimper. Humanity, left to itself, can accomplish nothing. And the purpose of this part of the prayer is precisely to make us realize that we need supernatural help and that all the power of the living God is at our disposal. I have proved this too — proved that a person can be instantly lifted out of his own inadequacy to the point where no harm can touch him and where he is and remains equal to anything even when things turn out very differently from what he had expected. The genuine dialogue becomes part of him.

The kingdom of God is where humanity is in a state of grace and all things move in divine order. Human needs are met by God's abundance, human limitations are dissolved by God's power, human rashness is tamed by God's discipline — all this is part of the kingdom of God. It is a quickening in our innermost heart, passing from person to person. It is a silent grace which nevertheless gives impetus to word and deed; it exists both as an action and an order. Everything that we need today is covered by this prayer. Contact with God is the one thing that gives sense and satisfaction to our lives and God is always ready and waiting — waiting with beneficent readiness, not tyrannical coercion. The kingdom of God is grace, which is why we pray for it; but the grace of God so often stands at the door and knocks without finding anyone to open.

Humans raise a barrier between themselves and God's kingdom in two ways — first by the kind of life they choose to lead and secondly by their demand for certain social conditions or their toleration of others.

But the absolute minimum is alertness and willingness to receive. In themselves, as purely human and natural beings, humans are graceless and their course through life graceless and unmerciful. In the long run their progress through life is destructive both for themselves and others. Despite their Promethean outpourings they are at the mercy of things and quite unequal to the tasks and problems they are faced with. That is the clue to the history of recent times where none of the pressing problems have been successfully met. If we cannot bring ourselves to turn completely to God we must at least consent to be receptive so that God can reach us. This prayer stipulates repentance on our part, and our consent to a revolution — that is, a willingness to uphold a social reorganization that will enable us once more to open our heart to God and thus become ready for the contact. The most pious prayer can become a blasphemy if the one who offers it tolerates or helps to further conditions which are fatal to humankind, which render him unacceptable to God or weaken his spiritual, moral or religious sense. This prayer asks a great deal of God — no less than himself. But at the same time it imposes a great responsibility on humanity. Whether it is really offered as prayer or whether it is mere pious cant depends on the way in which one accepts and carries out that responsibility.

Thy Will Be Done on Earth as It Is in Heaven

This is our prayer for freedom. It may not sound like it but it is so all the same. Humanity is set on a certain course. Any attempt to evade that course, to ignore it, set it aside or destroy it must inevitably lead to disaster. The very fact that we constantly have to take into account factors over which we have no control makes us cautious. We keep coming up against circumstances which impose all kinds of restraints on us, from polite considerations of tact and good manners to actual duty and obedience. Even on this level any pretense to self-sufficiency means self-deception, delusion, suicide. There is no creative "splendid isolation." And this is even more true on the plane of our supernatural obligations. God has a place in the definition of humanity both as *God from whom* and as *God to whom and by whom*. Any other concept we may form of ourselves is disastrous and likely to be fatal.

The link with God binds us to his order, his law — which is the reflection of his nature. It is a link with his freedom, his mysterious grandeur. These are the things a person must reckon with if he wants to remain human. God's order binds us both because it is an integral part of the natural structure of human existence and also as a point of contact with the requirements of the law. God's freedom lifts us beyond all this into the wider sphere of personal submission, vocation, trials, visitations and so on. Our greatness and worth — that which raises us above the average — is decided in this personal dialogue with the exacting God. But God's might, his hidden mystery, brings us up against obscure ways, dark visions, brilliant revelations, the mystery of the supernatural which cannot be put into words.

Only in voluntary acceptance of all this will we find freedom. Failing such acceptance we are a slave to our fears and the things we would like to hold on to. We must cut ourselves adrift and leave all things behind if we ever hope to find our true self. Until we have made complete severance we cannot experience this blessing — and once we have experienced it we will know it for a foretaste of heaven. The will of God in heaven is the ratification of God by God and the confirmation of God by the blessed. Self-acknowledgment and self-confirmation make the great jubilation of the Trinity, the torrential life of God. And the confirmation of God by those who have reached fulfillment is the substance of their fulfillment — they are caught up in the divine jubilation and blissful torrent of divine life. And of course the will of God, which is to be done, is always and fundamentally good will, healing will. The surrender, the encounter with God's freedom and God's mystery mean contact with salvation.

Give Us This Day Our Daily Bread

We can accept this petition as it stands, at its face value. It has been coupled with the words of our Lord "My meat and drink is to do the will of my Father" and it has been held to refer to the holy eucharist. These are pious reflections but here I am concerned with the prayer's literal reference to the recurrent hunger of humanity and the bread which is meant to satisfy it. The Lord's prayer teaches us to bring the perplexities of our everyday lives to God and talk them over with him. The affairs of the "earth" are now to be considered — bread, trespasses, struggle, evil. The things that occupy and trouble us in our daily lives are very real. Our Lord has taught us how to pray. Our cares and our blessing are the contents of the Lord's prayer.

Our daily bread really is God's concern: lack of bread and prayer for bread are part of our make-up and the prayer acknowledges these two fundamental factors. Philosophers have summed up one in the words *basis of life* as though they regarded it as an essential but altogether inferior necessity. Intellectual people often have that kind of snobbery. Of course one can idolize bread and make a god of one's stomach. But if one has endured hunger for weeks on end it is a very different matter. Anyone who has ever undergone such a trial knows that an unexpected crust of bread can seem like a real gift from heaven. I can vouch for this because I have personally experienced it. Only one who has known the effect hunger can have on every life impulse can appreciate the respect in which bread is held and what the perpetual struggle for daily bread really means. We will preach in vain about the kingdom of heaven, or even the kingdom on earth, as long as people go hungry and daily bread is something that must be struggled for. Bread always was one of the greatest mediums of temptation and still is so. Nothing can be more important than placing the problem of distribution of bread in the right hands. And the bread problem must always be a subject for prayer, otherwise we will lose ourselves in the material world. No matter how abundant and dependable it may be, bread still comes day by day from the eternal provider and we must realize this. Such truths and their implications must be kept transparently clear, or the consequences are dangerous.

That is why we are not enjoined to pray for overflowing barns and well-filled store houses; we are only told to pray for daily bread. The hazards and uncertainty of human life find an echo here, and the fact that life justifies itself in trust rather than in security. Anxiety regarding income, insurance, pensions, dividends and so on has been responsible for much destruction in recent years. We who are enduring a second war in these days of "welfare" and for the second time experiencing a bread-shortage know what it means. Bread is important. Freedom is even more important. But most important of all is unshaken loyalty and adoration without betrayal.

Forgive Us Our Trespasses as We Forgive Them . . .

It is as natural for humans to err as it is for them to need daily bread. Our urgent need for bread is not more real than are our faults. I am not referring here to original sin, that burden we have inherited from the first catastrophe at the dawn of creation. That is also a fact but it has been overemphasized so that it has produced only an echo. This underlining of original sin has led humankind to adopt two different attitudes — one because the natural strength of which we are conscious belies the fatigue and incapacity with which we have been credited. Some do not understand — and others pretend not to understand — that the incapacity refers to the supernatural order and its fulfillment. The scandalous revolt against God that we have witnessed in the western world has robbed this thought of most of its force. The second attitude is utter indifference to failure since humans are told that they cannot act otherwise. To regard sin not merely as a lapse but as a personal reproach and responsibility has become completely foreign to western mentality.

But I mean precisely this when I say that sin is part of our daily life. We fall into sin because we give up and fail. We are guilty in the fact that we are living in a given moment of history and we have allowed things to happen which are a reproach to us. There is such a thing as a personal attitude toward God and there is also a public attitude, that adopted by the community as a whole. Our generation is guilty, grievously guilty. It is very important that this should be acknowledged. This guilt must be washed away, we must be absolved from it — otherwise we shall perish. Humanity performs strange dances round its sin but instead of being rhythmic its movements look like epileptic contortions. Humans can try to escape from their guilt — that is forgivable because it is a natural reaction. They can try to deny it, they can dream in the manner of the ancient Greeks and try to argue it away. All this helps to blind their eyes and stifle their conscience — but the guilt remains. Deeds that have been committed are like endorsed checks — sooner or later they are bound to be presented. We can only gain remission of sin by repentance. We must recognize and acknowledge that sin inflicts a wound on God's creation, a wound that defies all the arts and strength of creative being. As sinners our only hope lies in turning to the healing forgiveness of God. This generation urgently needs persons prepared to stand before God for its sins.

God bids us place our hope of mercy in the mercy we are prepared to show. The sins of the world must vanish with transcendental guilt so that the world now and then may breathe again. As far as we are concerned this means that we must refrain from all bitterness against those who have wronged us. I bear them no grudge; I forgive even that charlatan who made such a travesty of German justice. They even arouse my pity. But I pity still more the people who have delivered themselves and their holy spirit into the hands of such monsters. God help us.

Lead Us Not into Temptation

We ought to offer this prayer very seriously. Our Lord knew what it was to be tempted and what bitter struggles temptation may entail. Who can be sure of himself? When things are going well we let these words pass over us negligently, thinking very little about them as if they really did not apply to us at all. And then all of a sudden the sky becomes overcast — a storm arises, and with the wind blowing from all directions at once we do not know which way to turn. Take this journey of mine up the perilous face of my cliff. How many hours of weakness and despair have had to be endured in making that climb, hours of sheer helplessness, of doubt, not knowing which was the best course. How is it that conditions suddenly get distorted, their balance disturbed and their threads twisted and entangled producing a pattern far from our intention and quite beyond our power to unravel? No one can escape the hour of temptation. It is only in that hour that we begin to sense our weakness and to have a faint inkling of the vital decisions we are expected to make. If only I can manage to keep a hold on this perilous perch and not faint and let go.

I have committed my soul to God and I rely on the help of my friends.

Temptation assails us from within and without. Compulsion, force, pain, humiliation, one's own cowardice, God's silence, complete inability to cope with an external situation, all these call for painful decisions. And added to all these there is fear, that creeping worm that eats its way into a person's very substance. The devil within may break loose — indignation, doubt, the overwhelming wish to live which cannot be suppressed. All these can cause many hours of bitter struggle and when it dies down the world no longer seems the same place. One's skin is turned to leather, crisscrossed with scars and wounds.

We have only God to fall back on in such a moment. This, and the knowledge that we have not brought the temptations upon ourselves voluntarily are our only hope. God bids us pray that we may be spared such trials. I advise everyone to take this admonition seriously to heart. What a witches' cauldron my own experience has been. How it will end, what still awaits me sitting here on the brink of the precipice, and how long I shall have to stay here before I must take the plunge, I have no idea. Nor do I know for certain that the gnawing worm within may not become active again. We must guard against every kind of false security — only then will we find access to God's great peace and omnipotence. How very different my feelings were during those hours in court. Then, although I knew from the start that I was doomed, I had no real sense of defeat. That was thanks to divine strength. And life from that moment took on a new meaning. It was clear and unmistakable that life is worth living and worth dying for. If this is true it applies in the fullest measure to moments of temptation when we cannot depend on our own strength alone.

Deliver Us from Evil

This part of the prayer again applies to a person involved in temptation. Resistance is not only a manifestation but a thing that weighs the outcome in the balance. We are under a strain and begin to doubt whether we shall find salvation. In temptation it is a question of deciding for or against God and the essence of temptation is that it robs our judgment of its clear-cut certainty in making decisions. No one can escape deciding for God but the danger of making the wrong decision is a thing one must pray to be spared. And incidentally this prayer requires far more humility and honesty than are usual nowadays.

The evil from which we pray to be delivered is not that which is most oppressive in life, such as poverty, worries, hardship, burdens, sacrifices, pain, injustice, tyranny and so on; it is the chain of circumstance that leads us into temptation, disturbing the balance, pushing life off-center, distorting the perspective. It will be seen at once that the so-called "good things" of life are just as liable to cause such disturbance as the painful and hard realities. These things all possess the potential power to lead or force us into temptation and by that I mean all the things that can possibly come between us and God.

Life is a contest, and this is emphasized by the words "deliver us from evil." The passage is even more eloquent than the one preceding it. In the natural course of existence we are again and again brought up against both the agony in the Garden and the temptation of the wilderness. There, too, genuine temptation had to be met, because our Lord was weak with hunger and because the devil found him vulnerable. The devil. Yes there is not only evil in this world, there is also the evil one; not only a principle of negation but also a tough and formidable anti-Christ. We should give thought to the fact that we must distinguish between the spirits. And to the fact that wherever self is stressed, as in strength that glories in its own might, power that idolizes itself, life that aims at "fulfilling itself" in its own way and by its own resources, in all these, not the truth, but the negation of truth may be suspected. And there is only one thing a person can really do about it — fall down on his knees and pray. Only after ten long years — ten years too late — do I fully realize this.

COME HOLY GHOST

The Holy Ghost is the breath of creation. As in the beginning the Spirit of God moved on the face of the waters, so now —

but in a much closer and more intimate way — God's Spirit reaches the human heart bringing us the capacity to grow to our fulfillment.

Theologically this is clear — the heart of grace is the Holy Ghost. That which makes us like Christ is the same indwelling Spirit — the principle of supernatural life in him and in us. Believing and hoping and loving, the heart beats of the supernatural life, are the created being's participation in the self-affirmation of God which is expressed in the Holy Ghost.

The cry of "come" can be interpreted in this way. It embodies the intensified hungry Advent-yearning. It is the will to break through barriers, to escape from fetters and confinement.

And Send from Heaven

From heaven — out of this world, of God's reality. From that place where all things are united in one, not scattered over the earth. The created being must cry out to some power beyond itself in order to acquire its share of strength; when we realize and acknowledge that our natural powers on their own are inadequate we have taken the first step toward salvation. We need the mission and the assignment God gives us, the permanent guidance and healing of God if we are to meet the forces of destiny on equal terms. And as we are beings limited in form and capacity by the set pattern to which we are created, and do not exist by our own strength and power, so too our potentialities are a free gift and a grace. Humans have always tended to forget this ever since the beginning of time — they always tend to fall in love with their own estimate of themselves. We all proceed from one failure to another and after every collapse we come out with less substance and more wounds — all of us. When we are tired and tempted to give up, instead of blaming fate and circumstances we should ask ourselves whether we are living sufficiently close to God, whether we have called on him earnestly enough. Help comes from the hills — and they are here, at hand; their help is simply waiting for us to apply for it. My life at this moment should prove this. Everything points to the fact that God has chosen this way to teach me this lesson. All that I was so sure of in my self-satisfied judgment and so-called wisdom has been shattered by the experiences and the disillusionment I have gone through. *God alone suffices.* These last few months have blown a great deal of my work sky high; according to the verdict perhaps my very existence on this earth must come to an end. Yet there have been miracles. God has taken my case entirely into his hands. I have learned how to send up my cry and to wait for the message of encouragement from the eternal hills.

Send Thy Radiant Light

Light is symbolic of one of the great longings of human life. Again and again we find ourselves benighted, sunk in deep gloom, without light to guide us. How could we even desire light if it were not for the eternal gift of grace which gives our spirit a vague intuition that darkness is not its natural and final state, that even in the darkest hour there is something to be hoped for, a state of fulfillment toward which the spirit must aspire. God created human beings as light-endowed, radiant beings, and as such sent us forth into the world; but we have blinded ourselves to this truth. Only a faint inkling of it remains. We are never more soul-sick than when we become confused and finds ourselves helpless to cope with a situation. That is the primary meaning of this prayer — it is a despairing cry for divine help to dispel our self-imposed, sinful darkness, wiping the dreams and the fear from our eyes so that they may see again. But there is also another imperative need for light in our lives; God's radiance dazzles us. We get presentiments and glimpses but they are transitory and usually lead nowhere. Those who are dedicated and prepared pray for divine light which will heighten their perception and raise them to realization of that fullness they have hitherto only dimly guessed at. Once a person has arrived at this stage he knows what the strength of God is even in the darkest and most hopeless situations of his life. When life becomes most serious our own ideas always wither or become childish. This has been proved again and again in our individual lives and in the life of the community.

Come Thou Father of the Poor

Three times there is this cry of "come" breaking from the depths of human misery and helplessness to the comforting presence of God. This cry is the arc that connects the created being with the Creator's divine fullness. In it the two realities meet in a simple and fundamental relationship. We recognize ourselves as pitiful creatures incapable of satisfying even our most pressing needs by our own efforts — and that is the key: we want to live and intend to live but do not possess the wherewithal for living. This applies to every part of life even in the middle of abundant material riches. One of our Lord's beatitudes refers to the poor in spirit. Yet the overcoming of need is the promise made to those who have it and it applies to all those who are still held in bondage by their need, whatever it is. How often I have sent up these three cries of "come" during these weeks of hunger — they have become my grace before meals.

To the person in need God's Spirit appears fatherly, that is as all-providing strength and power directed by love. That is as it should be. When we acknowledge our need, presenting ourself without vanity, self-assurance and so on in all our naked help-lessness, God manifests himself in miracles of love and pity. The effects may range from the ease of heartache and spiritual illu-mination to the satisfying of physical hunger and thirst. When we send up this cry we call upon the Spirit of creation. We are desperately poor; let us acknowledge our poverty and offer up our prayer for ourselves and our race.

Come Bounteous Giver

Three times the "poor soul" sends up its cry to the Creator and three times the healing, omnipotent Father hears that prayer. It is good for the soul to persist in its pleading. The Holy Ghost is the Spirit of fulfillment, inner strength, infinite abundance; it is the Spirit of fulfillment in its divine essence. God comes to the summit of expression in the Holy Ghost; all the passionate adherence of God to himself is affirmed and confirmed by the third Person of the Trinity. His law and divine order is really summed up here — what is unfinished must be completed, ful-filled; and that fulfillment is the Holy Ghost. *Bounteous giver.* Again I say the Holy Ghost is the breath of creation, the mighty current which would like to gather everything up and rush back to its original source. The soul which is weary and sick and con-scious of its poverty should call on the Holy Ghost. He is the giver; through him we can be shaped to the likeness of the Son. He gives us new life and makes us capable of living. He heartens us, strengthens our will, heightens our understanding so that we may believe and hope and love — that is so that we may draw nearer to God and live in unity with him. And he is the giver of gifts in the narrower, often forgotten, sense — the seven gifts of the Holy Ghost. These bring us new potentialities, enable us to live more abundantly. Our supernatural life is genuine life and therefore it is differentiated and the more faculties a person is

able to quicken the more fully he will live. Everything grows
and becomes more efficient under the creative blessing of the
bounteous giver. Human misery and need are things to be overcome and all this is very relevant to the problem. Nietzsche's
declarations and his dreams concerning superman eventually
depress and bore us — indeed in the end they seem despica-
ble. There is only one way to progress and that is by praying,
and praying in the right way. In my present situation what help
can I get from a concept of the greatness to which humanity
should attain — what use is that in this isolation and loneliness? But to feel the warm presence of the Spirit, to be aware
of his strengthening breath does help me along this lonely road.
When we remember that we can call on God as the bounteous
giver, *dator munerum,* the dispenser of blessings and strength,
then adverse circumstances lose their power. The Holy Spirit
finds ways and means to give us comfort; he has resources of
tenderness and attention far exceeding the arts of human love.

Come Light of Our Hearts

Once again we find God symbolized by light — it occurs again
and again. And the wonderful words "light of our hearts" indicate that we are here concerned with the Spirit of God in the
very center of life, bringing healing to its roots and its source.
Humans don't live and feel with their thoughts — nor do they
suffer through them until they develop into a passion or become
a burden to their hearts. Perplexity of heart is the greatest of all
confusions a person can fall into and the extent to which his
heart is committed is the measure of a human being. In other
words we are measured by our ability to love. That is the key
to a person's life and also to history — it solves many riddles
if we realize that the history of humankind is the history of
human passions. And the history of human folly is the history

of unenlightened hearts. Our risk lies in the fact that we can become confused and irresponsible, lacking sound instinct and good judgment, at that very center of our being where decisions are made. It is our great misfortune that this instinct so often fails us. The heart is the innermost core of a person where all capacities, wishes, needs, and longings are concentrated and find expression as decisions, impulses, love and surrender. So here, in the *very* center of our being, the temple of the Holy Ghost should be established. It is the nature of the Holy Spirit to penetrate and blend with the life impulses, purifying and completing them and thus imbuing them with its own intensity and assurance. *Light of heart.* We cannot pray for it too often or be too earnest in our plea that our hearts may keep their harmonious rhythm and their power of right feeling. Feeling is here the operative word — statement and explanation are of minor importance; feeling and instinct are the things that count. When the heart is in the right place, as they say, everything is in order. May the Holy Spirit have pity on this poor, foolish, hungry, frozen, lonely and forsaken heart and fill it with the warm assurance of its presence.

Best Comforter

Comforter. We ought to take this word in its simplest and most straightforward sense. To be comfortless is a state of mind and spirit that results from misery experienced and recognized as a condition, a fact, particularly if it is one's own. Therefore there can be no comfort in a facile denial of the comfortless condition. There can be no comfort until things are changed and the new conditions are those the spirit can rejoice in and be satisfied with. For the essence of comfort is that the mind and spirit are no longer troubled, that they are in a state of security, order and fulfillment. The genuine comforter must either establish this new state or so harmonize the old state with existing circumstances that the misery vanishes and the whole situation takes on a new character. Both depend entirely on the action of the Spirit in us. The *bounteous giver* and *father of the poor* overcome inherent human misery and the *light of our hearts* makes us aware of the change that is taking place. Through the power of this Spirit we are armed to meet and overcome our moments of despair. We have only to keep on believing and praying.

Sweet Guest of Souls

The verses that follow describe the various consolations bestowed on humankind by the Spirit of God. God does not dole out blessings one at a time. He is comfort and comforter. *Guest of souls;* actually present and present in a singularly personal way. True mystical experience is nothing less than the shatteringly conscious awareness of this continuous presence. The Spirit of God is the supreme comforter because it overcomes finally and absolutely the fundamental sensations of misery and helplessness by driving the poison out of them.

And, in spite of the necessary submission on the part of the creature, the whole of religion is a truly personal relationship and of nothing is this more true than of the divine intimacy between Creator and worshipper. It is an intimacy, a true friendship. The prayer refers to the presence of the divine friend as *dulcis,* sweet. We feel a bit embarrassed by the word in this connection. So many words have lost their original spiritual meaning and come down to us colored by human emotion instead of spiritual experience. Let us admit frankly that this word, like most with a deep religious meaning, has been taken from this sphere of human emotional life. All great and fundamental spiritual feelings are inter-related and belong to the same class. The sad thing is that nowadays neither love nor religion have any real bearing on the words used to express intense bliss or inexpressible intimacy. Both as worshippers and as people capable of love we have deteriorated sadly.

Sweet Refreshment

This phrase can only be really appreciated by those fortunate enough to know one of those people whose very presence is so infectious that it makes him a source of strength, security, joy and trust, so inspiring that it changes the whole atmosphere, dominating it. The spiritual joy and inspiration conveyed by *dulce* radiate like heat — the air becomes warm and friendly. *Refrigerium* means melting, dissolving — what warmth and shelter are to the wounded who have suffered exposure, the comfort of the Holy Spirit is to the soul; only the soul, being more sensitive, feels this far more acutely than the body.

Rest in Labor

These three prayers are the cry of the tormented soul yearning for contact with the healing strength of spirit. Here are human-kind's three fundamental needs which are provided for by the current of divine healing.

The first need is: *in labore* — "by the sweat of his brow" was the way it was put at the beginning. And out of this has grown the harassed, hunted person of today, totally enslaved to duty, never free from care, restless, hagridden. Duty, necessity, danger give him no respite from their imperative demands. And on top of all this are his personal difficulties — his anxiety for those he loves. This is what our life has come to. *In labore* — ceaseless strain, insecurity, helplessness — not knowing the answer to any of it. We have lost the freedom for which we were created and have condemned ourselves to perpetual bondage and fatigue.

And this titanic drama of human destiny is being played out on a stage that embraces the whole of humanity. Recent epochs decreed that *homo sapiens, homo speculativus, homo religiosus* and so on should be exterminated and replaced by *homo faber.* Now *homo faber* has arrived. Factories are the new cathedrals, machines are the magic symbols of today and the human being is the most easily convertible currency in this utilitarian world of machinery. Everyone has been drawn into this new order and none can escape its dictatorship. Life has opened a machine gun fire of demands on us and we cannot long withstand the onslaught — unless help comes from the hills. Unless we turn to that inner strength that lets us rise above all the trials that beset us. Only from within can we draw the calm that will lift us above the hectic rat-race even when we fulfill its demands and carry out our duties. Spirit has a way of adapting itself to our needs, entering completely into our life and giving relief just where the need is most pressing. Where it is heaviest the burden will be lightened and where help is most needed it will be most vividly experienced. The Holy Spirit will give us the great virtue of perseverance. With his help we shall prove stronger than the forces ranged against us, swifter than the hounds of care that pursue us in this desperate hunt our lives have become. He will give us quiet assurance and silent fulfillment to enable us to endure. And though we may often think we have reached the end of our resources, a new demand will find us not only ready but, in God's name, capable and willing to meet it. The one indispensable condition is that we remain receptive listening for the inner voice, otherwise we shall be drawn up in the sterile and stifling world of everyday realities. God's Spirit will pour itself through our every need, drown every noise, overcome all fatigue if only we will turn to it in faith and with desire. That is why our prayer today must be to the Creator Spirit, who works in us and fulfills our needs bringing us to our true selves in our personal lives.

This very day, this moment in which our heart is crushed by weariness and our strength seems to have ebbed away, precisely now in the middle of all this trouble we pray for the healing peace of God; *in labore requies.* All you tired people who are battling under strain and sorrow that threaten to undermine your loyalty and deprive you of love and strength, you who see your very existence threatened by circumstances you cannot control so that you hardly know how to hold the tattered rags of your lives together, believe me that this help is real and genuine and all these surface disturbances can serve to convince us of God's indisputable nearness and reality. Oh I know that these other things seem so much more real. But the waters of healing surge up within ourselves. God within us is like a fountain and we are guests invited to rest and refresh ourselves. We must discover this fountain within ourselves and let its healing waters flow over the parched land of our lives. Then the desert will blossom. He wants to quicken you. The word of God, given long ago, is fulfilled by his free-flowing Spirit. From within you will receive the strength and the spiritual assurance to conquer. How often I have proved this in the stress of these last dismal months of burden and depression — suddenly renewed strength would flood my whole being like sunrise. The peace after a storm that has blown itself out, the satisfaction that comes from a job well done would fill my whole being. Unless we find these inner fountains, these healing waters, no outward rest, no relaxation, will help us. But when the divine Spirit dawns on our consciousness then we are able to surpass ourselves. We are filled with that peace, that holy and restoring stillness which we associate with God's presence — in a cathedral for instance, in a magnificent countryside, in a cherished friendship.

Coolness in Heat

This is the second fundamental need of poor, exposed, defense-less humans. They are at the mercy of inner driving forces that alternately harass and handicap them till they are almost exhausted. These compulsions come from within; the sleeping volcano bursts into life and stirs up explosive energies which send the tattered remnants of reality flying in all directions. Hot blood and violent anger, the sudden assertion of the inborn urge to tyrannize — these and many other smoldering human impulses may turn into consuming fires. Outwardly most human lives go through a period of stress and alarm; it happens as naturally as a summer thunderstorm which may break suddenly or pursue its destructive course by slow and stealthy stages piling burden on burden, trouble on trouble till the heart and shoulders of the victim are weighed down. In short humans are vulnerable both to inner fire and external sparks — either can be fanned into a blaze and leave behind a path of destruction and trouble beyond human endurance. Then we are forced to look for new sources of help and restoration, for powers that can reestablish the balance and enable us to master our problems.

Coolness in heat; the Holy Spirit as the source of our power to cope with the contingencies of life. God's passion for himself, which finds expression through the human spirit, burns up a person's incipient passions. One's individuality is thereby strengthened and intensified. Such a person is equipped to meet the trials that assail him from both within and without; his decisions are unerring because he keeps the end in view and the measure in his hand. A courageous person is filled with the Holy Ghost; he is calm and clear headed. His chariot may indeed be drawn by spirited horses but they are well controlled.

Coolness in heat; a person in the midst of life's thunderstorm. This need springs from the fact that his heart is constantly being consumed by inner fires and the wings of his spirit are forever being hindered by his own wild and irresponsible impulses. Our souls and our memories are stamped with pictures — visions of refugees, of ruined houses, shattered possessions. It has all really happened. Yet these are only pictures, the reflections of humanity's inborn violence, the volcanic eruptions to which we have always been prone and always will be. Human power grows impotent, human strength turns to helplessness, human spirit becomes merely an instrument whereby we may measure frightfulness and drain the cup of misery to the last dregs instead of being a weapon enabling us to cope with difficulties and conquer them. This is really a case of fire fighting fire. The Holy Spirit appeared at the beginning as tongues of fire. That is God's way of dealing with the situation. God is no destroyer of the beings he has created. His will is that all shall be forgiven and redeemed and hence his fire is not consuming but healing. And in the breath of the Spirit human beings grow till they can control their demoniac wildness. The holy fire of God renders us impervious to the firebrands of destruction. And at one and the same time God is both fire and water. Only those who are filled with the Holy Ghost have the courage in these times to venture a word or deed of real importance. The gift of judgment, farsightedness, the power to undertake restoration go hand in hand with steadfastness and persistence. In times like these we must send up our cry to the Holy Ghost or we will be consumed.

Solace in Woe

The third fundamental need of human beings. Time and time again they are reduced to weeping and wailing, both individually and collectively. Trouble usually descends upon them out of the blue, often when their spirits are highest. Often trouble breaks loose at the height of a celebration when people are at ease and thoroughly pleased with themselves, lulled by their own self-esteem. Suddenly they are forced to recognize that the high opinion they had formed of themselves was an inebriated dream and no real ecstasy. Wine-tinted dreams can fashion shapely jars from broken pots but sobriety soon shatters them. Suddenly a person is faced with the naked truth and forced to make the age-old admission: I have wasted my substance. Or alternately the force of reality may come down and crush him in a very elementary fashion. All the laws he has transgressed rise in judgment on him. The triumphal march of a great life dwindles to a hard crusade, then to a procession of beggars and finally to a funeral procession that goes on and on. Once again human nature is brought up short not knowing which way to turn in this eternal circle of blood. The shriek of injured innocence mingles with the hoarse croak of despair from those who suffer chains and confinement imposed by the abuse of power and with the groans of those who perceive the universal trend and look desperately for a way out — only to discover that although they work until their hands are raw they cannot find one. All that seems to triumph is arrogance, vanity, belligerence, defamation. Such terrible waste of substance. Here we have the distress — the manifest distress — of humankind.

And again the word of comfort appears. Not a false word that will proclaim the situation harmless but an affirmation as real as the fetters on my wrists. When the Spirit reveals itself to human beings it gives us certain proof of God's creative freedom, of the powerful help God is capable of extending and willing to extend. The fact that one is lifted out of oneself and able to look at the situation from a new angle is in itself a great step forward. We then realize that we have resources, capacities and powers of which we previously had no notion. We can follow the undercurrents and implications better than we did before, the message and the purpose of things and circumstances become clearer. We remember the dedicated mission of John the Baptist calling on people to repent and return to God. We are able to compare the most distressing conditions to a fertile seed; it becomes a call to sacrifice, the only thing that can restore humanity's capacity to love. Warm currents of life flood our being, breaking like streams over the wilderness and making it fruitful. I vividly recall that night in the Lehrterstrasse and how I prayed to God that he might send death to deliver me because of the helplessness and pain I felt I could no longer endure, and the violence and hatred to which I was no longer equal. How I wrestled with God that night and finally in my great need crept to him, weeping. Not until morning did a great peace come to me, a blissful awareness of light, strength and warmth, bringing with it the conviction that I *must* see this thing through and at the same time the blessed assurance that I *should* see it through. *Solace in woe.* This is the Holy Spirit, the Comforter. This is the kind of creative dialogue he conducts with humankind. These are the secret blessings he dispenses which enable a person to live and endure.

O Blessed Light

Again we have the word light. The light that blesses, the blissful light. These words illustrate what I was trying to say just now. Humans are permitted to become conscious of God as a living reality that floods us with bliss. There are summer days when the light seems to envelop us like a tangible blessing. It can happen in a lovely alpine meadow or a rippling field of ripening grain or floating silently in a boat on a beautiful lake. Our consciousness is intensified and we feel at one with nature and

have a marvelous cognition of the ripening, healing and sanctifying powers the cosmos contains. Only a receptive, reverent
and observant person can experience this. It is a faint reflection of the saint's experience of blessed light — an awareness
that there are times when God enfolds his children in waves
of tenderness flooding their hearts and filling their whole being
with the blessed current of divine life. In God this is a constant
state — the state of grace, of divine son-ship. We are only conscious of it in rare moments of contact but such moments are
sufficient to see us through long days in the wilderness and long,
hopeless nights, because once we have been vouchsafed such an
overwhelming experience the impression never leaves us. There-
after we can detect God's quiet smile in all things and in all
conditions and circumstances.

Fill Our Inmost Heart

Back again to the connection between the light and the heart.
Here the reference has another application. Light in this context
does not primarily apply to the understanding, reason, spiritual perception. Here it represents the radiance of God's love
breaking out to touch us at the very center of our consciousness
and unsealing the fountains of grace which give humans a foretaste of heaven. Understanding and reason are intensified as the
individual is lifted up. Under the influence of this inner illumination we become more clear sighted, more intuitive, wiser. We
are enabled to strip the mask from falsity in circumstances and
in other people; we are equal to any emergency and can deal
with problems more kindly than if we were in an unenlightened
state — because we now know their rightful place in the scheme
of things, meet them on their own ground as it were, and see
through them to the very core of their secret hearts.

Our inmost heart really refers to the life lived intimately with God. Piety alone couldn't bring about this highly intensified radiation of the personal relationship. Friendship and love grow stronger on every plane in the loving contact of the dialogue. The same applies here. The only difference lies in the fact that here the partner is the Spirit of God for whose sanctifying presence we ardently pray.

Thy Faithful

I shall have something to say later about followers of the Holy Ghost. For the moment I only want to review what I have already said and examine it more closely. Like all intimacy this relationship with the Holy Ghost rests on trusting surrender and receptivity. God's Spirit never coerces even for our own good or to hasten our self-realization. The dialogue thus remains a genuine dialogue even though the creative force comes only from God and seeks us out and makes contact. If ever an intimacy needed to be guarded and cherished it is this one. Anyone who tries to enter this dialogue with coarse thoughts and uncouth habits will lose much grace and blessing. Such a person will miss so many whispered words of warning, silent indications of the tender solicitude and good will of God. There are times too when God's light will break like lightning over us, descend suddenly and violently, affecting our whole existence like a great boulder torn from a hillside and crashing into a lake. And in that too there are divine pointers which an unenlightened individual may easily overlook. For a sustained continuance of the dialogue alert watchfulness and sensitive receptivity are absolutely essential. These require a more complete surrender than humans in our natural state are capable of; they demand supernatural alertness, the constant crossing out of our own personal will in order that it may lose itself in God's. The trustful faith with which we approach God is the door through which the miracle of God's strength enters as he gives himself to us.

Without Thy Grace

An unfinished sentence, this, an incomplete theme. Therefore one shouldn't spend too much time meditating on it. Yet it has an important bearing on our life today for here we have a brief and pithy summary of all the folly and error of our race, and of its destiny. *Without thy grace.* We elected to live gracelessly, we trusted solely to our own strength, were bound only by our own laws, surrendered to our own whims and followed our own instincts. On those foundations we built our new towers. We have lifted our voices and celebrated triumphs, we have marched, we have worked, we have boasted and saved and squandered. And the outcome? Precisely *without thy grace* — a graceless life, a pitiless age, an age of inexorable fate, a time of horror and violence, of worthless life and senseless death. We ought not to be surprised that such a graceless life has translated itself into the kind of manifestation we are now enduring. And we who have been dragged down into the universal collapse — which perhaps we did not try to prevent by every means in our power — must in the midst of our destiny overcome that destiny, turning it into a cry for grace and mercy, for the healing waters of the Holy Ghost. Humanity ought never again to over-rate its capabilities or delude itself as we have done. Those who survive should take these lessons to heart and preach them with inspired zeal. The graceless way of living is presumptuous and leads to disaster. We are only truly human when we live in unity with God.

Nothing Is in the Human Being

Humanity is nothing without God. Sometimes we are tempted to declare that humanity is nothing at all. But this is because comparatively few people have the good fortune to meet a real human being. After all no one is above the law of transgression — *without thy grace.* We have all taken the wrong road and our empirical experience of humanity has demonstrated little but weakness, incapacity and extreme helplessness. Our yearning to excel, our desire to achieve and accomplish things indicate that our shortcomings are not fundamental but are a superficial effect. Our dissatisfaction with the conditions of our earthly existence is deep seated and constantly impels us to venture to try to improve our way of life.

We have it in us to conceive high ideals and work for their realization but if we are honest we will recognize the fact that we can do nothing on our own. Left to ourselves we are incomplete, not quite human. God is part of the definition of a human; inner unity with God is the primary condition for a fulfilled and successful life. The decision to recognize this is the greatest that we can make and the only one that will rescue us from the chaos in which we are involved. About turn — back to the beginning — that is the only solution and the way to achieve life's fulfillment.

Nothing Is Harmless

This applies to our makeup, to our total reality. Nothing is perfect and nothing can be described as potentially harmless. In plain words this means that there is a state, a condition of reality, in which things are not only out of order but actually dangerous, poisonous, destructive. We all know, individually, that there are times when everything we attempt seems to go wrong. All our efforts turn against us and end in bitter disappointment. It also sometimes applies to whole generations, to spiritual movements, to social and economic projects and so on. We see things getting out of hand; intentions and programs misfire, not only because the ideals have been betrayed by leaders and people, but because reality itself, proving too strong, has suddenly become antagonistic, difficult, intractable. Experience confirms the belief that facts that do not take God into account are inherently unreliable, and for sound order inherent shortcomings are fatal. There can be no progress or development when the foundations are faulty — indeed the structure then becomes definitely dangerous. In the last analysis there is no such thing as neutrality — there is absolutely nothing that does not matter. Decisions, conduct, intentions, all have either a positive or a negative value and if negative they are harmful and dangerous. Thus the sentence *nothing is harmless* should put us on our guard. The thought expressed is one in which we can recognize our need of an alliance with God, the initial and decisive step toward our own good. Anyone who rejects this partnership lays up a store of trouble for himself and is definitely acting against his own interests.

But our prayer applies to the terms of personal intimacy on which we ought to live with the Spirit of God, the Holy Ghost. And here the same thing is true, even more true. Intimacy with the Holy Ghost is grace in concrete form and is therefore a contact, a partnership. Moreover by his own being the Holy Ghost strengthens our spirit and gives it the capacity to achieve a fulfilled and successful life. He gives us mastery over our inherent weaknesses, our liability to err, our inhibitions and handicaps so that we not only conquer them but can rise above them. Humanity in a state of grace, through the Holy Ghost, is more capable of conducting its own life successfully and is also better equipped to help others. In our handling of everyday affairs we have clearer insight and better judgment, we are kinder and more generous. He bestows blessings and receives them.

Wash What Is Stained

Toil, heat and grief express fundamental conditions of human nature which always make themselves felt as long as one is on one's journey through life. They are not always so abnormally prevalent as they are today but they are nevertheless an indispensable part of our existence. And only when we fail to go through life in partnership with God do these things get the upper hand, bursting all bounds and overwhelming us with trouble of all kinds.

I am not concerned here with the material needs of humankind but with our own degeneration, our blunted faculties and spiritual poverty — all the burdens in fact which the kind of existence one leads have introduced into one's life and which have now become characteristic of one's nature. Just as there are virtues that can be acquired so also there are faults that result from repetition such as habitual unawareness of individuality, perpetual relinquishment of powers of decision, permanent weakening of the sense of reality, and so on. Faced with these shortcomings we find ourselves under a terrible strain and utterly helpless. If we lose our material possessions our vision is clear enough to enable us to regain them. We might through carelessness or sheer foolishness or some ill-judged idea allow our right hand to be cut off or suffer some other form of mutilation and then we have no personal power to put the thing right. These are misfortunes we might suffer but they do not come from any limitations of human nature but from the wrong use of freedom — hence one must accept responsibility for the misuse of one's free will. Being prone to such errors of judgment the only thing one can do is to turn again and again to God praying earnestly that the Holy Ghost may take pity on one's failings and let the healing current flow freely through one's life.

With an honesty that is quite shattering the verses that follow list humanity's most urgent requirements. Again and again they bring up the dominant failings of human life. And we must admit that all people experience both these failings and the needs mentioned earlier. And we today, perhaps more than at any other time, have fallen back on our last reserves as human beings and made serious inroads on them. For us the borderline is more sharply defined and our failure more obvious and more keenly felt. It all stresses the fact that it is more than time contemporary westerners returned to our natural human status determined by our relationship with God in humility, contact and unity. Of course we must clearly understand that God does not exist merely as a sort of medicine for ailing humanity. In the first place the Lord says: I will renew you, and in the second place it is not that God exists for humankind and our well-being, but that those who do not exist for God and live up to all the conditions God has laid down or may lay down are their own enemy and murderer.

There are moments in every person's life when we are filled with self-disgust, when consciousness of failure tears the mask from self-assurance and self-justification and reality stands revealed — even if only for a moment. Occasionally such a moment produces a permanent change and the mask is not resumed. Our natural tendency is to avoid these moments of truth. Pride, cowardice, and above all an intuitive feeling that the only way out of the situation will be to humble oneself and submit, tempt a person to declare reality unreal and to pronounce the counterfeit genuine.

The shock may come when a great wrong, or a succession of mischances, has sapped a person's self-confidence and forced him to take a closer look at himself. Everything depends on whether he takes this seriously or passes it off as a moment of "weakness" from which he speedily "recovers." In that case his last state is worse than his first — he becomes immunized to error, no longer able to distinguish the false from the true. Then we get cliches like "self-determination," the "right to live," "hunger for life" and so on. When this happens in the case of a gifted person, he can easily become an evil influence leading others astray, scattering sparks that ignite the inflammable material and bring about historic catastrophes. Such individuals are capable of dragging whole generations to ruin. Their contemporaries suddenly find themselves in a vicious circle, sharing responsibility for evils they are unable to rectify.

On the other hand by divine grace a person may be suddenly raised to a consciousness of how near he is to God. Then, too, he is bound to be shocked by the truth of his own unworthiness. None of us can escape the admission that we have made sad mistakes and to some extent bungled our lives. By acknowledging their fault humans recognize their weakness and their dependence on divine help and recognize also the danger of concluding an easy peace with the weaknesses of their own nature. Coming to terms with things our conscience cannot approve means that we must share the responsibility for them because they have our assent.

There is only one way to salvation and it is not achieved by trying to escape or failing to acknowledge our fault. We are saved not by denying our failures but by looking at them honestly and acknowledging them. This need not distress us — it is a salutary experience to be roused now and then to recognition of our mistakes and to make a fresh start. Woe to the person who gets bogged down in error, resigning himself to it through sheer fatigue — when that happens everything is lost. If in the midst of sin a person can hold on to the finer impulses of his nature they will show him the way back to his true self. Sin

always sullies and sometimes distorts reality. Only the Lord of
creation is capable of restoring it and he is always willing to do
so. All the sinner has to do is submit to God's word and surrender himself to the healing will. Submission is his contribution
to the cure. But the healing, creative intervention of God cannot be dispensed with and this is most potent at the moment of
contact with the Holy Ghost. It is in the bliss of that contact
that we come to full awareness of our human limitations and
the unworthiness of sin. And again all that we can do is to surrender ourselves absolutely in order that the Spirit of God may
do its work in the unity of contact.

The Holy Ghost floods our being like a healing stream and
no blemish can withstand its cleansing power. *Wash what is
stained.* This must be the prayer of all who long for unity with
God in the core of their being. Great benevolence and grace
are called for and God does not withhold these from his creation. Humans cannot live without this creative contact with
their Maker and these fountains are unsealed by honest and
complete surrender. This is the indispensable act on our part —
surrender and prayer.

Water What Is Barren

We have to keep reminding ourselves of the underlying theme
of the Whitsuntide liturgy — the devout dialogue between the
worshipper and the creative Spirit. When song dies in the heart
and the inner fountains have dried up, the waste land of our
life becomes a barren wilderness swept by raging sand storms.
There are moments of exaltation and inspiration when the
world seems almost too small and the stars are *very* near — but
this is often a kind of creative drunkenness quickly dispelled
on sober awakening to the realities of human weakness. Some
people have a natural creative gift, more penetrating insight and

a more skillful hand than others for the shaping of intractable material — but there are limits to this too; genius is also subject to frustration and sudden disappointment.

There are two kinds of sterility — personal barrenness and the barrenness of whole generations. A person may be sterile not only in his personal life but also, and much more terribly, in his contact with God, in the living dialogue with his Creator.

And a generation can be sterile; suddenly the creative fruitfulness of a whole race may dry up. Creative ideas are no longer born, nothing of any note is produced in art, literature, politics, philosophy, theology or religion.

These manifestations require much thought. They cannot merely be noted as facts and left at that. They are conditioned by fundamental laws of our existence.

The obvious and easiest explanation, which traces back the failure of creative substance to exhaustion and fatigue, simply does not suffice. There is not only supra-normal impulse and fertility — there is also a sub-normal level of sterility. And the fact of creative productivity ceasing indicates that fundamental laws are involved and that fundamental health is affected. And if this is conceded we must recognize that we are not concerned only with great creative achievements, though these also come under the same laws since the prerequisites for great achievement are exemplified by humans in their relationship with their fellow creatures and with God. When a person gets to a stage where adoration is no longer fruitful or seems strange and contrary to his nature, when his love has degenerated into superficial emotion and he doesn't want anything else, when he really only exists as a caricature of himself, then the sources dry up and a person's own wilderness starts to spread and encroach on the green and fertile land. The immediate cause may lie in outward conditions that sap a person's strength or regiment him into narrow channels. But underneath it all there is still the fundamental fact that the person has lost the sense of values, the instinct that should enable him to judge rightly. Another factor may be the false image he has formed of his own potentialities, either through conceit or through collective wrong thinking. In any case the actual cause is the failure of his critical judgment and his obstinate determination to go his own way, following his own blind impulses.

Here too the only solution is to reestablish the partnership with God. This is the only order by which we can properly regulate our life. It is the pattern to which we were created and the one we have got to live by. Where objective circumstances consequent on wrong decisions have become so hard and intolerable that they bow us down, it is no use waiting for a new order to emerge from a change of heart. Active steps must be taken to reorganize life in accordance with God's law, even at the expense, if need be, of a real clash.

This cannot be done without God's help. May he stir our hearts and give the necessary vision and courage to make the decisive step.

In the last analysis it is our lack of vitality that causes fatigue and exhaustion. The burdens God lays on us can be heavy and the road dreary and exhausting. We can only make an effort and bear strain up to a certain point. There are limits to our endurance and beyond that point we need help from outside.

And there is another wilderness which we must cross — the wilderness God ordains both as a test and a means of redemption. Let us go toward it bravely — but not without earnestly and trustfully reaching out for God's guiding hand. These wildernesses must be mastered — that of loneliness, of fear, of depression, of sacrifice. God who created wildernesses also made the streams that bring forth fruitfulness when they flow over barren land. Prayer and trust in his goodness bring his promises to pass.

Heal What Is Wounded

Humanity is in great distress when it is wounded. The desire to be whole and fulfilled is so strong that we regard every wound as an injustice. The further we are from fulfillment the greater the heights we will have to scale in our endeavor to attain it and as we go on we realize that no progress can be made without getting wounded now and then. Even when we are in sober earnest and honestly adhere to the partnership we still have to fight our way through to the hard core of reality, and suffer sorrow, privation and pain in our own person. Dumb nature hits out at us through its very dumbness and the rigidity of its rhythmic constitution which does not yield to our will without a struggle — and especially to that ultimate will which represents our innermost self. We attack one another in enmity, deliberately and thoughtlessly, through greed, through indifference, through hatred and sometimes through love. There is no end to the wounds we can inflict on each other, and sometimes the hardest blows of all are those sustained when God himself seems to be inflicting pain on his poor creatures. He named those who mourn and those who suffer among the blessed but so often that blessing seems to be nothing more than a promise, while we chafe under the conviction that our current suffering is due to an act of God. Poor wretches — we sometimes feel we would like to crawl into a hole like some stricken animal and hide where no more harm can come to us. But even that is no use. The ties of love, of duty, the bonds of everyday existence keep us at our posts in our greatest distress. And many have to carry not only their own misery around with them but to share the need and the sickness of others, of the great mass of humanity grown silent and weary.

I have frequently referred in these meditations to the dangers and setbacks we encounter at every level of existence, and

I don't want to go into that again. Let us leave the solution of
these problems to prayer. It is best that all the suffering and misery should be gathered up in one great cry for help. There are
times when this is the only thing that can be done. When all else
fails we remember God and appeal for help. And in the stillness
of this holy contact help assuredly comes. Sooner or later our
fruitless efforts to escape from our entanglements must cease;
we must realize their futility. Straining against the pricks never
helps — it only produces more worries. We must grow quiet
enough to realize God's omnipresence, to feel his comforting
hand and open our hearts from within, silently, letting his healing will have its way. Then the waters will flow over the arid
soil and things will start to grow again. If only we keep still.
God permits many wounds — but there are also miracles. We
are today — individually and collectively — fainting from want
and loss of blood. Things have gone so far that no one can help
us any more — neither friend, nor goodwill, nor comfort can do
us any good. Our last resource is to turn to the creative Spirit,
the Holy Ghost, which is ready and willing to pour out on us
the healing power of our Father, God.

Because of this we should never despair even in our darkest hours. We should remember that God shares our life, that
through the Holy Ghost we can be on the most intimate terms
with God and that God is always there, when outward pressure is at its worst, helping us to carry our burdens over the
roughest places on our weary road. There is no fiber of our
being that the healing Spirit cannot reach as long as we are willing to let it do its creative, healing work. It goes on in silence
within us and we should remind ourselves constantly that in
alliance with God we possess powers of recuperation which enable us to endure the most grievous wounds without flinching
and go on meeting the demands life makes on us. We should
have this inner confidence, not mere self-reliance, but because

we know beyond a shadow of doubt that God is sharing his life with us.

The worst wounds that can be inflicted on humans, or that they can inflict on themselves, are those of evil. When faith wavers, hope disappears, love grows cold, adoration ceases, doubt nags and the whole life is shrouded like a winter landscape in snow, when hatred and arrogance predominate, life is mortally wounded. That is the time to get into reverse, and let the Holy Ghost work from within building up a new life. From God's view point the world looks quite different and we must at all costs get back to the divine point of view. And a great many situations must be subjected to this process of conversion. The person who insists on isolation and never grows conscious of the inner presence of the Spirit is doomed to failure after failure. I am proving this each day and each hour. If I had tried to cope with all this mountain of trouble unaided I should have reached the end of my tether long ago. Natural logic keeps forcing its evil conclusions, like poison, on one's consciousness. To counter them one has to apply the logic of healing, of guidance and submission, on which decisions can be based when they have been patiently arrived at through prayer. The Holy Ghost constantly helps me over my hurdles in the small hours. I am aware of this and I do not doubt it. I could never have accomplished any of this on my own. Not even that night in the Lehrterstrasse. God heals. The healing strength of God lives in me and with me.

Bend What Is Rigid

Life knows nothing more injurious than creeping paralysis. A paralyzed life is utterly impoverished whether it realizes its condition or whether it has become so accustomed to paralysis that it thinks it normal. Movement, animation, is a primary law of life. It goes hand in hand with unfolding, growth. Sensation, which is inherent in all living things, craves for change; inertia is foreign to it because the very vitality of living drives it on to the desired goal of fulfillment. Paralysis is the exact opposite. It brings existence to a standstill at one particular point; it cuts across the law of progress with an untimely desire for a fixed destination.

A person can be rigid in many ways. He can have a one-track mind like the rich young man in the gospel. God would be doing such a man a kindness in destroying his possessions before calling him to the last judgment. This paralysis in the realm of things, this fixation about property, riches, gold, jewels, art and good living was characteristic of the last century. One half of the world's population lost their souls to material possessions; the other half spent their time protesting, not at the danger to humankind through this kind of bondage, but at the fact that it was not possible for them to lose their souls in the same way because they had not yet succeeded in gaining such possessions. Recent wars have destroyed houses, goods and much more besides. If a new freedom and a new outlook do not emerge from this destruction humankind will once again have missed a great opportunity.

Even more dangerous is that inner paralysis which induces us to betray the fundamental laws of our existence. No longer "living to all truth, to all goodness" we pull up short, set ourselves apart, rest on our laurels and lead the life of a pensioner. We no longer strain with all our might to achieve ideals, reaching for the stars. The command to love God with all one's heart, with all one's mind and with all one's strength no longer has any meaning for us; we treat it as something handed down like a legend, something that has served its turn and can be thrown aside. All the truths have already been discovered, we think — no need to go to the trouble of looking for any more. The world has grown dumb — we no longer hear the underground rumblings as the secret forces collect their strength for the great fulfillment which can only be brought about by humanity's conscious recognition and decision. Destiny, and God's Spirit operating from within, can save this kind of person from the hard fate in store by rekindling the divine spark in his heart. Here is a case that emphatically calls for bending, loosening, melting, making the intractable pliable. Present-day humanity's incapacity for love, for reverence, for appreciation has its roots in arrogance and in this petrifying of existence.

A pliable nature is a gift of grace rather than the outcome of effort or the operation of fate. In all sincerity humans must loyally observe the rule of the road along which they are traveling. Then the dialogue will be maintained and they will remain genuine partners in divine freedom and vitality.

Fate may be the cause of a paralysis which is the grimmest of all. When life itself transfixes a person, tying him hand and foot, shutting him up in a prison with no possible outlet, of what use then are all decisions to live abundantly? The paralysis of fear, the hardening brought about by bitter experience are often a mere defensive armor, but they can also endanger life itself. Only when God's strength plays a part in the drama will the inner vitality hold out, even if we fall. The restorative power of the Spirit must refresh our nature from within, rendering us capable of resisting temptation and of holding our own, no matter what fate may have in store for us. The love of God, and the patient loving hands of those whose lives have not been afflicted with paralysis, will help us in our struggle.

A life that has hardened into numbness is mortally sick. All that is vital in life succumbs to the hardening process. A numbed person deludes himself into believing that he cannot hear the inner voice that calls on him to shake off this numbness and rise out of himself. He is bound and fettered to himself and wastes away in that condition. He becomes incapable of living faith, as he is incapable of entering into the dialogue, the fundamental form of creative life in every respect. True faith, reverence, respect, love, adoration — all these are forms of the dialogue and all of them are stifled in the numbness brought about by the hardening of heart. So a person really ought to make every effort to maintain the dialogue and not to miss a single moment of contact with the invisible partner. More grievous than any external hardness or difficulty is this inner numbness, whether it results from habit, or fear, or shock, from pettiness or pride.

In the creative dialogue we find ourselves and make closer acquaintance with our underlying motives and our background. Hence the prayer for bending is actually a plea for our own life. Oh how a life can suffer from its own hardening and numbness. When I think back I realize how conceited I was about my own firmness. It was all self-deception and arrogance, this fine idea I had of my independence and so on. I had my suspicions about it even then, for I found that whenever I caused anyone pain that pain hurt me also. Contact with God helped me at such times and I noticed that the more honest it became the more I was forced to give up my arrogant attitude and my unloving approach. But I really owe the quickening of my intercourse with God chiefly to the intensifying of intercourse with my fellow human beings, which broke much fresh ground in me and brought it under cultivation for the first time.

When a person's heart softens and loses its numbness he actually brings about his own liberation. Like all surrender that is not prompted by creative assent this can be a painful business. But it is restorative and a step toward freedom — the torrent at last finds an outlet to its own ocean. The overcoming of icy isolation, of lack of love and self-sufficiency — that is the task of the Holy Ghost in us.

Melt What Is Frozen

In a collect — I think it is that of the day dedicated to St. Francis's stigmata — the words "world grown cold" occur. As the world turned to ice it was the time and the hour of this saint of love. *A world grown cold:* love turned cold is the deadly fate that threatens all life and must be overcome at all costs. We should recognize clearly what this horror means, whence it comes and how devastating it can be.

Science maintains that our earth will eventually end in another ice age. That is as may be; at the present stage of knowledge it may be regarded as possible. No one can tell what the future may hold in the way of new impulses and changes of emphasis as developments proceed. But no one can dispute that the culture of the west, where documents and monuments are at present being rapidly destroyed, has frozen to death. One is only human, and great, in so far as one is capable of loving. In the west it is long since humans loved greatly and had a passion for the absolute. They have had passions for things, for power, for authority, for pleasure, for possessions, but they have not been capable of a genuine passion for humankind. Everything had to have a purpose or an object. Humanity was no longer the target but only the means through which others could heighten and multiply their own experiences. Our hearts no longer trembled when we thought of ultimate realities like God, humanity, mission, and so on. Things were proclaimed, passed on and practiced as before but the actual creative source within us, the genuine impulse, the great surrender, even the passion, was lacking.

It is not easy to revive a smoldering fire. When humans have strayed from the current of reality they can do nothing about it at any rate on their own. At best they can revive their memory, give the assent of their will and pray for the fire from heaven that prepares, transforms, and rekindles.

The Holy Ghost is God's passion for himself. Humanity must make contact with this passion, must play its part in completing the circuit. Then true love will reign again in the world and humanity will be capable of living to the full. The indwelling presence of God must take possession of our senses, draw us out of ourselves, in order that we may be capable of genuine assent and contact. God must ratify himself in us and through us; then we shall live as we should. Then the holy fire will again become the heart of the earth and remain so.

Bend What Is Rigid — Melt What Is Frozen

Two characteristic features of our age come up before the seat of judgment — middle-class respectability and the bureaucratic Church.

At one time the middle-class style of life had its virtues and served a purpose. It was always threatened and it was also always a potential danger because it allied itself with human weakness and ran the risk that the possessions people hoarded, and which they needed for their task and mission, would end by mastering them. This was their particular form of numbness and hardening; the sense of duty died out and what remained was middle-class gluttony, idleness, comfort, ease and all that went with material possessions. Dividends, stock, shares, bank balances — these were the symbols of respectability, the ideals men strived for. There arose a type of person to whose hearts one might almost say God himself could find no access, because they were so hedged around with security and insurance. The type still flourishes. It laid down the lines on which our present progress is developing. The type has not been overcome because all the counter-movements have failed to negate the type — they merely object to the exclusion of sections of humanity from the type. Most modern movements set off with the object of enabling their adherents to live in the best possible material style. And even where the times and the spiritual connections have here and there carried the movements on they have still clung to the old middle-class mold in middle-class imperialism.

It is a pity that so much that gave momentum to the old system must now be brought up for judgment before *bend* and *melt* which alone can rouse humankind from its lethargy. And that there are so many persons the heat of the fire has not yet reached. A new alert type of person must be born of this trial of fire and of the penetrating radiance of the Spirit. He must be awake and alive, this new person, fully responsible, with far-seeing eyes and a listening heart. His soul must respond to the marching song and his spirit must carry the standard of freedom he has found and to which he has sworn allegiance.

The other type which must appear for judgment is no less important and quite as numerous in present-day life. In fact people of this type inside the Church are largely responsible for its bureaucratic pattern. The Church has made its own contribution to the emergence of the middle class. And the middle class has lost no opportunity to take advantage of the Church and to establish the ideals of human weakness, riches, power, luxury and security in the Church.

Of course there must be administration in the Church — statistics, auditors, official seals and so on. Nothing can alter that. But while it is in the nature of things that such organization should be centralized, in the ecclesiastical sphere this should be as little noticeable as possible. Human beings have become subjectively and objectively submerged, impersonalized, under ecclesiastical life and ecclesiastical guidance. It is useless to quote a list of examples. Only one thing need be stressed. The rule that ordains that leaders should have neither names nor faces has encouraged regimentation in our lives quite as much as the anonymous act and the control of the State, economics and political parties.

Here, too, appeals to a vital, personally courageous existence will be in vain until God calls the Church and its present system to account before the judgment seat of *bend* and *melt*. "None can pass through fire without being transformed." When we have passed through a hundred doors and all our bridges are burnt we get some inkling of the immense distance that must be covered if the name of God is to pass our lips. The Spirit, the life-giver, will help us emerge from all this rubble, not as human ruins but as persons with new horizons and new courage. We must forget a great deal and forsake much and we must invest a great deal more if we are to win back the whole. The earth is being ploughed and new seed sown. Let us cherish God's freedom and surrender ourselves to the truth and vitality of the Spirit.

Correct What Is Wrong

One of the saddest and most significant things about modern life is that it lacks instinct. Loss of instinct is the greatest deprivation either for a tamed animal or a human being who is exhausted. People today are completely without instinct. Under the fatal burden of our civilization, the overwhelming weight of our titanic dreams, the futile waste of our so-called self-realization and other vague ideas we have lost our natural instinct. And the mechanization and reorganization of our religious life have taken away our supernatural instinct as well. Very seldom is a natural taste for religion (which is a characteristic of those who consciously yield themselves to the indwelling Spirit) met with nowadays. The certainty which enabled us to distinguish between good and evil by our own inner standard, to decide between useful and harmful, between wisdom and folly, has vanished. This explains the immature behavior of so many Christians today. It has a much deeper cause than faulty upbringing or inadequate instruction. The religious profession, like other professions, suffers from this same lack.

Our deviation from the right road underlines the fundamental errors and the need for immediate repentance. As the whole theme of this prayer is life in the intimacy of the Holy Ghost, the loving creative contact between the Spirit of life and the created being, I think it is especially pertinent to the correction of this lack of instinct. Both as individual Christians, and as the corporate community, the Church, we have in recent times failed in our dealings with our neighbors, failed in our assessment of situations and spiritual realities, in the art of leading, in the presentation of our doctrine and in much else besides. We have every reason to be shocked and ashamed. Of course the Church still has skillful apologists, clever and compelling preachers, wise leaders; but the simple confidence that senses the right course and proceeds to act on it almost unconsciously is just not there.

Among the gifts of the Holy Ghost are listed prudence, wisdom and piety. These are natural attributes which provide penetration, the power to see connecting links to divine underlying factors and basic causes. These are the "intuitive" faculties with which the Holy Ghost endows us and which he keeps alive in us by his own life. They give us the "single eye" and safeguard us against blind conflict with reality which must in the end do us harm.

Give to Thy Faithful

Faith is the point of contact. I have already pointed out that this wonderful life of spirit can only grow and unfold in the sphere and atmosphere of personal intimacy. The first step is faith and that means faith as personal surrender. There is far more to this than the bare acceptance of truth as the rock on which God's Church is built. This is the very least a person can offer in the way of assent and receptivity. Anyone determined to limit his acceptance to the things he can grasp and understand is not going to get very close to the living God. Faith is our first step away from ourselves and toward God as center and absolute reality, to the exclusion of self and all pseudo realities. And the decision has to be translated into one personal thing — unconditional loyalty. Only then does it become vital, alive: in that moment our real consciousness of the Holy Ghost is born. But it only becomes active in us when we can realize it as the personal will of God for us and give the corresponding personal answer. Life has the same fundamental pattern even in the realm of the supernatural — the personal dialogue is the basis of spiritual vitality. Give to *thy* faithful the prayer says. It is exactly like the intercourse of two healthy human beings — the heart dares to mate with another because it finds itself at home with the chosen comrade whose worth is recognized. The Spirit does not use force, breaking in like a thief. God's holy will never coerces but responds to the cry of willing assent. And when that cry is raised, the slightest movement of the heart is sufficient to stir the ocean of God's munificent love into full flood.

We must make veneration of the Holy Ghost and the plea for his coming and his blessing our heart's constant prayer, particularly today as we see more and more what the destruction going on round us really means. It is in conditions like these that the word takes on its full meaning for us. Only in prayer can we go on, can we rise to the heights and use our full capacity for life.

Who Trust in Thee

Confidence is the fruit of faith. It is the condition that has not yet attained the full blessing of love but it embodies the sense of security we experience when we have firm ground under our feet, a foundation we can rely on. It puts our doubts to rest and allows us a sense of peace because we know we can depend on the integrity we have built up and on our capacity to measure up to life's demands and bear whatever burdens are in store. The decision I spoke of just now in relation to personal faith becomes something final, irrevocable and is the basis for the ensuing decision. Confidence means that something can be relied on in face of all doubt and reservation and appearances to the contrary.

But the condition of personal trust and confidence is something more. We can trust in things of proven value or those vouched for by reliable people. But this is because we have confidence in ourselves, in our expert knowledge and judgment or in the trustworthiness of the guarantors. But where the relationship between two persons is concerned, trust is only possible as a personal intimacy — not necessarily the supreme intimacy of love although love is the ultimate blessing and the harvest of trust.

The relationship between humanity and God, in spite of the distance between them and the humble reverence necessary on our part, is a relationship built on personal trust. God bases many of his promises on the trust we should place in him. Many miracles and graces depend on the trust with which they are prayed for and expected. In this respect we have a certain advantage over God — an advantage we rarely realize and so often fail to make use of. Our Lord called his disciples men of little faith when they did not trust him to cope with a few manifestations, laws of nature or consequences of natural logic. We must at the very least arrive at a state of mind that will make certain that things do not fail because we had insufficient faith to let God handle them.

Realization of our wonderful life in the Holy Ghost also rests on our trust. Despite our indwelling Spirit we often feel tired and frightened and disheartened because we do not trust the Spirit of God sufficiently for him to be able to make something of us. We believe more in our own unworthiness than in the creative impulse of God — who is living our lives jointly with us. It all hinges on trust, on whether we are willing to receive God's creative blessing and let it fulfill our lives, making us efficient, living souls. Blessed are those that hunger and thirst. . . .

5

The Last Stage

AFTER THE VERDICT

It has become an odd sort of life I am leading. It is so easy to get used to existence again that one has to keep reminding oneself that death is round the corner. Condemned to death. The thought refuses to penetrate; it almost needs force to drive it home. The thing that makes this kind of death so singular is that one feels so vibrantly alive with the will to live unbroken and every nerve tingling with life. A malevolent external force is the only thing that can end it. The usual intimations of approaching death are therefore lacking. One of these days the door will open, the jailer will say, "Pack up. The car will be here in half an hour." We have often heard this and know exactly what it is like.

Actually I had thought to be taken to Plotzensee straight away last Thursday evening. But a new timetable is in force and we, apparently, are the first people to come under it. Or could it be that appeals have been made? I hardly think so. Here everything is subjective — not even bureaucratic procedure but undisguised subjectivity. The man Freisler is able, nervous, vain and arrogant. He is playing a part and his opponent must be made to look inferior. In this sort of dialogue the advantage of having the upper hand is obvious.

While it was all going on I felt as if I were a mere spectator. It was rather like a bad Pullach debate only that the defense kept changing and the accuser decided who was in the right. His fellow judges, the "people," were a bunch of ordinary, dutiful individuals who had put on their Sunday suits very ceremoniously for the occasion and took themselves very seriously indeed sitting there in judgment with Herr President in his red robe. They were good biddable SS men, obediently fulfilling the role of the "people" — which is to say "yes."

Everything was as per schedule — nothing missing; the Grand Entrance with an awe-inspiring muster of police — each of us had two men with him. Behind us, the public, mostly gestapo and so on; their faces are good-natured, average faces, very accustomed to this sort of thing, the average type representing "the" Germany. The other Germany is not represented, or is in the process of being condemned to death. All the performance needed was an overture and a finale at the end — or at least a fanfare.

The proceedings themselves were handled slickly and ruthlessly — so ruthlessly that no word in the defendants' favor was even permitted. The only questions asked were those that suited the accusers' purpose and the findings, naturally, were in accordance.

Our case was aimed at the destruction of Moltke and myself and all the rest was mere window dressing. I knew from the moment we began that my fate was already sealed. The questions were all prepared and followed a definite plan and woe betide any answer that did not fit into the prearranged pattern. Scholasticism and Jesuitism were paraded as the real villains. It is a common belief that a Jesuit commits a crime every time he

draws breath. He can say and do and prove whatever he likes —
no one ever believes him.

The slanders on the Church, incidents singled out from
Church history, the smirching of the Order and so on were very
grim. I had to keep a tight grip on myself to stop myself explod-
ing. But if I had let go it would have ruined all our chances. It
was a great opportunity for the actor to declare his opponent a
clever, dangerous, beaten man and then show off as being, himself, immensely superior. From the moment he started it was
all over. I strongly advise my brothers in the Order to keep
away from these trials where one is not a human being but an
object. And all under an inflated rigmarole of legal terms and
phrases. Just before this I had been reading Plato who said that
the greatest injustice is that performed in the name of justice.

Our own crime was that of heresy against the third Reich.
Someone ought to remind Freisler what would have happened
if Moltke's defense plan had been used. And how many of
the men he (F) has condemned are being missed now. Anyone who dares cast any doubts on the Nazi system is of course
a heretic — and former judgments on heretics are child's play
compared to the refined and deadly retribution practiced by
these people.

Moltke's plight might not have been so bad if he had not
been "tied up with the Church" which laid him open to the
charge of "re-Christianizing intentions." He had consorted with
bishops and Jesuits. What fools we were when we tried to make
preparation for this trial — it had nothing whatever to do with
facts or truth. This was not a court of justice but a function.
An unmistakable echo and nothing else. I just can't understand
how any person can go on doing this sort of thing day after day.

The final session was on Thursday and all round everything
else went on as usual — rather like a prize-giving in a small
school which hadn't even the proper room for it. I thought

Moltke and I would be taken to the Plotzensee immediately afterwards but we are still here.

The sentence seemed just as unreal as the proceedings of the two previous days. I kept the Host with me and before the final session I said Mass and took communion — my last meal. I wanted to be prepared. But here I am, still waiting.

Up to now the Lord has helped me wonderfully. I am not yet scared and not yet beaten. The hour of human weakness will no doubt come and sometimes I am depressed when I think of all the things I hoped to do. But I am now a man internally free and far more genuine and realized than I was before. Only now have I sufficient insight to see the thing as a whole.

To be quite honest I do not yet believe in my execution. I don't know why. Perhaps our Father, God, has some great grace in store for me and will enable me to pass through this wilderness without having to perish in it. During the proceedings, even when it was clear there would be no miracle, I felt lifted above it all and quite untouched by all that was going on. Was that a miracle? If not, what was it? I am really in some embarrassment before God and must think it out.

All these long months of misfortune fit into some special pattern. From the first I was so sure everything would turn out well. God always strengthened me in that conviction. These last few days I have doubted and wondered whether my will to live has been sublimated into religious delusions or something like that. Yet all these unmistakable moments of exaltation in the midst of misery; my confidence and unshakable faith even when I was being beaten up, the certain "in spite of it all" that kept my spirits up and made me so sure that they would not succeed in destroying me; those consolations in prayer and in the Blessed Sacrament, the moments of grace; the signs I prayed for that were vouchsafed again and again — must I put them all away from me now? Does God ask the sacrifice which I will not deny him — or is he testing my faith and my trust to the last limit of endurance? As I was being taken to Berlin for the preliminary hearing I suddenly remembered the unexploded bomb in St. Ignatius's House and quite distinctly I heard the words "It will not explode."

And the second special thing about this week is that everything I did to better my situation went wrong and in fact made it worse. It was the same during the recent hearing. The change of lawyers which at first seemed so promising was a bad mistake. As the new man became aware of the anti-Jesuit complex he told me, while the proceedings were still in progress, that as a matter of fact he was against Jesuits too. Sending Freisler the pamphlet *Man and History* was a mistake also — it only gave him the impression I was clever and therefore more dangerous. Statistics prepared for our defense were used against us. The whole proceedings led to one disaster after another. And on top of all this the quite unforeseen misfortune that we remain here, still alive, when we had prepared ourselves to die last Thursday. And so on.

What is God's purpose in all this? Is it a further lesson with regard to complete freedom and absolute surrender? Does he want us to drain the chalice to the dregs and are these hours of waiting preparation for an extraordinary Advent? Or is he testing our faith?

What should I do to remain loyal — go on hoping despite the hopelessness of it all? Or should I relax? Ought I to resign myself to the inevitable and is it cowardice not to do this and to go on hoping? Should I simply stand still, free and ready to take whatever God sends? I can't yet see the way clear before me; I must go on praying for light and guidance. And then there is the accepted sacrifice of the past seven months. It is terrible the way a person keeps on going over these things in his heart. But at least I will look at them honestly under the impulse of the Holy Spirit.

When I compare my icy calm during the court proceedings with the fear I felt, for instance, during the bombing of Munich, I realize how much I have changed. But the question keeps coming back — was this change the purpose of it all — or is this inner exaltation and help the miracle I asked for?

I don't know. Logically there is no hope at all. The atmosphere here, so far as I am concerned, is so hostile that an appeal has not the slightest chance of succeeding. So is it madness to hope — or conceit, or cowardice, or grace? Often I just sit before God looking at him questioningly.

But one thing is gradually becoming clear — I must surrender myself completely. This is seed-time, not harvest. God sows the seed and some time or other he will do the reaping. The one thing I must do is to make sure the seed falls on fertile ground. And I must arm myself against the pain and depression that sometimes almost defeat me. If this is the way God has chosen — and everything indicates that it is — then I must willingly and without rancor make it my way. May others at some future time find it possible to have a better and happier life because we died in this hour of trial.

I ask my friends not to mourn, but to pray for me and help me as long as I have need of help. And to be quite clear in their own minds that I was sacrificed, not conquered. It never occurred to me that my life would end like this. I had spread my sails to the wind and set my course for a great voyage, flags flying, ready to brave every storm that blew. But it could be they were false flags or my course wrongly set or the ship a pirate and its cargo contraband. I don't know. And I will not sink to cheap jibes at the world in order to raise my spirits. To be quite honest I don't want to die, particularly now that I feel I could do more important work and deliver a new message about values I have only just discovered and understood. But it has turned out otherwise. God keep me in his providence and give me strength to meet what is before me.

It only remains for me to thank a great many people for their help and loyalty and belief in me, and for the love they have shown me. First and foremost my brethren in the Order who gave me a genuine and beautiful vision of life. And the many sincere people I was privileged to meet. I remember very clearly the times when we were able to meet freely and discuss the tasks in front of us. Do not give up, ever. Never cease to cherish the people in your hearts — the poor forsaken and betrayed people who are so helpless. For in spite of all their outward display and loud self-assurance, deep down they are lonely and frightened. If through one person's life there is a little more love and kindness, a little more light and truth in the world, then he will not have lived in vain.

Nor must I forget those to whom I owe so much. May those I have hurt forgive me — I am sorry for having injured them. May those to whom I have been untrue forgive me — I am sorry for having failed them. May those to whom I have been proud and overbearing forgive me — I repent my arrogance. And may those to whom I have been unloving forgive me — I repent my hardness. Oh yes — long hours spent in this cell with fettered wrists and my body and spirit tormented must have broken down a great deal that was hard in me. Much that was unworthy and worthless has been committed to the flames.

So farewell. My offense is that I believed in Germany and her eventual emergence from this dark hour of error and distress, that I refused to accept that accumulation of arrogance, pride and force that is the Nazi way of life, and that I did this as a Christian and a Jesuit. These are the values for which I am here now on the brink waiting for the thrust that will send me over. Germany will be reborn, once this time has passed, in a new form based on reality with Christ and his Church recognized again as being the answer to the secret yearning of this earth and its people, with the Order the home of proved men — men who today are hated because they are misunderstood in their voluntary dedication or feared as a reproach in the prevailing state of pathetic, immeasurable human bondage. These are the thoughts with which I go to my death.

And so to conclude I will do what I so often did with my fettered hands and what I will gladly do again and again as long as I have a breath left — I will give my blessing. I will bless this land and the people; I will bless the Church and pray that her fountains may flow again fresher and more freely; I will bless all those who have believed in me and trusted me, all those I have wronged and all those who have been good to me — often too good.

God be with you and protect you. Help my poor old parents through these days of trial and keep them in your thoughts. God help you all.

I will honestly and patiently await God's will. I will trust him till they come to fetch me. I will do my best to ensure that this blessing, too, shall not find me broken and in despair.

LETTER TO THE BRETHREN

Dear Brethren,

Here I am at the parting of the ways and I must take the other road after all. The death sentence has been passed and the atmosphere is so charged with enmity and hatred that no appeal has any hope of succeeding.

I thank the Order and my brethren for all their goodness and loyalty and help, especially during these last weeks. I ask pardon for much that was untrue and unjust; and I beg that a little help and care may be given to my aged, sick parents.

The actual reason for my condemnation was that I happened to be, and chose to remain, a Jesuit. There was nothing to show that I had any connection with the attempt on Hitler's life so I was acquitted on that count. The rest of the accusations were far less serious and more factual. There was one underlying theme — a Jesuit is *a priori* an enemy and betrayer of the Reich. So the whole proceedings turned into a sort of comedy developing a theme. It was not justice — it was simply the carrying out of the determination to destroy.

May God shield you all. I ask for your prayers. And I will do my best to catch up, on the other side, with all that I have left undone here on earth.

Towards noon I will celebrate Mass once more and then in God's name take the road under his providence and guidance.

> In God's blessing and protection,
> Your grateful,
> Alfred Delp, S.J.

EDGEWOOD

EDGEWOOD

BY KAREN MCQUESTION

For readers everywhere. You matter.

One night that changed everything. If I'd known what was going to happen would I still have gone out walking after midnight?

Absolutely.

—Russ Becker

Remember tonight... for it is the beginning of always.

–Dante Alighieri

CHAPTER ONE

——— o ———

I couldn't believe it was happening again. Couldn't sleep, couldn't sleep, couldn't sleep. It was a Monday night; school started the next day at 7:20 a.m., and I was exhausted, but my body didn't care. I shifted in bed and punched my pillow into different shapes, like that would help, even though it never did before.

Finally, after midnight came and went, I dealt with it in my usual way—I got up. I got out of bed, threw on some jeans and a hooded sweatshirt, and tiptoed downstairs. When I got to the back door, I paused to pick up the Nikes I kept next to the mat and slipped out into the night. Once outside, I pulled on my shoes and headed out. Just me and the night air. I was never afraid to be out alone at night because I kept undercover. Even though I was a pretty tall guy, almost six feet, I was able to stay hidden in the shadows. I relished the time alone with my thoughts. But mostly I looked forward to getting back home when I was done with my walk so I could finally get some sleep.

The weather was cool and a little clammy. Not too bad, pretty warm for spring in Wisconsin, and there weren't any mosquitoes

1

yet. Our next-door neighbor had used his outdoor fireplace earlier in the evening and a faint smoky smell still lingered.

I walked around to the sidewalk in front. My house was dark except for the one lamp my mom always kept on in the living room to scare off burglars.

I didn't stay there for long. I had a certain route I did every night and it didn't involve roads. I preferred cutting through yards, fields, and parking lots. I told myself that if I just covered this route I could go home and go to sleep. It was a little psychological game I played, and it worked like nothing else did. I didn't know it yet, but tonight was going to be different.

It's amazing how many people are up at two in the morning. Driving or working mostly. There are others too, people like me who just seem to be awake for no reason at all, pacing in their houses, watching late-night TV, reading. They can't sleep and I can't sleep. It makes me feel better when I see them through their windows and know I'm not the only one.

That night started off the usual way. I did my route through a residential section on the other side of town. There were a few houses that were always lit up, occupied by people like me still awake at that hour. I'd pause by each house watching them through the window, feeling a sense of kinship even though they never noticed me lurking outside. After that, I headed for the strip mall three blocks from my house and wandered around behind the building before taking my usual path through the industrial park toward the old, boarded-up train station.

I was almost to the train station when I noticed a series of bright lights moving fast in the sky overhead. I stopped, trying to figure out what it was. It wasn't a plane or a flare or any kind of reflection. More like a blur of shooting stars. Except that shooting stars were usually higher in the sky, I thought. This thing was

heading downward and breaking apart as it traveled, almost like fireworks, but dispersing in a more random way. It looked a little bit like photos I've seen of an aurora borealis, but I was sure if something like that was going to happen I'd have heard about it.

I wished someone else was around to see this thing, to tell me what they thought it was. I sure couldn't figure it out. Then I heard the rush of air as it arced in the sky. It seemed to be dropping down at a slower rate now, almost defying gravity, and broke apart, scattering sparks as it went. The pieces fell to the ground in a slow, lazy motion, like an artistic explosion. The whole thing landed close, maybe only a block away, on the other side of the train station. Despite the slow descent, when it finally hit, the whole mass came down hard. I swear the earth vibrated on impact. The soles of my feet tingled in a weird way, and I found myself moving toward the thing, whatever it was. I wanted to get a closer look.

I darted around a building that had once been a train station decades before. It was boarded up and there were signs warning people not to trespass. I walked over the tracks, now unused and in disrepair, over to the other side. The field beyond glowed with fragments of something, like someone had tipped over a charcoal grill the size of a water tower. The embers glowed blue and gold, beautiful like jewels. I got closer and noticed the glowing chunks were different sizes but that overall they formed a swirling pattern that covered the entire field. How could it have landed in such a perfect spiral?

Heat emanated off the field, but nothing was on fire or even smoking. So weird. I walked into the center of the pattern, thinking the temperature might drive me back, but it wasn't as hot as I would have thought. What could have caused this? A meteor, a shooting star, a weapon, a fireworks display? Standing in the

center of the swirl, it was so bright I could have read a book, but it wasn't blinding, just glowing. I suddenly felt good and energetic, like I do after going for a run on a sunny day. Whatever this thing was, it was having a positive effect on me.

A scattering of fragments fell all around me, but I wasn't worried about getting hit or burned. The sensation was pleasant, like the feeling of the sun coming out from behind a cloud on a gloomy day.

The pieces on the ground sparkled. *Twinkle, twinkle, little star...*

You know how sometimes you stop to look at something interesting and then after a few minutes, you're done looking and you move on? Well, this wasn't like that. I could have stood there forever, that's how I felt. I walked until I was right in the middle of the swirl pattern and planted myself, content to stand there and take it all in. I didn't leave until the light of the embers had faded to a soft glow. Finally, when I realized how much time had passed, I reluctantly headed for home, still not sure what I had experienced, but confident that it would be on the news tomorrow.

Something that incredible didn't happen without the world noticing.

CHAPTER TWO

———— o ————

For the past few months, there have been nights when I can't sleep, no matter what. I'm tired, exhausted even. I close my eyes and wait for it, wait to slip into blissful slumber, to go into a sleep coma, to fall into unconsciousness. I'm always ready for a visit from Mr. Sandman, but the bastard never shows up.

When I first had developed this problem, my parents took me to a psychiatrist, Dr. Anton. Nice guy, Dr. Anton, burly and kind, with a little goatee, always suited up with a tweed jacket and gray pants. He wore a bow tie. I thought it made him look goofy, but my mom said it gave him a "snazzy" look, whatever that means.

Dr. Anton specialized in pediatric sleep disorders. He was a good listener, I gave him that much. When I talked he tilted his head to one side, and the expression on his face showed he really cared. "We're going to get through this, Russ," he said, like we were in this thing together. "I'm going to teach you how to send your body cues that it's time to sleep." He suggested dimming the lights, drinking warm milk, and not going on the computer or playing video games too close to bedtime. Unfortunately for me,

he was opposed to sleeping pills. "You just need to retrain your body's circadian rhythm," he said.

I tried all his suggestions and more. I exercised to tire myself out, ran a fan for white noise, and visualized lying in a hammock on a deserted beach. I took melatonin for a few nights and night-time cold medicine after that. Nothing helped. I stopped going to Dr. Anton after a while because I felt like such a failure. I lied and told him I was all better, sleeping like a baby now, which was actually the truth since babies are up all night long. My parents were relieved I'd outgrown my insomniac phase.

At some point I figured out that walking was the only thing that helped. After an hour or two, I was able to come back home and zonk out. I was still tired during the day, but it was almost the end of the school year and soon enough it wouldn't make a difference.

I didn't inherit this problem from my parents. Every night they tried to stay up for the late-night news, but they usually didn't make it. It was so easy for them. My dad could even fall asleep in his recliner with the TV on. I'd look at him with his head tipped back and mouth open, making snorting noises, and I wished some of that would rub off on me. Not the noises, but you know what I mean.

The first few times I went out at night I thought for sure I'd get caught, that my parents would hear the back door open and close, or check my bed and worry that I was gone. I even left notes in the beginning—*Couldn't sleep. Went for a walk. Be back soon.* But the notes weren't necessary, as I soon found out. No one woke up. No one wondered where I was. Ironically enough, my folks slept right through my insomnia.

Being outside at night was cool, even in the beginning when there was still snow on the ground. I got a thrill from being where

I wasn't supposed to be. If the cops ever stopped me, I'd be in big trouble for violating curfew, but I was careful and darted into the bushes whenever I spotted headlights in the distance.

After the first week or two, I found myself going the exact same way. I always started out walking behind the strip mall. Sometimes I found interesting stuff by the dumpsters. The grocery store in particular threw out lots of perfectly good things, dented canned goods and bananas that didn't look too bad. Someone, somewhere, would have been glad to get that stuff, but instead it was thrown out. What a waste.

After going past the strip mall, I went through the industrial park, three blocks of small factories. I wasn't really sure what went on inside the buildings—welding and machines for molding rubber parts was my best guess, based on my observations. When I came by, I saw men hanging around the back loading docks, working sometimes, but other times smoking. Occasionally, I lingered and listened to them talk. They had this sort of easy back and forth trash talk that was funny. Razzing each other about their beer bellies and who lost the latest bet. I knew Bruno's booming voice, and Tim, Mike, and Dougie by sight. I felt a sort of kinship with them. When they handed out cigars because Tim's wife had a baby boy, I wished I could step out of the shadows and join them in slapping the new father on the back. Just one of the guys.

My favorite part of the route was the houses. I stayed out of my own neighborhood—that would just have been creepy. Instead, I went to a section on the edge of town, Old Edgewood. It was the complete opposite of where I lived, *New* Edgewood. Clever, huh?

The houses in Old Edgewood were smallish and close together like mine, but that was the only similarity. Mostly brick

with big porches, they had more character than the houses in New Edgewood. The thick tree trunks were good camouflage. I could stand on the sidewalk, and as long as I was behind the trees I could watch without being seen. I know that makes me sound like some kind of perv, but it's not like that, really. I was just interested in how they handled being up at night, and after a while I felt like I knew some of these people. At least I knew their nighttime habits, what they did when they couldn't sleep.

I grew kind of fond of all the nighttime people and found myself labeling them. There was Grandma Nelly, and the Woman-Who-Played-the-Piano. Third-Shift-Guy lived on Elm Street. If I got there early enough he was leaving for work as I was arriving. Three doors down from him was Knitting-Lady. Always knitting, all the time. There were others, but the ones I mentioned were the regulars. I wondered how many of them tried to sleep, but just couldn't. Did they lie in bed like I did, feeling like their heads might explode if they had to stay there one more minute?

I ended my nighttime route by looping past the abandoned train station on the outskirts of town. The building itself was old and boarded up, but still pretty solid. There had been some talk by the local historical committee to have it restored, but that never happened. Beyond the train station were the tracks, no longer in use, and beyond that, what seemed like an endless field. Signs on the building warned about trespassing, so no one ever went there but me, or at least that's how it felt. I liked ending with a trip to the train station. It was forbidden and dark. A little scary. It made going home seem like a relief.

Each night, I thought this trek outside might be my last. It was ridiculous, I thought, to be roaming around when I was so tired and all I really wanted to do was sleep. I had to figure out a

way to sleep without leaving the house. But a solution never came and I just kept going.

You might be wondering—why didn't I just do this walk thing earlier? Eight, nine, ten o'clock? If I did that, I'd be back in plenty of time for a normal bedtime. Don't think it hadn't occurred to me. I tried it, more than once, and it didn't work. It only worked when I left after my usual bedtime. I knew it was just a head game, but I didn't know what else to do.

Like I said before, my parents have no trouble falling asleep. "I wish I had your energy," my mom says, as if energy has anything to do with it. She's a speech pathologist at a school (not mine, thank God), and pretty worn out most of the time. She and my dad are in their late fifties, a lot older than my friends' parents. One drawback to having older parents is that I don't have any living grandparents; the last one died when I was a little kid. I do have an older sister, Carly, but I don't have much in common with her. I was born when Carly was still in high school. Her son, my nephew Frank, is only five and a half years younger than me. I was what people call an "oops" or "change of life" baby.

My mom told me that when she learned she was pregnant with me they were over the moon with excitement, but Carly said otherwise. Her version is that Mom cried and cried when she first found out.

I know that having me put a damper on my parents' plans. They were just about done with the whole child-rearing thing when I came along. Knowing this makes me feel bad, but there's not too much I can do about it. Carly was hell on wheels, even she admits that. She drank and smoked pot and flunked classes and wrecked the car. I heard my dad say they couldn't go through that again, that they're glad I'm a good kid. I figure it's the least I can

do. I don't want them to worry about me and my psychological problems.

So I keep my troubles to myself. When I can't sleep, which is most of the time, I walk at night. I do my rounds, going from the mall to the industrial park to the houses, and then I go home and crawl into bed.

CHAPTER THREE

———— o ————

That night after seeing the light explosion I fell into a deep sleep as soon as my head touched the pillow. I actually remember sinking through all the stages of sleep. Down, down, down I went, into a sinkhole of comfort and warmth. I had dreams, vivid colorful dreams, and I remembered them when the alarm went off, but somewhere between me hitting the snooze button and my mother yelling up the stairs, they completely left my brain.

I did a quick look online to see if there was anything in the news about meteors or shooting stars or weird lights in the sky, but there was nothing at all. Nada.

It was starting to feel like one of those vivid dreams that seem real when you first open your eyes, but fade the longer you're awake. I didn't have too much time to think about it, though, since I needed to get my stuff together and head for school. As the day progressed, I somehow managed to put it out of my mind. Until last hour when I had science with Mr. Specter.

Specter was one of the better teachers at my school. He was almost as old as my parents, and he didn't try to relate to the

kids, something I liked. Nothing worse than teachers who act like they know the latest slang or ask about rock bands or popular YA novels, like they're one of us. Mr. Specter just did what he was supposed to do. He taught us science. He totally loved the subject—that much was clear. I was taking what everyone called dummy science, a class called Science Samplers, which consisted of units in biology, chemistry, and natural science. Basically, Specter covered whatever he was interested in. It seemed to vary from year to year and class to class, but no one ever complained because he was brilliant and funny and interesting. We saw films on technology, and he did magic tricks and explained how they were done, and he encouraged us to bring in things to share like a sort of high school show-and-tell. One kid brought in his uncle's taxidermied squirrel, which started a whole conversation about how it was done and why. Another student in my class brought in fossils she found on vacation, and then we were all about fossils for the next week. You didn't know what you might get in Specter's class, but it was never dull, and that's saying a lot when you're a sophomore in high school.

That day, I sat down in my seat, the middle of the row closest to the door. I settled in and dropped my book and notebook on the desk. We hardly ever used the textbook, but I felt compelled to keep bringing it anyway. The rest of the class filtered in bit by bit, but Mr. Specter wasn't upfront like he usually was. The bell rang and still he wasn't there. A few kids speculated that we would be on our own. There was talk of leaving, but no one did. Some pulled out their phones and several of the girls started talking, the way girls do sometimes, kind of show-offy, laughing and smiling in the direction of guys they liked, hoping the guys would notice and drift over by them. I wasn't the kind anyone wanted, so I kept quiet and took it all in.

Finally, half an hour later, out of complete boredom, I opened my notebook and started doodling randomly. Without realizing what I was doing, I started sketching the light show from the night before, first as it appeared in the sky and then how it looked on the ground. In the background, I drew the abandoned train station, quickly and with great detail. I'm usually terrible at drawing, but this turned out good, surprisingly good. My hand had a life of its own. It knew where each line and dot belonged, like someone else was drawing it through me. Without even thinking about it, I sketched a figure standing in the middle of the field, right in the center of the glowing swirl, arms raised upward. It was a picture of me, although I didn't remember standing quite that way.

When I glanced up, I saw that the girl in front of me, Mallory Nassif, had turned around in her seat and was watching me draw. I didn't know Mallory that well. She was the sort of girl who blended in with the crowd, until you noticed her, and then she clearly stood out. She had big doe-eyes fringed with long lashes, shiny dark hair always in a ponytail, and this really nice laugh that carried across the lunchroom. Her skin was the color of coffee with cream. I sometimes got that tan by the middle of summer, if I was out a lot, but her coloring came naturally. Besides what I saw in front of me, all I knew about her was that she'd been the new girl the beginning of this school year, and she played on the field hockey team. Our eyes met for a second and then she gestured to my notebook. "Whatcha drawing there, Russ?" she asked.

I stared, surprised she even knew my name. I started to say something about how it was nothing, just a doodle, but before I could get the words out, the door flew open and Mr. Specter strode in. I shut my notebook.

13

"Okay, people," he bellowed, heading to the front of the room. "Settle down. Free time is over. Now it's my turn." He seemed a little out of breath, and not himself, frankly. He wore a button-down shirt with a sweater vest over it and a pair of creased gray trousers, per usual. His wire-rimmed glasses had slid to the end of his nose and perspiration shone on his forehead.

"You okay, Mr. Specter?" asked one of girls. Emily, a total suck-up. "You're not sick, are you?'

"I'm fine, Emily," he said. "Just coming back from a meeting that ran a little late." He shuffled through some papers on his desk and went to his computer to send attendance to the office. Everyone was quiet now. We all respected Mr. Specter. He was a real teacher. "Now," he said, walking away from his desk and standing front and center. "I thought we'd talk about astronomy today."

"I'm a Capricorn!" This from Chris Jennings, a guy I was friends with in grade school, back before I had good taste in people.

"That would be astrology, Mr. Jennings." Mr. Specter pulled a handkerchief out of his pants pocket and mopped his brow. "Another fascinating subject, but not one that's included in our curriculum." Our curriculum—what a joke. As if we had a set schedule. "No, I'm talking about *astronomy*, the study of objects and matter outside the earth's atmosphere and of their physical and chemical properties." He looked at us over his glasses. "That's an exact dictionary definition, a rather narrow view in my opinion. Astronomy is so much more than that." He glanced around the room. "William Shakespeare said, 'It is not in the stars to hold our destiny, but in ourselves.' Does anyone know what that means?"

Mallory raised her hand, and when he nodded, she said, "That's not quite right, Mr. Specter. The actual line is from the

play *Julius Caesar* and it goes like this: 'Men at some time are masters of their fates: The fault, dear Brutus, is not in our stars, but in ourselves, that we are underlings.'"

I thought Mr. Specter might be irritated at being corrected, but he just nodded. "Well done, Ms. Nassif. And what exactly does that mean?" He glanced around the room. Mallory started to answer, but he brushed her off saying, "Let's give someone else a turn, shall we?"

He pointed to a kid in the front row, who shrugged his shoulders and said, "Yeah, I got nothing."

Mr. Specter leaned back against the whiteboard. "Come now, there are twenty-four students in this room. Miss Nassif can't be the only one with a brain in her head."

Whoa, kind of harsh. Especially coming from Mr. Specter, who wasn't usually demanding at all.

"Can you repeat the quote?" someone called out.

Mr. Specter raised his eyebrows at Mallory, who sat up straight and repeated, "Men at some time are masters of their fates: The fault, dear Brutus, is not in our stars, but in ourselves, that we are underlings."

"What is this, English class?" another guy grumbled. "I want to do science."

Mr. Specter ignored him and walked up to me. "Mr. Becker, would you care to tell us what that means?" He leaned over and drummed his fingers against my notebook.

I nervously cleared my throat. "Umm, I think it means we determine our own fate. It's not what happens to us in life, it's what we do about it."

Mr. Specter gave me a penetrating look and then nodded. "Very good." He walked briskly to the front of the room. "Last night a phenomenal astrological event happened only a few miles

away from here. If you were awake last night around one in the morning, you would have seen it. Does anyone know what I'm talking about?"

I knew immediately what he was talking about, but I wasn't about to fess up to being out that late at night. "Come on now," he said, when a minute or so had passed. "This was spectacular. Someone had to have seen it."

"Tell us what it was," Chris Jennings said. "Maybe I saw it and didn't know it."

"You would have known it," Mr. Specter said, more quietly this time. He looked around the room searching each face, one at a time. "Extra credit for anyone who can tell me about it," he said in a cajoling tone. I looked down at my desk, not wanting to meet his eyes.

"Come on, Mr. S., give us a clue," one of the girls said.

"No clues."

He walked down the first row, the one closest to the door. "Anyone who saw it and can accurately describe it will be excused from having to do the final project and will automatically receive an A for said project." That made everyone take notice.

"Whoa."

"Cool!"

"No fair. I can't help it if I didn't see it."

"Ooh, ooh." Allie Westfahl raised her hand.

"Yes, Miss Westfahl?"

"I remember now. I was looking out my window last night and I saw an eclipse."

"Nice try, but that's not it."

Mr. Specter moved methodically through the room, row by row, desk by desk, pausing by each student and placing a hand on their shoulder. If they didn't look at him, he'd say their

name until they glanced up. No one knew what he was talking about.

Except me. He was five students away and I wasn't sure how I was going to handle this.

Now four students to go before he got to me. "Brad?" Mr. Specter said, but Brad shook his head.

Three students. My heart sped up a bit. I concentrated on not looking flustered.

In front of me, I heard a strangulated gargling noise that made me look up despite myself. It was Mallory Nassif. Her head trembled and then shook, making her ponytail swing back and forth. She fell out of her desk chair and onto the floor in the aisle, her head hitting the linoleum with a loud thwack.

Once she was on the ground, it was pandemonium. One of the girls screamed and people were shouting different things all at once.

"Someone should call the office."

"Screw the office, call 911."

One girl said, "I heard that for seizures you should stick something in their mouth to keep them from swallowing their tongue."

It didn't seem like a seizure though, because once she landed on the floor, she stopped shaking and fell limp. Mr. Specter quickly took over, sending one girl down to get help from the office and telling the rest of us to move the desks away from Mallory's body. Body, like she was dead. The whole thing was pretty surreal. Mallory was completely still, not even flinching when he knelt down next to her and put his fingers on her neck. "I have a pulse and she's breathing," he said to no one in particular. By the time Mrs. Schroeder, the woman from the health room, came to the door, Mallory's eyes had fluttered open and

he'd helped her to sit up. "Easy now," he said, in a kind way. She looked around, seemingly confused.

Some of the girls fussed and made idiotic comments. A few pulled out their phones even though it was against school rules. I'm not sure if they were posting to Facebook or texting or what, but it seemed pretty insensitive to me. When Mrs. Schroeder and Mr. Specter helped Mallory to her feet, everyone clapped like they would for an injured player getting up at a sports event. She looked unsteady, and the adults decided she should get checked out by a doctor. "I think I just got lightheaded," Mallory protested. "I didn't eat breakfast this morning and my blood sugar is low. I'm probably fine."

I didn't think she could be fine, not the way her head smacked against the floor like a dropped cantaloupe.

"It's best to get it checked out," Mrs. Schroeder said in a soothing way, easing Mallory toward the door. Emily gathered up Mallory's things and followed along like the suck-up she was. They were barely out the door when the bell rang and class was over.

CHAPTER FOUR

— o —

That night, out of habit more than compulsion, I left the house around midnight and did my usual route, thinking about Mr. Specter's class as I walked. So weird that he'd brought up the astronomical event I'd seen the night before. How was it that he knew about it but it wasn't mentioned on the news or anywhere online? I wasn't about to say what I knew in class, even with his bribe. Extra credit, big deal. Like that would make me confess to being out in the middle of the night. And there was something odd about the way he asked, too. He wanted the information a little too badly. Suspicious.

I was still thinking about this during my nighttime walk when I got to Old Edgewood. One of my first stops was a house where a really old lady lived. She had to be ancient, eighty-five or so. The drapes were always open, so I could see her clearly through the window. She slept sitting up in a recliner, but sometimes she shuffled around using a walker. Mostly she watched television, but she never looked interested in what was on. No one was ever with her: no nurse, no family members. She seemed pretty frail to be alone. I looked up her address online and got a

name. Nelly Smith, that was her. Even though it was the middle of the night, I never saw her in a bathrobe. It must have been cold in her house because she always wore sweatpants and an oversized sweatshirt (usually decorated with birds or ladybugs).

None of my grandparents were living, so I started to think of Mrs. Smith as Grandma Nelly. I thought about going back to her house in the daytime and offering to run errands for her, or maybe getting her groceries. But in the morning I felt differently. I didn't really know her, after all. Maybe she was mean or crazy. I mean, why didn't she have family or friends looking after her? If she was a lovable old lady they'd be there, right?

That Wednesday I rested next to a tree in Mrs. Smith's front yard, like I always did, pressing my back against the rough bark. I heard a truck rumbling in the distance. The front porch light was on, but inside the only source of illumination was a floor lamp in the front room. She wasn't in her chair, but that wasn't unusual. Nelly Smith was elderly, but she wasn't dead yet. Maybe she went to the bathroom or to the kitchen for a snack. I waited for what seemed like a long time, but there was no movement in the house. Odder still was the fact that her walker stood next to her chair. I'd never seen her without it, not in all my weeks of visiting her yard.

I almost wrote it off—almost left to go to my next stop, but something made me stay and creep closer to the house until I was on the front porch looking directly into the front window. I had a view of the whole living room—the television still on, the recliner upright, and Nelly Smith lying in a crumpled heap on the floor.

CHAPTER FIVE

———— o ————

I don't know how long I stood on Nelly Smith's porch peering through her window. Thirty seconds, ten minutes, forever? My breath caught in my chest and I felt my heart accelerate: buh-bum, buh-bum, buh-bum. She wasn't moving and I couldn't tell if she was breathing, but that didn't mean she was dead. Still she was old and obviously not in great shape, so the dead thing was a real possibility. I shifted my weight and looked around the neighborhood, unsure what to do. Flag down a passing car? Knock on a neighbor's door? And then what? Doing any of these things would lead to questions about who I was and why I was far from home on a stranger's porch in the middle of the night. Even to me it sounded suspicious.

I lifted my hand to press the doorbell and then let it drop to my side when I realized how stupid that was. Like I'd ring the doorbell and Nelly Smith, who was either dead or stroked out, would rise up when she heard it, come to the door, and assure me that she was fine, really, just resting on the floor. What was I thinking?

I pulled my cell phone out of my hoodie pocket. Damn. My battery was dead. I was looking down at it when I noticed the doormat beneath my feet. It was one of those brown bristly types that usually say "WELCOME." This one, however, said "GO AWAY." The old woman had a sense of humor, anyway. Under different circumstances I would have laughed.

On impulse I stepped aside, leaned over, and lifted the mat. Aha—a key. Didn't Ms. Smith know that putting a key under the mat was like inviting criminals into your home? Luckily, Old Edgewood wasn't known for break-ins.

I picked up the key, opened the screen door, and unlocked the front door like I lived there. I tucked the key back under the mat before opening the door. "Mrs. Smith?" I called out before stepping over the threshold. Man, was I in trouble if she thought I was breaking in. Not likely since there was no response. Cautiously I went in, crossing the room to Mrs. Smith's body. She was curled up on her side, a cordless phone on the floor next to her head. I knelt down and put my fingertips against her neck, not knowing what the hell I was doing, but recalling something I saw in a movie in seventh grade. Her skin was cold to the touch. *Please God, don't let her be dead. I have a big test tomorrow and I'm so tired. I really don't need this right now.*

I moved my hand closer to her throat but couldn't find a pulse. Oh man, this was terrible. "Mrs. Smith," I said, "I'm Russ Becker. Just hang on. I'm going to call for help, okay?" No answer, but saying the words made me feel better, like someone was in charge. I picked up her phone, stood, and dialed 911. I heard my own voice say, "I need someone to come right away."

CHAPTER SIX

---o---

"**R**uss, you look terrible," my friend Justin said, when he'd caught up to me at my locker the next day at school. "Smoking all that crack is catching up to you."

"Get it right. I don't smoke crack anymore," I said, playing along. "It's meth all the way now, and I'm not stopping until my teeth rot in my head." I bent down to unload my backpack.

"Whatever you're doing, it can't be good. You look half dead." His voice took on a more serious tone. "You're not still roaming around at night, are you?"

"Just now and then," I said, "when I have trouble sleeping."

Justin was the only one I'd told about my late-night walks. He'd been worried when I told him, saying I really should go back to Dr. Anton and beg for sleeping pills. "Dude, that's his job to push the pharmaceuticals. Tell him you need it." He wouldn't shut up about it and kept bringing it up until I finally told him I had it under control.

"Did you have trouble last night?"

"Nope, last night I slept like a baby," I said, slamming my locker shut. In fact, I hadn't slept at all. After running all the way

home, I'd lain awake in bed as jittery as if I'd downed a four-pack of Red Bull.

I kept replaying the whole thing in my mind, the way I picked the phone off the floor and called for help. I was standing next to Mrs. Smith's body, talking to the operator when I felt a tug on the bottom of my jeans. I jumped a little—anyone would have—and told the 911 lady, "She's coming around. She just moved."

"Good," she said calmly. "Just stay with her and keep talking to me. Help is on the way."

I squatted down next to her, the phone still up against my ear. I patted her arm. "It's going to be okay. They're sending an ambulance. It'll be here soon."

She gave me a wide-eyed stare. "You shouldn't have done it," she said, her voice raspy. "I didn't want to come back." Confused, clearly.

I stayed by her side until I heard the ambulance pull up in the driveway, and then I set the phone on the floor and went out the door to meet them. Something about the way the two men exited the vehicle, one carrying what looked like a large toolbox, spooked me. Going through my head were the words, *You're not supposed to be here.*

My flight instinct kicked in then, and without thinking, I took off, running past them into the darkness. One of them yelled, "Hey!" as I went by. I never looked back.

I only slowed when my own house was in sight. Quietly, I eased my way through the back door and up the stairs, careful to skip the creaky step. My house was a bungalow, one bedroom down, two up. My parents' room was on the first level, which gave me the upstairs, complete with bathroom, all to myself. My friends thought it was cool that I had my own space. I didn't think too much about it, except when I was coming and going and wondered if they could hear me on the stairs.

In a way, getting up that morning was easy. I was already awake when my alarm went off. I felt like I'd been hit by a bus, but otherwise I was okay. I stumbled into the shower and felt a little better. Standing under a spray of warm water is a quick but short-term fix to most of life's problems.

I decided that if I got through school without walking into any walls or dozing off, the day would be a success. Besides Justin's inference that I resembled something you'd normally find in a septic tank, no one else noticed I was a wreck.

I was at my locker after lunch when Mallory came up next to me. "Russ Becker?" she said, sternly.

I closed my locker and slung my backpack over one shoulder. "Mallory, are you okay?"

"Of course I'm okay. Why wouldn't I be?"

"You clunked your head pretty hard when you had that seizure in Specter's class."

She waved away my concerns. "Oh that. Just a diversion. I was faking it."

"Really? Why would you do that?"

"Why I did it isn't important right now." She leaned close to me in a seductive way, but her words were more accusatory than sexy. "Here's the thing. I saw you last night."

"Last night?"

"In the middle of the night. I live right next door to that old lady's house and I saw you running away when the ambulance got there. What happened?"

My stomach lurched. What kind of eyesight did she have? It was dark and I was running very, very fast. "I really don't know what you're talking about," I said.

"I know what I saw. I saw you." She tilted her head to one side, waiting.

"You must have me confused with someone else."

"So you're saying it wasn't you?"

"Nope, not me," I said, trying to be nonchalant.

"I was eight feet away. I know it was you."

"I have to get going or I'll be late for class. See you later." I stepped around her and staggered a little, the lack of sleep kicking my butt at last.

"We're not done, Russell Becker," Mallory called after me. "Don't think I'm going to just let this go."

CHAPTER SEVEN

———— o ————

I completely crashed when I got home from school. I left a note
for my mom to find when she got home from work. *Mom,
Taking a nap. Wake me in time for dinner. Russ.*

If life were fair, I'd have been able to stay awake until ten
o'clock and get a good night's sleep like a normal person. But I
was too tired. Life was so not fair.

Mom woke me by calling my cell. She never walked up the
stairs if she could help it. Five minutes later, I sat at the table with
my mom and dad, chewing on garlic toast and listening to them
discuss their respective days. Nothing good ever seemed to happen at their jobs, at least nothing they ever mentioned.

At six o'clock, my mom turned on the small TV she kept on
the kitchen counter. We always watched the news during dinner,
a tradition that would have horrified my health teacher had she
known. Apparently watching TV during meals is the primary
cause of the breakdown of the American family. Not to mention that a person statistically consumes more calories watching
a screen than conversing. All of America was going to become

obese and disconnected from its loved ones, and it would be the fault of technology. According to Ms. Hadley, anyway.

We sat quietly through the newscast teasers: the promise of unseasonably warm weather, upcoming predictions for the local ball team, a man gets a life-saving kidney donation from a brother he'd never met, a local woman gets a most unusual visit. Blah, blah, blah. It's always something.

I was only half-listening, my mouth full of spaghetti, when they got to the local woman story at the end of the forecast. The female half of the anchor team, Madeline Park, covered the story. "Yesterday, Nelly Smith of Poplar Drive in Old Edgewood had an unusual late-night experience."

I sat up straight. The food in my mouth suddenly congealed and felt like wet cement.

Madeline Park kept talking even as I was having trouble breathing. "Mrs. Smith, who is eighty-six years old and lives alone, experienced a heart attack at approximately one a.m. this morning. Paramedics were dispatched to the home after receiving a 911 call from the residence. The call was placed by an unidentified man, who was not on the scene when they arrived. At the hospital, Mrs. Smith told our reporter that despite her door being locked, an unknown man entered her home and brought her back from the dead. Police say there was no sign of a break-in."

Mom sprinkled Parmesan cheese on her noodles. Thankfully, neither she nor Dad were looking in my direction. I was sure my face would have given me away.

The news broke away to a shot of the Smith home. Across the bottom of the screen it said: *Local woman believes she died and was revived by a stranger in her home.* Then the shot switched to a reporter, Patrick Doolan, who stood in front of the house and repeated most of what Madeline Park had already said.

28

"Why do they always recap like that?" Mom asked.

Dad shrugged. "Filler. It's damn annoying."

On the screen Patrick Doolan said, "In a fascinating account, Mrs. Smith told me she remembers being in pain and then leaving her body and floating upwards toward a beautiful light where she was met by deceased family members. The next thing she recalled was being pulled back to earth by the touch of the unknown man who called 911. Mrs. Smith is resting comfortably at the hospital and declined being on camera. With us is her neighbor, Mallory Nassif, who saw the ambulance arrive from her home next door. She has some insights of her own on the situation." He held the microphone out and the camera zoomed in on Mallory's face. "Mallory, can you tell us what you observed last night?" I felt like I was going to throw up.

She smiled, straight at me, it seemed. "I got up in the middle of the night to get a drink of water and happened to look out the window as the ambulance was leaving, around two fifteen. My mom and I check on Mrs. Smith sometimes, so we know her really well. I heard she's in stable condition now, and I'm going to visit her tomorrow."

Patrick Doolan's voice in the background: "What do you think of Mrs. Smith's assertion that the person who called 911 was a complete stranger who somehow got into her locked home and revived her from death?"

"I think it's possible," she said. "Why not?"

"Some would find the idea unbelievable," Patrick Doolan said. "What would you say to those skeptics?"

Mallory smiled again. "I think Mrs. Smith knows if her door was locked. And the house was open when the paramedics got there, so no one broke in. And if she said she died and came back, I'm willing to believe it. Miracles happen sometimes."

"There you have it, folks." Patrick Doolan's face filled the screen. "A miracle on Poplar Drive."

Back in the studio, Madeline Park said, "We love a happy ending here at News Center Five. And I love that young woman's attitude. I'm willing to believe in miracles, too."

As Madeline exchanged small talk with her co-anchor, Dad got up and turned the TV off. Somewhere along the line I'd started breathing again. I hoped my face had recovered from the shock.

"What do you make of that?" my dad asked.

"Weird." Mom took a sip of water.

"Okay, forget about the back from the dead thing. Focusing just on the unknown stranger—they must have the guy's voice recorded on the 911 call," Dad said.

"Yes, but he didn't identify himself," Mom said.

"Hmmm." Dad shifted into problem-solving mode. "Sounds like a case for *CSI*. Here's what they should do—dust for fingerprints, look for strands of hair, check for footprints inside and out, and test for DNA. A person can't even walk through a room without leaving something behind."

"I'm sure Edgewood doesn't have much of a forensics department," Mom said. "Besides, no crime was committed, right?"

"True, but an investigation would rule out paranormal entities. And clearly it was someone who wasn't supposed to be there—a would-be burglar or something."

I hoped no one in the room could hear the pounding of my heart. I said, "Why does it have to be a criminal? Couldn't it just be a passing Good Samaritan? Someone going for a walk who noticed something wrong?"

"At one in the morning?" my mother questioned. "What kind of person is out for a walk at that time?"

I shrugged. "People who work the late shift?"

"But wouldn't someone like that stick around? Why run off when the ambulance arrived?"

I had nothing to say to that.

Dad said, "I like that your tendency is to think the best about people, Russ, I really do, but in this case, I think there's more going on. It'll come out eventually, you wait and see."

When he said that, a chill went up my spine, the kind you read about in horror stories. I'm not sure why I felt so guilty. I hadn't done anything wrong, and in fact, if you really thought about it, I'd done a good thing. I saved Grandma Nelly's life, right? What would it hurt to tell my parents it was me? Sure they'd be upset that I'd gone out at night, and Mom would be hurt I hadn't told her I'd had more problems sleeping. I'd probably have to go back to Dr. Anton and he'd try to dig deeper into my psyche, or whatever you call it, trying to find out the root of my problem. And I sure didn't want that. But maybe I could downplay the whole thing, say that last night was the only time I had trouble sleeping, the first time I'd gone for a walk at night. Of course, once Mom and Dad knew, they'd be watching me all the time and that would be the end of my late-night walks. And then how would I ever fall asleep?

"I forgot to tell you, Russ," Mom said. "You got a phone call while you were napping. Some girl."

My hand, holding a forkful of spaghetti, froze. "Who was it?"

"I don't know. She said it was important. I gave her your cell number."

CHAPTER EIGHT

———————— o ————————

After dinner I went upstairs to do my homework. That was the official version, anyway—doing homework. I spent most school nights up in my room. I had my own TV, game system, laptop, and phone, so there was no reason to be anywhere else in the house. Mom and Dad never questioned how I spent my time, probably because I had a 3.6 GPA and, unlike Carly, I'd never had any visits from the police. Having her come first made everything easier.

I sat on my bed and checked my cell. No message from the mystery girl, the one I feared would be Mallory Nassif, but there was one from a friend. I had a circle of guys I hung out with, but Justin and Mick were my main friends. This was Mick's voice mail message: "You loser. Answer me, dammit." Typical. He'd left me seven text messages, most of them complete gibberish.

I called him back.

Me: "Sup?"

Mick: "What are you doing right now?"

Me: "Homework."

Mick: "Ha! Good one. Seriously, you have to go online now and watch this thing. Funny, so damn funny. You're gonna die. I'm sending you the link."

Me: "Okay."

Mick: "What's wrong with you?"

Me: "Nothing."

Mick: "Your nothing sounds depressed. Don't kill yourself, okay? Whatever it is can't be that bad."

Me: "Do you know Mallory Nassif?"

Mick: "Not as much as I'd like to."

Here I have to stop and explain that Mick is sort of a wannabe womanizer. He never got any action in that department, but he made comments about every girl who walked by. And he was always convinced he was on the verge of getting some. He was delusional that way.

Mick: "Why? Is she asking about me?"

Me: "You wish. I just asked because she was on the news."

Mick: "Mallory Nassif was on the news saying she wanted me?" (He choked out a kind of heh, heh, heh laugh.)

Me (ignoring him): "No, her neighbor had a heart attack."

Mick: "Someone our age?"

Me: "No, a really old lady."

Mick (sounding bored): "Oh. Well, that stuff happens when you're old, right?"

This is the part where I got really annoyed. Yes, that kind of stuff happens when you're old, but it's different when you see the person lying on the floor. Then it's a really horrible thing. Being there, I was *involved*. But I didn't want to tell Mick that. At least not yet. Something inside of me said I should keep it to myself. "I gotta go," I said. "I have a math test tomorrow."

"Give me a break," he said, and started going on about something he saw on Comedy Central. I hung up while he was still talking, the way I always did. Most people would think it was rude, but it was just the way we did things.

I'd been having some trouble with math, so I knew I had to study if there was any chance of getting an A that semester. My friends thought getting good grades came easy for me. I never let on how many hours I spent poring over textbooks and making notes at home. Sometimes, during study hall, I even went to the math lab, the refuge of the truly desperate. Unlike some of the kids I knew, I was on my own. Once I reached sixth grade, my parents refused to help me with my homework, saying too much had changed since they went to school. My mom, in fact, claimed not to know anything besides basic addition, subtraction, division, and multiplication. Hard to believe she had a master's degree.

I was knee-deep in logarithms when my cell phone went off. My eyes still on my notebook, I answered. "Yeah?"

"Russ?"

I had a sinking feeling. I sat up straight. "Yes?'

"It's me. I told you I wasn't going to let this go." There was a long pause where neither of us spoke, and then Mallory said, "Are you there, Russ?"

"Yeah, I'm here."

"Well, don't you have anything to say?"

"What do you want me to say?"

She sighed heavily, for my benefit, I thought. "I think this would work better if we both cut the crap. I know about the lights in the field, and I know you were at Mrs. Smith's last night and so do you. Pretending differently doesn't change things."

I picked up a pen and started drawing spirals in the margins in my notebook, a nervous habit I'd had since grade school. "Just say I was in your neighborhood last night," I finally said. "And I'm not saying I was, but *if* I was—so what? It's not like it's a crime or anything. And no one can prove it either way."

"I'm not interested in proving it," she said. "I know what I know. I saw you there as sure as I know anything in this world."

"Is there a reason for this phone call?" I said. "Because I'm in the middle of something right now and don't have time to play games."

"I'm not playing games." Now she sounded indignant. "I'm calling to invite you to join my group. This is completely secret. I wouldn't ask just anyone, but if you aren't interested—"

"What kind of group?" I asked. I had to admit, she got my attention.

"I'm not telling you about it unless you're in for sure," she said. "It's strictly confidential."

This girl was insane. "I'm not joining some group I don't know anything about," I said. "If that's a condition, forget it."

"This is an opportunity to be part of something important," she said, emphasizing each word. "You are part of this whether you know it or not. We need each other—you're going to find that out sooner or later."

There was a long pause, for dramatic effect on her part, I guessed, and on my end, because what the hell do you say to that? "This is a church youth group, isn't it?"

"No."

I guessed again. "A service organization?"

"No."

"An exclusive academic club?"

"No, no, and double no," she said and laughed. "Do you really think I'm that type of person?"

"Frankly, I don't know what type of person you are, Mallory Nassif. I know you believe in miracles on Poplar Drive, and you play field hockey. That's all I know." I looked down at the notebook page, which was now covered in doodles. I wrote, CRAZY in large letters and circled it three times.

"I'll tell you what," Mallory said. "Just meet with us and then make your decision. I think you'd be a good fit."

I cleared my throat. Her proposition sounded interesting, but I doubted it was as great as she was making it out to be.

She continued without waiting for an answer. "Tomorrow night at midnight. I'll text directions for where to meet beforehand."

"Midnight?"

"That's when we meet," she said. "Are you interested or not?"

"Tomorrow night is a school night."

"Yeah, so what? So was last night."

She had a point. Chances were pretty good I'd be up and wandering around anyway. "What kind of group meets in the middle of the night?" I asked.

"Come and find out, if you're interested. And if you have the nerve."

"Okay," I said finally.

"Okay what?"

"I'll think about it."

"You do that." Then Mallory laughed again, a really great laugh, like she'd won an argument. She was certain I'd show up, that much was sure. As for me, I still hadn't decided.

CHAPTER NINE

———— o ————

I hated to admit it, but Mallory Nassif had gotten to me. Inviting me to join some secret group, but not giving me the details, was, I'm sure, supposed to make me insanely curious, and it worked. The next day, I found myself thinking about what she'd said. What if this was some type of dark cult? Would there be blood oaths or black robes? What if her group did things that were illegal? Or maybe she was messing with me and there was no group. It could all be a big practical joke. My mind whirred with all the possibilities, making me distracted during class.

"Mr. Becker, would you like to join our discussion?" Ms. Birnbaum asked. It was one of those smart-ass questions teachers use that I really hate. Along with: *Would you care to let the rest of us in on the joke?* and *Are we interrupting your sleep?* Teachers think they're being clever, but the truth is, it's just annoying. If students could answer the way they wanted to they'd say, *No I don't want to join the class discussion because frankly, it sucks. And if I wanted to let you all in on the joke, I would have done it already. Finally, yes, you are interrupting my sleep. Could you keep it down?*

Maybe I was just in a mood. Lack of sleep will do that to you.

I looked for Mallory between classes and spotted her a few times, walking down the halls. I saw her at lunch too. She was always with at least one other girl, so I couldn't talk to her. I've noticed that girls always travel in packs if they have a choice. Today, like every other day, Mallory's hair was pulled back in her usual ponytail. I heard her burst out laughing at one point and it made me smile. Her laughter was explosive and happy-sounding. No one could duplicate that noise if they tried.

I finally caught her eye at the end of the day. I was getting something out of my locker when she walked past with Amelia Schuster. Amelia was talking a mile a minute and gesturing wildly, and Mallory was nodding like she totally agreed with everything she said. As they approached I reached out to get Mallory's attention, but she shook her head like, *not here.* Funny how I was able to read so much into that one gesture. I would have felt like she was giving me the brush-off if not for what she did next. She winked at me, and then grinned. It was fast, over in a split second. I was the only one who saw it, which made it kind of cool.

I started almost obsessively checking my phone for the directions to the meeting place once I got home. I got a few other texts, but nothing from Mallory. I went from thinking I wasn't going to meet her secret group at the secret place, to being afraid she wasn't going to follow through. What if my reluctance kept me out of the group? Wouldn't that be a hell of a thing?

Dinner with my folks that evening consisted of meatloaf and a salad. I poured a lot of ketchup on the meatloaf to offset the dryness, and when I looked up I caught my parents exchanging an amused look. "Meatloaf not to your liking, Russ?" my dad asked.

"Nope, it's fine," I said.

My mom changed the subject. "Did I tell you Frank is spending the weekend here?"

Inwardly I groaned. This was very bad news. Frank was my sister Carly's son. My nephew. His full name was Frank Shrapnel Becker, if you can believe it. My sister wanted to give him a tough guy name. This was during her biker chick phase. The phase passed, but the poor kid was saddled with the name Frank Shrapnel forever. Unbelievable. Comparatively speaking, my middle name "David," which was kind of boring, was preferable.

Frank spent so much time at our house it was like we shared custody. He was really cute when he was little. Back then my mom did most of the caretaking. Now that he was ten, he'd latched onto me, following me around the house talking nonstop and asking a million questions. Sometimes it was cool. The kid was pretty good at video games and sometimes I was up for that. Lately not so much.

"No, you didn't tell me that," I said. "What's the story?"

"What do you mean, what's the story?"

"Why is he coming over?"

My mom gave me a slight frown. "He's our grandson. Does there have to be a reason?"

"Carly is going to some enlightenment workshop," my dad said. "Her new boyfriend is some new age guru."

I took a sip of my milk. "I hope you don't think I'm going to be entertaining him. I have a lot of plans for the weekend." Or at least I would have plans, now that I knew.

"Don't be that way, Russ," Mom said. "He adores you. All he wants is a little attention. Is that asking too much?"

"His mother should be the one paying attention," I said. "She can't wait to get rid of him."

My mom looked like I'd slapped her, and I immediately regretted saying it. Carly was a crappy mother, but it wasn't my parents' fault. They'd set a good example. She just chose not to follow it.

"Regardless," Dad said. "Frank shouldn't be punished for her lack of maternal instincts. Mom and I are going to take him to a movie and to the mall, but we can't keep him occupied the whole time. We'd like your help."

"We really do appreciate it," Mom added. I believed her. They did appreciate my help. It was my flaky sister who expected everything and appreciated nothing. When Frank was a baby, she dumped him at our house every chance she could. It got to be less as the years went on, but he still spent a fair share of his time here.

"Okay," I said. "I'll hang out with the kid."

After dinner I cleared the table for my mom, then went upstairs for the night. I checked my phone constantly. Just after eight, when I'd almost given up hope, I was rewarded with a text from Mallory. She said: "Important meet-up at midnight behind the ball bearing factory. 276 Industry Drive. See you there."

Now that I got the message, I started to have funny feelings about the whole thing. The thing that bothered me was the location. I knew Industry Drive. It was part of my route. I had no idea there was a ball bearing factory there. You learn something new every day. If she was some kind of psycho who belonged to a gang or something, her group could jump me and do who knows what. Not saying that would happen, but it did cross my mind. What kind of group meets in the industrial park at midnight during the week? It was weird. Not interesting-weird—bizarre-weird.

I thought about my life. I had my friends, school, homework, my family. And this summer I would get my driver's license and

a job. I had a lot going on. I didn't need Mallory and her secret club. Not to mention I was tired and needed to get caught up on my sleep. And I actually felt like I could sleep tonight, which was rare.

Forget it. I wasn't going to go.

At ten o'clock I shut everything down, washed up, and climbed between the sheets. I closed my eyes and regulated my breathing the way Dr. Anton taught me. In, out. In, out. An hour later I was still concentrating on inhaling and exhaling, but now I was frustrated. I couldn't sleep and I really wanted to sleep. Damn, I was tired. Why wouldn't my body cooperate?

The house creaked and outside I heard street noises: a car driving past and the slamming of a car door. Someone was either coming or going. Curious, I got out of bed and went to the window. I separated the slats of the blinds and looked down to see my neighbor arriving home with bags of groceries. Nothing interesting there.

I turned to go back to bed, but realized that I was now wide awake. More than wide awake, really. Hyper-awake. I looked at the clock: eleven forty. I did some mental arithmetic and calculated that if I got dressed and moved quickly, I could still make it to the ball bearing factory by midnight.

CHAPTER TEN

———○———

It was completely quiet except for the slapping of my shoes against the pavement. When I took a shortcut through an empty field near the industrial park, I slowed my pace. The streetlights were further apart than in the residential section, and I couldn't see very well. I stopped at one point and opened my phone to check the time. Good, I still had a few minutes. I would make it.

When I got to the other side of the field, I cut over to the street. Industry Drive. All the streets here had the same theme going. Manufacturing Street, Production Avenue, Assembly Circle. Whoever came up with these names probably thought they were pretty clever.

I was more visible than I wanted to be, but I had to walk along the curb in order to spot the addresses on the buildings. Some of them didn't have numbers at all, at least not that I could see. Finally I came to the right place: 276 Industry Drive. Metal Castings Inc. the sign said. The parking lot was half full, and lights were on inside. People working the night shift.

I went past the parking lot to the other side of the building and eased my way toward the back. Behind the building was another parking area, but this one lacked cars. Stacks of metal rods randomly dotted the lot. A few dumpsters were lined up to one side. A lone light post illuminated the lot, but it didn't give much light. The asphalt pavement was cracked and buckled. When a slight breeze kicked up, I got a whiff of hot metal and grease. If the odor was that strong outside, I could only imagine how the workers smelled after working in the building for eight hours.

This empty lot didn't look like the kind of place a secret society would meet. I stood and listened for a few minutes, but I didn't hear any footsteps or voices. Where were they? That's when it hit me—Mallory had gotten me good. I'd actually gone to the back of a factory at midnight looking for a top-secret organization. What kind of idiot would do that? I looked at my phone: 12:04.

I imagined her having a good laugh at my expense. It really wasn't all that great of a practical joke. I felt like an idiot for having fallen for it. Stupid Mallory with her great laugh and intriguing invitation.

I checked my phone one more time. Nothing. I weighed my options—walk around a little more, maybe even do my usual route, or just go home? Home, I decided. I stuck the phone in my pocket and walked to the front of the building.

When I turned the corner, I walked right into Mallory, and I mean right into her—we collided face-to-face, and she sort of bounced off of me, but not before I stepped on her foot. "Hey," she said, like I'd hurt her. "Where are you running off to, Becker?"

"Home," I said indignantly. "I was here at the right time and you weren't, so I was going home."

She stood so close to me I had to look down to see her face. "You sure are impatient. It's been what, all of three minutes?"

"I just don't appreciate being jerked around, Mallory Nassif." I stretched her name out for emphasis: Na-seeeef.

She held a finger up to her lips and then spoke quietly. "We've been here the whole time. In back behind the dumpsters. We kept waiting for you to come back, but you kept clinging to the side of the building like a big baby."

"I looked," I said. "And I didn't hear anything. I wasn't going to go scouting around behind some dumpsters."

"You have to be bolder than that if you want to be part of our group," Mallory whispered. "Come on." She grabbed my sleeve and pulled me along. "I want you to meet the others." She turned on a small flashlight and led me to the back. Her grip was firm and deliberate. We stepped around piles of industrial junk, metal rods and bins of small parts I hadn't noticed from my hiding spot. She maneuvered around them like she'd done this before many times.

As we approached, two other kids stepped out from behind the dumpsters. A small girl wearing a black sweatshirt with the hood up, her face barely visible, and a tall, skinny guy with glasses. The guy had a knit cap set back on head, so that only a little of his white-blond hair stuck out. I didn't recognize either of them. Mallory led me to them and finally released her grip on my arm. This was Mallory's secret society? Not to be mean, but I wasn't seeing much here.

Mallory pointed. "Russ, this is Nadia and Jameson." The girl kept her head down but gave a little wave. "Jameson, Nadia, this is Russ." Jameson nodded an acknowledgement, real serious-like. Mallory turned to me. "I told them all about you."

"But you didn't tell me anything about them," I said. They were not an impressive group at all. Nadia kept looking down at her shoes, and Jameson, shifting from side to side, looked a little uncomfortable too. With one finger he pushed his glasses up and then stared at me, like I was the odd one.

"What do you want to know?" Mallory asked.

"Everything," I said.

"We have to hide," Nadia said, her face still aimed at the ground. "Someone is coming."

I turned, but didn't see anything and was about to say as much, but the other three were already in motion.

"Come on," Jameson hissed to me, and I found myself ducking behind the dumpsters with the rest of them.

"What are we doing?" I asked Nadia, who was crouched beside me. She didn't answer. I turned to Mallory, but she shook her head and put her fingers to her lips. The crazy girl had lured me here for some kind of wacked-out grade school game. I usually was pretty good about reading people, but I'd really messed up this time. Somehow she'd pulled me into this weirdness, she and her strange friends.

And then, we did hear someone coming. I heard the shuffle of footsteps as someone approached the dumpster, then the creak of the cover being lifted and the sound of a bag of trash being thrown in.

Were we going to jump out and scare them? Eavesdrop? What was going on? I looked at the other three, who were frozen in place.

When it was completely quiet, I turned to Mallory and said, "What the hell was that about?"

She shrugged. "We don't want to get caught out at night."

Well, duh. I tried again. "So why the ball bearing factory? What's the significance?"

"No significance. It was chosen randomly as a place to meet," Mallory said. "We like to switch it up." She turned to Nadia. "Are you ready?" In response, Nadia's hood bobbed up and down.

Then Nadia stepped toward me, her arm outstretched like she wanted to shake hands, but when I went to grab it, she withdrew abruptly and looked at Mallory in alarm. "What?" I asked. "Did I do something wrong?"

"Don't move," Mallory said. "Keep your arms at your side and stand still."

Nadia stepped forward again. Without touching me, she ran her hand up and down my sides, and then front and back, like they do with those handheld security scanners at the airport. What was this all about? I gave Mallory a befuddled look, hoping she'd clue me in, but all three of them looked super serious, like this was a real thing. Just when I thought it was over, Nadia reached up and grabbed me by the shoulders. "Look at me," she said. I found myself looking down at her hooded face. Even though her face was shadowed, the intense way she stared gave me the creepiest feeling. I felt exposed and ashamed, like she'd walked in on me dancing naked in my bedroom. Not that I dance naked in my bedroom. Okay, I have, but it was only the one time and no one had walked in on me. Still, I had some context.

Finally Nadia let go of me and said, "He checks out okay."

"What the hell was that all about?" I asked.

Mallory, clearly the leader of this group, said, "Nadia has a talent for sizing people up. We weren't about to confide in you until we knew you were okay. Too dangerous."

"Really," I said, folding my arms. I didn't mean to sound sarcastic, but I knew I did sound that way, at least a little. I couldn't help it. This was starting to remind me of the secret clubs third graders invent. Pretty soon they'd be showing me their clubhouse and their secret handshake. "So how exactly was she sizing me up?"

"That's part of a bigger story."

"Yeah? Well, I'm all ears, so feel free to fill me in anytime now."

CHAPTER ELEVEN

———— o ————

I had to wait to find out. Jameson suddenly announced he was hungry and Mallory said they'd fill me in at the all-night diner on Highway 63. Rosie's Diner had been there since my parents were kids (back then it was Melvin's Diner), and I'd been there a million times, mostly after our high school football games. I knew the place was open all night, but it had never occurred to me to go there during my walks. Wouldn't a teenager in a diner after midnight arouse suspicion? That was my thought anyway, but Jameson, Nadia, and Mallory didn't seem concerned about it. They walked in the door like the regulars they apparently were. The place was empty, except for one old man sitting at the counter. I recognized him from around town. He looked like a bum, disheveled in flannel shirt and worn work pants, shuffling around like he was feeble-minded. Sometimes I saw him at the library, dozing in a chair by the magazines. When we saw him out in public, my mom always greeted him and they exchanged pleasantries, but she was like that with everyone. I'd never looked closely at the old guy, but Mallory greeted him warmly, placing a hand on his back and saying, "Hey, Gordy, what's up?"

He swiveled in his chair to answer. "The sky, the stars, the moon." He chortled more than was warranted, and Mallory laughed too. I got the impression it was a standard joke between them.

The owner, Rosie, who was also the waitress, motioned us over to what she said was their usual booth. I slid in first and was glad when Mallory sat next to me.

"You added a new person to your group," Rosie said, bringing menus. "You're not a trio anymore."

"He's on probation," Mallory said, giving my arm a poke. "We're still testing him out."

Rosie laughed. "If he's a good tipper, I say you keep him."

Oh, shoot, the mention of tipping reminded me that I had no money with me at all. Mallory's group knew their order without even looking at the menu. Without exception, they all ordered breakfast by giving her a number.

"Okay, so I've got two number fours, and a number six for the tall gentleman by the window," Rosie said, jotting the order down on a pad. She looked up. "The usual drinks?" They nodded.

She turned her attention to me. I handed her the menu and said, "I'm not really hungry. I'll just have a glass of water, thanks."

Mallory spoke up. "He'll have a number four like me. And an orange juice. My treat."

"Hey," I said, "you don't have to do that." Was my face red? It felt red.

She shrugged. "It's the least I can do since you made the trip out here." The waitress jotted down my order and walked away before I could cancel it. I guess I was having the number four, whatever that was.

"You don't have to pay for my food," I said.

Mallory said, "Call it payback."

"For what?"

"For saving Nelly Smith's life," Nadia piped up, her head aimed at the table.

I turned to Mallory. "You told them?"

"I didn't have to. They were with me that night. They saw you running away." She took a sip of her ice water. "But I would have told them, if they didn't already know. We don't have any secrets in this group."

"What exactly is this group?" I asked. Jameson was busy stacking the jelly packets so they were perfectly symmetrical, and Nadia still had her hood up. Mallory was the only one who seemed to have it together as far as I could tell.

Jameson gave me a steely-eyed look over his glasses. "We're geniuses with superpowers."

I couldn't help myself—I laughed. He'd said it with a completely straight face, but I couldn't imagine he was serious. I looked from Nadia to Jameson to Mallory. They didn't look like geniuses with superpowers.

Jameson looked disgusted. He said to Mallory, "I told you this was a bad idea. I can tell already that he's not going to work out."

Rosie came with our drinks. It was orange juice all around, except for Jameson, who had coffee. Nadia pulled the wrapper off her straw and twisted it around her finger. After the waitress walked away, I said, "I'm sorry for laughing, but come on. You're joking right?"

"It's no joke," Mallory said, lowering her voice.

"You're all geniuses?"

Nadia's head bobbed up and down under her hood. Jameson glared at me.

"That's how we met," Mallory said. "At a group for accelerated homeschoolers doing college-level work."

Now I was confused. "But you're not homeschooled."

"Not this year," Mallory said. "But I was before. The only rea-son I'm going to school now is that I wanted to see what I was missing. Going to dances, having a locker, doing labs in science class. The usual high school stuff. I wanted to play field hockey and complain about the cafeteria food. Plus, my folks thought it would be good for me socially."

"And has it been good for you?" I asked, and then added, "Socially, I mean."

Before she had a chance to answer, Jameson spoke up. "Mallory won't tell you this herself, but she's brilliant. A day at your high school for her would be like you spending time with kindergartners." His tone wasn't hostile, exactly, but it wasn't friendly either. I could tell he wanted me to know the pecking order. A guy thing.

"Okay, I get it, you're all smarter than me," I said. "You can feel superior if you want."

"It's not that we're smarter exactly," Mallory said. "It's just with academics—"

"No, he's right," Jameson said, interrupting. "We're smarter. You don't have to apologize for it, Mallory. It's okay to say it. Russ here probably has other things he's good at."

"I know I'm pretty average. I don't have a problem with that," I said. "I get good grades, but I spend a lot of time study-ing." Jameson nodded like he agreed with me. What a jerk. I changed the subject. "So what kind of superpowers are we talk-ing about?"

"So how did you know to help Nelly Smith?" Mallory asked, ignoring my question. "Why were you out at night to begin with?" She squeezed my arm in a way that made me want to cooperate. We could get back to the superpower question later.

51

"I have trouble sleeping," I said, "The only thing that seems to help is walking at night."

Nadia looked at me with surprise. Mallory had a triumphant look on her face, and I saw her catch Jameson's eye, but his expression didn't change.

"Why do you have trouble sleeping?" Mallory asked.

"I don't know why. I just can't."

"What made you think to go for a walk? It's kind of a weird thing to do."

I thought for a moment and then shrugged. "I don't know. I just sort of felt compelled to go outside. The house seemed confining. I had to get out. And then, after it helped, I kept doing it."

Rosie came with a tray then and set the food in front of us with crisp efficiency. Man, the cook here was fast. "Be careful, the plates are hot," she said, and pulled a bottle of Tabasco sauce out of her pocket, which she set in front of Nadia. "Do you need anything else?"

"No, we're good," Jameson said, speaking for the group. "Thanks."

Everyone turned their attention to the food. The salt shaker was passed around, and Nadia coated her fried eggs with enough Tabasco to burn the stomach lining of a cow. Everyone picked up their forks and began eating. I followed their lead and dug into my hash browns. I was hungrier than I'd thought.

"So Russ," Mallory said. "You have trouble sleeping and then you go walking. That's it, basically?" She took a sip of orange juice while she waited for me to answer.

"I guess. It's the only thing that helps."

"Does anyone else know you go out at night?" Jameson asked.

"No. I go out and I'm back before my folks even know the difference."

"And you always follow the same route." This from Mallory. She said it as a statement, not a question.

"You've been watching me?"

"Not on purpose," Jameson said. "But we can't seem to avoid you. Everywhere we went, there you were." He smirked at Nadia, who grinned in response.

"There aren't too many people out at night," Mallory said. "So when we started to see you lurking in the shadows it got our attention. We only followed you to make sure you weren't doing anything wrong."

"You were following me?" Creepy. How could I not have known that?

"Only at first," Jameson said. "We figured out pretty quickly that you were harmless." He emptied a sugar packet into his coffee and swirled it around, his spoon clinking loudly. I guess they never covered stirring without hitting the side of the coffee cup in genius school.

"So," Mallory said cheerily, "want to join our group?"

"Um, no," I said. "Why would I?"

Nadia turned to Mallory. "You forgot to tell him what we're all about."

"It got lost in the interrogation," I said, taking a sip of orange juice.

"Okay, short answer," Mallory said. "There's some kind of weird astronomical phenomenon happening. Those exposed to it seem to become affected in some way."

A light bulb went on in my head as I realized what she was talking about. The lights in the sky. So I wasn't the only one who'd experienced it. "You saw it too, then, the other night? The lights that came down out of the sky and landed in a spiral?"

The three of them exchanged a look that I couldn't quite decipher. Mallory sucked in a deep breath. "No, not this time."

"It's happened before?" I asked.

Mallory nodded. "We saw it about a year ago. It came in streaks and then landed in a perfect Fibonacci spiral on the ground. We studied it until it burned out, but none of us could figure out what it was. Later on, we all started to experience different things. *Unusual* things."

Nadia said, "It put some kind of spell on us. It was intoxicating."

"How did you know I saw the same thing?" Now they had my complete attention.

"Because you sketched it in Specter's class," Mallory said. "You drew it exactly the way we saw it. And then Specter started asking about it. I put two and two together."

"Tell him about what happened afterward," Jameson said in a forced voice. "After we saw it."

"This was last year. A few days after we saw the 'lights' as you call them, we went back to the site to collect evidence. We'd been so mesmerized by what we saw that it didn't occur to us to pick up some of the pieces, so we went back." Mallory spoke in hushed tones. "And this is when it gets really weird. It was all gone."

"Gone?"

"Not there anymore," Jameson said, his voice tinged with sarcasm.

"I know what *gone* means," I said. "I just don't understand. How could all the pieces be gone? There were like thousands of them. Maybe they blended in with the rest of the dirt?"

"No, they were gone. Someone had come and scraped the field clean," Jameson said, and then regretfully added, "I should have picked up samples when we first saw them. I missed my chance."

Nadia patted his arm, but he didn't seem to appreciate her attempt to console him.

"No one is blaming you, Jameson," Mallory said. "It's not that big of a deal. It's just," she said, leaning toward me, "that we wanted to analyze the pieces. Their properties don't correlate with what we know about energy and matter. They retain light and low-level heat, but they aren't hot per se. Sometimes the light intensifies after it's gone out, like those trick birthday candles that relight. It seems to permanently affect those who come into contact with it, but not consistently. Each of us had a different side effect, for lack of a different word."

"I'd give my right arm to be able to study a chunk of that stuff," Jameson said.

"Whatever it is, the properties of energy don't seem to apply," Nadia said, shrugging. "And the effects on human beings seem randomly generated."

"Just one little piece, that's all I'd need," Jameson said.

My food sat on my plate. I set down my fork. I was done. "So now you all have superpowers?"

"I like to call them *enhanced abilities*," Mallory said, her fingers making quotes around the last two words.

Jameson smirked. "I just called them superpowers for your benefit, Russell."

"You don't need to dumb down your vocabulary on my account," I said. "Even if you use big words, trust me, I'll be able to follow along."

Rosie came back with a pot of coffee and topped up Jameson's cup. While she was there, the group was silent.

"So what are these enhanced abilities?" I asked, once the waitress walked away. I gave each of them the once-over, trying to figure it out for myself, but came up short. Mallory looked like a typical pretty high school girl. Jameson, with his pasty white skin and lanky build, resembled an albino giraffe with glasses.

And Nadia, well, since she lurked behind her hood the whole time, I wasn't sure what to make of her. From her spiky bangs and big dark eyes, she could have been an anime character. None of them would ever be mistaken for a superhero. There was a long pause, and when no one answered I said, "Am I supposed to guess?"

I saw Nadia look at Jameson, and even though they didn't speak, there was something going on there. Their eyes flickered slightly and their facial expressions gave them away. I looked at Mallory to see if she'd fill me in, but she was looking intently at the other two. It was so quiet that when Nadia spoke, it was almost startling.

"Show him, Jameson," she said.

Jameson grinned like he'd been waiting for this moment. He rubbed his hands together. "So, Russ, how well do you know your science?"

I shrugged. "Okay, I guess. I'm getting an A in the class."

"Good for you!" Jameson said, in a clearly condescending way.

"Of course I'm in the dummy class, something called Science Samplers," I said. "Hey wait a minute." I pointed to Mallory. "If you're a genius, what are you doing in my class?"

She looked sheepish. "I tested out of all the math classes the school offered. I'm taking Specter's class as an elective."

"Oh."

"And what was the deal with your faked seizure?"

"I had to do something. You were just about to tell Mr. Specter about the lights."

"Eyes over here, Russ," Jameson said, waving a hand and snapping his fingers. "Let's get back on track."

Nadia said, "Just show him what you can do." Her dark eyes shone bright and she fidgeted slightly with anticipation. "It's very impressive," she said to me.

"I want to explain a little something first," Jameson said. "This might be a little advanced for you, Russ, but try to keep up. It has to do with energy. For the sake of simplification, let's say there are two basic types of energy: kinetic and potential. Potential energy is stored energy. If I lift up a jelly packet I exert energy that will become kinetic energy when the packet is dropped." He held one up at eye level and released it so that it fell to the table.

"Oh for God's sake, just demonstrate what you can do," Mallory said.

Jameson held up a hand. "Patience, Mallory, he's getting this, I can tell." He turned to me. "Kinetic energy, on the other hand, is the energy of motion. The faster the body moves, the more kinetic energy is produced. If I put this same jelly packet on a slide at a playground and it hurtles its way down to the bottom, the potential energy is converted into kinetic energy. Still with me, Russ?"

I nodded.

"Thus, the greater the mass and speed of an object the more kinetic energy there will be."

"I hope there's a point to all of this," I said, glancing up at the clock on the opposite wall. I was out much later than usual, and it was making me nervous.

"Oh there's a point all right."

I looked back down at the table to see the jelly packet, moving on its own, sliding in circles in front of Jameson, seemingly directed

by the subtle movements on his pointer finger. He wagged his finger back and forth and around and round, and the jelly packet, half a foot away, followed along. "Jump, little jelly, jump," Jameson said gleefully, and it did just that, leaping up and down off the tabletop like a bouncy ball. He reached out and snatched it in midair.

I felt my mouth drop open. "How are you doing that?"

"It's not kinetic *or* potential energy," he said, still directing the jelly. "It's a completely new kind. I call it Jameson energy."

CHAPTER TWELVE

———— o ————

Mallory nudged me like, *See I told you this was big*, and an expression of pure delight crossed her face. Nadia, too, looked charmed as she gave him a silent clap, clap, clap of applause. I hoped I didn't look as dumfounded as I felt.

Jameson handed me the jelly packet and numbly I took it. There was nothing extraordinary about it, no strings, nothing attached, no heat emanating from it. It was like all the others, a minute plastic container covered with a peel-off top decorated with a bunch of purple grapes. The only difference between this one and the other jelly packets was its ability to do gymnastics. "Being exposed to the lights one night, a year ago, gave you the ability to move objects without touching them?" I said.

Jameson grinned, showing all his teeth. "I told you he'd get it, Mallory. Such a smart boy." He took off his glasses and polished them with the front of his shirt.

"Okay, enough with the sarcasm," Mallory said. The waitress came to top up the coffee and Mallory waved her away. "Just the check please."

"How is this possible?" I set the jelly packet down. Part of me couldn't even fathom what I'd seen. It was a trick, it had to be. Magicians and illusionists had been pulling off stunts more mind-blowing than this for centuries. If someone could saw a girl in half or make an elephant disappear, making a small object move couldn't be that difficult.

Mallory leaned toward me and said softly, "After being exposed to the energy fragments each of us discovered we'd picked up an ability, and all of us have something different." She put a reassuring hand on my arm. "I know it can be kind of freaky if you aren't expecting it."

"So what's your superpower?" I asked.

"Me? I guess you'd call it mind control."

"Mind control? Like 'these aren't the droids you're looking for'?" I said, quoting Obi-Wan from *Star Wars*.

"Something like that. I'm still figuring it out. *We're* all still figuring it out." Mallory looked at the others and they nodded. "None of us knew the lights had affected us until odd stuff started happening. I didn't know I could do mind control. At first it just seemed like everyone was agreeing with me about everything, and I was so confused. Now I can actually feel it coursing through my body and I can kind of control it."

"Why would you want to control it?" I asked. How awesome would it be to have everyone agree with you all the time?

Mallory shook her head. "When I first realized I could do it, I did it all the time. I mean, it was really cool to get my way with everything, but it took a weird turn. Now I'm careful. When I exert control over people, it seems to pull energy from them. It makes them tired, and they get headaches and muscle and joint pain. It made my mother so sick, she was in bed for two days."

I wasn't sure if I believed what I was hearing, but if she was acting, her performance was perfect. I didn't want to believe that this pretty girl was lying to me, but it all seemed too incredible. "Can you show me how it works?"

"I will, I promise," she said. "But not tonight."

"And your power?" I said, looking at Nadia. "What did you get?'

"I can read people. I can see their thoughts, tell if they're lying, see what they've done in the past. When I look in their eyes, I know them. I can see the essence of their soul." Nadia looked down at her hands as she spoke, so all I saw was the top of her hoodie.

"Interesting," I said. And it was interesting. Interesting that two out of three of the powers were things no one else could actually see, while Jameson's was basically a parlor trick. I wasn't a genius, but I wasn't a fool either. And I wasn't about to be the butt of a practical joke. Mrs. Becker didn't raise a fool (unless you counted my sister, Carly, but that was a different story).

"And you brought back a dead person," Nadia said. "So it's pretty easy to figure out what your superpower is."

"Oh, no," I said. "That wasn't me. I mean, I was there, but I didn't bring her back from the dead."

"Did she have a pulse?" Jameson asked.

"Not that I could find. But," and here I held a hand up for emphasis, "that doesn't mean she was dead. Her pulse was probably too faint for me to detect. I was pretty rattled. A trained professional probably could have found a pulse."

"So you're saying she wasn't completely dead, just a little bit dead."

"No, I—" The way Jameson twisted my words was starting to get me mad. "She wasn't dead at all, so I couldn't have brought her back to life."

"But you did bring her back to life," Nadia said.

"Whatever." I didn't want to argue about it, but I knew I was right. I'm a fairly observant guy when it comes to new things going on in my own life. I noticed right away when I started getting armpit hair. I sure wouldn't miss suddenly getting a superpower.

The waitress brought the bill, and everyone scrambled out of the booth. I followed, still trying to process what I'd just been told. At the register, Mallory paid for everyone. Nadia and Jameson didn't even look in their pockets or try to pay.

"Thanks for the food," I said as we left the diner, the door slamming shut behind us. "It's been great."

Mallory said. "Thanks for the food? It's been great? That's all you have to say after we told you this huge secret involving superpowers?"

"You don't even have any questions?" This from Nadia, who trailed behind us. She hadn't pulled her hood down the entire time we were in the diner, and now she was completely hidden behind it.

"Only a million of them." It was true, I could have talked about it all night, but it was later than the time I normally got home, and that made me worried. I'd never been caught being out at night before, but that didn't mean I wouldn't this time. Just my luck I'd get in the house at the same moment my mom was getting up to go to the bathroom. Why someone couldn't go a whole night without peeing was beyond me, but I often heard the downstairs toilet flushing at night, and I always knew it was her. She blamed it on menopause. Actually, she blamed a lot of things on menopause. "I have to get home," I said, shoving my hands in my pockets. "We can talk later, right?"

Mallory nodded. "I'll explain it all to you after school. Just remember that what we've told you is strictly confidential. Only the four of us know this."

"Wait. So you've known about this for a year, and none of you have told *anyone* else?" We'd been crossing the parking lot, but now I stopped to face them. "Why not?"

Nadia's head was down. Her voice floated out from under her hood. "In comic books they never tell."

"Well, yeah…" It was true, but this wasn't a comic book, and I wasn't Peter Parker. Telling someone in authority seemed like a good way to go.

"The main reason we decided not to tell anyone is that we think it might be dangerous at this point," Mallory said. "You need to trust me on this. Don't tell anyone, or Google anything about this, or text anyone. That can all be traced. We have to do this old school and talk face-to-face. Someone else knows about this, and they're trying to find us. We're still trying to figure out who knows and what they want. When we do, we might go public. For now, we're keeping it to ourselves."

"How do you know that someone knows and is trying to find you?"

"Mr. Specter knew, for one," she said, ticking off on her fingers. "And the fact that it's not in the news or online. There are other things too. Someone is hunting for us. I'll tell you more next time." She looked up at the night sky. It was a clear night and above us the stars shone brightly. "Just be careful, Russ. I think if we stick together we can figure this thing out."

"What do you mean someone is hunting for us?"

"Maybe hunting is the wrong word. Trying to get us to come forward is more like it. I'll tell you more tomorrow."

"For now, just keep your mouth shut, if that's possible," Jameson said, pointing a finger at me. "Try not to screw things up."

"I can keep a secret," I said, matching his rude tone.

"I hope so," Jameson said, pushing his glasses up with one long, pointed finger. "Mallory vouched for you. If it were up to me, you wouldn't be here."

"Yeah, I got that," I said. The guy clearly had a serious problem with me and I wasn't sure why, but I wasn't going to take his abuse even if he was a friend of Mallory's.

CHAPTER THIRTEEN

———— o ————

We said good night and parted ways. I started to head for home, but somewhere along the way, a thought nagged at me that I needed to go back to the abandoned train station and check out the field where I'd seen the lights. Mallory's group said they'd gone back a few days after their sighting and the fragments were gone, all gone. I had no idea how that could be. It would take one person forever to pick up the individual pieces. Even a crew of people couldn't possibly get them all. There were thousands, maybe tens of thousands of fragments. There had to be some proof left behind. If I recovered a piece I would definitely one-up that smug bastard Jameson, who thought he was better than me. Okay, maybe he was smarter. So what? That didn't mean I had nothing to contribute. What had he said? *I'd give my right arm to be able to study a chunk of that stuff.* I didn't want his right arm, or any part of him at all, but I'd love to see the look on his face if I had a piece of something he wanted.

I made my way toward the field as quickly as possible. When I was nearly to the train station, I saw the lights off in the distance. Not the kind of lights I'd seen falling from the sky earlier in the

week. These were man-made lights, accompanied by the buzzing of some kind of electrical equipment. I walked up a small hill and darted behind the boarded-up train station building before peeking around the corner.

The field had been marked off like a crime scene. Each corner was staked and connected by yellow tape. Bright lights on tripods illuminated the space where the light spiral had been just a few nights ago. Two armed guards stood on either side of the field, each of them carrying a gun in a shoulder holster. Their guns weren't as long as rifles, but they were bigger than handguns. From this distance it was hard to identify them exactly. I didn't recognize their uniforms either. Not the police or any military that I was aware of. What could this be all about? They were guarding rocks?

Inside the taped area, at least a dozen men walked slowly while waving a device like a metal detector over the ground. They wore white jumpsuits that zipped up the front. Their hands sported oversized white gloves like Mickey Mouse. No one spoke, but the device made an odd, high-pitched EMF noise I found maddening. Back and forth the men walked in slow, careful steps, their gaze on the ground. They were looking for the pieces of stone that had fallen from the sky, I was sure of it. The event had happened two nights ago. Maybe they'd picked up most of it already and now were checking to make sure they got it all?

As I watched, one of the devices went off, making an annoying beeping noise like an old-fashioned alarm clock. The worker turned off the alarm, tucked the device under his arm, and bent at the waist to pick something up. I couldn't see what it was, but he was able to hold it in the palm of his hand, so it wasn't big. He walked over to a man who stood just outside the perimeter.

I hadn't noticed that man before. He was dressed differently from the others—no white suit for him, so clearly he wasn't one

of the workers. I only saw his back, but he was trim and tall, and dressed in dark clothing. He had the authoritative stance of someone in charge. He was overseeing this operation, was my take on it. The worker showed the boss whatever it was he'd picked up, and when he got a nod of approval, plunked it into what looked like a cylindrical container the size of a garbage can. The two exchanged a few words, and the next thing I knew, the worker was headed my way, the detector tucked under his arm.

Oh man, he was coming right at me. This couldn't be good. If I was spotted I was so screwed. If I started running now, I thought it would attract attention. I froze and shrank back against the building. Involuntarily, I raised my hand to my mouth, willing myself silent. On my side of the building it was fairly dark. Maybe I would be okay.

And then I had another thought. What if the boss man had noticed me lurking and sent him to grab me? What had Mallory said about getting found out? That it would be dangerous. That was the word she used. Dangerous, as in life-threatening. I didn't even want to know what those armed guards would do to a trespasser.

I heard the worker rustling through the tall grass, getting closer and closer. My heart pounded so loudly I was afraid it would give me away. But no one else could hear that, could they?

In the distance I still heard the buzzing and the movement of the other men, but it was the one walking toward me I worried about. Closer, closer, closer. He cleared his throat in a threatening way. Just when I thought I should make a run for it, the worker stopped walking. I was in the back of the building and he was around the adjacent side, so close I was willing to bet I could reach my arm around the corner and touch him. Near enough he could jump out and grab me.

But neither of those things happened, because the next thing I heard was the sound of a zipper and the unmistakable sound (and smell) of pee hitting the side of the building. The guy wasn't coming to find me; he just needed to take a whiz. I looked up at the starry sky and thanked God. What a relief. I exhaled silently and gave my heart permission to slow down.

As soon as the guy was done I vowed to head straight home to the safety of my bedroom. And never leave again. I wasn't made for this much stress. I waited while the guy peed, and peed, and peed some more. Man, he really had to go. I leaned my head back against the building and let myself relax, just a little bit. In a minute I'd hear him walk back to the work site and then I'd be safe.

I heard the stream taper off, and a zipper being yanked up. And then a click and the EMF humming like he'd turned the detector back on. A few seconds later, his detector made the raucous beeping sound it had made earlier in the field. Startled, I jumped. Over the noise, I heard him say, "What the hell?" to himself, and then he shouted back to the others, "I've got something here."

I didn't wait around to see what happened next. I ran. I ran as fast as I could, which suddenly didn't seem fast enough. I heard the guy yell, "Hey!" and knew I'd been spotted.

There was a small incline behind the building and I was out in the open. Not great, but that's the way it was. I didn't have time to think about it much anyway. I was on fast-forward, my legs fueled by adrenaline and fear.

I'd have more places to hide once I got to the houses of Old Edgewood, the neighborhood where Nelly Smith (now in the hospital) resided. But that was three blocks away. Behind me I heard the pounding feet and a voice calling out for me to stop,

but there was distance between us, and besides, I was younger and faster.

When I reached the road, I made a rookie move and looked behind me. I told myself it was just a quick glance to assess the situation, but it turned out to be a big mistake. Two men were coming after me. The worker who'd stopped to pee was the closest of the two, the detector dangling from his hand; periodically it would beep, which was weird, since we weren't anywhere near the field with the fragments. The other guy was one of the armed guards, a burly man whose large shoulders and overall build made him resemble the Hulk. Despite their advanced ages, they were speedy, and my pause to look helped them to gain on me.

I'd been on the track team in middle school, but I heard how competitive things got in high school and didn't even bother joining my freshman year. A good decision, I'd thought at the time, since I'm really not much of an athlete. Since middle school, I've played baseball with the local rec team over the summer and disc golf and basketball with my friends just for fun, but that was the extent of it. None of it had prepared me for this night.

"Halt!" one of the men shouted behind me.

"Stop or I'll shoot!"

Halt. Stop or I'll shoot. Unreal. Like in a movie, or a dream. It occurred to me then that maybe I was in the middle of an extremely vivid nightmare, one of those where all your senses are engaged right down to the bite of the night air and the frantic realization your life was in danger. The situation was bizarre enough to be a nightmare, but it felt too real. I was out of breath, panting, but still my legs kept pumping, almost on their own. Fear is a powerful motivator.

I felt something hit the base of my neck. The sensation was followed by a sharp sting and a burning sensation, but I didn't

have time to think about it. The pain, and the fact that I was close to Old Edgewood, gave me a surge of strength. In a minute I'd no longer be out in the open, but close to houses and trees and fences. Places to hide.

Despite the burning on my back, I just kept moving. When I got to the edge of the residential section, I leapt over the curb. I had a stitch in my side like I used to get as a kid when I ran with my mouth open. I'd been sweating so hard my T-shirt was glued to my body. My sweatshirt suddenly felt overly warm, but the dark color also gave me some protection. I ran in between the houses and made a dash for the thick shrubbery that divided two properties. The pounding of the men's footsteps seemed to be getting further away, but I didn't let up. I gulped in air and crouched down between two rows of bushes. Although there were streetlights there, I was a ways back from the road and almost invisible in the shrubbery. As an added bonus, I could push through to the neighboring yard if I needed to.

I kept low to the ground and listened. My hands rested on the ground and I got a whiff of my own perspiration mixed with the smell of dewy grass. Even though I'd dodged them, the men weren't giving up. Their voices drifted from the street, talking about me.

"Where did he go?"

"We couldn't have lost him."

The sound of a car approaching made me hopeful. Maybe it would make them wary and they'd retreat. With any luck, it would be a cop and my worries would be over. A guy in a white suit accompanied by a dude carrying a gun would have some explaining to do.

The car stopped, its brakes squealing slightly, and I held my breath, listening intently. Instead of a cop asking what they were

doing out and about in the middle of the night, I heard the sound of multiple car doors opening and the footsteps of the passengers leaping out. Then men's voices, all talking at once.

"Quick, before we lose him!"

"Which way did he go?"

"Did you get a good look at him?"

"Men, spread out and comb the area. He couldn't have gotten far."

This was starting to sound like an FBI manhunt. For trespassing? I was in so much trouble. Would I be better off running or staying put? I couldn't decide. When I'd been running I didn't have much time to think or feel—I was too busy fleeing. Now I felt a tidal wave of terror come over me. Panicked, I peered out of my hiding place, trying to decide what to do. *Think, think, think.* I watched as four men in white dispersed, all of them holding their buzzing detectors in front of them. The armed guard conferred with the man in the dark clothing, the one I'd thought was the boss of the operation.

A front door creaked open and an old woman dressed in a green bathrobe stepped out onto the porch. "What's going on out here?" Her tone was sharp. No one I'd want to mess with.

"No need to get alarmed, ma'am. Just a civil defense drill," the boss said.

She shook a finger at him. "A civil defense drill? In the middle of the night? I've never heard of such a thing. I'm calling the police!"

"Please, ma'am." The man's voice got louder as he approached. "Let me show you some identification. That should ease your mind." He walked briskly up the walkway and onto the porch.

"Get off my property! I don't want to see any—"

Silence. I held my breath, wondering what he'd done to make her stop mid-sentence, but when I peeked out, all I could see was

the two of them standing side-by-side, his hand on her arm. He spoke so softly I could just hear him. "Just go inside and go back to sleep. Forget you ever saw us."

She looked around, confused. "Go back to bed?"

"Yes, that's right. You'll sleep soundly, and when you wake up you won't remember any of this."

"All right then," she said, turning and going back into the house.

The boss walked back to the car, and he and the armed guard got in and drove away. As I watched the taillights go off in the distance, I felt relief wash over me. I wiped my sweat-slicked hands on the front of my jeans and blinked back tears.

Only then did I stop to think about the throbbing on the back of my neck. I reached up to rub the spot and found it sticky and wet. When I pulled my fingers away and looked, I realized that what I'd thought was sweat plastering my shirt to my body was actually blood. I had no idea how this had happened. The men who'd been chasing me hadn't even come close. But something clearly had made contact with my neck, causing the stinging sensation. And that something had broken the skin.

I didn't have time to think about it. I had to go at least a mile before I got home, and I needed to do it without getting caught. I looked up and down the street before crawling out of my hiding place. Lights were on in a few of the houses, and the streetlamps lit up the road, but the trees, mature and abundant in this part of town, would help me hide along the way.

CHAPTER FOURTEEN

---○---

I'd gone through Old Edgewood so many times before that I knew all the good hiding places. I darted between parked cars and behind hedges. Crouched behind garages and moved stealthily between trees. The men in white had their detectors on, so I knew I'd hear them if they were close. Meanwhile, I could be absolutely silent. I tried not to think about the man with the gun. Maybe he and the boss had left for good.

I came to Knitting-Lady's house. Looking through her front window, I noticed she was up to her usual routine. Seeing her working at her knitting made my world seem normal again. For a moment I could fool myself into thinking I wasn't being hunted by men in white suits and a man with a gun. *Hunted?* Wasn't that the word Mallory had used? And here I'd thought she was being overly dramatic.

Leaning against a tree trunk in front of Knitting-Lady's house, I allowed myself the luxury of a few moments' rest. I watched as she yanked at a skein of pale pink yarn, then resumed her work, fingers effortlessly manipulating the yarn into something that would (I guessed) eventually be a scarf. Observing

her going through the motions was soothing; I let my brain whir with all that had happened. Even though I'd essentially been spying over at the train station, I hadn't seen anything of interest. Why should the men even care that I'd been there? And why spread out and search with their detectors on? I thought about how weird it was that the old lady had changed her mind about calling the police. She almost sounded drugged. Maybe the boss man had hypnotized her? Or maybe it was mind control, like Mallory talked about. None of it made sense. I looked at my cell phone and groaned when I saw it was half past three. My alarm would go off in three hours.

Reluctantly I left Knitting-Lady's yard and continued carefully toward home: through the industrial park and past the strip mall, until I was finally in New Edgewood at last. My side of town lacked the foliage, but the houses were closer together. I was familiar with every barking dog, every motion-sensor light, and every residence that contained a fellow insomniac who might be looking out the window. I avoided all of it. I didn't see any further signs of the men who'd been chasing me, and I decided they must have given up. The worst was over.

When I got to the back door of my house, I felt a surge of happiness so enormous it trumped Christmas morning. It was bigger than the feeling I got hitting my first winning home run. Home had never looked so good, and I could easily imagine a life where I would never leave it, and would stay cocooned safely inside for the rest of my days. I opened the screen door and turned the knob slowly to keep the noise down. Once inside, with the door shut behind me, I wiped my feet on the mat and, after considering how dirty they were, leaned over to take off my shoes.

From my parents' room came a shuffling noise and then the squeak of a door opening. I froze. If my mother was headed to

the bathroom, she might not even come this way. Turns out, she wasn't going to the bathroom.

"Russ?" Once she'd called my name I knew there was no getting out of this. "Russ, is that you?"

"Yeah, it's me." The good news was that since Mom hadn't ventured out of her room she couldn't see me. If I was lucky, she would stay where she was and I could bluff my way through this.

"Oh thank God, I thought someone had broken into the house."

"Nope, just me."

"What are you doing up, honey?" she asked, her voice floating through the darkness. "Trouble sleeping?" Even without seeing her, I could picture her forehead furrowed in concern.

"No, I just woke up hungry, so I had a snack." I thought fast. She'd certainly heard the outside door open and close. I needed an explanation. "Then I noticed the garbage was full, so I took it out."

"Oh. Well, thank you."

"Good night, Mom."

"Good night, Russ. Get some sleep."

"I will."

She retreated back into the room. When the door clicked shut, I went into the kitchen to check the garbage. It was almost empty, just as I'd thought it would be. Earlier, after dinner, I'd taken it out without even being asked. Luckily, my mom hadn't remembered my kind gesture. Menopause was turning out to be my friend.

I headed up the stairs and straight to the bathroom to check out my wound. I looked in the mirror and it was like seeing someone else. My hair stuck up funny, and there were dark circles under my eyes. The right side of my sweatshirt was dark with

blood, and there were streaks of it on my right cheek. I must have touched my face with my bloody hand. My hands were streaked with dried blood as well, but I'd wiped most of it onto my clothes. I pulled at the neckline of the sweatshirt to get a better look, and the motion made me wince. Oh man, did that hurt! I ignored the pain and took off all my clothes, one piece at a time, and piled them in the corner, careful not to let the bloody part touch the floor. My parents rarely came up here, but I wasn't taking any chances that my clothes would stain the rug or vinyl flooring.

I twisted around in front of the mirror, trying to get a look at the source of the pain on the back of my neck. Could I have snagged my shoulder on something attached to the train station building and not realized it until later? The wound was circular, like I'd been poked with a large skewer, and it was still bleeding, though not quite as badly. I placed my hand over it to see if I could stop the flow, and my fingers got oddly warm. Pressing on the wound felt comforting and lessened the pain. I kept the pressure on, my fingers getting warmer and warmer, like they had a fever of their own. Beneath my touch, there was a sudden movement, like something jerking free. It reminded me of when I was a kid and my dad pulled a sliver out of my palm. A pinch, a pull, and before I could even say ouch, he'd gotten it out. But no one was doing this, it was just happening on its own. Something was rising out of the wound at the base of my neck; I could feel it making its way to the surface.

And then it was right under my fingertips, a small, bloody lump. I stared at it for a second before turning on the faucet and rinsing it off.

It was a bullet.

I blinked a few times, trying to readjust my eyes. A bullet. I'd gotten shot and not even realized it. They *were* trying to kill me.

If this was a crime show I'd know what caliber this was and could trace it back to its origins. But this wasn't a crime show, and I knew nothing about guns or bullets besides what I'd learned through games. And getting shot at in real life wasn't exciting—it was terrifying.

Shaken up and shivering, I stepped into the shower. A risk because my mother had a knack for hearing running water, even when she was asleep. Later she would certainly ask why I'd taken a shower so early, but there was no getting around it. I needed to clean off the blood and get a good look at the wound.

I knew I'd promised Mallory and her two sidekicks that I'd keep this a secret, but the situation was starting to feel bigger than anything I could handle alone. A bullet wound needed medical attention, and there would be no way to explain how it happened except to tell the truth. And maybe the truth was what was needed. Tell the police, let them handle it. A bunch of high school kids were no match for men with guns.

When I got out of the shower, I felt a lot better. I wrapped a towel around my middle and went back to the mirror to check out the wound, but I didn't see it from that angle. I twisted around, thinking I was looking at the wrong shoulder, but I still couldn't locate it. Finally, I got a hand mirror and checked out my entire back side, from the base of my neck to the bottom of my spine. The skin was unbroken. There was no indication that I'd ever had an injury, much less gotten shot. I looked down at the blood-soaked pile of clothes for confirmation that I wasn't losing my mind. I reached down and touched the sweatshirt, and when I looked at my fingers they were tinged with red.

And there on the counter next to the sink was the bullet, right where I'd left it.

Fresh blood and a bullet. But no wound. This was crazy.

CHAPTER FIFTEEN

———— o ————

It was cold in my room, so I pulled on sweatpants and a clean T-shirt before sliding into bed. I was certain I wouldn't sleep, sure it would be impossible with everything that had happened. So it was a pretty big shock when the music went off and I jolted awake. I reflexively hit the snooze button and opened my eyes a crack, trying to sort through the realities of the night.

Staggering out of bed, I went to the bathroom to splash water on my face. After I'd pressed a towel to my face, I noticed the bullet next to the soap dish and toothpaste. Nothing says "shot at by a guy with a gun" like the existence of a bullet. Glancing downward I saw my bloody clothing, still in a haphazard pile on the floor. So last night had really happened then. I looked at my face in the mirror, bloodshot eyes with dark half-moons underneath, and I knew there was no way I'd be walking the halls of my high school today pretending it was just a normal day. I trudged down the stairs to tell my mother I was taking a sick day.

"What's wrong?" she asked, turning away from eggs in a frying pan. She set her spatula down to place a hand on my forehead.

"No fever, but you do look terrible." Her worried eyes met mine. "Is it your stomach?"

"My stomach, my head, you name it." All true. Then I added, "I think I'm coming down with the flu." Not true.

"Maybe your snack in the middle of the night wasn't such a good idea?"

"No, Mom, I don't think that was it."

She looked so concerned, I felt guilty. "Okay then," she said. "Go back to bed and I'll call in for you. Unless you want to try eating something first?"

"No, I think I just need rest."

She nodded. "Oh, I almost forgot. Carly is dropping Frank off right after school. I'll leave a note on the table saying you're sleeping so he doesn't bother you."

"You know he's still going to come up to my room, don't you?" I said, shaking my head. There were no boundaries in my nephew's world. Carly didn't raise him right, that was why.

"Be nice, Russ." Mom sighed. "Frank is family."

Like I needed to be reminded of that. As I headed back upstairs, I heard my dad come into the kitchen.

"What's wrong?" Dad asked.

I paused to hear Mom's response. She said, "Russ is sick. He's staying home today."

Dad chuckled sympathetically. "There's some bug going around the office—headache, stomach problems, achiness. It comes out of nowhere and hangs on for a day or two."

"That must be it," Mom said. "That's what he has."

The power of a good reputation. They never doubted me for a moment. If Carly had pulled the same thing in high school, they would have assumed she was hung over or else faking it so she could spend the day with her loser friends. It almost wasn't fair. I

headed up to my room and plopped into bed, ready to sleep like a pharaoh in a tomb—alone and for a long, long time.

I woke up a few times during the morning when I heard my phone ping with text messages.

From Justin: *Dude, u pulling a Ferris?*

Mick: *Get your sorry self down here. If the rest of us have to suffer through a Friday, so do you.*

Mallory: *Are you OK?*

And then not too much later, I heard from all of them again.

Mick: *Don't make me come get you.*

Justin: *You better be doing something awesome.*

Mallory: *Now I'm worried. Please let me know you're OK.*

I was too tired to do much more than text back "*I'm OK*" to Mallory. The others would have to wait.

I got up around one to eat some soup and a sandwich, then checked the local news online, but there was nothing about an excavation near the old train station, or anything about men in white suits running rampant through the streets of Old Edgewood, with buzzing detectors in hand. Remembering what Mallory had said, I didn't Google anything on the subject. *That can all be traced.* I didn't believe her then, but I believed her now. Whatever I'd seen last night was dangerous, and I wasn't looking for trouble. My room was my cocoon, and I didn't want to be found. Let other people figure out what was going on. I wasn't brave enough to risk my life getting involved.

I wasn't even a little bit brave. I wanted my old life back, the one where I studied for tests and diligently went to school, not doing anything that would make me stand out from the crowd. The worst things I did involved TPing houses with my friends, thinking endlessly about sex, and taking a drag off something that was not a cigarette at Melissa Reinhardt's pool party last

summer. Even those minor infractions would have shocked my parents, who were convinced I was the world's best son. Which was fine by me.

I crawled under the covers and closed my eyes again, but this time I fell into a dream. It was nighttime, nearly pitch black, and I was running from the men with the detectors. There were no houses in sight, just an endless stretch of open field. Panting, exhausted, I kept going, but it was no use, they were closing in on me. My legs were heavy and I couldn't get any traction. The white-suited men were right behind me now, the buzzing from their devices like bees swarming behind my head. I opened my mouth to scream, but nothing came out. One of the men grabbed my arm and I tried to pull away, but he had a tight grip. I knew I only had moments left to live. "No," I said, "please no." I couldn't see his face, but he was shaking my arm and saying, "Russ, Russ, wake up!"

It took all I had, but I swam to the surface and pulled myself out of my sleep. When I opened my eyes, I was back in my bed with Mallory's face right above me. "Russ, it was just a dream. You were dreaming." She put her hand on my forehead, the way my mother had earlier that morning, but I liked the feel of Mallory's hand a whole lot better. This felt as unreal as the past few minutes, like the chasing had been a dream within a dream.

"Mallory?" I sat up and rubbed my eyes. "What are you doing here?" Yep, she was here all right, sitting on the edge of my bed. Only a sheet, a blanket, and a comforter separated my body from hers.

Her dark eyes narrowed in concern. "When you weren't in school, I worried. I thought maybe we freaked you out last night, or else something had happened to you."

"Who let you in the house?" I glanced at my alarm clock. It was just after two. School wouldn't even be out yet. "Aren't you supposed to be in class?"

She shrugged. "I stopped at the health room and said I had cramps. I told them all I had left was study hall, so they let me go early. And then I came here, and when no one answered my knock, I came in the back door. It wasn't locked."

"Wait. You just came into my house?" Such nerve. I never could have done that. I didn't know if I should admire her or what.

"I was *really* worried."

"Oh." Wow, what a rush I was getting from the fact that this beautiful girl was worried about me. It was almost worth getting shot at.

"You really should lock your doors," she said, stating the obvious.

"When I came in last night, I must have forgotten."

"So you're really just home sick?"

"Not quite," I said. "Something happened last night after I left you guys." I ran my fingers over my head, wondering how my hair looked.

"I had a feeling something was up," she said.

"Wait here," I said. She scooted back and I slid out from under the covers, glad I was wearing sweatpants and a T-shirt instead of any of my usual nighttime choices. I went into the bathroom to get the bullet and snuck a look at myself in the mirror while I was there. Not too bad, considering.

When I got back to my room, I saw she had moved off the bed and over to my desk chair. Walking in and spotting her there, hair pulled away from her face (which highlighted her chiseled cheekbones), chin lifted, and hands folded in her lap, she looked like a girl way out of my league. A few days earlier, after she'd fallen out of her chair in science class, I'd come home and looked up the name Nassif, and discovered it was Egyptian. Right now

I could easily believe she was of Egyptian nobility, a descendent of Cleopatra. Hard to imagine that someone like Mallory was in my bedroom because she'd been worried about me. This was the kind of scenario my friend Mick always talked about. If he could see me now.

I placed the bullet on the desk in front of her. "I got a little gift last night, over by the train station."

She picked it up and examined it, then looked up at me questioningly. "A bullet?"

I sat on the end of the bed, and she swiveled in the chair to face me. I started at the beginning. "Last night, after we left the diner, I just had to go back to the field where I saw the lights." I told the whole story, every detail. I felt a little like I was rambling, but she leaned forward and took in every word, fascinated.

When I was done, Mallory sat back with her arms folded. "So I was right then," she said, in a satisfied way.

"You knew all this?"

"No, I didn't know anything about the field or the men trying to kill you. I'm talking about your superpower. You can *heal* people." When I didn't say anything, she added. "First Nelly Smith, and now yourself."

"You think *I* made the wound go away? That I touched it and just like that—*poof*—all better?"

"Of course. Do you think bullets rise up out of people on their own? And why didn't getting shot kill you in the first place? It hit your neck, for crying out loud. You should be dead or paralyzed!" Her eyes shone with excitement. "And that's why Nelly Smith came back. When you went to feel her pulse, you resuscitated her."

"Well, I don't know about that…" If that were true, wouldn't I know? I didn't feel any special healing energy coursing through me, I just put my fingers over the wound.

"What's healing, but cells regenerating?" she said. "And that requires energy. We all picked up energy from the light source, and each of us utilizes it differently. Jameson can move objects; I can affect people's thinking—"

"Mind control," I said.

"More or less. And Nadia can read people and see their pasts. She's scary good at it, actually. She sees right through the veneer and into their deepest places. It's hard for her to do, actually, because she usually doesn't like to be so close to people."

"You know what? You need to tell me everything you know," I said. "I want to know what you saw and how you figured out you got these so-called 'abilities' and how you know we're being hunted. You didn't seem all that shocked that someone was trying to kill me. I feel like I walked into the middle of a movie. Time to fill me in."

CHAPTER SIXTEEN

---○---

Mallory got up and sat right next to me on the bed. Having her so close made my heart race, but the move, I quickly figured out, wasn't for intimacy, but comfort. That and also because she wanted to keep our conversation confidential. She leaned against my headboard, her legs extended, and began. For the next hour, it all spilled out. Her hands fluttered like birds while she spoke, and her voice rose and fell with the storytelling. If I hadn't known what she was saying was true, I'd have thought it was something from a graphic novel, it was that farfetched.

"I met Nadia and Jameson through my homeschooling group," she said. "The group has these socials once a month. The three of us are the only ones at the high school level around here, and all of us were in the accelerated college-level program, so we had that in common too."

Here we go again, I thought. All of you are smart, while me? Not so much. But maybe she didn't mean it that way. It was entirely possible I was being overly sensitive.

"Nadia's parents never let her leave the house unless a family member is with her. And I mean *never ever*. I thought my

parents were strict, but they're nothing in comparison. Her mother is so overprotective it's ridiculous. She doesn't even let Nadia have her own phone, so we always have to call the house and ask for Nadia. They screen her calls, believe it or not. Luckily they let Jameson and I get through, but we still have to go through some small talk before they hand the phone over to Nadia."

"Why are they that way?" I asked.

"Because Nadia was attacked on a city bus three years ago. She doesn't like to talk about it, so don't ask," she added, as if I would. "Anyway, the three of us started calling each other, first to talk about schoolwork and then just to hang out."

They started going out at night, Mallory said, when all of them discovered, at around the same time, that all of them had trouble sleeping. They were restless; it was like they were *compelled* to go outside, like their houses were suddenly confining. So they met up outside and walked. For Nadia, it was sweet freedom after being caged by her mother's worry.

The first time they went out, it was going to be a onetime thing, or so they thought. But when they didn't get caught, there was no reason to stop. "At night, it's like the world is ours," Mallory said, getting a faraway look. "Everything has a different feel at night. It was like we stumbled onto some secret place." Coincidentally, they all wanted to go out on the same nights. All three got that restless urge at the same time.

"And we were drawn to go to certain places," she said. "We didn't think much of it. We sort of just went with it."

"And the diner?" I asked.

She nodded. "One day we got hungry and decided to risk it. We told the waitress, Rosie, that we were college students and she seemed cool with it. Now we go all the time. No one else is ever

86

there at that time of night, except sometimes that old guy, Gordy, but he wouldn't hurt a fly."

"And how long did you do this walking around before you saw the lights?"

"About two months, I think?" Mallory said. "We were on the other end of town when we saw them in the sky, and by the time we got to the field, they were there on the ground in a perfect Fibonacci spiral. We walked through it and were just awed. I mean, none of us had ever seen anything like it. I'm not sure anyone else has either. We were so dumbstruck we didn't even think to collect samples, something Jameson still hasn't gotten over." She wrinkled her nose. "When we went back to the field during the day, it had been bulldozed. The whole surface had been scraped and carted away, by someone, we don't know who. It took a long while for the grass to grow back, but it did."

"So who did it?"

"We never found out. The property around the old train station is owned by the city. I made some calls to the city office using a disposable cell phone, but no one would tell us anything. Every person I talked to said they didn't know what I was talking about. They sure were curious about me though. The receptionist put us through to the mayor, and he wanted to know who I was and *why* I was asking. He demanded to know, in fact. I finally hung up on him."

Then, she said, it got even weirder. They saw signs posted around town offering rewards for anyone who could supply information about a meteor event, and they listed the date that the lights had appeared in the sky. "Of course it wasn't a meteor event, but they had to call it something."

I snapped my fingers and pointed. "I remember those signs. They were on the bulletin board at the supermarket, right?" My

friend Justin had made jokes about making up a story to collect the money.

She nodded. "And the post office and a lot of other places too. But the odd thing is that the media didn't cover the event, and no one else seemed to have seen the lights either." Nadia was paranoid right from the start, Mallory said. She was the one who told them they shouldn't talk about it, or use their real phones, or look online for information. "I thought she was being a little extreme," Mallory said, shifting her position so her legs were tucked under her. "But we soon found out she was right about everything. I used the computers at the library to do searches and signed in with the name 'Marsina Follys,' which is, as I'm sure you already figured out, an anagram of my actual name, Mallory Nassif."

I tried to look as smart as she thought I was. "Of course."

"My searches came up with nothing. I just couldn't believe it. I was at the computer for an hour putting in every search term I could think of, but there was no record of it ever happening. If I hadn't had Nadia and Jameson with me I would have thought I'd been hallucinating. A week later, Jameson was at the library studying, and two men in suits came in, looking very official. He noticed them right away. He overheard them say they were from the FBI and they wanted to speak to whoever is in charge of Internet use at the library. The head librarian—you know Mrs. Wick? She came out and was all flustered. They wanted to see the signup sheet and wanted to know what the protocol was for using the computers. They inspected the sheet and compared them to something they had, and then one of them says they need to have the contact information for Marsina Follys. Jameson said the hair on the back of his neck stood up when he heard this. Mrs. Wick looked up Marsina Follys on the library computer behind

the counter, and of course there's no record of anyone by that name in the system. One of the men actually pushed her aside to see for himself, and then they reamed her out for not checking IDs. Jameson said she looked ready to pass out, poor thing."

"And that's why you think it's dangerous."

"Oh, it gets better." Mallory was enjoying telling this story. It was as if she'd been dying to share it with someone for ages and finally could. She began counting down on her fingers. "So far we have a strange astronomical event no one seems to know about. Then the field is cleared of evidence and signs go up looking for witnesses. And then the *FBI*," and here she put finger quotes around the word, "is looking for whoever was searching for information about this whole thing. At this point, our minds are blown by the implications here. Jameson starts reading everything he can about astronomy, and Nadia researches FBI procedure to see if the library incident was done by the books. We thought we were onto something, but little did we know it was just the beginning. A few days after Mrs. Wick was visited by the suits, the three of us went out night walking again. We stopped for something to eat at the diner, and when Jameson went to reach for a salt shaker, it skidded across the table right to him." She laughed. "You should have seen the look on his face. It wasn't long after that when Nadia discovered she can tell if people are telling the truth or not and gets a sense of who they are and what they're all about. If she touches them and looks in their eyes, she can see their past, or at least bits of it. She says it's as clear as watching a movie, but it comes all at once, not in regular time."

"And you found out you can do mind control," I said, filling in the rest.

"Yes." She smiled right at me, and I found it impossible not to look at her big, dark eyes.

I felt myself leaning toward her in fact, wanting to—wait! I straightened up. "Are you doing it right now?"

"No!" She reached over and slapped me playfully on the arm. "I wouldn't do that to you, at least not without asking you first, like if you want a demonstration."

"Yeah, I don't think I want a demonstration, at least not on me," I said, feeling a flush of embarrassment. I thought about the hypnosis guy on the Discovery Channel who made people do ridiculous things, like profess their love to complete strangers or dance to imaginary music. I was capable of humiliating myself on my own. I didn't need any help, thanks.

"How fascinating that you can heal people," she said. "Imagine what you could do with that."

"I don't think that's what it was," I said. "I'm still figuring it out, but there has to be another answer."

As if not hearing me, she continued the discussion, going in a different direction entirely. I've noticed that girls do this a lot. My dad will be talking about something in the news and my mom will interrupt him to ask if the car is due for an oil change. At least Mallory stayed on the subject somewhat. "We've done some brainstorming to try to determine who's behind the library visit. If it's not the government, it might be some corporation trying to develop the power from the stones."

The government or an evil corporation, both major movie clichés. "Maybe the light particles were sent by aliens," I joked.

"That had occurred to us," she said. "We really can't rule anything out at this point. But more likely, it's a natural phenomenon that hasn't occurred before. Or at least it hasn't been reported. Scientists are always discovering new things. That's the joy of science. As our body of evidence grows, the truths of

science change along with it. It's more fluid than most people think."

"So why don't you go to the authorities with this information?" I asked. "Or tell your parents?"

"Don't even think of telling anyone," she said. "I mean it. We've got good reasons not to go public with this."

"But doesn't it make sense to inform—"

I was interrupted by noises downstairs: the sound of the front door opening and closing, and the usual sounds of Frank and Carly arriving. Carly calling out, "Hello, anybody here?" followed by her yelling at Frank to take off his shoes and put his backpack in the front hall closet.

I groaned. "Oh no."

"What is it?"

"My sister is dropping off my nephew. He's staying with us for the weekend."

"Oh, that's nice," she said, in a way that indicated she'd never met Frank Shrapnel. "How old is he?"

"He's ten," I said. "It's just—" But it was too late to explain because now Frank was clomping up the stairs. His timing had always been bad, but today was the absolute worst.

"Frank, come back here!" Carly called after him, and then just when I didn't think it could get any worse, I heard her footsteps clattering behind his.

The door flew open revealing Frank, his shaggy hair all askew, his eyes bright with excitement, "Hey, Russ, guess what?" And then he saw Mallory and he transitioned from overeager-Frank to shy-Frank. "Hi," he said.

She waved back "Hello there."

Carly's face popped through the doorframe. "I tried to stop him, Russ! Really I did. Oh, hello…" She spotted Mallory perched

on my bed, and you could read the shock on her face. Nobody expects much from old Russ, that's for sure. An instant later, a smug smile formed on her lips, like she totally had something on me. "What have we here?" she asked. I could have killed her for acting like this was a big deal.

"Mallory, this is my sister Carly and my nephew Frank," I said, gesturing.

Mallory got up and crossed the room to where Carly stood, and politely extended her hand. "It's nice to meet you. I'm Mallory Nassif, a friend of Russ's," she said. "I brought his homework over for him."

Carly shook her hand and looked over at me. "You were home sick today?"

"You would have known that if you'd read Mom's note on the kitchen table."

"Sorry," she said, not sounding sorry at all. She ran her fingers through her hair and checked out the room, as if maybe there was more to see. Carly was nearly grown when I was born, but you couldn't tell that by looking at her. She was thirty but appeared much younger, and since she kept up with the kind of music, games, movies, and clothes that were current, she felt like we were peers, but we weren't, and even though I knew she wanted us to be friends, it was never going to happen.

It wasn't always like that. When I was little, she used to take me to the park and out for ice cream. She read books to me and we played hide-and-seek. I loved Carly then. But one day, when I was four, she just took off and we didn't see or hear from her for over a year. My mother told me that every day for weeks I'd sit on our front stoop waiting for her to return. My memories are fuzzy, but I remember looking down the street wishing she'd

come back to me. By the time she did, more than twelve months later and pregnant with Frank, I didn't trust her anymore.

So much about Carly was unstable. After barely graduating from high school, she'd had one loser job after another. Cell phones were another matter. She was always losing them or changing her phone number. Men came and went in her life. The identity of Frank's father was this big mystery. Carly never named him. My guess was that Frank was the product of a drunken one-night stand and she didn't catch the guy's name.

Carly had a busy social life and men loved her. I'm not sure why. One after another, it was like they had lined up, waiting for their turn. Her pattern was that she'd begin dating a guy, and we'd hear her talk about him nonstop. She'd say that this one was different; he was more caring, more enlightened, more responsible, blah, blah, blah. She'd start bringing him around and we'd be subjected to him at Thanksgiving and family birthdays. Just when I got used to a guy, she'd dump him. Any number of them would have married her, but she wasn't going for it. My mom thought she was searching for something and not finding it. My dad said he was glad she was supporting herself and not living with us. I was beyond caring. "So you brought Russ his homework and then the two of you were just hanging out here, in *Russ's bedroom*, talking?" She grinned and I wanted to tell her off, but I knew enough to ignore her. She loved to tease me and thought it was big fun. Not so fun on my end.

"We were just wrapping things up," Mallory said. "Russ, if you're feeling better tomorrow night give me a call and we can go out for wings."

"Sounds good," I said, following her out the door to the stairs. I pushed past Frank and Carly, who still lingered in the

doorway like they had nothing better to do than intrude on my personal life.

When Mallory and I got to the front door, she stopped and turned to me, whispering, "Seriously, don't breathe a word of any of this. There's more. I'll tell you tomorrow." I got a warm little shiver from the feel of her lips so close to my ear.

"Tell me now," I whispered back.

She laughed. "No way, I need more time to get it all out."

"Are we really going out for wings?" I asked.

She pulled back and shrugged. "Might as well. We have to eat, right? I'll pick you up at six?"

"Six is fine," I said, holding the door open for her. I watched her walk down the driveway to a silver car parked across the street. She stopped to fish car keys out of her purse and beeped the door open. When she pulled away from the curb, she glanced back and gave me a wave, which I returned. A bunch of sophomores at my school already had their driver's licenses, but I was young for my grade and wouldn't turn sixteen until June. Watching her speed down the street, I couldn't wait for my turn at the wheel. I was tired of walking and having my mom drive me everywhere.

I guess I shouldn't have been shocked to turn and see Carly standing right behind me, but I was. Frank had already commandeered the PS3 up in my room; I could hear the sounds of a game above me. You always knew when Frank was over: the kid couldn't keep quiet for anything. But my sister was another matter. She was a sneaky thing—quiet as a cat. Probably from years of practice as a teenager sneaking out of the house late at night and taking the family car without permission. I waited for her to make some snarky comment, but all she did was put her hand on

my forehead. "Oh yeah," she said, her face scrunched in concern. "I can see why you stayed home today. You've definitely got it."

"Got what?"

"The looove disease." Carly's face lit up and she thrust a fist in the air, pleased with herself.

"Okay, enough already." For once though, I wasn't all that annoyed with her.

"And she drives too!" Carly punched me lightly on the arm. "An older woman, Russ! You dog, you!" She could barely contain her excitement.

"She's just a friend." I tried to hold back a smile without much luck.

"A friend? Just a friend, and she whispers in your ear like that?"

"A good friend."

"Just a good friend?"

I grinned. "A *very* good friend."

"That's how it starts," she said, twirling around with her arms stretched high. "Next thing you know, you'll have moved to the next level and then—watch out! Fireworks! Trust me on this. I know these things."

"Yes, because you're the expert when it comes to relationships." I meant it as a joke, but it came out wrong. As soon as the words were out of my mouth I knew it was the wrong thing to say. Her face fell, like a balloon deflating, and she stopped dancing. She'd been happy and we were getting along for once, and just like that, the mood shifted. I'd ruined the moment.

"That wasn't nice, Russ," she said. "In fact, it was kind of cruel."

"I'm sorry. I didn't mean it like that."

"I know I'm not good at relationships. I try, but I'm just not." Her voice was raw. She looked on the verge of tears. And suddenly I felt a kind of tenderness toward her I hadn't felt since I was four years old. Carly must have felt something too, because she reached up and ruffled my hair the way she did when I was a kid. I wanted to pull away, but I didn't. She smiled, just a little. "When I was your age, I found true love, and it hasn't happened since. I keep looking for it, but nothing compares. I guess I should be glad I had it once, even if it was over far too soon."

"What happened?" I asked.

Carly exhaled and didn't speak for so long I didn't think she was going to answer. Finally she said, "He died."

"Oh." Talk about shocked. I wasn't expecting that answer. I wanted to know more, but the finality in her voice told me this was all I was going to get. "I'm really sorry, Carly."

She gave me a rueful pat. "Real love doesn't come around all that often. If you find it with this girl, hold on to it. And don't let anyone tell you you're too young."

CHAPTER SEVENTEEN

———— o ————

My mother was impressed with how quickly I recovered after spending a day at home sick. "The resilience of youth," she said to my dad across the table at dinnertime. She thought I had the flu and couldn't believe my appetite. If she knew how quickly I'd bounced back from being shot, she'd have been really impressed. I'd just taken a second helping of lasagna and salad. Next to me, Frank waited for his turn to take more. The kid copied everything I did.

"I slept most of the day," I said, sliding the salad bowl over to my nephew.

"Sleep," Dad said, nodding approvingly. "That's just what your body needs when you're sick."

"Russ had a girl over when my mom and I got here." Frank poked at the salad with the tongs, oblivious to how much I wished he would just, for once in his life, shut up.

"A girl?" My parents exchanged puzzled looks.

I played it cool. "Mallory Nassif from my science class dropped off my homework on her way home. We're working on a project together."

"Oh, how nice," Mom said. "I don't think you've ever mentioned someone named Mallory before."

"You'll probably get to meet her tomorrow night," I said, oh so casually. "A bunch of us are going out for wings, and I think she's driving." A slight edit with the addition of "a bunch of us." Necessary to keep the questions at bay.

"She's really hot," Frank said, even though he was still chewing. With every word he revealed the mushed-up lasagna in his mouth. Gross.

"We don't objectify women in this house," my mom admonished Frank. "I'm sure Mallory has a lot of wonderful qualities besides being attractive."

"She's a genius," I said. "Like an actual genius."

"I'd expect nothing less," my dad said solemnly, and then to my surprise, the subject changed and they started talking about their plans for the weekend. I, Russ Becker, had a hot genius girl in my house when no one else was home, and neither of my parents were even all that curious. The advantage of a good reputation was also a disadvantage. No one thought I was capable of doing anything wrong.

* * *

I spent Friday night playing video games with Frank. I didn't have a reason not to. Since I hadn't gone to school, I had no homework, and leaving the house in the evening after being home sick wouldn't have gone over well with my mom. Sometimes, as they say, it's best to choose your battles. Besides, I was going out with Mallory on Saturday night. I had a lot to look forward to.

We drank bottles of Sprecher root beer while we played, and I was careful to set the caps aside in case Frank wanted to take

them home. He collected everything: stones, bottle caps, coins. Mom thought it was his attempt to have permanency and order in his life. I thought the kid just liked junk.

Frank had his own room at our house: Carly's old bedroom, cleaned out and repainted long ago. Unfortunately, it was on the second floor, right next to mine, so every time he stayed over, he encroached on my privacy. From the outside our home looked a lot like a first grader's drawing of a house: a square base topped with a triangular roof, black shutters on either side of symmetrically-spaced windows, and a brick chimney off to one side. My folks called it a Milwaukee bungalow, which just meant it was like a lot of houses in our neighborhood. The upstairs was made up of two bedrooms and a bathroom. Small, but all mine when Frank wasn't around.

Not that I should complain. For a ten-year-old, Frank wasn't too bad, just a little too eager to please. To make me happy, he always used to let me win when we played games, even when I figured out what he was doing and told him to stop it. I fixed that problem by playing games with co-op. He totally loved that. We were "war buddies"—that was his term, anyway. The whole evening he was yelling things like, "Don't worry, Russ, I've got your back." My mom peeked in a few times, and once I saw her mouth, *Thank you, Russ,* like she knew playing with Frank was a huge favor for me.

The next day, after lunch, my parents told Frank to get his jacket because they were taking him to the mall to buy new shoes. Afterward they were going to a movie at the multiplex. Frank invited me along, begged, in fact. "Come on, Russ, it'll be fun!" Like that would work.

I told him I had too much homework and pointed up the stairs. "I wish I could, but I'm going to be spending all afternoon

on a paper," I said. "You can tell me all about the movie when you get back. If you like it, I probably will too." That made him happy, I could tell. The kid was high maintenance, but easy to please. Carly really needed to spend more time with Frank. Either that or she should have given him a brother close in age. It made me feel lucky that I had my parents around all the time. Frank got shortchanged in the family department with no dad, an absentee mom, and no siblings. At least he had grandparents who loved him. And he had me too, of course. I did what I could.

I watched from my bedroom window as Dad backed the car down to the street, and then, a second later, as the car pulled forward into the driveway again. Frank got out and came tearing up to the house, his arms and legs flailing, like he had no control over them. I heard the front door being flung open, and I headed to the top of the stairs. I yelled down, "What did you forget?"

He didn't answer, but came up the stairs holding my old Nikes, which he thrust at me. "Your shoes were all muddy and Grandma had me clean them for you. They were on the front porch drying out and Grandpa said I better bring 'em in, in case you want to go somewhere."

"Oh, thanks," I said, taking them from him. I never bothered cleaning them because I only used them for my nighttime walks, but my mother didn't know that. I turned them over and saw that the underside was spotless. Mom must have had Frank scrub the grooves with a brush. "Good job." His face lit up at the praise, which was kind of sweet and pathetic at the same time.

"I had to really work at it," he said. "I took a butter knife to pry the mud and all the gravel out. Grandma said I did a better job than you probably would have done."

"Well done," I said.

Outside, a loud honk. Dad got impatient at times.

"I gotta go," Frank said, and off he went, bounding down the stairs two at a time and swinging off the banister at the bottom. He yelled up, "See you later, Russ!"

"Later, dude." I went back into my room where I spent the next five hours counting down to my (fingers crossed) date with Mallory. I'd never been on a date before, unless you counted the homecoming dance freshman year when I'd been matched up with Justin's girlfriend's friend, a quiet girl named Katy who went to a different school. We went with eight other couples, and Katy seemed more interested in the group dynamic than in talking to me. There were a few awkward dances and, at the end of the evening, one brief, very disappointing kiss. The next day, my mom, always nosy, wanted to know if I was going to see Katy again. When I shrugged, she said, "No chemistry, huh?" which pretty much said it all. And then my mother sighed and said, "In high school, the one you like never likes you." I'm sure she had a story and a life lesson there from her high school days, but I didn't ask.

With Mallory I wasn't sure if there was chemistry on her end, but I was feeling it on mine. I wondered if it counted as a date if only one person knew it was a date. I decided it would, as long as I paid for the meal, which is what I intended to do.

Mick texted. He was at Justin's and they were bored, as usual. The day before, I'd told them I had to stay home because Frank was over and I'd just taken a sick day. This recent text asked what I was doing tonight. I told him I was going out for wings with Mallory Nassif, and got the kind of response I've come to expect from him.

Mick: *No way.*

Me: *Way.*

Mick: *You're lying. Stop. Lying. Now.*

Me: *She's picking me up at 6:00.*

Mick: *Unbelievable. Has she lost her mind?*

Me: *At 6:00 she will be at my house to pick me up. For wings!*

Then Justin, not content to let Mick have all the fun, starting texting me too.

Justin: *What's this I hear? Mallory Nassif is on drugs and will go out with just about anyone?*

Mick: *Dude, turns out you're not the only one. Mallory's picking me up at 5:00!*

Me: *Stop already.*

Mick: *And we're skipping the wings and going straight to bed. Heh.*

Me: *You guys are losers.*

A few days ago we would have gone back and forth like this forever and I would have thought it was hilarious. Now they irritated me. I didn't like the joking about Mallory, but that wasn't all of it. They just seemed juvenile. I told them I had to go and ignored the next few texts that came in. Eventually they gave up and my phone grew quiet.

At six sharp, I was looking out my bedroom window when I saw Mallory's car pull into my driveway. At the same time, my phone rang. It was her. "I'll be right out," I said, and bounded happily down the stairs, much like Frank Shrapnel had a few hours earlier. I was glad my parents weren't home. Much easier without them lurking around, wanting to know everything.

My mood plummeted when I got outside and saw Jameson sitting up front in the passenger seat. My spot. Judging from the expression on his face, he wasn't all that thrilled to see me either. I got in behind and said (to the back of his head), "Hey, Jameson, glad you could join us."

Mallory made that wonderful melodic laugh of hers, but Jameson didn't react at all. The guy was a statue; he didn't even move his head. When Mallory glanced back, I pointed to Jameson and said, "You'd think a guy named after whiskey would be the life of the party, but apparently not."

She said, "Before we go, I want to do a little experiment, if you don't mind, Russ."

Jameson turned around now and both of them were looking at me a little too intently for my comfort level. "Okay, what do you have in mind?"

Mallory held up her right hand and wiggled her fingers. "I cut myself picking up pieces of a glass that broke in the dishwasher." Sure enough, her pointer finger was covered with a bandage. "I was hoping you could fix it." She peeled the bandage off and thrust her hand toward me; the top part of her finger had a small, jagged cut edged in dried blood.

"Fix it?"

"Don't play dumb," Jameson said. "You know what she wants. Touch her hand and make it go away."

"I told you that I don't—"

"Please?" Mallory asked sweetly. "For me? Just try."

"Okay." I had no idea how a person healed someone, but I could try to fake my way through it. I shook my hands, like a pianist before a big concert, and then leaned forward to take her hand in mine. I sandwiched her fingers between my two palms and closed my eyes, willing the cells in her skin to regenerate. *Heal*, I thought. *Heal*. There was a lot at stake and I wanted to come through, even if it were only to win Mallory's admiration and be part of the group. I held her hand for a minute or more, but no matter how hard I tried, I didn't feel healing powers coursing through my body. Truthfully, I felt nothing, except

completely ridiculous, especially when I opened my eyes and saw both of them staring at me. "I was concentrating," I explained. I took my hands away and Mallory inspected her finger. Without even seeing it, I knew the results.

"It didn't work," she said, clearly disappointed.

"What a surprise," Jameson said, every word tinged with sarcasm.

"Look, I never said I could heal people. You were the ones who came up with that conclusion."

"Maybe you just need time," Mallory said. "Maybe with practice..."

"Yeah, that's it." Jameson, again with the sarcasm.

"Or maybe it works a different way," she said. "Like you have to be standing a certain way or have a certain mindset. We can try again later. Let's just wait and see."

As if we had a choice. She sighed and turned the key, revving the engine. As we drove off down the road, I said, "Are we picking up Nadia?"

"Nadia never goes out," Jameson said, no expression in his voice.

I said, "That's not entirely true. I saw her out just the other night."

Mallory said, "Her mother never lets her out of her sight. Nadia sneaks out for our night walks. We all do."

"Well I knew that." It was coming back to me now. "Didn't you say that Nadia was attacked on a bus a few years ago? And that's why her mother is so overprotective and never lets her go anywhere?"

"Well, if you knew that why did you ask?" Jameson somehow managed to sound patronizing and bored at the same time. For a pencil-necked geek, he sure had a lot of confidence.

"Boys, boys," Mallory said. "Can't we all get along?" She turned down a side road that led to the outskirts of town. Something about it felt wrong.

"Where are we going?" I had a sudden sick feeling that I knew *exactly* where we were going, and I didn't like the idea at all.

"I thought that first we'd go past the field and see if there's any sign of the activity you saw the other night."

Jameson said, "Mallory told me about the claimed events. I'd like to take a look and see for myself."

It took me a second to process his insinuation that I was lying. "They weren't just claims," I said. "Everything I told Mallory was true. I saw a crew of men with detectors combing the field. Two armed guards were there and a guy who looked like he was supervising. When they saw me they chased me and shot at me. If you don't believe me, I can show you the bullet."

"That won't be necessary. I believe you have *a* bullet."

Complete silence. What he was implying, of course, was that I made up the whole story and was using some random bullet as proof. Mallory didn't come to my defense, and she had seemed to believe me Friday afternoon. "Going to the field is not a good idea," I said. "What if they're there and they recognize me?"

"The field is really far from the road," Mallory said. "They won't even be able to see our faces from that distance. We'll just swing by."

The last time I swung by the field someone had tried to kill me. I definitely had a bad feeling about this.

CHAPTER EIGHTEEN

———— o ————

When we got to the field, it couldn't have looked more deserted and less menacing. Of course, I told myself, everything looks safer in the light of day.

"The guys with the guns must have gone home," Jameson said to no one in particular, but I got it—he was needling me.

"I guess that trying to kill me tired them out," I said.

Mallory slowed the car to a stop. "I want to get a closer look." Before I could stop her, she was out of the car and walking up the incline toward the train station building. Jameson got out as well, leaving me in the back seat by myself. Fear kept me there for a moment, but peer pressure is a powerful thing and a second later I was right on his heels.

"I thought you were afraid," Jameson said, not turning around. "Or was it terrified?"

I wanted to make a smart-mouthed comment, but I'd decided a while earlier that I was better than that. Let Jameson be petty and superior and possessive of Mallory. All of those things made him look small and insecure. I would rise above his condescension. "I'm not afraid for me," I said. "I know I can outrun and

outsmart them. You, on the other hand, might need some protection."

He muttered something under his breath and kept going. Ahead of us, Mallory had reached the site and stopped. She stared at the ground intently, and when we approached, she said, "Amazing."

"What is it?"

"There's nothing," she said. "No signs that there were light fragments. No signs that anyone has been walking here. Didn't you say this area was staked out?" She looked up at me.

I nodded. "Like a crime scene. There were stakes in each corner connected by yellow tape. The men were walking inside of it."

She had a puzzled look on her face. "It doesn't look like anything's been disturbed."

"The grass has been trampled," I pointed out.

"It's spring. Everything looks like that after the snow melts," Jameson said.

I hated to admit it, but he was right.

"The last time the lights fell from the sky somebody actually scraped the top layer of the field and took it away." Mallory crouched down and touched the dirt. "I wonder why they did it differently this time."

"Probably because you made those phone calls asking about it," I said. "They decided not to draw so much attention to the field this time around."

"That's probably it," Jameson said, and he gave me a look that reminded me a little bit of admiration. "And if so, that means that the guys who shot at Russ are either from the government or someone who's got them in their pocket."

"Or they're aliens," I said, joking.

Mallory stood up and wiped her hands together to brush off the dirt. "No, we pretty much ruled out aliens, remember?"

"Maybe you did, but I'm still mulling it over," I said. "You know what they say—the truth is out there."

We wandered around a bit, pacing our way around the field, but nothing indicated that a big event had happened there just two days earlier. The unused train tracks were built on wood ties that were now crumbling, weeds growing in between the rails. The building, off in the distance, was the same. Just an old boarded-up structure with peeling paint and a cracked slab of concrete on either side of it. It was hard to believe I'd been afraid to come back here.

"Hey, Russ, want to see something cool?" Jameson asked after we'd inspected nearly every inch of the ground. Without waiting for a reply, he took his phone out of his pocket and held it loosely in his palm. As I watched, it levitated and zoomed around my head and zipped back to Jameson, who let it hover for a moment before he reached out to snatch it in midair.

"That is cool." I wasn't quite as flabbergasted as I'd been with the jelly packet, but I had to admit that Jameson could do something incredible. I was still doubtful that I would ever be able to heal people. (And even if I *had* healed myself before, could I do it again? Maybe Mallory was right and the circumstances had to be just right.)

"Show-off." Mallory poked Jameson's arm.

"That's nothing," he said. "I've been practicing with weights every day. I can move things farther and heavier than I ever could before, and my powers seem to get stronger with practice."

"A renewable energy," Mallory said thoughtfully. "I've noticed that with me, too. I haven't really been practicing though. It seems immoral somehow to make people do things without their consent."

"I could get past that," Jameson said.

I had a sudden thought. "So if you can move things with your mind, what makes you think you can't do other things too? Maybe you can also do mind control like Mallory and read people like Nadia. Have you even tried to do other things? Hey, maybe you can fly or turn invisible."

Jameson scowled. "It's been a year. If we had other abilities, they would have manifested themselves by now." He was back to the old Jameson, the one who knew better than me. Apparently our truce had been short-lived.

Heading back to the car, I held my hand out for Mallory as we approached the incline. It wasn't much of a drop, but she still took my hand for support, and I felt a surge of victory over poor Jameson, who, walking ahead of us, didn't even notice. "At my house yesterday we were interrupted right when you were going to tell me why we can't talk to the authorities," I said.

She squeezed my hand as we made our way over the last small bump and then let go when the ground leveled off. "Other kids before us have had this happen, and when they tried to tell, they disappeared or were killed."

I stopped. "You know this for a fact?"

Her face turned grave. "Fairly certain. Over the past thirty-five years a disproportionate number of teenagers from this area have suddenly died or disappeared, many of them after reporting seeing strange things in the sky. Some of their families also disappeared—just moved out of the area without a forwarding address. Like they were...relocated or something."

"How do you know this?"

"I spent hundreds of hours at the library looking at old copies of the local newspaper and the high school newspaper." She gave me a smile. "They actually used to print up little newspapers and sell them at the school. Isn't that cute?"

I was still stuck on the idea of missing teenagers. "Like how many are we talking about who died or disappeared?"

"Over the last thirty-five years there were maybe a dozen? I can show you a list if you want."

"Yeah, I think I'd like to see that," I said. It wasn't that I didn't believe her, because I did, but sometimes seeing something on a page helps my mind to make sense of things. And I needed to make sense of this.

"And here's another strange thing," Mallory said. "No one else seems to have observed the lights except for teenagers. Instead, on the dates the kids see the events, there are next-day reports of adults having had trouble staying awake that night—falling asleep at the wheel, dozing on the job, that kind of thing—which leads me to believe the light particles energize and draw some people, notably some teenagers, while having the opposite effect on adults. Some of the teenagers mentioned feeling compelled to go outside at night long before the lights appeared."

"Just like us."

Mallory nodded. "Exactly."

"Why would that be?"

She shrugged. "It would be hard to say without more information. I can only make conclusions based on the information at hand."

Because we'd paused to talk, Jameson had reached the car ahead of us, and now I saw that he appeared to be leaning over someone who was actually *inside* the car. Jameson's back was to us, and he was blocking our view, but I could see that the back door was open and he was hovering over a man who was slumped in the back seat in what had been my spot.

Jameson turned around and gestured frantically. "You guys, come quick! Hurry!" Mallory broke into a run, and I was right

behind her. Judging from Jameson's wide eyes and the way he bellowed, I knew it was something major. Still, when Mallory pushed Jameson aside, it took me a moment to register that it was Gordy, the old guy from the diner, who was lying across the back seat of the car.

"What happened?" I asked.

Mallory said, "Where'd he come from?"

"I don't know. I don't know." For once Jameson didn't look smug and sure. "I got to the car and there he was, just laying there. I think he's dead."

"Not dead yet." Gordy's voice came out soft and raspy. His whole body shuddered.

Mallory leaned in, giving me a view of her backside. "What happened, Gordy? Did someone do something to you?" she asked, and when he didn't answer, she whispered reassurances to him, telling him everything would be okay from now on. When she straightened up she went into take-charge mode—first handing Jameson the keys and telling him to get a blanket out of the trunk. I was next. "Help me move him," she ordered, and just like that I was pressed into service, following her instructions to pull Gordy further into the car so that his dangling legs were inside and we could close the car door. When Jameson came back with a green plaid blanket she folded it up and handed it to me. "Lift him up and cushion his head with it." She took the keys from Jameson and got into the front seat, barking orders as she went.

"Let's move."

"Hang in there, Gordy. We're going for help."

"Jameson, call the hospital and tell them we're on our way to the ER."

"Shouldn't we call 911?" Jameson asked.

"No!" Mallory yelled. "Just do what I tell you to do."

I was on the side of the car opposite the curb, trying to lift Gordy's head onto the folded-up blanket. The length of his body took up the entire back seat, begging the question: "Where am I going to sit?"

Mallory turned around and frowned. "Put his head on your lap, of course. Come on, Russ, get serious. We have an emergency here."

As if I weren't being serious. I sat on the edge of the seat and cautiously lifted his head as I slid in. When I shut the back door, his eyes fluttered. For the split second they were open, they locked on mine and he smiled briefly. "Hold tight, sir, we're going to the hospital," I said. He nodded slightly.

Jameson called Mercy Hospital to let them know we would be arriving to the ER soon. Listening to his end of the conversation, it was clear that not having all the answers rattled him. He couldn't tell the hospital Gordy's last name, his age, or even what was wrong with him. At one point they must have questioned the validity of the call because he said, "No, I'm not joking."

Mercy Hospital was in the city, a half hour away, but Mallory managed to get there in twenty minutes. She paused at red lights, looked both ways, and went through; she passed people in no-passing zones; she went eighty-five on the highway. Jameson said, "Jeez!" when she passed a semi on the two-lane highway and we found ourselves heading straight toward another car. Luckily, she was able to maneuver back into our lane with split-second timing. "If there's a cop around we're in trouble," Jameson added.

"I hope there is a cop around," she said. "We've got a dying man in the back seat who needs medical attention."

"Well, if we had called 911..." Jameson said.

Mallory gave him a sharp look and frowned. "And bring attention to us being at the field? Are you out of your mind?"

I sat in the back, not making stupid comments like some people, just taking it all in. I held my breath during the most harrowing turns, but otherwise, I didn't let myself get rattled at all. For the most part, I kept my gaze on Gordy. It would have been hard not to, considering he was right there, his head on the blanket on my lap. His wrinkled, dirty hands were pulled up to his whiskered chin. His mouth was slack, revealing two missing teeth. The teeth he still had were ragged and yellowed, probably from cigarettes. An acrid stink of smoke wafted off of him, reminding me of the overflowing ashtray in my great-aunt Trudy's car. I also got a whiff of the smell of burning rubber.

Gordy grunted occasionally like he was in pain, and I uttered things like, "Hang in there, sir," and "We'll be there soon." I'm not sure it helped, but it was the best I could do.

When we finally arrived at the entrance of the emergency room, I cracked open a window to air out the car. That burning odor was really getting to me.

Mallory threw the car into park, and she and Jameson ran inside to get help.

"We're here now, at the hospital," I said to Gordy, running a hand over his arm in a tentative show of compassion. I'd been wary of touching him, because I was afraid of hurting him and also because it's weird to be in such close contact with a complete stranger. Uncomfortably intimate. I was glad trained medical professionals would take over from here. I looked out the car window for signs that help was coming.

"Son?"

Startled, I looked down. "Yes?"

The old man's eyes were wide open now and he looked alert. I watched as he swallowed; his tongue flicked out over his cracked

lips, as if to wet them, but it didn't seem to help. "I tried so hard to get you back. So, so hard..."

"Are you talking to me?"

"I'm sorry I failed. So sorry."

"Mr. Gordy? Sir...I'm afraid I don't understand. What are you sorry for?"

Now his eyes narrowed, like he was trying to focus. "No, not you." Gordy exhaled and turned his head, mumbling. "I got confused. I meant the other one."

"What other one?"

"You look like him."

"Who?"

"My son."

His son? He was clearly delusional. Any son he had would have been at least fifty. I wouldn't be arriving at that age for a long, long time. "Do you want me to call your son?" I asked. "And let him know you're at the hospital?"

Gordy's forehead furrowed in thought. "No, not my son. My grandson. I'm so confused..." His eyes rolled as if he had no control over them. "But you can't call him. He's locked up—a prisoner. They have him." His hand flapped over the side of his pants. "Take it out of my pocket. You'll need it."

I wasn't following him at all. "Maybe if you tell me where he's a prisoner, I could contact him for you?"

"There's no time." His fingers trembled as he motioned to his pocket. "Get it out of my pocket."

I looked at the hospital, wondering what was taking them so long. Why did they have to leave me here with this mixed-up old man? "Maybe you should just hang on to it for now," I said. "When you're better, you'll need it." I patted his arm in what I hoped was a comforting way, but he shook off my touch.

"Take it," he said, this time his voice louder. "It will help you." His breathing was labored now. "He's still out there."

Oh, jeez. How could I not do what he asked, even if it didn't make sense? It was obviously important to him. Too bad it involved sticking my hand in his pants. There's sort of an unspoken rule that a guy never puts his hand in another guy's pocket. It's bad enough when I spot a dude making suspicious motions in his *own* pocket, much less me maneuvering in someone else's. I did a quick check out the window to make sure no one would see and think I was either robbing Gordy or making some perv move, and then I stuck my fingers in his pocket but felt nothing. "I'm sorry, sir. There's nothing in your pocket."

"Not that one." He grunted and grabbed my hand, forcing it to the seam alongside his thigh. "It's hidden, so they wouldn't find it."

I patted where he indicated and felt something below the surface of the cloth. I could see the stitching where the fabric came together. I couldn't see a pocket, and yet... I leaned over to inspect it, and then pulled at the seam. It came apart with the ripping sound of Velcro. The old man was right; he did have a hidden pocket.

I pulled out a folded piece of paper and held it in front of his face. "Is this what you want me to have?" It was thick, like it was wrapped around something. The whole wad was held together with a rubber band.

Gordy nodded and closed his eyes. A thin string of spittle formed on his lower lip, grossing me out a little bit. I wasn't cut out for dealing with sick people. He croaked out a few words. "Always carry it with you."

"Sure, I will," I said, patting his arm. "Don't worry about a thing."

"Don't tell anybody," he said. "You must keep it a secret." This last line came out in a wheeze. He was having trouble getting the words out. "You must find him."

"I promise."

I had started to unfold the paper when I noticed movement outside the car—Mallory and Jameson (finally!) rushing through the opening of the glass doors. Behind them, two men in scrubs pushed a gurney as big as a twin bed. "Here we go," I said to no one in particular. I slid out from under Gordy, making sure not to jolt his head as I left the car, then stuck the folded up wad of paper into my jeans pocket. The hospital attendants quickly went to work, wheeling him through the double doors with the three of us trailing behind.

The woman at the reception desk stopped Mallory by holding up a clipboard and saying they needed information about the patient. Jameson stayed glued to her side, but I kept going right behind Gordy and the two men. Someone buzzed us through a set of doors, and they picked up the pace until we were nearly running. Other people joined us as we moved down a corridor, a man and a woman, both wearing white jackets, their collars looped by stethoscopes. Doctors, I assumed.

After they wheeled the bed into a room shaped like a large curtained cubicle, the men in scrubs stepped away. The woman, who seemed to be a doctor, leaned over Gordy and clasped his arm. "Sir, you're at Mercy Hospital. Can you tell me if you're in any pain?" Gordy moaned, but didn't answer. She looked at me. "What's his name?"

"Gordy."

"Gordy," she said, this time more loudly. "We want to help you, but first we need some information." Other people had gath-

ered behind us, and she rattled off commands for an EKG and blood to be drawn. "Have you taken any medication today, sir?"

"No." Forcing the word out clearly took great effort.

She put the buds of her stethoscope in her ears and leaned over to listen to his heart. "Erratic heartbeat. Let's get moving with that EKG!"

Like a well-designed machine, the team sprang to action, one woman attaching a blood pressure cuff, another clipping what looked like a clothespin to his finger. A third unbuttoned Gordy's shirt, then unpeeled adhesive backings off electrodes and fastened them to his chest. I walked around to the foot of the bed to get out of their way.

"Did he fall?"

I was studying the bottom of Gordy's shoes and didn't realize the doctor was talking to me until she snapped her fingers in front of my face. "Was he injured? Did he fall? Did he complain of pain?"

"He was shocked." I pointed to the soles of his feet. Each one had a quarter-sized hole rimmed in charred black. Electricity had surged through his body and out his feet, melting a hole in his shoes. "With electricity. Shocked."

She came over to look where I was pointing. "Are you sure?"

I gulped and nodded.

"How did it happen?"

"I don't know," I said, and it was the truth. I didn't know *how* it happened, but I knew in my heart that he'd been shocked and I sensed it was on *purpose*. Even in the car I had somehow known this, but it took the scorched holes in his shoes to confirm it. Someone had done this to him.

But why?

CHAPTER NINETEEN

———— o ————

They hustled me out of the room so quickly I couldn't even look back. A heavyset young woman escorted me to a waiting area, which wasn't much more than a few padded chairs in a corner. "Someone will come and let you know how your grandfather is doing," she said. I didn't contradict her on the grandfather thing; it was easier that way. I sat down, unsure what to do next now that I was apart from the others. After seeing the blackened holes in the soles of Gordy's shoes, I wasn't about to look at what he'd given me out in public. I decided to wait a few minutes before I texted Mallory to see what she thought we should do next.

The TV suspended in the corner was on mute, which was just as well. They never had the right channels on in waiting rooms. Down the hall, I heard the sounds of controlled chaos: the squeaky wheels of carts being moved quickly, voices volleying back and forth, the electric beeps of machines monitoring vitals and keeping people alive. The ER had a slightly antiseptic odor, but above it I still smelled the smoke that had emanated from Gordy. It was in my nostrils now; I couldn't get away from it.

How excruciating would it be to have electricity surge through your body strong enough to shoot holes through the bottoms of your shoes? It had to have been horrible. He was a tough old geezer, still conscious and talking, even if he was confused. Soon enough we could ask him what had happened. Another piece of a puzzle that needed to be solved. I never asked to be part of this, but I was in too deep to turn back now.

I leaned my head back against the wall. What a night. What a week. Until recently, all I worried about was getting a good night's sleep and making it through sophomore year. Next summer I'd be sixteen, and that meant driving and a job and money. Now I had other things on my mind. Why would someone shoot at me? Who would electrocute an old man? And less important, but still puzzling—why would Mallory bring Jameson along on what was supposed to be our evening? I leaned forward and rested my head in my hands, suddenly tired.

I closed my eyes, but wasn't sleeping. Not even close. I still heard all the hospital noises. My eyelids couldn't quite shut out the fluorescent lights. Suddenly, I found that if I concentrated I could feel the electricity all around me, like being in the middle of a hot tub and knowing where the jets are located by feel. I felt it in every one of the millions of cells of my body, and I also felt it outside of my body too, as it coursed through the building. It was absolutely, mind-blowingly amazing. Like discovering I had picked up an extra sense somewhere along the way. Even with my eyes closed, I could visualize the electricity in the walls, the way it flowed through wires to outlets and then poured from the outlets into electrical cords, activating machines and powering lights. Somehow, crazy as it sounds, I understood that the electricity and I were one and the same. I almost had a handle on how that could be when I heard my name being called. "Russ!"

I looked up to see Mallory and Jameson jogging down the hall toward me.

I stood up to meet them halfway. "Can you feel it?" I asked when we were close. I held out my hands and whispered, "It just happened suddenly. I can source the electricity. I'm not sure how, but I can just feel it all around me."

Jameson said, "Why didn't you answer your phone?" He sounded irritated.

"My phone didn't go off."

"We have to leave right away," Mallory said.

I looked down the hall to where I'd left Gordy. "Can't we wait to see how he does?"

"We should have left already," she hissed, grabbing my arm and pulling me down the hallway. Jameson walked behind us, like he was her backup.

We passed the cubicle where the staff still hovered over Gordy. I paused. "Shouldn't we—"

Both of them said, "No!" in slightly hushed tones, and I let it go.

Mallory steered me down a hallway I hadn't seen before. I was sure she was turned around, so I said, pointing, "I think the way out is that way."

She didn't even pause, but just said, "We're using another way out."

When we got to the end of the corridor, Jameson hit a button to open the door. The sign said, "Caution, Door Swings Toward You," so we stood back, and when the door began opening, Mallory, still pulling me along, wasted no time, but slid through the opening, followed by Jameson, who was so close behind us he actually stepped on my heel as we exited the hospital on the side of the building.

"What's going on?" I asked as we made our way through row after row of parked vehicles. "Where's the car?"

"I moved it over here," Mallory said, not slowing down at all. When we got to her vehicle, she unlocked the doors with a beep and slid into the front seat. Jameson and I quickly got into our respective spots, and she was zooming out of the lot before I even had the chance to put my seat belt on.

"Good grief, was that close," she said as we turned onto the road and sped away. I glanced back and saw the hospital getting smaller through the rear window. "I just about had a heart attack when I saw those men come in. I was afraid they were going to see us."

CHAPTER TWENTY

———— o ————

"What men?" I asked, but my words were drowned out by Jameson, who had his hands raised in the air like he was on a roller coaster. "That was wild!" he yelled, stretching the word "wild" so it went on and on. "I can't believe we did that! I can't believe how you messed with that nurse's mind. And did you see how I made that cart tip over? We rule!" He paused to punch Mallory's shoulder. "Woo-hoo! I've never had a feeling like that before. That was awesome."

Mallory gave him a sideways glance. "Awesome, but very scary."

"What happened?" I asked.

Jameson turned completely around to tell me the story and narrated using his hands for emphasis. I'd never seen the guy so hyped before. It was like someone reanimated a corpse. The way he told the story involved telling me every detail, complimenting himself on his quick thinking and his use of telekinesis as a distraction.

I could have told the story in about three sentences, but he went on for fifteen minutes. According to Jameson, this is how it

went: After I left them in the reception area, Mallory pretended to fill out the form to make the nurse happy. She didn't give them our names, and she didn't know anything about Gordy, so she filled in some nonsense and used mind control to make the nurse think the form was complete and that he was completely insured.

"You should have seen it!" Jameson crowed. "Mallory is like, 'The form has all the information you need,'" and the woman is like, "Oh good, he's got complete coverage."

"Then I went out and moved the car so it wasn't blocking the entrance," Mallory added.

And after that, Jameson said, two men came in—the same two men Jameson had seen at the library. "We were sitting in the waiting area at the time," Mallory said. "Texting you. Or trying to text you."

I pulled my phone out of my pocket. Sure enough, they'd texted me, but my phone was on silent.

Jameson said, "The two men were dressed the same way as when I saw them at the library. Dark suits, black shoes, ties, like businessmen. They walked right up to the desk and asked about a patient who had just been brought into the ER, Gordon Hofstetter. One of them said Mr. Hofstetter was his father." He made a dismissive noise. "Like anyone was going to believe that."

"You should have seen the look on Jameson's face when he saw those two guys," Mallory said. "I thought he was going to curl up in a ball and start whimpering."

"That's not true," he said, giving her a steely-eyed look. "Why would you say that?" He turned back to me. "The woman at the desk asked them to wait while she went and checked, and then to distract them, I knocked over a cart full of supplies." He tapped his forehead. "Using only the power of my mind, Russ."

Mallory interjected the next part. "So I took advantage of the commotion to follow the nurse into the examining area. When I caught up to her, I did my mind magic and told her that a middle-aged woman named Marge Schaeffer had brought Gordy to the hospital. I even gave her a description."

"And this worked?" I asked incredulously.

Mallory's head bobbed up and down. "She would have testified in a court of law. Tomorrow she's going to have a headache."

When the nurse came back, she told the men that Marge Schaeffer had brought Mr. Hofstetter in and described her exactly as Mallory had specified. And when a bunch of guys came into the hospital carrying a buddy who'd been beaten in a bar fight, it was enough of a distraction that Jameson and Mallory were able to follow another staff member through the double doors to come and find me.

"So that's why we went out the side door?" I asked. "To avoid the men in the suits?"

"Of course," Jameson said, smug as usual.

"And why are we dancing around these guys again?" I leaned forward to address my question to Mallory. I'd had enough of Jameson. "Why not just ask them what the story is? For all we know, they're the good guys."

The car screeched over to the side of the road so fast I thought my head would snap off. Mallory threw the car into park, put on the four-way flashers, and twisted around to face me. "Russell Becker, I hope you're joking." Her voice was raised and her face contorted in anger.

Jameson said, "I had my doubts about this guy from the beginning. I told you that. I say you wipe him out."

I held up a hand to block Jameson's face out of my view and kept it there. "It's hard to believe you're both geniuses because

you're acting like idiots. I'm not saying we tell anyone about the light particles or the field, or your powers. But what's wrong with saying we found an old man who needed medical help? How are we going to get more information if we just skulk around dodging people?"

Mallory shook her head. "Are you not the same guy who was freaked out just yesterday because you'd been chased and shot at the night before? Do I really have to explain to you how dangerous it would be to voluntarily come forward?"

"But isn't it even more dangerous keeping it just to ourselves?"

Jameson batted at my hand. I lowered it and gave him a smile before continuing. "Look at it this way. If something happens to us, wouldn't you want our families to have some information about what's going on? Maybe, if the other kids had gone to the media, the ones you say were killed or disappeared, they'd have been protected by the authorities. Maybe they would have stayed safe."

Jameson dramatically lowered his head in his hands and wailed. "Mallory, I can't believe you vouched for this guy. A chimp has more sense."

"Mallory?" I wanted to hear her reaction and not his; right now, I'd have said she looked conflicted.

"So what exactly are you proposing?" she asked. "Who do we tell—our parents, the police, the FBI? And what exactly do we tell them? The whole truth or only part of it? Are you prepared for the repercussions? Have you even *thought* about the possible repercussions? Because we have. We've worked out every possible scenario, and believe me, none of them are good." When I didn't say anything, she said, "I'll tell you what, Russ. You go ahead and tell anyone anything you want. Nobody is going to stop you."

Jameson said, "*I* would stop him and—"

"But here's the thing," she said, waving Jameson's words away. "None of us is going to back you up either. If you say we're involved, we'll say you're crazy and we don't know what you're talking about."

"You'll be on your own, pal," Jameson said. "We're not backing you up. We'll say you're crazy."

"Yeah, I think I got that since Mallory said the exact same thing a second ago."

Mallory said, "Look, we've all been through a lot recently. Russ, would it be possible for you to think about this for the next few days before you do anything?"

A few days? What could possibly happen in the next few days? Sure, I could wait. "Yeah, I guess so."

"You better keep it to yourself," Jameson said. "Do you know how much trouble Nadia would be in if her mother found out she'd been going out at night?"

That would be the least of our troubles. "I already agreed not to say anything. Just yet," I added.

"Well I'm glad that's settled." Mallory started up the engine and fiddled with the radio, finally settling on an old Nirvana song. Something about a mulatto and an albino and a mosquito. The lyrics made absolutely no sense, but hearing a familiar song pulled me back into my everyday world and made me feel better. After flicking on the turn signal, Mallory did a cursory back-and-forth glance at the road before pulling off the shoulder, and then we were back on our way. We didn't go far before she said, "I hope you guys don't mind if I cut the evening short. I have a bad headache and I want to go home."

"No wings?" Jameson sounded disappointed. "But I'm starting to really get hungry."

"Maybe another time." She met my eyes in the rearview mirror. "Okay with you, Russ?"

"Of course." The thought of going out for wings with Jameson there spoiled the whole date night concept. "Whatever you want, Mallory."

We dropped Jameson off first. Turned out he lived in a biggish house in the wealthy end of town. Rich Edgewood. No surprise there. I had him pegged as a privileged sort of guy. We drove up the circular drive and under an overhang, the kind you see in front of hotels. White pillars flanked either side, and a stone lion sat to the left of the enormous door. "Well, here you are," Mallory said, her voice full of false cheer. "The end of another wonderful Saturday night."

He had his hand on the door, but he didn't seem like he wanted to leave. "Thanks for driving, Mallory. When I get my license, we can go in my dad's Corvette." He leaned forward like he wanted to kiss her or something, but she just looked straight ahead.

"That would be great," she said, and then to me, "Russ, why don't you get in front?"

I scrambled out of the car, and Jameson was forced to get out. He stood on the porch and waved as we drove away. I glanced back and said, "I thought he'd never leave."

Mallory laughed, and suddenly all was right with the world. "He's not too bad. A little insecure so sometimes he acts superior, but overall he's okay."

"A little insecure and acting superior doesn't sound okay to me."

"He's the only one of us who's a true genius," she said. "Nadia and I are in accelerated classes and we both do exceptionally well, but Jameson is way beyond either of us. He actually has an IQ of

like 186 or something. Of course, the IQ test as a measurement of intelligence is a matter of debate."

"Of course."

"Still, he's undeniably gifted academically."

"Sure. Yeah, I can see it." I tapped my fingers on the dashboard. "But he can be kind of a whiny baby at times." She smiled but didn't contradict me. Neither of us spoke for a time, Mallory because she was driving, and me because I was starting to pick up on electricity again. I felt it coming from the engine compartment through the radio. At its source, which I knew to be the battery, the car electricity felt different than what I'd experienced at the hospital, and different yet from the power lines I sensed as we drove past. So odd, being able to pick up on electricity; it was like being able to see in the dark. I wondered at the fact that electricity is all around us, yet people go through their days oblivious to its presence.

Mallory turned off the radio and my eyes opened. "What's on your mind, Russ?" she said softly. "The look on your face is freaking me out a little."

"I'm concentrating," I explained. "On the electricity. I can feel it now. It started in the hospital. I was aware of it surging and pulsing all around me. I can sense it even when I close my eyes, and if I really quiet my mind, it's like it speaks to me. I know where it's coming from and how strong it is. You know what I'm talking about. You guys have had this happen, right?"

She shook her head. "No."

"But you can sense it?" I gestured to the electrical poles that dotted the roadside. "Outside it hums like music through the wires." I patted the dashboard. "And I can feel how it powers the radio. So amazing."

"So this sensing thing is happening to you right now?"

"Well, yes. It's not like something that happens now and again. It's there all the time. It just is."

"Hmmm…" She turned into my subdivision. "The light particles do appear to affect everyone differently, based on what I've seen with the three of us. And what you experienced on your night was in all probability different than what we experienced, so it would make sense that you were affected differently as well."

"When I was out in the field, and the particles fell all around me, I felt—"

"Wait a minute!" For the second time that night Mallory suddenly pulled the car over to the side of the road. This time a little more smoothly. "The particles fell all around you? You stood inside the spiral while the light fragments came down around you?"

"It was mostly done falling by the time I got there," I said. "But while I was in the middle of the spiral, more did come down, yeah."

"And it didn't burn you?"

"No, the pieces glowed, but they were warm, not hot."

"Huh." With one hand she smoothed the wheel to the left and continued the drive to my house. "I wonder what that means…"

"I don't know."

We drove on. I noticed that the sun had dropped in the sky while we were at the hospital. The headlights of the car lit the road ahead of us, and I felt the way the electricity reached from the battery to the headlamps to make that happen. How had I gone a lifetime not even noticing this?

Finally, Mallory pulled into my driveway. It seemed like a day had passed since she'd first picked me up, but it had been only a few hours. "Well, this it, I guess," she said.

I unclasped my seat belt before extending my right hand. "Thanks for a nice evening and for driving."

"No problem."

I thrust my hand closer. "Take my hand, Mallory."

"What?"

I ignored her puzzled expression. "It's a social custom. Maybe you've heard of it? Shaking hands? Put it there."

Still bemused, Mallory gave me her hand. I sandwiched it between mine and focused all my thoughts and energy on our touch. We were two separate people linked by skin and bone and blood and energy. Especially energy. The energy from me hummed right at the point of contact. From the look on her face I could tell she felt it too. Her head tilted toward me and her eyes lit up with amazement. "Whoa," she whispered.

And then, it felt done. Abruptly, I let go and her hand dropped. I said, "Thanks again, Mallory. See you at school."

I was halfway to my front door when she rolled down her window. "Russ?"

"Yes?"

She waved her hand out the car window. "The cut on my finger is gone."

I nodded. I knew it would be.

CHAPTER TWENTY-ONE

———————— o ————————

Later that night, when I was almost asleep, it occurred to me that maybe I could use my powers to heal Gordy. I sat up in bed, turned on my nightstand lamp, and rubbed my eyes. If Jameson and Mallory hadn't been so eager to leave the hospital, I might have thought of it while I was still there. Now it was after midnight and I had no way to get to the hospital. For my own peace of mind, I looked up the number to Mercy Hospital and called the front desk to inquire about Gordon Hofstetter.

The woman who answered the phone asked me to spell his last name.

I gave it my best guess. "I think it's spelled H-O-F-S-T-E-T-T-E-R. First name, Gordon. He came into the ER earlier this evening." I was careful to speak quietly, knowing that Frank was asleep on the other side of the wall. Nothing worse than a hyped-up ten-year-old awake after midnight.

I heard the sounds of a keyboard clicking before she came back on the line and said, "I'm sorry, we don't have a patient by that name."

"Does that mean he was released?"

"I'm sorry, sir. I can't give out that information. Hospital policy." She did sound a little sorry, anyway.

I hung up feeling better. Best-case scenario—Gordy had been stabilized and released. They didn't keep anyone at the hospital anymore if they didn't have to. Last I saw, the old guy was doing pretty well. Considering he'd been electrocuted.

Thinking about Gordy nudged something in my brain. When I remembered what I'd forgotten, I almost smacked my forehead with my palm like they do in the movies. I still had his wad of paper in my jeans pocket. Or at least I thought I did. Oh man, I hoped it hadn't fallen out at some point.

I got up and crossed the room to where my clothes were on the floor in a crumpled heap. It only took a second to check my pocket. Relieved, I found the folded paper still there.

Sitting cross-legged on my bed, I took off the rubber band and unfolded the paper to find it was wrapped around a silver medallion. As large as a belt buckle, it was octagonal in shape and had what looked like a clear gemstone in the center. I held it up to the light and found that it looked more like glass than crystal—old glass, the kind with ripples in it. Around the glass, a spiral pattern was etched. The same kind of spiral I'd seen in the field.

I set the medallion down and turned my attention to the paper, but it was blank except for some light scribbles. Just something to wrap the medallion in? No, there were some numbers and some shapes, so light I could barely see them. I set it aside for now.

I folded the medallion back in the paper and tucked it under my keyboard on my desk. It would be safe enough there. I'd figure it out tomorrow.

I turned out the light and settled back under the covers, happy that it was Saturday night, because that meant I had another day

before the school week started up again. I'd had an unbelievable week, but I wanted a break from thinking about it. Maybe things would die down and life would get back on track.

Sunday was usually my time to do homework and relax, except for the weekends Frank stayed over, and then the day had a whole new meaning, as I was reminded the very next morning. "We're going to the comic book store!" he said, bouncing around the kitchen. It was nearly noon, and he'd been up for ages while I tried to sleep in. For at least two hours I'd overheard Frank pleading with my mom to let him wake me up, while she held firm, saying he should let me sleep. I appreciated it. She would be justly rewarded when Mother's Day rolled around. "Comic book store, comic book store!" The kid was like Tigger on steroids.

I spooned more Lucky Charms into my mouth and regarded him with amusement. The school had him tested for ADD and it had been ruled out, but I wasn't entirely convinced. "We aren't going for a while," I told him, "so you might as well find something to do for the next hour."

"Not a whole hour," he wailed. "Why can't we leave when you're done with your cereal?"

"Sorry, Frank. I'm not doing anything until I take a shower."

An hour later, Dad gave us each twenty dollars and dropped us off at the entrance to the strip mall. "A little something for my two favorite guys," he said, pulling out his wallet and ceremonially handing us each a crumpled bill. I almost turned down the money. It's a little embarrassing at my age, but then I thought, *Hey, twenty dollars! For nothing.* And Dad seemed so happy to be handing it out I didn't want to hurt his feelings.

"Thanks, Dad," I said, tucking it into my pocket.

"You're welcome, son."

The strip mall parking lot was known for being crowded; cars often had to pull over or back up to let other cars through. It was a poor design, according to my dad, and he said the lanes were oddly configured. This was his excuse for dropping us off at the entrance instead of driving us right up to the door. Truthfully, I preferred it that way. If anyone from my high school was there I'd rather they not see my dad driving me like I was a sixth grader. Walking wasn't that much cooler, but it was better anyway.

Ahead of us on the sidewalk, three boys about Frank's age were running in circles trying to push each other into the parking lot, in front of oncoming cars. Compared to them, Frank looked like a rocket scientist. I was just about to make a comment, when Frank said, "Russ, can I ask you a question?"

"I think you already did."

He continued without acknowledging my cleverness. "Why doesn't my dad love me?"

"What?" My legs stopped mid-stride and he stopped walking too. "Who told you that?"

Frank's head drooped and his lower lip quivered. Jeez, the kid was practically crying. It was hard to believe that only ten minutes earlier he'd been jumping-out-of-his-skin excited about comic books. Talk about a mood switch.

"Was it your mom? Did she say that?" I asked, anger rising from my chest.

"No." He shook his head and toed a crack in the sidewalk.

"Who then?"

"No one ever talks about him," Frank said. "What's his name? What's he like?" He looked up and I could see his eyes had filled with tears.

"I don't know. I never met him. Neither have Grandma or Grandpa."

A woman with a stroller approached and expertly maneuvered over the curb and around us. When I turned my attention back to Frank, I saw that he was waiting for me to say more. I leaned over to look him in the eye. "Here's the thing, Frank, I don't know anything about your dad. Your mom is the only one who would be able to tell you anything about him. I honestly don't know if he loves you or if he doesn't love you. But I'll tell you one thing, if he doesn't, it's his loss." I rested my hand on Frank's shoulder. "Because you're just about the greatest kid I know."

"Really?" He looked at me with those needy puppy dog eyes, and I felt a surge of anger at his father for putting him through this.

"Yeah, really. If you want to know the truth, I feel sorry for the guy. He's got this really cool son and he's missing out. Meanwhile, I'm lucky because I get to hang out with you on the weekends."

"Mom said you think I'm annoying. She told me not to bother you so much."

Oh Carly, I thought, *why would you say that to him?* I punched him on the arm. "Okay, you can be a little bit annoying at times, but I can deal with it. We're war buddies, right?"

He wiped his eyes with his knuckles. "Don't tell anyone we talked about this, okay, Russ?"

"Talked about what?" I said, and then gestured for him to keep walking. "Come on. It's Sunday afternoon. Let's go hang at the comic book store."

Power House Comics had been around since before I was born. Comic books took up most of the store, but the place also carried trading cards, posters, and collectibles like superhero figures. As generous as my dad had been, twenty dollars wouldn't

go far, but if Frank came up short I was willing to kick in some of my own money.

A jangling bell signaled our entrance. The place was fairly busy for a Sunday, but no one looked up. A dozen customers, mostly teenagers, flipped through classic comic books in free-standing fixtures, looking for that one rare find. Those comics were sealed in plastic so they'd retain their value, while the newer ones were displayed in revolving racks. Frank went right to the racks. Comic books weren't an investment for him; he just liked to read them. Buying new, he'd get more for his twenty dollars.

Some kind of crazy techno music filled the place, and two teenage girls swayed to the music in front of a glass case displaying action figures. Girls often came into the store, hoping to catch the eyes of the guys, but it rarely worked. Generally speaking, comic book aficionados are serious customers and a little on the shy side. Not a good combination for picking up chicks.

I wandered around a little bit, killing time while Frank decided what to spend his money on. We'd be here at least an hour or two, and then I knew he'd expect we'd walk down to the frozen custard shop afterward where he'd have a cone and I'd have a root beer float. In a way, I reflected, my dad and I were Frank's only male influences, if you didn't count Carly's revolving-door boyfriends, and I didn't. I decided to be nicer to the kid from now on.

I leaned against a glass counter and pretended to study the contents, very old comic books dating from the 1960s. I put my hands flat on the counter and, closing my eyes, paid attention to the electricity in the store. I sensed the flow into the fluorescent lights overhead and the cash register at the main counter behind me. The electricity didn't always come in one continuous stream. Like water flowing through the tap, there were variances. I took

a deep breath and tried to figure out what I was supposed to be doing with this new awareness. I didn't know if it was connected to the way I'd healed Mallory's finger or not. Probably not, I decided. It felt like two separate things.

"Can I help you?"

Jolted out of my thoughts, I glanced up to see a familiar face. "Mr. Specter?"

He grinned. "Mr. Becker. Imagine seeing one of my favorite students here at Power House Comics." Mr. Specter looked just as he had in science class earlier in the week: same glasses, white shirt, and sweater vest. It was him, no doubt about it, but I still had trouble believing what I was seeing. Looped around his neck was a plastic-covered tag with his name, Samuel Specter, topped by the store logo.

"You work here?"

"Yes, I do. Sometimes." He took off his glasses and wiped them with a handkerchief he'd produced from his vest pocket. "The owner is a good friend of mine. I fill in when he's short-handed."

I had trouble wrapping my brain around this. I mean, I knew teachers didn't make a lot of money, but I'd never seen one working in a store before. "Do you like comic books?"

"I have a certain fondness for the genre," he said, putting his glasses on and carefully folding the handkerchief into a neat triangle before tucking it back into his pocket. "In my opinion, comic books are an incredible art form like no other. And of course, like many readers, I have a special regard for the super-hero concept."

"Oh."

He pointed to the comics in the case below. "I love reading about ordinary men who acquire superpowers through

extraordinary means, and who then grapple with everything that comes along with it—defeating villains, moral dilemmas, secrets from family and friends, alter egos. There's no end of possibilities, wouldn't you say?"

"I guess so." Was I imagining things, or was he staring me down? What did he know, if anything? I glanced back to see Frank talking to the three boys we'd seen on the sidewalk outside. The smart ones who were trying to push each other in front of oncoming cars. Frank had a comic book clutched to his chest, and one of the others, an obnoxious-looking boy wearing a backwards baseball cap, was trying to take it away from him. "Excuse me," I said to Mr. Specter. "I have to check on my nephew."

I hurried over to Frank's side and caught the other boys making taunting noises, but I couldn't make out the words. "What's going on here?" I demanded. The three looked to be a little older than Frank, and all of them were full of undeserved swagger. The ringleader, Backwards Cap Boy, had "bully" written all over his face. I can tell you right now that under the same circumstances, at their age, I would have backed away from a bigger teenager, but not these three. They had balls of steel.

"We're just talking to Frank," Backwards Cap said. "Right, Frankie?" The other two kids, one with a weasel face and one who looked not too bright, stood alongside their leader, grinning like they thought the whole thing was funny.

Frank didn't say anything, but held the comic book to his front, his forehead aimed at the carpet. "Whatever you're doing, you're done now," I said to them and grabbed Frank's arm, pulling him over to the other side of the store. In low tones I asked, "What were those punks doing? You can tell me."

He glanced their way and I thought I saw fear in his eyes. "It's okay, Russ. They were just playing around."

"It didn't look like playing around to me."

"I don't mind them, really."

I considered for a moment, and let it drop. "Well, okay, if you say so, but I'm sticking to your side from now on." We spent the next hour looking through racks of comic books. I told Frank I'd make up the difference if he went over his twenty-buck limit, and he reacted like Christmas came early. I watched Mr. Specter as he worked behind the register, making small talk, ringing up sales, giving change. He did a good impression of a store clerk and he never looked my way, so why did I feel like he was spying on me? At the same time I also kept an eye on the three punks. Such little scumbags, so full of themselves. I was relieved when they left the store. They didn't buy anything, of course.

When it was time to check out, Frank, feeling shy, tried to get me to handle the transaction, but I told him he had to take care of it himself. Mr. Specter greeted us when we walked up to the counter. "So you're Russ's nephew?" he asked.

"Uh-huh." Frank set his comics down.

"Mr. Specter is my science teacher," I said, although why I bothered to explain I didn't know. Frank didn't seem to care.

"I taught Carly Becker too, way back when," Mr. Specter said. "Is she a relation of yours?"

"She's my mom!" Frank said, suddenly interested.

"I didn't know you had my sister as a student," I said. Most of my teachers were Carly's age. It never occurred to me that she and I would have had a teacher in common. I'd heard enough about her high school years that I could only imagine his opinion of her.

"Oh yes, indeed, she was a memorable student." He picked up a comic book and scanned it, then worked his way through Frank's pile. "A freethinker."

That's one way to put it, I thought.

"Did my mom get good grades in your class?" Frank asked. Inwardly I winced, since I was sure of the answer.

"It was a long time ago, and I don't remember what grade she earned," Mr. Specter said. "I do remember some spirited discussions in that class. She and the Hofstetter boy were quite the pair. They always had something to say."

The name Hofstetter hit me right between the eyes. How many could there be in Edgewood? There had to be a connection. "The Hofstetter boy—is he related to Gordon Hofstetter?"

Mr. Specter nodded. "*Was* related. His grandson. A sad, sad story. The boy died in a car accident his junior year. Gordon never got over it." He looked at Frank. "That will be twenty-two dollars and sixty-eight cents, young man."

I had to know more. "Do you know Gordon Hofstetter?"

Frank fished around in his pocket for his money, and not finding it, started emptying his pocket, one thing at a time. Bottle caps, gum wrappers, loose change. The kid carried around more junk than anyone I knew. Mr. Specter didn't get impatient; he just smiled and answered my question. "Gordon and I were once good friends, but we've drifted apart. He's had a lot of troubles, poor soul."

"Alcohol?"

"That came later. Gordon had a sad life. His wife died giving birth to their only child. He raised that child, a boy, by himself. It was hard. And then years later, his only grandchild, David, died in a horrible accident. David was a good kid. He'd just gotten his driver's license and must have been driving too fast. They're not sure what happened, but his car went down the embankment on Highway 12 and exploded. The firefighters came to the scene too late to do anything but contain the fire."

"How terrible." I tried to look sympathetic, but I didn't really feel that way, maybe because I didn't know the family. Instead, I was fascinated by the thought that maybe this David Hofstetter was the true love my sister had mentioned. Her words echoed in my mind: *When I was your age, I found true love, and it hasn't happened since. I keep looking for it, but nothing compares.* And then: *He died.* My parents had to know about this. How was it that no one ever mentioned it to me?

Mr. Specter absentmindedly fingered one of Frank's bottle caps. "Gordon never got over it. And after that, David's parents moved away to California and Gordon felt abandoned and alone. It's no wonder he turned to the bottle to drown his sorrows."

"Found it," Frank said, triumphantly holding his twenty in the air for a second before handing it over. I got out my wallet and gave Mr. Specter a five-dollar bill to cover the balance.

The cash drawer opened with an old-fashioned ding, and Mr. Specter made change, which Frank was going to take until I cleared my throat and moved his hand aside. I was putting the singles in my wallet and Frank was scooping his junk off the counter when Mr. Specter said, "What's this?"

I glanced up to see him pick something up from the counter. He peered intently at it over the top of his glasses.

"That's a stone from my collection," Frank said.

"He collects everything," I explained. "The kid has buckets filled with stuff."

"I'm sort of a collector myself," Mr. Specter said. "Would you consider selling this to me?"

Frank said, "Maybe."

"I'll give you twenty dollars for it."

Frank's eyes got big. "Twenty dollars? Sure thing!"

Mr. Specter moved quickly, putting the stone in his pocket and opening the cash register drawer. "I'll tell you what, young man, I'll even give you a brand-new twenty." He handed Frank a crisp bill, and the kid bounced forward on the balls of his feet to reach over the counter to take it.

This whole exchange confused me. None of the junk in Frank's pocket was worth even one dollar, much less twenty. Mr. Specter must have seen the other kids picking on Frank and decided to do something nice to make up for it. It was a kind gesture, but a little weird. "You don't need to do that," I said to Mr. Specter. "That's a lot of money for a stone."

"Believe me, it's my pleasure to do business with a budding geologist."

Frank admired the money, a smile on his face. "Whoa! This has turned out to be an awesome day. First Grandpa gives me twenty dollars, and now I got this one."

"I'm happy it worked out for both of us," Mr. Specter said.

"But—" I started to object, but another customer stood behind us, waiting to check out, and Mr. Specter motioned for him to come forward.

"See you in school tomorrow, Mr. Becker," he said, dismissing us.

CHAPTER TWENTY-TWO

---o---

As Frank and I walked out of the store, the kid was still talking about what a good day he was having and how great it was to hang out with Uncle Russ. Not exactly a thank-you, but I took it that way anyhow. If it weren't for me, he'd have been back at the house watching TV all afternoon.

We headed down the sidewalk toward the frozen custard shop, and when we got there, I saw the place was half filled and that the three punks were sitting up front by the display case, underneath a sign that said: TODAY'S FLAVOR: MINT CHOCOLATE CHIP.

"Hey, Frank, how's it going?" Weasel-Face said in this really smart-mouth way. If he'd been my size, I would have been tempted to call him out. I'll give Frank credit though, he ignored him and kept his gaze on the glass cooler full of the different tubs of frozen custard.

"I don't know why you look, you always wind up getting the same thing," I said.

Sure enough, five minutes later we were at a table, me with my root beer float and Frank with his double dip chocolate

waffle cone. We sat at a table as far away from the three boys as possible, but I kept my eye on them. I know most kids that age are obnoxious, but these three idiots took it to a new level. Backwards-Cap was the definite leader, and the other two followed everything he did. When he laughed (this annoying, donkey-like bray), the other two did too. When people went up to the counter to order, he'd repeat what they said in a mocking way. I wanted to smack the kid. When Backwards-Cap stuck his foot out to trip an old lady with a cane (she saw it and walked around), I was ready to get up and say something, but Frank, reading the intention on my face, said, "Let it go, Russ, just let it go."

"What are their names?" I asked.

He regarded me suspiciously. "Why do you want to know?'

"Don't worry, I'm not going to make a big scene or report them or anything. I just want to know." When he didn't answer I leaned forward, my voice low. "The one who doesn't know how to wear a baseball cap, what's his name?" He looked nervously in their direction. "Frank Shrapnel," I said, poking the table with mock impatience. "I believe I asked you a question." He grinned. Frank loved it when I used his middle name.

"That's Kyle," he said. "I don't know the other kids. They're all a year ahead of me."

Kyle. In old books and movies, bullies had names like Sluggo or Scut Farkus. Kyle wasn't a threatening-sounding name at all. "So what's Kyle's last name?"

"You're not going to call his house or anything?" He looked over at the three punks, a worried look on his face.

"No, I swear this is just between us. It won't go any farther."

"It's Bischmann. Kyle Bischmann."

"And he gives you grief about not having a dad."

Frank nodded and put his cone up to his mouth to lick away a drip.

Kyle Bischmann. What kind of insensitive dirtbag torments someone about their missing father? I watched Kyle across the room, laughing his stupid braying laugh, and suddenly I found myself madder than I've ever been in my life. At my side, my curled fists pulsed with spasms of barely-contained energy. I seriously wanted to kill the kid. Pictures filled my head—flashes of me pounding on Kyle Bischmann and his moron friends. Another picture came to me too, and this one was even worse: me shooting lightning bolts from my palms into their chests and watching them recoil in pain as their flesh sizzled. I felt my muscles strain like I was lifting weights at the gym. "Look," I said to Frank, my voice a deep growl I barely recognized, "if Bischboy every does anything to you, anything at all, you let me know and I'll take care of him for you."

Frank's eyes got wide with delight and he laughed. "Bischboy! That's really funny, Russ. I'm going to tell everyone at school that you said that."

And just like that, I snapped out of it and my anger faded. Kyle turned from a monster who had to be destroyed to a stupid eleven-year-old kid who thought he was hot stuff. I shuddered, thinking how close I'd come to getting up and walloping him across the face. How would that have looked? I outweighed Kyle by fifty pounds. If I'd lost control and hit him unprovoked, who would be the bully then? I probably would have gotten hauled off to jail.

I shook my head. "He's just a jerk," I said to Frank. "He's got nothing on you."

"He comes to my class for math," Frank said. "He got held back in a few subjects." We sat for a few minutes without talking.

When the frozen custard in his cone was nearly gone, he started nibbling on the edges of his waffle cone. "This is really good."

Kyle and his cohorts made a point to walk right past us as they left the place. "Bye, Frankie," Kyle said.

Frank didn't even look up. "Bye, Kyle. See you in math."

Kyle looked a little startled, but he didn't say anything back, just kept going.

At that moment, I saw Frank with a new admiration. You think you know someone and then you see another side of them and you realize there's more there than you gave them credit for. "You are one cool little dude," I said, and his cheeks flushed pink at the praise. He wasn't such a bad kid. I'd have to start pointing out his positive traits more often.

We were finishing up when I said, making small talk, "What are you going to do with that twenty dollars you got from Mr. Specter?"

He shrugged. "I don't know. Maybe give it to my mom. She comes up short a lot."

I'd heard that expression from Carly more than once. She borrowed money from my folks all the time and that was always her excuse. "I'm coming up short this month." My mom wasn't all that sympathetic, but my dad was a sucker for her sad stories. She never asked me for money, which was good because I wouldn't have given her any. "You shouldn't have to give your mom money," I said. "Parents give kids money, not the other way around. Grown-ups are supposed to be the responsible ones."

"Yeah, I know. She just has problems." Frank sighed and I saw how her problems sometimes became his problems and how that weighed heavily on him. No wonder he liked coming to our house where he could just be a kid. "Besides, it's just extra money

for a stone I got from the mud on your shoes, and Grandma already paid me two dollars for cleaning the shoes."

Wait a minute—I reached over and grabbed his arm. "Let me get this straight. You got that stone out of the bottom of my shoe?" His words triggered something, and my head reeled with the sequence of events that must have occurred for this to have happened. I saw it in a collage of images: me walking at night in a damp field among (apparently) magic light particles; Frank cleaning the bottom of my shoes the next day; him (I now knew) removing a stone from bottom of said shoe and keeping it, and finally, Mr. Specter buying that same stone from Frank. As I was figuring this out, Frank had a worried look on his face like he was afraid that answering my question would get him in trouble. I tried again. "So you're saying that the stone Mr. Specter bought from you came from my shoe?"

His head bobbed up and down. "Grandma told me to clean 'em. They were all crusty and gross with mud, and she said she'd give me two dollars if I could get the bottoms spotless. I had to pry a lot of junk out with a butter knife, and then I washed 'em in the sink in the basement. It took me like forever. But I found a cool stone wedged in there, and she said I could keep it for my collection." His eyes widened. "You're hurting my arm, Russ."

"Sorry." I released my grip. "What did the stone look like?"

"I don't know." His shoulders came up and he raised his palms. "Like a stone?"

"Describe it."

"Russ, Grandma said I could keep it." He rubbed his arm.

"I know, Frank, I'm not mad that you took it. I just need to know what it looked like. Think."

"It was sort of round-ish."

"How big?"

"You saw it on the counter."

"I wasn't paying attention. I was busy talking to Mr. Specter. About how big was it, Frank?"

His forehead scrunched in thought. "Maybe the size of a nickel?"

Okay, now we were getting somewhere. "What else?" I asked.

He looked down at the table, concentrating. "It had these sparkles in it."

"Like fool's gold?" I said.

"You mean pyrite?"

"Yes," I said. I couldn't believe he knew the actual word. "Like pyrite."

"No, it didn't have gold on it. The sparkles were *inside of* it."

"Inside of it?"

He nodded. "It kind of glowed sometimes. Like there was a little, teeny-tiny flashlight inside of it."

I couldn't help myself. I slapped my palm against the tabletop. "You had a stone that glowed all by itself and you didn't think to mention it to anyone?"

"It only glowed *sometimes*," he said, defensively. "And not really that much. You could barely see it unless it was completely dark." As if that made a difference.

I buried my head in my hands. How had this happened? I couldn't believe we just handed the stone over to Mr. Specter. And how would he have known what it was? Had it started to glow on the counter and I didn't notice? I could just imagine Jameson's reaction when I shared this story. He already thought I was mentally challenged. This would confirm it. I got up suddenly, my chair scraping against the flooring. "Come on, Frank. Let's go."

"Where are we going?'

"To get that stone back."

I headed down the sidewalk at a fast clip, dodging an old couple and darting around a teenage girl who carried a crying toddler on her hip. Frank was on my heels, jogging along, just barely keeping up. "Wait, Russ!" he called out. "What are you talking about? I can't get it back. I already sold it to the guy."

"He took advantage of a kid," I said, not slowing. "We need to get it back."

The door to Power House Comics jangled as I went through, but I didn't even stop to hold it open for Frank. The kid was ten. He knew how doors worked. I went straight to the front counter where we'd just checked out less than an hour before. No one was at the register, but I wasn't going anywhere until we got this thing worked out. Behind the counter, a drape covered a doorway leading to the back room. I said, loudly, "Excuse me, could I get some help?" It was exactly the kind of thing my dad did sometimes. When he did it, I wanted to sink into the carpeting from embarrassment. Right now Frank, standing next to me with the bag of comic books under his arm, looked like he wanted to sink into the carpeting himself.

"Let's just go, Russ," he said, still trying to make everything okay. "I don't mind that he took advantage of me."

I shushed him. "Let me handle this."

A dark-haired man with excessively long sideburns came through the curtain. He was about forty or so, with a beer gut covered by a large T-shirt with the Flash logo across the front. His name tag identified him as Kevin Adams, owner of Power House Comics. I'd seen him in here many times before, but didn't really know him. "Sorry about that," he said, brushing his hands together. "What can I help you gentlemen with?"

"I'd like to talk to Mr. Specter," I said, my hand resting on Frank's fidgety arm.

"You just missed him," he said, a bit too cheerfully as far as I was concerned. "Finished working and headed out about ten minutes ago."

"Do you know where he went?" I glanced down at my nephew, who seemed relieved that there wouldn't be a showdown after all.

Kevin Adams shrugged. "If I had to guess, I'd say he went home. Is there something I can help you with?"

"No, that's okay," I said.

As we walked out of the store, Frank said, "Well, I guess that's it then. I'll just keep the money."

"You can keep the money," I said, "but this isn't over. I'll see Mr. Specter in school tomorrow and I'll talk to him then."

CHAPTER TWENTY-THREE

○

Mondays tend to be long anyway, since they start off the school week, but this one was the worst. I had science class last hour, and since I'd decided to talk to Mr. Specter afterward, the whole day felt like a countdown. At lunch I saw Mallory across the cafeteria, but I couldn't catch her eye. I hadn't yet filled her in on the stone issue, since I no longer trusted phones or computers. Without them, communication was limited to notes and face-to-face contact, which really sucked. Now I knew how people felt during the Dark Ages. I probably wouldn't be able to talk to her until science class or after school.

At lunchtime I sat with Mick, Justin and his girlfriend, and a few of her friends. The number of kids at our table had grown over time (freshman year it had just been the three of us), but I didn't feel like I really knew any of the new ones all that well. Mostly I listened, which served me well today, because I had a lot on my mind.

The day before, after I'd called my dad to pick us up from the strip mall, Frank and I had waited outside of the custard shop. He leaned against the side of the building and cracked open one

of his new comic books, eager to get started. I knew the feeling of having a brand-new story and wanting to get at it right away. I also was glad not to have to talk anymore, so I didn't take it personally.

While I lingered on the sidewalk, I happened to glance into the frozen custard shop and saw that the closest table to the window was occupied by an uptight-looking middle-aged woman sitting across from what looked like a teenager in a sweatshirt with the hood up. The woman didn't look happy. She had a scowl on her face, and from the way she jabbed her finger toward her kid, she was pissed about something. I watched the whole thing out of the corner of my eye, feeling sorry for whoever was on the receiving end of the verbal abuse. If that were me, I'd hide under my hoodie too.

When the woman got up from the table, the teenager finally raised her head, and when I caught a glimpse of her face, I saw, with a shock, that it was Nadia. She recognized me at the same moment, and a look of understanding passed between us. The angry woman, I realized, had to be the mother who never let her out of her sight.

Nadia nodded and then slowly raised a hand and pressed it to the window, first her palm and then her outstretched fingers. From my side I could tell exactly where the flesh made contact with the glass. Like handprints made in kindergarten, the impression showed the surface of her hand in perfect clarity. I saw the bands dividing each knuckle and the swoop of a lifeline across her palm. Without even thinking, I put my hand on the other side and we connected through the glass, my hand covering her much smaller one. It was a show of solidarity, a sign we had a secret between us.

Nadia smiled, the first time I'd ever seen her do so. At the same moment, she lifted her chin and pushed her hood back

slightly. It was then I noticed the scarring on one side of her face, the skin rippled like fried bacon. The damaged skin covered part of her forehead and all of her cheek to the top of her chin. The scars were deeper in color than the rest of her face, making them stand out even more. Something terrible had happened to her, and she wanted me to see. I nodded to let her know I understood, and I did. It was if she'd spoken through the glass. *This is who I am. This is why I stay hidden.* I didn't think she showed her face to too many people. I knew I should feel honored that she'd let me into her world, and I was, of course, but it also made me want to know more. Nadia had been attacked on a city bus, Mallory had said. Whatever had happened had left its mark.

I watched as a tear slowly dripped down her good cheek. She blinked twice before wiping it away with her free hand. And then, in an instant, Nadia dropped her hand from the window and the hood went forward as well, covering everything. Her mother returned with two sundaes, and they sat silently and began to eat them. Nadia never looked in my direction again. When Dad pulled up and Frank and I got in the car, I glanced back to see her still working on her sundae, her head down, the plastic spoon moving back and forth from the cup to her mouth. What normally would be something fun—going out for a treat—felt sad and socially limited. Who wants to go on an outing with your mom when you're in high school? Especially a mother who criticizes you in public. Nadia's life was the worst.

When we got home from the strip mall, Carly was already there, waiting to pick up Frank. My dad had said she was at an enlightenment workshop with her new boyfriend, but she didn't look enlightened to me. If anything, she looked a little tired and was showing her age more than usual. "Hey there, Russ, how

goes it?" She ruffled Frank's hair. "I hope the kid didn't give you any trouble."

"Never," I said. "Frank is always great to hang out with."

Frank beamed. It took so little to make him happy.

Carly said, "I'm glad he's well behaved at his grandparent's house. Sometimes he's kind of mouthy to his mother."

"I find that hard to believe," I said.

They packed up Frank's backpack and were out the door before I had a chance to swear him to secrecy about the exchange with Mr. Specter in the comic book store. But then I realized, if he hadn't told anyone he'd had a stone that glowed on its own prior to this, chances were good it wouldn't come up again. Frank had a tendency to prattle on about absolutely nothing. He'd tell me every single detail of an episode of *Scooby-Doo*, but forget to convey Carly's instructions about medication he was supposed to be taking while he was at our house for the weekend. It was probably safe to assume the subject of the glowing stone would never come up. At least I hoped so.

I was remembering all of this while I was chewing on my cafeteria pizza the next day in school when Justin interrupted my thoughts. "What do you think, Russ?"

"About what?"

Everyone at the table laughed. "I told you he was in another place," Justin said, smacking his forehead with the palm of his hand, and I realized that they must have been watching me while I was lost in thought.

"I have a lot on my mind lately," I said, which was the absolute truth. They resumed talking, and I did my level best to pay attention, even adding a few comments here and there to prove I was present, but between my thoughts and the abundance of electricity in the cafeteria, it wasn't easy. I never knew how much

current flowed into the space behind the counter. Lights and coolers and microwaves and ovens. The school kitchen sucked massive amounts of electricity. If I tried, I could shut out my awareness of it in the same way I could ignore annoying background noise, but it took a little effort.

One of the lunch ladies, Mrs. Whitehouse, came by our table and stopped to tell Justin he'd dropped a napkin on the floor. Mrs. Whitehouse operated under the assumption she had a rapport with the kids, which, believe me, she did not. It was sad to watch. When you went through the line, she'd sometimes randomly bellow out, "Who's in the house?" and then cup a hand around her ear and wait for someone to call out, "Mrs. Whitehouse is in the house!" There were always a few girls nice enough to humor her. I never joined in and neither did any of my friends, even though she reportedly gave extra servings to students who played along. After everyone finished getting their food, she usually came out from behind the counter to visit tables. She joked about how growing kids should eat their vegetables and took informal surveys about the food as if we'd be getting more options in the future, but that never happened.

Today, Mrs. Whitehouse showed interest in our group, asking if kids still read the *Twilight* books (she was outspokenly in favor of team Edward). I watched as she chatted with Mick about books made into movies, and I wished she would go away. None of the other school employees felt compelled to pal around with the kids. She thought she was a teenager, from the way she acted. Truthfully, it was hard to gauge her age. Her hair was dark with no gray, and she didn't have any wrinkles, but there was something that made her seem dated. Maybe it was her shape. She wasn't really fat, but she was proportioned funny with a noticeably large midsection and drumstick legs. Carly remembered her from her

high school days, so she'd been working here since before I was born, which gave me something to go on. Mrs. Whitehouse had been wearing that hair net for a really long time.

When the bell rang (also powered by electricity), Mrs. Whitehouse shuffled off and Lindsey, one of the girls from my table, made a point to come up to me and say, "Whatever you're going through, Russ, I understand. If you need someone to listen, I'm here for you." She was a cute girl and seemed nice enough. Mick, always putting his own womanizing spin on things, referred to her as "doable." Lindsey patted my arm in a reassuring way and leaned forward so that I could see down the front of her scoop-necked shirt. Normally that would have totally made me lose my mind with lust, and *that* would have led to complete social-awkwardness, but I could see Mallory across the cafeteria and Lindsey held (almost) no appeal for me. "Thanks," I said. "Good to know."

Two hours later I slid into my spot in science class, so jazzed up I felt like I might jump out of my skin. Sometime during this hour, I needed to tell Mallory about the stone—how I had it and lost it without even realizing I had it in the first place. And when the hour was over, I would have to confront Mr. Specter about the stone and tell him I needed it back. I wasn't good at standing up to adults. I'd seen other kids argue with teachers, usually about grades, and also usually without success. I'd never felt that strongly about a grade, probably because I did pretty well. Before today, I couldn't imagine challenging a teacher about anything. Now I had no choice.

Mallory walked in with another girl just as the bell rang, leaving me unable to talk to her before class. I heard her laugh and it annoyed me a little bit. How could she laugh while I was in crisis mode?

"We need to talk," I whispered as she took her seat in front of me.

She looked startled, but nodded. "After school."

For fifty minutes, I was so preoccupied with what was to come, I barely heard a word Mr. Specter said. I was glad he didn't call on me during the class discussion. Maybe he sensed I had a storm cloud hovering overhead, ready to burst. Mallory, too, was quieter than usual.

I kept thinking about the powers Mallory, Jameson, and Nadia had, and my own discovery too that I could heal Mallory's cut. If I could do that and take a bullet out of the back of my neck too, what else could I do? I imagined walking through a hospital and putting my hands on patients in an effort to heal them. Would it work? And if it did, and the word got out, what then? Would people line up in front of my house begging for my help? I imagined a crowd pulling at me, every one of them with a heartbreaking story, all of them wanting my full attention and my ability to heal. How could I not do it? But if *I* could do it, the news would spread and more and more and more people would come. And soon there would be thousands and the numbers would grow. It was a scary thought.

After playing out this scenario in my head, I knew I didn't want it. Not because I didn't want to help, but because I had the sense my ability wasn't supposed to be used randomly. None of our powers were intended to be used randomly. There was, I sensed, a purpose. I just didn't know what that purpose could be.

When the bell rang and everyone else gathered up their things, I went up to the front of the room. Mr. Specter had opened his briefcase on his desk and he was riffling through the contents. I stood and waited.

"Yes, Mr. Becker?" He hadn't looked up at all, yet somehow he knew I was there.

"The stone you bought from my nephew at the comic book store yesterday?"

"Yes?" Now he looked up and glanced at me over his glasses.

"It has some significance for me. I'd like to buy it back from you."

"Okay." He shuffled a stack of paper and attached a top sheet with a paperclip.

"That's okay?"

"Fine with me," he said.

That wasn't what I was expecting to hear. "You don't mind?"

"Of course not. Why would I mind?" He sounded almost bored. "It's a stone. If it has some significance for you, certainly you should have it."

I exhaled in relief. Out in the hallway, kids let out pent-up energy—lockers slammed, voices yelled back and forth, music blasted. "I have the twenty dollars with me," I said, pulling the bill out of my pocket and looking at him expectantly.

"Surely you don't think I brought a stone with me to school?"

I stared blankly. Stupidly, for some reason, I *had* thought he'd have it with him. "Oh, I guess not. Well, if you bring it tomorrow..."

"I'd rather not conduct business at school, if you don't mind," Mr. Specter said. "It might have the look of impropriety. If you'd like to stop by my house this evening around seven, we could do the exchange then. You know where I live?"

"Yeah." Everyone knew where he lived. He owned a red brick house; his backyard abutted the high school football field. You could see his entire roof from the bleachers. Some kids once got into trouble for throwing tennis balls over the fence during a football game. Several of the balls made it into his rain gutters,

which caused overflow problems during the next storm. Or so I heard.

He snapped his briefcase shut. "Is there anything else, Mr. Becker?" he asked, pleasantly enough.

"No, that would be it."

"To make it sound like an acceptable outing, perhaps you can tell your parents you need an hour at my house to watch a special science demonstration for extra credit. Sound good?"

When I nodded mutely, Mr. Specter said, "Well then, I'll see you tonight around seven."

He walked briskly out of the room while I stood there wondering how he knew I'd been wondering what excuse to give my parents. Maybe just a lucky guess.

CHAPTER TWENTY-FOUR

———— o ————

"Don't argue with me, Russ. I'm coming and that's all there is to it," Mallory said, as she drove me home from school. I'd gratefully accepted her offer of a ride home after science class ended that day. It beat taking the bus or walking, that's for sure. I'd hoped people would notice us together in the parking lot but no such luck. None of my friends were around, and everyone else was busy with their own thing. High-schoolers can be so self-involved.

I'd just explained about the stone, and that I was going to Mr. Specter's that evening, when Mallory announced she was going with me. I told her it wasn't necessary, but secretly I welcomed it. For one, I'd be going somewhere with Mallory (and not Jameson this time), and for another, she could drive, which eliminated parental involvement. And lastly, the whole thing kind of weirded me out. It would be nice to have someone else along. Safety in numbers.

I used Mr. Specter's lie and told my folks I was going to his house to see a science demonstration. "It'll take about an hour,"

I said, and they nodded agreeably despite the fact that the whole concept was absurd. What teacher requires kids to go to his house ever, much less on a school night for extra credit? Why a Monday? What kind of demonstration? But true to form, neither of them asked. I was already getting an A in science. Presumably with a little extra credit I could bump it up to a more acceptable A+.

Maybe part of their easy acceptance came with the knowledge they didn't have to drive me. When I told them Mallory Nassif was picking me up, they didn't question that either. Again, I'm just too good of a kid to ever do anything wrong in their eyes. Lying to them now made me feel terrible, but it couldn't be avoided.

So now Mallory and I were headed to Specter's house, with Jameson nowhere in sight. I didn't miss that guy at all. Maybe I'd suggest we stop at Starbucks afterward and I could worm my way into her heart over a chai latte or whatever it is she liked to drink. Stopping somewhere for ice cream was another thought. The truth of it was, I didn't care what we did, I just liked being with her. Something about her made me want to be as near to her as possible.

Maybe Carly was right and I did have the love disease. Lately I thought about Mallory all the time. I found myself replaying our conversations in my head over and over again when I was alone in my room. I'd memorized every expression on her face, the way she frowned slightly when she was deep in thought, the way she burst out laughing when something funny caught her off guard, the look of concern she had when people were injured, like when we'd found Gordy. Making her laugh was the best, like winning a prize. I found myself making funny little comments on a regular basis, trying to amuse her. I was a rat pulling levers,

hoping a food pellet would come my way. It was craziness, but I couldn't seem to stop.

Guys my age get stereotyped as being all about sex all the time. "Hormones are raging," is what my health teacher, Ms. Hadley, was fond of saying. Some of that is true, but the hormone thing isn't just a teenager thing. I don't think I'm any moodier than, say, my mom, who admits to having emotional swings and wicked hot flashes (she calls them power surges, as if that makes it better). And I probably don't think about sex any more than the average guy in his thirties. The thing they never talk about is that besides thinking about sex, guys my age also think about other things: the way it would feel to wrap my arms around her, how I like to picture myself protecting her from harm, what it would be like to press my forehead against hers and look right into her big dark eyes. I see movies with couples making out and I mentally insert myself with Mallory. I wonder sometimes—what would she do if I suddenly kissed her? These are the kinds of things I'd never tell my friends, or anyone else for that matter, but it's all true.

I wasn't one hundred percent sure if I was in love with Mallory Nassif, but I knew I wanted her to love me. I craved having her by my side, hearing the sound of her voice, having her full attention. I wanted to feel her body pressed against me and her lips against my ear. If she loved me, I wouldn't need anything else.

As a passenger in her car, it was easy to watch her without seeming too obvious. I liked watching her fiddle with the radio, and I got a rush when she looked to me for approval when she got to a certain song. I always agreed with her choice. Whatever Mallory wanted worked for me.

"Nadia said she saw you yesterday," Mallory said, breaking the silence between us. She paused at a stop sign before turning left.

"Yeah, at the custard shop. After the whole thing happened at the comic book store. She was with her mother. We didn't talk." We were only a block away from our destination and would be at Mr. Specter's in about two minutes. If I was going to ask, I'd have to make it quick. "How did her face get scarred like that?"

"You saw it?" Mallory asked incredulously.

"Just for a second. She pulled her hood back."

"On *purpose*?"

"I guess so. It seemed like she wanted to show me."

Mallory shook her head. "Unbelievable. When Jameson asked about her face, she wouldn't talk to him for a week. Why would she show you, someone she barely knows?"

"I can't tell you."

"Hmmm. So odd." Mallory exhaled loudly. "Nadia is sort of a puzzle to me. She doesn't open up much. I knew her about a year before she even talked about it."

I tried again. "What happened? Was she burned?"

"In a way." She tapped at the steering wheel with her fingers, as if debating whether to elaborate.

"If you don't want to tell me…"

"No, I can tell you," Mallory said finally. "This is what happened. She was riding the bus, going to visit a friend, when some crazy man came on board carrying an open container full of this liquid. He started raving about our imperialistic society, and he wouldn't sit down, and he wouldn't pay the fare. When the bus driver told him to get out, he flung the liquid up in the air. It turned out to be battery acid. Nadia got hit in the face. The driver got splashed pretty badly too. A couple of other passengers tackled the guy and they called the police. It was awful."

"Battery acid?" How horrific. It was like something from a movie. "I don't remember hearing about this," I said. "Was it

in the news?" We were pulling up in front of Mr. Specter's now. On the opposite side of the street the curb was lined with cars. Someone had company over.

"It happened in Illinois. They moved here two years ago."

"And that's why her mother never lets her out of her sight."

"It's worse than that," Mallory said. "Nadia could get plastic surgery and it would make her face look a million times better, but her mother won't let her do it."

"Too expensive?"

"No, it's not the money. In fact, insurance would cover it. Her mother won't let her fix her face as punishment. It's because Nadia didn't have her parents' permission to be on the bus that day."

I let the words sink in. "But that's cruel," I said, shocked. "She has to be deformed forever because she did something wrong once?" I couldn't imagine my own parents ever acting that unreasonably, no matter what I did. I complained about them sometimes, but I knew that overall they wanted me to be happy and do well. We were all on the same team for the most part.

"The woman is certifiably insane and just a horrible person," Mallory said. "Nadia can't wait until she turns eighteen because then she can arrange to have the surgery herself. But in the meantime..."

"She's stuck," I said, finishing for her. And then, almost to myself, "Wow, that's a lot of years of suffering." And the most important years too. Being disfigured anytime was horrible, but having it happen when you're a teenager was worse yet.

Mallory turned the key and the engine went silent. "Let's get this over with," she said. "I'm eager to see this glowing stone."

We walked up the pathway leading to the front porch with me in the lead, since the pavement was too narrow for two people

side by side. Besides, as Mallory had said, this meeting was sort of my thing. "You do the talking," she said, giving my back a nudge. Her fingertips trailed down my spine, giving me the shivers. "I'm just tagging along."

The front door opened before I could even knock. As we stepped onto the concrete stoop, Mr. Specter pushed open the screen door to greet us. "Good evening, Mr. Becker," he said. "Oh good, you brought Miss Nassif along with you. Perfect." He nodded at Mallory. "Please, come in."

I'd never been inside Mr. Specter's house and I didn't know anyone who had, so I wasn't sure what to expect. Judging from the front entryway and living room, he believed in keeping things orderly. I'd heard he lived alone, so this was all his doing: the gray mat just inside the door where we wiped our feet, the coat rack and umbrella stand in the corner. In the living room beyond, I saw a couch and two chairs arranged around a coffee table, two end tables, and a lamp. There was no TV or anything else. Furniture displays at stores looked homier. "I don't spend much time up here," he said, as if reading my mind. "My den is where you'll find evidence of life. I spend most of my time there." He beckoned with one long finger. "Follow me."

Like faithful dogs, Mallory and I quietly trailed him past the living room and through the kitchen. When he opened a door leading to the basement stairs, I said, "The stone is down there?"

He said, "Of course," and proceeded confidently down the stairs, clearly not doubting we'd follow him. I had an uneasy feeling about this.

I stepped back to see if Mallory was feeling it too, but her face didn't show any concern. She took my movement for good manners, as if I were saying—*Ladies first!*

"Thank you, Russ."

I paused at the top, uncertain, but when she was halfway down I came to my senses and followed. This was Mr. Specter, after all. The science teacher at my high school. It's not like he'd have a dungeon in his basement, knock us unconscious, and lock us up. I'd told my parents I was going to be here and Mallory's car was parked in front. If I didn't come home, this is where my parents would come looking. Still. Why not have the stone upstairs? He had known I was coming to get it since this afternoon.

My nose wrinkled as I got a whiff of something, and at the same time Mallory said, puzzled, "I smell popcorn!" At the landing at the bottom, I smelled it too. Fresh buttered popcorn. Making the turn, I saw that Mr. Specter's basement had been converted to actual living space—no cement block walls and iron support beams here. Instead, the walls had been covered with drywall, the ceiling tiled, the floor carpeted. Bookshelves on either side of a closed door lined the wall opposite the stairwell. A horseshoe-shaped sectional sofa with a coffee table in the middle took up a good portion of the room.

And sitting on that sofa were my psychiatrist, Dr. Anton; Mrs. Whitehouse, the lunch lady; Kevin Adams, the owner of Power House Comics; and Rosie, the waitress from the diner—all of them munching on popcorn and drinking tall glasses of what looked like lemonade. When Mallory and I walked into the room, they stopped what they were doing and turned their attention to us.

"Speak of the devil," said Mrs. Whitehouse. "Or should I say devils?" She popped a kernel of popcorn in her mouth and laughed an insidious cackle.

CHAPTER TWENTY-FIVE

———— o ————

Mallory backed up a step and said, "Sorry for interrupting."
"You aren't interrupting, Miss Nassif," Mr. Specter said.
"Please take a seat. We'd like to talk to you."

"Just a minute," I said, taking hold of Mallory's arm. "What's this all about?"

"A book club?" Mallory asked, her voice tentative.

"It's not a book club," I said. "They're here because of us."

"You say that like it's a bad thing," Dr. Anton said, his head tipped to one side in a show of empathy. "This isn't anything you need to worry about. We just want to talk to you. Just a friendly chat." Somehow it didn't feel like a friendly chat. All of them stood up now, and I did a mental tally—there were five of them and two of us, but we were closer to the exit and we were younger. Maybe if we ran...

Mallory leaned against me. For the first time, I saw a look of alarm cross her face. All along she'd been saying someone was looking for us. She'd used the word "hunted," but even after I'd been shot and despite spotting the men in business suits at the

hospital, I sensed it hadn't felt truly menacing to her until now. Is it paranoia if people really are out to get you?

"I think we need to go," Mallory said. "My mom is expecting me back soon."

"This was never about getting the stone back, was it?" I asked Mr. Specter accusingly. "You had this planned all along."

"Really, Mr. Becker," he said. "What an imagination. We only first talked about it after school. I couldn't have planned this too far in advance, could I now?"

Rosie got up off the couch, her face crinkled in motherly concern. "You're scaring these young people, Sam. Stop it." She came up to Mallory. "We just want to talk to you, honey. That's it. We want to help you, if we can. You'll be free to go anytime." She turned and waved an arm at the group. "Look at us. Do any of these people look like they mean you harm?" I surveyed the group and saw her logic. None of them looked capable of doing anything nefarious. Still, you never know. I'd watched enough movies to know the ones you least expected always turned out to be the villains.

"We're just going to be talking?" Mallory said.

"I promise you, honey, it's just talk. We want to give you some information. Nothing painful." Her manner was reassuring; her tone was soothing. "All we ask is that you keep everything we say here confidential."

"It can't leave this basement," Mr. Specter said.

"We're listening," I said, crossing my arms.

"Oh, don't be like that," Mrs. Whitehouse said. "Really."

"Please, sit down," Rosie said, gently pulling on Mallory's elbow and leading her over to one end of the sectional. I shrugged and sat down too, resting one arm protectively behind Mallory on the back of the sofa. "You'll see," Rosie said. "This is gonna be painless." She smiled in a friendly way.

"So what's the deal?" I asked. "You all know each other?"

Mr. Specter cleared his throat. "Yes, we've all known each other since high school."

Mallory leaned forward, her interest piqued. "You went to high school together?"

"Yes, indeed. Well, except for Arthur." Mr. Specter waved at Dr. Anton. "He went to the boy's prep, St. Mark's Academy. It's not there anymore."

"Which is a pity," Dr. Anton said. "It was a good school. But poorly run. If it weren't for some very avoidable financial troubles it would still be around."

"We all met when we were walking around at night," Mrs. Whitehouse said. "Just like you and your friends." As much as I didn't like Mrs. Whitehouse, I was glad someone was getting to the point.

Mallory turned to me, her eyes wide. Rosie pushed the bowl of popcorn in front of us, and Mallory took a few kernels before asking, "Did you see the lights too?"

"We all saw them," Mr. Specter said, and the group nodded in confirmation. "We met right there on the field. Before then, none of us knew the others had been out night walking too."

"It was incredible," Kevin Adams said. "I can still see those particles glowing in an enormous spiral on the field. Right away I knew we were experiencing something most people only dream of." His eyes shone and I could imagine a teenage version of him. His younger self would be slimmer, and his Elvis hair and sideburns would look less out of place, I thought, on a younger, hipster-type. I tried to imagine the five people in the room—the lunch lady, comic book store owner, teacher, psychiatrist, and waitress—as teenagers so long ago, standing in the field marveling over a cosmic occurrence.

"And then, the changes began," Rosie said. "We began to experience unusual things. You know what I'm talking about?" Mallory nodded and Rosie continued. "I myself noticed I could read minds. I won't lie; it freaked me out a little bit. I got used to it, though." She chuckled. "And I found out that what people say is very different from what they're thinking." Rosie reached for the pitcher on the coffee table, filled two plastic cups with lemonade, and handed them to Mallory and me. Even when she wasn't working at the diner she still couldn't resist giving people food and drink.

Mrs. Whitehouse raised her hand and said, "My turn." Her voice got louder. "I discovered almost right away that I could heat things up just by touching them. My hand never changed temperature, but if I focused, whatever I touched got hotter and hotter. It was a big help when I got the job in the lunchroom right after high school." She tucked her hair behind her ear, which made me realize exactly what looked off about her. Without her hair net, her head looked oddly bare.

There was a pause, and Mallory said, "What about the rest of you?"

Kevin Adams said, "Mine didn't come for weeks, and at first I thought I'd been left out. And then, one day, I could see through things like I had X-ray vision. I went to Vegas in my early twenties and cleaned up at the card table. Eventually the casino owners figured something was up. They thought I was cheating and kicked me out, but by then I had made a small fortune. I used my winnings to buy the comic book store."

"What about you, Dr. Anton?" I asked. For a fleeting moment, I wondered if he could read minds too, and if so, if he'd done it while I was his patient. That would have been a terrible intrusion.

"Mine was a little boring, I'm afraid," he said, stroking his goatee. "I realized at some point that I could charge things.

Electrical things. Old batteries and the like. It came in handy on occasion, but it wasn't terribly useful."

"Dr. Anton is being modest," Mr. Specter said. "He was a human conductor of electricity, a marvel of science. It was truly amazing to see."

"He *was*," I said, suddenly realizing they'd all spoken in past tense. "So, not anymore?"

"No," Mr. Specter said, shaking his head. "The abilities don't last indefinitely." He leaned forward, his hands on his knees, and scanned the room, looking at the others. "When was the last time any of you were able to use your gifts? Or even were able to feel them?"

There was a collective murmur among the group. No one seemed able to pinpoint exactly when it had happened. "It just faded away," Dr. Anton said.

"By the time I turned forty it was all over," Rosie said. "It just got to be less and less and then it was gone."

Kevin Adams said, "I lost my X-ray vision about the same time I lost the ability to run a mile without stopping. Now I'm huffing and puffing after a block or so. Don't get any older if you don't have to, kids."

The other adults laughed. "Too many donuts, Kev," said Mrs. Whitehouse, patting her own considerable stomach. "I told you they'd slow ya down."

Mr. Specter said, "Let's not get off track here. There are things Mallory and Russ need to know before they leave this room." He fixed his eyes on me. "This is what we've learned over the past few decades, Russ. It seems that every sixteen years or so the light particles come, sometimes two years in a row and always near the field at the train station. At least that's the case locally. The particles fall in other places in the world on a different time schedule, but just for our purposes we'll talk about Edgewood."

Dr. Anton said, "Certain types of people seem compelled to come into contact with the particles. They have trouble sleeping for months leading up to the event. Their homes start to feel claustrophobic. For inexplicable reasons they feel the urge to walk at night."

"Certain types of people?" I said.

"Sophomores in high school," Mrs. Whitehouse said, firmly.

"Just sophomores?" I asked, exchanging a look with Mallory.

"So far." Mr. Specter got up and started pacing as he spoke. I recognized it as something he did in class. "We think it has something to do with cell growth of the individual at a specific age—sixteen years old, plus or minus six months or so."

"And all of these individuals are exceptionally smart," Dr. Anton said.

"*Exceptionally* smart?" I said. "I don't think so."

"I know I don't seem smart," Mrs. Whitehouse said, her face turning red, "but actually—"

"I don't think he was referring to you," Mr. Specter said, overriding her. "Were you, Mr. Becker?"

"No, sorry if you thought that." I hadn't been talking about her, but I could see where the mix-up occurred. "I meant me. I'm not exceptionally smart."

"Every one of the teenagers affected has had exceptional intellectual abilities, including you, Russ," Dr. Anton said. "Remember the tests I had you do when your parents first brought you in?"

I remembered. I'd filled out pages and pages of Scantron forms, all the while wondering what they had to do with having trouble falling asleep. "Yeah?"

"You scored quite high," Dr. Anton said. "Nearly genius level. I suspect that if you'd been less sleep-deprived you'd have done even better."

"So why do I have to work so hard to get good grades?"

"Because high school is boring," Rosie said. "Good lord, it's amazing you children learn anything the way schools are set up. No offense," she said, smiling up at Mr. Specter.

"None taken," he said.

"We know it's happened before to other kids," Mallory said. "And that some of them disappeared or died. Why?"

Mr. Specter took off his glasses and wiped them on the front of his shirt. The room got noticeably quieter and everyone's gaze was aimed at the floor. I wondered if maybe this was news to them, if maybe Mallory had stumbled upon a pattern they hadn't noticed.

"You weren't aware of this?" I said.

"No, we all know about it," Rosie said, her voice quavering. "We lost some good people that way." Her voice broke the spell of silence. The rest of them lifted their heads and nodded thoughtfully.

"So why did it happen?" Mallory set down her glass of lemonade and searched their faces. "Where did all those kids go? Why did some of them die?"

"I'll take this one, Sam, if you don't mind," Dr. Anton said. "It's because of the Associates. There's an organization, they call themselves the Associates. They run pretty much everything."

"Everything where?" I asked.

"Everything everywhere," Dr. Anton said. "Everything in the world of any consequence is controlled by the Associates."

CHAPTER TWENTY-SIX

———————— o ————————

"Everything in the world?" Mallory said. "What do you mean? I've never heard of them."

"*Everything* might be a bit of an exaggeration," Mrs. Whitehouse said. "They don't do business in every single country."

"Just the ones they care about," Mr. Specter said. He perched on the end of the couch opposite us. "They don't, for instance, seem to care much about Canada, which is a big mistake on their part."

"Don't underestimate the Canadians, I always say. They seem all nice and polite and apologetic, but when it comes right down to it, they're survivors." Rosie stood up with the pitcher. "Does anyone need a top-up on their lemonade?"

Mallory held out her cup. "So what does this have to do with us?"

"The Associates have always been around," Mr. Specter said. "They were the ones who orchestrated the presidential assassination of 1865. They wreaked havoc with the financial world in the twenties and started the Great Depression. They've been behind every military action—"

"Sam, that's enough," Rosie said firmly. "You're scaring them." She sat down and put the pitcher on the table. She spoke directly to us. "In a nutshell—the Associates like to cause problems, because people are easier to manipulate when they're hungry and desperate and panic-stricken. And the Associates are all about power and money. Greed. It's an old story."

"How can this be?" Mallory said. "Wouldn't people know?"

"Most people don't know," said Kevin Adams. "And the ones who try to tell are discredited or killed. Those of us who do know—and there are hundreds of us—have to proceed very cautiously. We have a whole network of people working behind the scenes doing whatever we can to offset their evil. One of the ways we try to get the word out is through disguised mass media."

"Disguised mass media?" I'd never heard that term before and couldn't even imagine what it meant. If something was disguised, wouldn't that mean hidden? How could it be mass media then?

"Through comic books!" Mallory said, her eyes lighting up.

Kevin pointed a finger at her. "Bingo, little lady. She's a smart one," he added, looking at Mr. Specter. "Comic books have more truth than people know. Movies too. We're trying to get people used to certain concepts, so that if news of the Associates and what they're doing becomes public, it won't be a complete shock. We're seeing progress too, now that comic books and graphic novels are becoming more mainstream."

"I think we need to get back to the main reason for this meeting," Mrs. Whitehouse said, brushing her hands together to wipe off popcorn salt. "We need to warn these kids about the recruiters."

"Ah yes, the recruiters," Mr. Specter said. "If it becomes known to the Associates that you have supernatural powers, you

will be recruited to work for them. We need to avoid that at all costs."

"That won't happen," Mallory said firmly. "My parents would never allow it. They want my high school experience to be a priority."

"I'm sorry to have to tell you this, but the Associates don't take no for an answer," Mr. Specter said. "It wouldn't be optional."

"Oh."

I'd gotten good at reading Mallory's face. All those hours of staring at her had paid off. I saw that she understood what he was saying, and that she also got that he'd indirectly answered the question about the kids who'd died or disappeared. Those were the kids who'd said no to the recruiters.

"How would they find out about us?" I asked. "And what can we do to avoid them?"

"Keep a low profile," Rosie said. "Walking around at night out in the open is probably not a good idea, no matter how good the eggs are at the diner." She smiled kindly, and I found myself smiling back, despite the seriousness of the discussion.

"Don't show anyone your powers," Kevin Adams said. "I know it's tempting, but keep it to yourself. They have eyes everywhere."

Mrs. Whitehouse jumped in. "Act normal at school and with your other friends. Don't give anyone any reason to be suspicious."

"Remember," Dr. Anton said, "we're here for you. You aren't alone in this."

"We'd like to talk to the other two young people as well, if you can arrange that," Mr. Specter said. "Nadia and Jameson?"

"How do you know—?" I started to ask, but was interrupted by Mallory.

"That's out of the question," she said. "Both of them are homeschooled, and Nadia isn't allowed anywhere without a family member. And Jameson, well, he can be difficult at times. I'm not sure I can get him to come."

Mr. Specter sighed. "Ask anyway. We can always try another avenue if they won't come willingly. Jameson's father plays golf at the country club where Dr. Anton is a member. We may be able to arrange a different kind of meeting."

"How is it that you know so much about us?" I asked.

"We had a rough idea of when to expect the light particles," Kevin Adams said. "And we've been watching all the kids in Edgewood for months. We have the advantage over the Associates that way. They come sniffing around after the lights appear. By then, we'd hoped we'd be able to warn the kids who were affected."

"Now that we've filled you in," Mr. Specter said, leaning forward with his elbows resting on his knees, "we'd like to make you an offer we think you'll find very interesting."

"Still listening," I said.

"We'd like the two of you and Nadia and Jameson to join our group," said Dr. Anton.

"Join the five of you?" Mallory's index finger swooped in an arc from person to person like she was counting. "In doing what?"

"It's not just the five of us," Kevin Adams said. "Remember me mentioning that there's hundreds of us quietly opposing the Associates? We're just one small faction of a bigger group called the Praetorian Guard."

"The Praetorian Guard?" I said it slowly, pronouncing each syllable.

"Exactly," Kevin said. "That's the name of our organization. Sometimes P.G. for short."

"How'd you come up with that?" Mallory asked.

"The name 'The Justice League' was already taken," Kevin said, chuckling. None of his friends joined in with laughter, so I was guessing it was an old joke. "But seriously, the Praetorian Guard has been around for a very long time. We haven't been able to defeat the Associates yet, but not for lack of trying. Our organization began when groups around the world realized we were all fighting a common enemy. We banded together, all of us combining our strengths and uniting against the Associates." His tone got serious, and he fixed his eyes on Mallory and me. "You are being called to join an organization that is making the world a better place. With your powers and our know-how, we have a real shot at destroying the Associates. So what do you think?"

"I don't have a lot of free time this semester. What exactly would you want us to do?" Mallory said, asking the very thing I'd been wondering myself.

"Well, it depends on your powers," Dr. Anton said. "We would test each of you to determine—"

A loud noise upstairs startled all of us and caused the doctor to stop mid-sentence. Someone was pounding on the door, ringing the doorbell, and yelling something undistinguishable all at the same time. It sounded like a woman's voice, and she was furious.

"What in the world?" Rosie said.

"I'll get rid of whoever that is," Mr. Specter said, standing. "Probably a student prank." He crossed the basement but stopped before going up the stairs. "None of you move a muscle," he said, finger pointing. "Everyone stay right here."

His footsteps on the stairs were nearly drowned out by the noises at his front door. The ringing, banging, and yelling had

escalated. She wasn't going to be easily turned away, whoever it was.

"Where was I?" Dr. Anton asked us, stroking his goatee.

"You said you'd test us?" Mallory offered, but it was no use. The distractions upstairs were too great, especially now that we heard Mr. Specter's raised voice in response to the woman's yelling. Everyone in the room looked up in alarm as we heard frantic movement on the floorboards above our heads. The woman was calling out something and now I could make out the words: "Russ! Where are you, Russ?"

My jaw dropped in shock. "It's my sister," I said to Mallory.

CHAPTER TWENTY-SEVEN

―――――――― ○ ――――――――

Carly clomped down the basement stairs, Mr. Specter on her heels. In the stairwell I heard her yell, "You people have a lot of nerve. If you think I'm going to let this happen again…" And then she turned the corner at the bottom landing and was in the room with us. I stood up and so did everyone else.

"Carly?" I said. "What are you doing here?"

"Russ, thank God," she said, walking over to me. "You didn't agree to anything, did you?"

"We were just talking," Mallory said.

"Talking. That's how it starts," Carly said. From her tone, I knew she was gearing up for a big blow-up. I'd seen it before. "You people are pathetic," she said to the group, her voice shaking in anger. "Sixteen years later and you're still meeting here with your popcorn and lemonade. Still playing at saving the world."

"Now, Carly," Rosie said, but she might as well have been a speck of dust for all the notice my sister took.

Carly crossed the room and jabbed a finger toward Dr. Anton. "I'm the most disappointed in you. You're supposed to be helping kids and instead you're exploiting them. Haven't you

heard of doctor-patient confidentiality? If I'd known at the time that my parents had Russ seeing you, I would have put a stop to it right away."

"Please, Carly," Dr. Anton said, in the reassuring manner that I remembered quite well from my time as his patient.

"Don't 'please Carly' me, I've heard it all before. You better watch it. My family could sue you for violating Russ's rights and you'd lose your license. How would you like that?"

"You don't need to get so worked up. I've done nothing to violate Russ's rights."

Carly waved a dismissive arm, as if to brush him away, and turned her attention to Kevin Adams. "And you! Reading comic books all day has done a number on your brain. You can play at superheroes all day if you want, but when you start involving my family—"

"Whoa, whoa, wait a minute there," he said, holding up both hands.

"Please have a seat, Carly," Mr. Specter said. He tried to guide her by her elbow, but she angrily shook him off.

"I'm not finished yet. The two of you should be ashamed of yourselves," Carly said, looking directly at Mr. Specter and Mrs. Whitehouse. "Working in a high school and using your position of authority to wrangle students into your stupid game. How unethical is that?"

Mr. Specter looked rattled, but he kept his voice calm. "I'm not sure what you think is happening here, but I assure you—"

"Keep your nice talk for someone else," Carly said. "I know what you're all about, and as far as I'm concerned it's your fault Gordon Hofstetter is dead. If you hadn't encouraged him with your spy games he'd still be alive. I say enough already. Do what you want, but don't involve my family. This ends *now*." She beckoned. "Come on, Russ, we're leaving."

I don't usually do everything Carly tells me to, just the opposite, in fact, but her mention of Gordon Hofstetter's death kept me from questioning her. Two nights ago we'd taken him to the hospital. I'd held the old man in my arms and told him everything was going to be okay. He was in bad shape, but alive. And now he was dead? And this group of people was somehow connected?

Carly said, "You too, Mallory. We're not leaving without you." Mallory hesitated for only a moment, and then, seeing I was leaving, she came too. I guessed she didn't want to be there without me.

Carly rested a hand on my shoulder. A little awkward since she's shorter than me. Normally, I would have pulled away, but my brain was spinning from everything we'd heard that evening and I wasn't feeling like myself anymore. She couldn't resist one last retort. "Leave these kids alone, or you'll be answering to me."

We trudged up the stairs in silence. None of them tried to follow us, as I thought they might. Carly led us to the front door and didn't speak until we were outside. "Do you have everything you came with?" she asked.

We both said yes, and then I asked, "How did you know I was here?"

"Frank told me about selling the stone to Mr. Specter. I went over to the house to talk to you, and Mom said you were here. It wouldn't take a rocket scientist to figure it out." She pulled at my sleeve. "Come on, let's get out of here."

As we fast-walked down the driveway to the cars parked at the curb, Mallory asked my sister, "You knew Mr. Hofstetter?"

"Yes," Carly said, not stopping. "I knew him. I was in love with his grandson David. He's dead too. It happened sixteen years ago, but I remember like it was yesterday." Her voice was

bitter. "They said David died in a car accident, but I knew it wasn't an accident. Gordon knew it too, and he's been watching and waiting for the lights to come back. Just recently he's been digging around, making phone calls and asking questions. He told me he was onto something, and I begged him to stop. I told him it was dangerous. Sure enough they zapped him just to shut him up. I have a friend who works at the hospital and she said the cause of death was listed as heart failure. Another complete cover-up. I guess it doesn't matter. In the end they got him too."

"Who?" Mallory asked. "Who got him?"

Carly said, "The Associates, of course. Didn't those idiots clue you in?"

"How is it you know all this?" I asked. It was a warm evening; the outside air had a hint of humidity, especially noticeable after having been in a basement.

Carly paused to get her car keys out of her purse. When she finally spoke, she didn't answer my question. "Associating with these people is dangerous," she said, gesturing to the house with a tilt of her head. "If someone was watching, you could be killed. Believe me, I know. Avoid them at all costs."

"But I have to see Mr. Specter at school," I said.

"And Mrs. Whitehouse too," Mallory said. "There's no getting around eating in the cafeteria."

Carly said, "That's different. I mean, don't see them outside of your normal routine. Like tonight." When we got to curb, she looked up and down the street and exhaled in relief when she saw it was quiet. "Mallory, I'm going to follow you home. Go straight home and walk right into the house. And this is important: never use your phone or computer to talk to anyone about this. It can be traced."

"We figured out that much. We've been careful," Mallory said, fishing through her own purse and pulling out a key ring.

I realized at that second I was being robbed of the rest of the night with Mallory. My imagined stop at Starbucks wasn't going to happen. It seemed I couldn't get ahead in this relationship no matter what, but I guess that was the least of my worries at this point.

"I'll see you tomorrow at school," I said, but my words were swallowed up by Carly repeating her instructions. "Go straight home and lock the door behind you. Don't talk about this to anyone."

"She heard you the first time." I leaned against the car, thinking that Carly had a lot of explaining to do. "We're not mentally challenged."

"I know that," Carly said. "Get in the car."

Carly drove an ancient, beat-up Honda she called "old reliable." It got great gas mileage and gave a smooth ride, but the seats were worn and the dashboard dusty. Still, if someone wanted to play a cassette tape, this would be the car to have. Empty Diet Coke bottles on the floor in the back scuttled from side to side with every turn. It drove me crazy, but Carly didn't seem to notice.

Mallory pulled away from the curb, and Carly and I kept pace right behind her, only a car length between us. "So," Carly said. "I take it you and Mallory have both been in contact with the light particles?"

"Yes."

"And you've each developed supernatural powers?"

"Yes."

"Great," she said glumly. "Which ones?"

"Mallory can do mind control," I said, "and it seems that I can heal people."

"Really." Carly tapped on the steering wheel, and her forehead scrunched in thought. She reached over to turn on the

radio, then seemed to think better of it and returned her hand to the wheel.

"I can also sense electricity," I said. "I can tell where it's coming from and how strong it is." That wasn't all though. I thought about how best to describe it. "Sometimes it feels like the electricity and I are one and the same."

"That's a new one. Are there any others?"

"Any other powers? Not that I know of."

"No, I meant any other kids."

"Oh, yeah. There's Jameson. He can move objects with his mind. And Nadia. She can read people and see their past events. It's like she can see into people's—"

"You don't need to explain. I know what it means," Carly said.

"How do you know about all this?" I asked. "Did you see the lights when you were in high school?"

"No," she said. "Not me. I was home that night, sleeping. But David Hofstetter, my boyfriend at the time, he'd been restless for months. He was out that night and saw it. Told me all about it the next day. He said it was like the universe had chosen him to experience something magical." Carly snorted. "Some magic." She continued, her voice dull. "There were four other kids there when David saw the lights. A few years later they were all gone. Either dead or they'd joined forces with the Associates."

"Do Mom and Dad know about this?"

Carly turned to me, her eyebrows raised in alarm. "No! And you better not say anything to them either. Tell. No. One. Talking is a death sentence. You need to warn those other kids too. My advice? Don't use your powers, don't talk about it, go about your normal business. Live a regular teenage life. The Associates will eventually lose interest and go somewhere else."

It was a lot to digest. We drove in silence, me thinking and Carly concentrating on keeping Mallory's car in sight. At stop signs Mallory would lift a hand, and I always waved back, even though it made me look like a goof.

"How is it you know about Mr. Specter and his group?" I asked.

"Those people," Carly said, spitting out the words. "Can you believe that all five of them stayed in Edgewood and got jobs that centered around teenagers just so they could see which kids would become affected? They never got over the glory years when they were the ones with the powers. They'll coast on that forever."

She still didn't answer my question. I tried wording it differently. "How do you know all this?"

"They approached David and offered him the same deal they were going to give you. And you know how that turned out for him." Carly sighed. "He was so excited about joining forces with them. He wanted to make a difference. Save the world."

"Saving the world is an admirable goal," I said, trying to put a positive slant on it. "What exactly was he going to do for them?"

Carly said, "They have some headquarters in the basement of Rosie's Diner, and they have a whole computer setup where they share information with the rest of the Praetorian Guard groups all over the world. Supposedly he was going on some secret mission. They were going to arrange it and it was a big deal." She dismissively flapped a hand in the air to show what she thought of that. "Then he died and I think those five were more disappointed about the mission being cancelled than anything else. Not too much happens in Edgewood. I think they've been itching for their share of the excitement for the past sixteen years."

"I didn't know Rosie's Diner had a basement."

"It's a *secret* basement." The sarcasm on the word "secret" was hard-hitting. "It's all very high-tech and confidential."

"Confidential? But you know about it."

"David told me everything. I don't think they counted on that happening."

So much for telling a teenager to keep a secret, I thought. Mr. Specter's bunch had to hate the idea that Carly knew so much about their organization.

"Where exactly does she live?" Carly asked when Mallory turned away from the residential section to loop around the industrial park. I knew what she was doing—going the long way so we'd pass the old train station and the field. I felt like I wanted to see it too, for some reason. Even now, with the light fragments gone, it was pulling us back.

"Old Edgewood," I said. "She must be taking the long way around."

Carly frowned, irritated. "Is your friend brain-damaged? I thought I was being pretty clear when I said to go *straight* home."

"She's not brain damaged," I said, irate. "If anything she's super smart. This is just a slight detour. Big deal. It adds all of three minutes. What could happen?"

The words were no sooner past my lips than Mallory slammed on the brakes to avoid a car that had pulled out in front of her. We skidded to a halt too, just stopping as the front end of our car made contact with Mallory's back bumper. Carly swore loudly, using the profanity my mother hated most (taking the Lord's name in vain), and I made a grab for the dashboard, as if that would help.

The car that caused our near accident had completely stopped, blocking our way. Mallory tapped on her horn, but Carly wasn't

nearly as polite. She leaned on the horn and rolled down her window. "Move it!" she yelled, sticking her head out the window.

When I saw two men, both dressed in dark suits, get out of the car and approach Mallory's side of the car, I realized they weren't going to be leaving any time soon.

CHAPTER TWENTY-EIGHT

———— o ————

I frantically unbuckled my seat belt and was halfway out the door as Carly said, "Russ, do *not* get out of this car. I'm telling you…" But I didn't hear much beyond that because I'd already left the car and was running around it to get to Mallory.

I moved as fast as I could, adrenaline coursing through my veins. There wasn't a clear thought in my head as to what I was going to do next. All I knew was that I needed to get to Mallory. Both men were by the driver's side now. They'd somehow gotten the door open; one of them was trying to pull her out. She struggled back, but wasn't saying a word. With no other sound besides the music from Mallory's radio, the whole scene felt surreal, like watching a movie.

One of the men had a good grip on Mallory's arms now and was pulling her out of the car head first. In a moment she'd be jerked out.

I didn't see any weapons or anything else. Just two guys in suits, one holding the door, the other yanking on Mallory. Both looked to be in their early thirties. They had an identical generic look: tall, medium build, short hair.

"Hey!" I called out as I got closer. "Stop it!" In a second I was alongside them, but they didn't pay any attention to me. "Hey," I yelled again, and this time I put my hands on the arms of Mallory's attacker, determined to pull him off of her.

In the background I heard Carly screaming for me to come back to the car. When it became clear I wasn't coming back, she changed tactics. "I'm calling the police," she yelled, getting out of the car, but not moving any closer. "The cops will be here in two minutes." This was for the benefit of the men, who didn't seem at all worried. "Two minutes! I'm warning you."

"Let go of her," I yelled, lunging toward Mallory's attacker. I grabbed hold of his arms and pulled, but he had biceps like steel. I was a weakling compared to him, but I couldn't give up because now I caught sight of Mallory's face. She looked stunned and afraid. Seeing me she found her voice. "Please, let me go! Please." Hearing her plead was heartbreaking.

The man holding the door shoved me aside like I was a little kid, and I fell backwards onto the ground where I wound up looking up at the sky. The impact knocked the air out of my lungs. My head hit so hard that my vision was affected—seeing stars is how they show it in comic books, and that wasn't too far from the truth. I pushed myself up off the asphalt and staggered to my feet unsteadily, like a drunk. Blinking, I saw that the one man had Mallory out of the car, and that she'd reacted by pulling her legs up to become dead weight. She screamed. No words, just the raw shrieks of someone completely terrified. The other guy grabbed hold of her legs, and the two carried her toward their car, which I now noticed had the trunk popped open.

I ran in front of them and physically blocked them. Mallory's eyes locked on mine as she kicked and flailed. I knew I was her last hope. "Put her down," I said.

They paused briefly before the taller of the two, the one holding Mallory's legs, pulled something out of his pocket and pointed it at me. The device in his hand looked like a toy gun— black plastic with yellow stripes on the side. A taser. An instant later, I felt a surge of electricity shoot into my chest.

The blast knocked me to my knees, and then I keeled over onto the pavement. I felt the voltage radiate from the point of impact, and for a second I thought my heart would stop. An intense pain made every muscle in my body contract. Every nerve ending screamed in agony.

Mallory screamed, "Russ!"

And then, something happened. Instead of the voltage defeating me, it expanded in my body and I turned it around and took control of it. The guy had no idea what he'd set off. I *was* the master of electricity, and he'd just given me more. Not only that, but he'd really pissed me off.

Like an acrobat, I leaped up. Purely on instinct, I blasted him back, electricity shooting out of my palm into his chest. I threw what looked like a splash of lightning, and I did it with a vengeance. Until that moment I didn't know I was capable of doing such a thing, but once I did it, it felt like my birthright. The man fell to his knees and clutched his front. In the process, he dropped the taser, which skidded several feet away from him. And then he screamed a truly horrible scream that echoed off the buildings of the industrial park. No one was around to hear it, except us.

The second guy released Mallory, and she dropped to the ground. "Tim?" he said. Seeing his buddy convulsing in pain, his attention shifted to me. He took a step toward me, his face contorted in anger. He pulled something out of his pocket; I didn't wait to see what it was, but let out another jolt of electricity. This time, not as much. Like sticking my thumb over the garden hose

to hamper the flow of water, I found I could control the amount of electricity discharged from my hands.

Flailing, he staggered back, and then he dropped to his knees. The handgun he'd pulled out of his pocket clattered to the ground. Like his partner, he wound up doubled over on the road, shrieking from the shock.

Mallory managed to get up, and she took a step back as if they might suddenly regain the ability to grab her again. She gave me a look of wide-eyed wonder. "How did you do that?" she asked.

Carly came rushing up and gaped as she saw the men writhing in pain on the road. "Oh man," she said after a moment. "That's something I haven't seen in a really long time."

I looked at my palms expecting to see a change, but my hands were the same as they'd always been. The skin was intact, not red or injured or any different than before.

Mallory asked, "What happened exactly?"

Carly said, "Russ just shot lightning bolts out of his hands and electrocuted two of the Associates."

Mallory's mouth dropped open. "How?" The question was directed at me, but my sister answered instead.

"His body generates electricity and he expels it through his hands. I've seen it done before," Carly said. "David could do it. The Associates desperately wanted him for that reason."

I stared at the men down on the ground, writhing in pain. They'd been stunned, and I was stunned in a different way. I'd jolted them reflexively, wanting to save Mallory from being abducted, and it had worked. But seeing them in so much pain, and knowing I had caused it, made me feel terrible, after the fact. This wasn't a comic book. These were real people—adult men with mothers and fathers, and maybe wives and children.

All my life, I'd never looked for a fight. It just wasn't my personality. And this? This was so far removed from who I was. Or who I had been, anyway.

While I stared numbly at them moaning and clutching themselves, Mallory and Carly debated what to do next. Mallory, still shaking, suggested we back up our cars and leave the men there, then drive home using another route. "Circle back and take the main roads," she said. Carly agreed, and added we should call 911 anonymously and have an ambulance sent to this location. They discussed taking the taser and gun with us, and decided against it.

Listening to them, I knew their plan sucked. You don't leave injured men behind, even if they are the enemy. And in their present state, these guys could talk. We'd never be safe then. Somehow, some way, the Associates would be back and they'd try to get us again, especially now that they knew what I could do. No, we needed to finish this.

Carly had her phone out and was just about to call when I said, "Don't even. There's a change of plan. We're doing this my way."

I thought Carly was going to override me like she's done nearly my entire life, but seeing me shoot electricity out of my palms apparently gave her a new respect for old Russ. "What did you have in mind?" she said.

"I want to try something," I said. "Using both my and Mallory's powers, I think we can make this whole problem go away."

CHAPTER TWENTY-NINE

○

After I explained my idea, Mallory and Carly looked impressed. "That could actually work," Carly said.

"But I'd have to touch them," Mallory said, looking down at the men fearfully. They were quieter now, moaning quietly, their bodies still wracked with pain. "I don't really want to touch them."

"You don't have to worry about that," I said. "I won't let them hurt you. If they try anything else, I'm ready for them." I curled my hands into fists, certain I could summon electric charges again if I needed to. It was a reassuring thought. Now I knew how weight-lifting guys felt when they flexed their muscles: prepared, capable, strong. Powerful. No wonder they acted so confidently.

"I think if you're going to do this you should do it quickly." Carly glanced nervously down the road. "Before someone else comes along and we have to explain what happened."

"Are you ready?" I asked Mallory. She still looked worried, but she nodded. "We can do this," I said to her. "Together."

We both bent down over the first man, the one who'd tasered me, and I rolled him onto his back. Kneeling down and putting

my hands on his chest, I tried to remember what I'd done when I'd healed Mallory's cut. I knew I'd had a certain mindset, an emotion I'd tried to infuse from my hands to hers. Positive, loving energy. Easy to do with Mallory, but with this guy? Not so much. It might even be impossible, but I had to try.

I held my hands firmly against him and focused all my thoughts and energy on the connection between us. We were two separate people linked now by skin and bone and blood and energy. Especially energy. Just like with Mallory, the energy from me hummed right at the point of contact and spread into his body until I could feel his cells beginning to recover from the very injury I'd inflicted. The man's face grew less tense as I lifted away the pain. I raised my chin to Mallory to indicate it was her turn. Still hovering over us, Carly held the phone, ready to call 911 if this whole thing backfired.

Mallory reluctantly placed her hands next to mine on the man's chest. His eyes fluttered open at her touch, which seemed to unnerve her.

"Go ahead," I said. "It's going to be fine." She swallowed and then began just as he was reaching awareness. Somehow Mallory and I managed to be perfectly in sync. It reminded me of practicing CPR as a team, although in this case we were giving healing and false memory instead of life.

She leaned over and spoke directly to him. "Listen carefully. This is the truth. You and your partner investigated all the kids in Edgewood and found that none of them came into contact with the light particles on the field. You've seen nothing out of the ordinary. You've concluded without a doubt that none of the teenagers in this town were affected by the light particles."

The other man, sprawled a few feet away, lifted his head and said, "Don't listen to them, Tim. Be strong." He tried to sit up but couldn't.

Carly nudged him with her foot. "Mind your own business."

"Don't forget about the other part," I said to Mallory. I felt my hands getting warmer as I delivered healing power. In my mind's eye, I saw the damage I'd inflicted and I also sensed his body repairing itself with my energy.

"Oh yeah." Mallory shifted closer. "No matter what anyone tells you, you will be firm in your belief that nothing of importance happened in Edgewood. The person who was chased by your colleagues on Thursday night was just randomly walking by. He saw nothing."

"Good." I gave her an approving look.

Then she added a little something of her own. "Repeat what I just told you."

The other man moaned and said, "No, Tim, no." We ignored him.

Tim said, "Nothing happened in Edgewood. No teenagers came into contact with the light particles. We saw no evidence of anything out of the ordinary. The man who came by the field on Thursday night was a random passerby and is of no consequence."

"Perfect," Mallory said. "Are you sure?"

"Yes."

"How sure?" she asked.

"I would stake my life on it."

My part in this was over. Just like the sensation I had when Mallory's cut was healed, I felt done. I held up my hands. "Finished," I said.

Mallory kept her palms pressed against the guy's chest. "I want you to get up and stand next to your car. When your partner comes to the car, I want you both to get in and drive away. If you recall stopping, you'll remember that one of you had to

get out to pee. If you feel sick tomorrow, you'll think you both picked up a flu bug. Leave Edgewood as soon as possible. You understand me, Tim?"

"Yes, I understand." And just like that, he rose up, brushed the dirt off his suit, and walked over to the waiting car. He was a human robot and Mallory was the one doing the programming.

We watched him until Carly said, "Come on, come on. Let's get going!"

We both crouched over the other man and placed our hands over his chest. Since I hadn't blasted him quite as hard, he was more aware and in less pain than the other guy. "Not going to listen," he said in a soft voice when Mallory started her speech, but within a few minutes, he too was agreeing with everything she said. I concentrated on sending healing energy through my hands while she told him our version of reality, complete with their stop to pee and the flu bug they both might pick up the next day. "Do you understand?" she asked.

"Yes, I understand," he said.

"Repeat it back to me."

And he did. I looked up at Carly like—*Can you believe this?* But she looked less awed than me, probably because she'd had sixteen years to get used to the idea of teenagers with superpowers.

"One more thing," Mallory said. "I need to know who the top person is in your organization. I want a name."

I gave her an appreciative look. She truly was a genius.

"I can't say," he said.

"You need to tell me." Her voice was firm.

"No," he said. "I don't know."

"You don't know who's in charge?" I asked. "Or you don't want to tell?" Mallory and I exchanged puzzled looks. Why wasn't her mind control working?

The man didn't answer me. It seemed that only Mallory could ask the questions and get a response. She repeated what I'd said. "You don't know who's in charge?"

"No one knows, except those at the top." He talked like someone who was half-asleep. "We call him the commander."

"Who do you report to then?" Mallory asked.

"My division leader—Miller."

"What's Miller's full name?"

"Just Miller. I don't know any more than that."

Just a last name, and a pretty generic one at that. Mallory's eyes met mine and she shrugged. "Okay then," she said, and proceeded to reiterate the rest of the story. From the way she stressed how they were going to feel sick the next day, I got the feeling she was pretty sure this mind control was going to give them a kind of next day hangover. "Do you understand?" she asked.

"Yes."

"Okay then, get up and join your friend." Mallory's voice was kindly, like she was instructing a six-year-old.

"Hurry up, hurry up!" Carly said. "This is taking too long."

The man didn't hurry up, but walked at a steady clip. We got back into our cars and watched as the men climbed into their car, put their seat belts on, and drove away.

"Do you think it will work?" I asked Carly.

"Your guess is as good as mine," she said. "It seemed to."

We followed Mallory the rest of the way home in silence, not even listening to the radio. After Mallory's car was safely inside a closed garage door, Carly drove me home. "Are you coming in?" I asked as we pulled into the driveway.

"No, I have to get back," she said. "Frank is at the neighbor's. I said I'd only be gone a short time, and I hate to make him wait."

"Okay." Maybe she was a better mom than I gave her credit for. I started to get out of the car and then thought of something. "Carly?"

"Yeah?"

"Thanks for watching out for me."

"You don't have to thank me for that. You know I love you, right, Russ?"

That last sentence took me by surprise, mostly because we were not a family who professed our love for each other. My dad always said the Beckers were from proud German stock. We were hard workers, on time, reliable. We'd do anything for each other, but we weren't huggers or kissers or people who gushed. Maybe though, we should be.

"Yeah, I know," I said. I realized that I hadn't quite known how she felt about me until that moment. Carly had always been a peripheral person in my life. Always there, but not really there. Flitting in and out of the house, lurking on the edges. We shared parents, but she felt like a young aunt or a much older cousin, not a sister. "But thanks for saying it anyway."

"You're welcome." And then in true Carly fashion she had to throw in some lingo, just to show me she was up to date. "You know I've got your back, Russ. That's how I roll."

I didn't have the heart to tell her that I didn't know anyone my age who talked like that unless they were being ironic.

CHAPTER THIRTY

---○---

I slipped into the house and past my parents, who were, as usual, in front of the television, although they didn't seem to be watching it. Mom flipped through a magazine, while Dad had his head tilted back and eyes closed. I knew if I mentioned this later he'd claim he was resting. He never admitted to falling asleep in the recliner. As I went by, I said, "I'm back. Good night," and I headed upstairs before my mother asked any questions and I'd have to lie about the fictional science demonstration at Mr. Specter's house.

I'd just plunked myself on my bed and turned on my laptop when I heard my mother's heavy footsteps coming up the stairs. Inwardly I groaned. She never came up unless I was in trouble or she wanted to have a heart-to-heart talk. I hadn't done anything wrong that I knew of—my grades were good, I'd completed my chores like a good son, and I'd cleaned up the mess in my bathroom, and thrown away the bloody clothes. No, I couldn't be in any trouble. This had to be a talk. Not really what I needed right now.

She came up the stairs so slowly it pained me to listen. Mom relied on the railing a lot, and I heard her grab the bar, pull, and

step all the way to the top. When she opened the door it was no surprise, but I played along and looked up as if it was. "Hey, Mom," I said. "What's up?"

"You ran off so quickly that I didn't get a chance to talk to you," she said. Oh no. I was right. We were having a talk.

"What about?"

"Can I sit down?" she asked, motioning to my desk chair.

I could hardly say no, seeing as how she owned the place. "Sure."

She sat and looked at me intently. "I'm worried about Carly."

Whew. So this wasn't about me. I thought carefully about what to say. If I've learned anything about dealing with parents it's that you can get yourself in a lot of trouble talking too much, so my rule was to say as little as possible. "I just saw Carly. She stopped in at Mr. Specter's to give me a ride home and she seemed fine." Mom didn't look convinced, so I added, "I don't think you need to worry about her."

"While you were gone she came flying in here, and then she became all upset when she found out about you going to Mr. Specter's house. She accused Dad and me of being terrible parents, of not thinking things through." Her eyes looked sad and she got a worried vertical crease in the middle of her forehead.

Time for some damage control. I said, "I don't know what she's talking about. You guys aren't terrible. I think you're great. I couldn't ask for better parents."

Mom looked relieved. "I'm glad to hear you say that. Carly seemed to think that it was suspicious that Mr. Specter would have students over to his house. Frankly, I didn't think anything of it, but after she said that, I did think it was unusual. Mr. Specter, he didn't ask you to do anything you were uncomfortable with, did he?"

"What do you mean?"

"Well, with all the talk of adults taking advantage of kids these days…"

"Oh my God, Mom, that's so sick. Do you really think someone could take advantage of me that way? I'm not six."

She looked relieved. Mission accomplished. "Of course not. That's what I thought. Carly just made it sound so sinister."

"Mr. Specter's a good guy. A little unconventional, as teachers go, but solid."

"I'm glad to hear it." She folded her hands in her lap. "Carly also seemed upset about something else. Maybe she mentioned a Mr. Hofstetter who died recently?"

"Yeah, she mentioned him. A really old guy, right?"

Mom nodded. "You've probably seen him around town. Nice man. He's been all alone for years now."

"Carly said she knew his grandson."

"She told you about David?" Mom looked startled.

"Just his name and that she knew him in high school. She said he died in a car accident." I hesitated, about to say that I knew they'd been dating, then remembered my philosophy about saying as little as possible and let it go.

"And that's all she said?"

"Sure. What else is there?"

"Nothing. I just wondered." She stared down at the floor like she was thinking, and didn't say anything for what seemed like the longest time.

"I wouldn't worry about Carly," I finally said. "She was probably just in a mood. You know how she gets."

"I know." Mom patted the arm of my chair and then stood. "Okay then, I'm glad we touched base."

"Me too, Mom. Stop by anytime. It's always a pleasure."

"Smart aleck," Mom said, but I could tell she was amused. She paused at the door. "One more thing. Dad and I are going to Mr. Hofstetter's funeral tomorrow night and we'd like you to come with us."

"How come?"

"Do you have other plans?"

"Well, no…" Couldn't she see how weird this was? Why would she ask me to go to the funeral of someone I didn't know?

"I'd really appreciate it." She stood in the doorway like she had all night and wouldn't be moving until I said yes. "Please, Russ. The poor man had very little family."

And that's my problem? But the look on her face was persuasive. "Okay," I said. "If it's important to you, of course I'll go."

"Carly is going too."

"And Frank?"

Mom said, "No, not Frank. Why would he go?"

More importantly, why would any of us go? But I didn't question it. "I don't know. I just wondered. Never mind."

"Good night, son," she said. "I love you."

As she clomped down the stairs I reflected on the fact that for the second time this evening a family member had told me they loved me. Suddenly people felt the need to say how much they cherished me. Very weird.

All this talk of Gordon Hofstetter's funeral reminded me of the medallion he'd given me. I got up off the bed and pulled it out from under my keyboard, then unfolded the paper to get a closer look. I turned on the desk light. If my dad were here, he'd say something corny like, "Time to shed a little light on the subject," and then he'd chuckle like he thought it was hilarious. Both of my parents were really easily amused. With the light on I could see more clearly though. Like a coin from the Civil War era, the

medallion just looked old. The spiral design, I thought, had to be connected to the pattern the light fragments made on the field. Mr. Specter's group had told us that this had happened in other parts of the world too, and many times in the past. Maybe this medallion had historical significance, an artifact from another era. I was tempted to look online and see if I could find another medallion like it, but I knew that was a bad idea.

I was less certain about the paper. The scribbles on it were so light they were hard to read. Someone had sketched some shapes over most of the paper, and along one edge were a series of numbers that meant nothing to me. Some kind of code, maybe? Then again, the paper might be nothing but an old sheet of paper he'd grabbed to wrap the medallion in.

In the car at the hospital Gordon Hofstetter had said someone (his son?) was being held prisoner, but his thinking seemed to be muddled, probably because the poor guy had just been electrocuted. For all I knew he was thinking of a movie or TV show. He'd also said I should carry this medallion and paper with me always. He himself kept it in a secret pocket, so he obviously thought it had some value. I got out my wallet and stuck the wad behind the plastic covered compartment where most people put their driver's license. It was a safe enough place; I almost always carried my wallet with me, and no one ever looked in it but me.

I read a few chapters from my psychology textbook before turning in for the night. I used to think psychology was my most interesting class, but now that I had the ability to blast people with electricity and heal injuries, the scientific study of the human mind and behaviors seemed downright mundane. Reading did make me tired though, which was what I was going for. After getting ready for bed, I shut off the light and climbed under the covers, ready to get some sleep. I thought back to all

my nights of insomnia. Preparation, apparently, for the night I needed to be up to see the light particles fall from the sky. I'd been drawn to the field. It was my destiny to be there on the one night that changed everything.

I thought about Dr. Anton and the fact that he was a child psychiatrist with a specialty in sleep disorders. He'd deliberately gone into a field that would help him identify night walkers like me. And Kevin Adams, owner of a store geared to kids. He probably waited for kids to come in asking about cosmic events in comic books. Mr. Specter and Mrs. Whitehouse at school—watching the sophomores to see if they showed signs of exposure—and Rosie, staying open all night, her diner a beacon for those who couldn't sleep.

Could they be trusted? Carly didn't think so, but I was a pretty good judge of people and I thought they were okay. A bunch of grown-up nerds playing at saving the world? Yes. But well intended, I thought.

I was almost asleep when I heard it. A female voice, undulating like a shimmer in my mind. *Russ?*

If it had been a real voice, one spoken aloud, I would have sat up and turned on my bedside lamp, but it wasn't a real voice. It was a thought, or a memory, or a figment of my imagination.

Russ? Can you hear me?

I stared at the ceiling, which was softly illuminated by the light of my clock radio, and wondered if I was losing my mind.

It's me, Nadia.

"Nadia?"

She laughed, and it reminded me of Tinkerbell in a production of *Peter Pan* my mother had dragged me to when I was a kid. A delighted, pleased-with-herself laugh. Her voice came through again: *I just figured out I could do this!*

I smiled. "How?"

I was in bed wishing I wasn't trapped in the house all the time and the next thing I knew I was rising out of my bed and over the house and then I came here. It was like flying, Russ! I can't believe I can do this. I'm free!

"So is your body still asleep back home?"

I don't know. I guess.

She seemed unconcerned about her physical self back at home. What if something happened and she couldn't get back? "Aren't you worried about being out of your body? Like this might be dangerous?"

I still feel linked to my body, like I'm somehow tethered to it. I know I can go back anytime I want.

"So you're not worried at all?"

I felt the equivalent of a shrug on her part, and then she said, *I don't feel worried. I feel euphoric, like someone opened the door to my cage.*

I tried again: "But don't you feel like getting all these abilities is confusing and overwhelming and scary?"

No, I love it. Love it. Now I can tolerate the hell that is my life.

"Well, be careful."

You don't have to speak out loud. I can pick up on your thoughts.

Okay. Be careful.

What could go wrong? I'm going to go see Mallory next. The sound of her voice in my thoughts had a different quality than her real world voice. Happy. She sounded happy.

Okay.

Should I tell her you said hi?

No, that's not necessary.

Because you like her, right?

Of course I like Mallory. I like all of you. Which was a little white lie, since I wasn't all that crazy about Jameson. I didn't exactly hate him or anything, but I wouldn't miss him if he were gone. I wondered how much of my thoughts Nadia could read. Like right now, could she tell I was wondering how much she could read, or could she only pick up on the messages I wanted to give her?

She said: *All the guys like Mallory. She's the obvious choice.*

She's very likeable.

She told me you can shoot lightning bolts out of your palms. And that you're getting good at healing.

Working on it, yeah.

You need to be careful with that. It makes you stand out.

I'm always careful, Nadia. You do the same.

Good night then.

Good night.

The air in the room felt different after she left. The sparkle was gone. As I dozed off I thought about everything that had happened in the last week. Nadia didn't find any of it confusing or overwhelming or scary, but I sure did. What could possibly happen from here?

CHAPTER THIRTY-ONE

○

I was pretty preoccupied in school the next day, thinking about everything that had happened in the last eight days. Part of me wondered if I'd imagined having Nadia visit the night before, but no—it seemed real enough. The next morning I remembered the correct term for this type of out-of-body experience: astral projection. Not knowing had been bugging the crap out of me, but I didn't dare look it up online. Not being able to Google things was really setting me back.

By now I was used to feeling electricity all around me in the same way I was used to breathing. I generally don't notice air unless something about it changes a lot, and that's an apt comparison. Being able to direct the electricity was another thing, and I couldn't resist trying it out from time to time, just because. In English class I sat all the way in the back in the last row by the window. While my teacher, Ms. Lawson, droned on about something or other, I combated boredom by passing electricity back and forth between my hands. I kept it very low level so that it was barely perceptible, except to me. I'd been so zoned out that

I didn't realize we were about to watch a video clip, and when Ms. Lawson turned out the lights, I was so startled that the electricity between my hands sparked, lighting up the area over my desk. I stopped right then, of course, but the damage had been done.

"Russ Becker!" Ms. Lawson turned the lights back on. "What is it you have there?" My stomach dropped as she marched over to me; every kid in the room turned to stare.

I stammered, "No-no-nothing," which made me look really guilty.

"Cell phone use is not allowed during school hours," she said, repeating something we'd all heard a million times. Now she stood over me, giving me an unflattering view of the inside of her nostrils.

"I know, ma'am," I said. "I don't have mine with me."

"Then what was that light I saw?"

"Static electricity," I said. "The soles of these shoes are a problem that way."

It was pretty lame, but since my desktop was completely clear, except for a notebook and pen, and I wouldn't have had time to hide anything, she let it go at that. I made a pact with myself to be more careful in the future. It didn't take much to arouse suspicions.

At my last class at the end of the day, I slid into my seat in Mr. Specter's class, eager to talk to Mallory, but she was busy speaking to a girl in the seat in front of her. I gave her ponytail a gentle yank, and when she finally turned around, I said, "I got a visit from Nadia last night."

"Me too," she said, looking thoughtful. "Wasn't that bizarre? I couldn't believe it. Kind of creepy, but she seemed pretty happy about it."

"She said she felt free."

"I guess if one of us was going to develop that particular talent, I'm glad it was her."

And then class began and our time ran out. Not that there was much to discuss besides the wow factor of having a friend who could do astral projection. I was getting to the point that nothing much surprised me anymore.

When class was over, Mr. Specter called out, "Mr. Becker, could I talk to you for a moment?"

What could I do? I nodded and watched as Mallory picked up her books, preparing to leave. I'd hoped to talk to her, but this was the last class of the day and she'd soon be gone. Our discussion would have to wait.

I gathered up my stuff and went to the front of the room where Mr. Specter stood waiting next to his desk. I'd always liked him as a teacher. He had passion and was entertaining. Plus, his class was an easy A for me. Last night had changed things. I still liked him as a teacher, but I didn't entirely trust him. "Yes?"

Other students lingered in the back of the room. They weren't paying any attention to us, but he lowered his voice anyway. "I wanted to touch base with you about the subject of last night."

He paused for so long that I finally said, "I'm listening."

"I know your sister is biased against me and my colleagues," he said. "But I want you to know that our offer of help still stands. We'd love to serve as mentors to you and your friends. We can help ensure your safety."

"I'll keep that in mind."

Mr. Specter looked at me over his glasses. "It sounds like you're dismissing me."

"No, just weighing my options," I said, glancing back. Mallory had already left the room. "There's a lot to think about. You understand, I'm sure."

He sighed. "Yes, I understand more than you know. Well, if you change your mind, I'm available any time of the day or night. Feel free to call or come over." He went behind his desk, opened a drawer, and pulled out a business card. "Keep this with you at all times. You never know when you'll need it."

This was the second time someone told me to carry something with me always—first Gordy's medallion and now this card. I took it from his hand and stuck it in my pocket. "Thanks, I'll do that."

* * *

Almost five hours later I walked into the funeral parlor wearing my best and only suit, the one that had been hanging in my closet under a plastic sleeve since the homecoming dance the year before. We arrived early, a bad habit in my family. My parents walked on either side of me, like guards escorting a prisoner. It felt like that too.

"How long do we have to stay?" I asked out of the side of my mouth. My mother gave me a sharp look which indicated we'd be staying as long as necessary, and that she'd be deciding what constituted necessary.

Once inside the entryway, we were greeted by a guy who seemed to be the funeral home butler. He ushered us through a doorway on our left. While my parents signed the guest book, I surveyed the nearly empty room. The place was fancy, with heavy velvet drapes and fussy-looking furniture. Floral wallpaper covered the walls; the pictures were framed landscapes topped with their own spotlights. On the far end of the room, rows of folding chairs faced an open casket surrounded by flowers. The air smelled like floral-scented fabric softener. Up front, my sister

Carly stood talking to the only other people in the room, an older couple.

When Carly saw us walk in, her face dropped in disapproval and her mouth set in irritation. I've seen that look before—the storm before the even bigger storm. She rushed over to confront my mother. "What is Russ doing here?"

"You look very nice, Carly," my mother said in a level tone. And Carly did look nice. For her it was a conservative look— knee-length black skirt and frilly gray button-down top with some kind of clunky silver necklace. She wore such high heels she was nearly my height.

"Take him home," she hissed. "He shouldn't be here."

I was about to say I didn't even *want* to be here, when I saw, coming up behind Carly, the couple she'd been talking to up front by the coffin. The woman led the way. "Good evening," she said softly, extending her hand toward my parents. "I'm Marian Hofstetter."

Carly switched from irritated to charming and introduced our parents to the Hofstetters. (It turned out that Marian's husband was John Hofstetter, Gordy's son.) Both sets of parents remembered each other from when Carly had been dating the Hofstetters' son, so many years before, but no one spoke David's name. The four adults did the usual exchange. My parents: *Our condolences on your loss,* and the Hofstetters: *Thank you for coming.* I saw a pained look on Carly's face. Perhaps she was thinking that if David hadn't died, they'd be married by now with a bunch of kids, and this couple would be her in-laws. Maybe she thought that would be a better version of her life and that she'd be happier. If only. Of course, we wouldn't have Frank Shrapnel then, which was hard to conceptualize. What would holidays be like without that kid?

"And who is this?" Mrs. Hofstetter said, and I realized she was repeating herself but I hadn't heard the question the first time because I'd been lost in thought.

"This is our son, Russ," my dad said, gripping my shoulders and steering me closer, which was incredibly weird, not to mention rude.

"Hi," I said, sticking out my hand.

But she didn't take my hand, just gave me such an uncomfortably piercing look I was tempted to look away. Then she did something really odd. She placed her hands on either side of my face and said, "Russ? That's your name?" Mrs. Hofstetter stared as if I were under a microscope. Between my family's behavior and this, I wasn't sure what to think.

When I nodded, she pulled her hands away. I said, "My name is actually Russell, but no one calls me anything but Russ."

"It's a lovely name," she said, looking at her husband, who wasn't doing anything but standing there. "I guess I'm just surprised because I didn't know Carly had a brother." There was an accusatory note in her voice I couldn't quite understand.

"It wasn't a secret," Carly pointed out.

But Mrs. Hofstetter's attention was on me and me alone. "How old are you, Russ?"

"Fifteen." It sounded young, even to me. "I'll be sixteen this summer."

"I see," she said, and then I heard the hushed voices of other people entering the room, which seemed to break the spell.

"I'm sorry for your loss," I said to both of them.

"Thank you," Mr. Hofstetter said.

I sensed someone behind me and felt a tap on my shoulder. To my surprise, it was Mallory. I gave her a big smile until I noticed Jameson lurking like a snake right behind her. "This is

my good friend Mallory Nassif," I said. "Mallory, this is Mr. and Mrs. Hofstetter. Gordon Hofstetter was Mr. Hofstetter's father." I purposely left Jameson out. He could maneuver his own introduction.

Mallory was good with the social graces. "I was sorry to hear about your father's death," she said, her head tilting sympathetically to one side. "I saw him often at the diner in town and enjoyed talking to him. He was a very sweet man."

During all of this, Carly looked uncomfortable, like she wished we all would just go away. Probably, I surmised, it was because she knew the Hofstetters and we were intruders. Well, too bad. I might not have known Gordon Hofstetter for as long as she had, but I was with him the night he died. Maybe I didn't even want to be at the funeral, but I was entitled to attend.

People drifted in behind us, and Mr. Hofstetter thanked us for coming and said, "If you'll excuse us, I think we have a few other people we need to talk to." His wife reluctantly followed him to the front of the room.

After I'd introduced Mallory and Jameson to my parents, and we'd done the walk up to the front to pay our respects (Gordy, with his slicked-back hair and a dark brown suit and tie, did not look like himself at all), my folks said it was time to take a seat for the service.

I'd wanted to sit with Mallory, but my mom was clear that we were there as a family. "You can see your friends anytime," she said, directing me with a firm hold on the back of my arm.

We sat up front, Dad on one side of me, Carly on the other. My dad, who normally never showed any interest in my social life, felt compelled to whisper (loudly), "That Mallory is awfully cute." He nudged me repeatedly with his elbow until I gave him a head bob of acknowledgment. Parents.

Next to me, Carly swiveled in her seat; she seemed to be taking inventory of the crowd. "Oh great," she said, through gritted teeth. "Look what the cat dragged in."

I followed her nod to see that the place was nearly full. Scanning the faces, I locked in on the ones Carly had noticed: Mr. Specter, Kevin Adams, Mrs. Whitehouse, and Rosie. The only notable absence of the five was Dr. Anton. "What are they doing here?" I whispered to my sister.

She shrugged. "Paying their respects, I guess."

"But not Dr. Anton?"

"Maybe he had something better to do."

When the service started, a minister stepped up to the podium and asked us to join him in praying for Mr. Hofstetter. I checked the time on my phone and looked back to see if I could catch Mallory's eye, but unlike me, she was praying. I did, however, catch Jameson's eye. The dweeb's arm extended over the back of Mallory's chair, and he had a smug look on his face. Well, let him have his fun. Sneaking an arm behind her hardly counted as anything.

When the minister stepped away, John Hofstetter took his place at the podium, thanking us for being there to honor the memory of his father. He talked about Gordon Hofstetter's forty-year career with the electric company and his devotion as a father, husband, and grandfather. I felt a flush of shame at how I'd thought of him as just an old guy. I'd been judgmental, something I hate in other people. I wondered, is it hypocritical to judge people for being judgmental? I thought it probably was.

My attention jerked back to the present when I saw Carly noticeably tensing. Her hands clutched her purse, and I noticed her mouth tighten.

Mr. Hofstetter was saying, "Many of you remember my son, David. He would be thirty-two if he'd lived, but unfortunately he

died in a car accident when he was sixteen. My father never got over David's death. He was our only child and his only grandchild. My wife and I found it too hard to live here with all the reminders of our son, which is why we moved out of state. We encouraged Dad to come with us, but he was firm in wanting to stay in Edgewood. He couldn't accept David's death as an accident, and for years he pressed the police to investigate further. I want to thank everyone here who was kind to my father in his last years, especially Carly Becker, who checked in on him from time to time and performed many other kindnesses."

My parents and I looked at Carly in amazement. It was like she'd been living a double life: outwardly a self-absorbed, too-cool-for-school young mom, but secretly acting as Mother Teresa bringing comfort to the elderly. Her face gave nothing away; she just listened. Mr. Hofstetter talked on about Edgewood as a community of neighbors who cared about each other, and the crowd nodded in agreement. Personally, I'd never given Gordon Hofstetter much notice until he was dying in my arms. Some neighbor I was, I thought with shame.

When Mr. Hofstetter finished, the minister came back to address the crowd. "You know," he said, "I was just reflecting on how fitting it is that we're celebrating Gordon Hofstetter's life the week prior to Easter Sunday, which is when Christians celebrate the resurrection of our Lord. It is a beautiful reminder that death is not final and that the soul lives on forever. May Gordon's eternal soul rest in peace. Amen." Several people in the crowd murmured "Amen," in response.

The only reason I knew the holiday was coming up was because there was no school on Friday and I had off the following week. The vacation from school was far more important to me than church or dying eggs or chocolate bunnies. Frank always

came over to decorate eggs with us, and even though I had to be dragged to the table to participate, I had to admit, when I dipped my eggs into the colored vinegar solution, that there was some fun in this family tradition. I drew the line at hunting for eggs in the backyard, though, and let Frank have that all to himself.

My mind wandered to what the minister had said, that "the soul lives on forever." It reminded me of Nadia's nighttime visit to my room. Was the glimmering wisp hovering around my ceiling her soul, or just some part of her conscious mind doing some roaming? And did it even matter?

As we got up to leave, Mrs. Hofstetter sliced through the crowd to seek out Carly. "I want to thank you again," she said, pulling my sister into an awkward embrace, "for everything you did for my father-in-law."

Carly looked sheepish. "I didn't do all that much."

"Oh, but you did. We relied on your reports, and all those times you drove him to the doctor! I'm not sure how he'd have managed otherwise. Well, we're grateful, is all." She turned to my parents. "You have a fine daughter. You must be very proud of her."

"Of course," Dad said. He spoke for both of them since Mom was stunned speechless.

"We're cleaning out Gordon's apartment the rest of the week," Mrs. Hofstetter said to Carly. "I know he had some of David's things. If there's something you'd like, you're welcome to it. Just stop by."

"Maybe I will," Carly said. "Maybe I will."

CHAPTER THIRTY-TWO

———— o ————

By the next day I'd decided our ploy had worked—Mallory's mind control had taken hold, the two guys had reported back to their superiors that there was nothing of interest in Edgewood, and all was right with the world. There weren't going to be any Associates sniffing around for teenagers with superpowers and trying to recruit us. We were free. Just four kids who could do incredible things. As long as we didn't get too bold and make ourselves known, we could live our lives as usual.

That's the conclusion Nadia and I'd come to anyway, on Wednesday during one of our nighttime talks in my bedroom. I'd found myself looking forward to hearing from her around the same time every evening. She entered my room like a heat shimmer. I'd sprawl out on my bed with the lights off, and we'd talk until one of us got tired and then, reluctantly, we'd call it quits and I'd drift off to sleep.

Tell me again, she said.

Nadia loved hearing the story of Mallory's botched abduction. How I stopped the bad guys by shooting electricity out of my palms and how Mallory reprogrammed their brains. I admit

to ratcheting up the story to make myself sound slightly more heroic, but that's what stories are for, right? I answered: *Don't you get sick of hearing about it?*

No, I love imaging it. I wish I could have been there. I could sense the wistfulness behind her words.

Maybe your mom will ease up soon and we'll get to do something together.

Not likely.

I changed the subject. *Does Mallory tell the story about the two guys the same way I do?*

I don't know. I never asked her.

How come?

A long pause. *I don't talk to Mallory like this anymore. She says it creeps her out when I astral project to her. Does it creep you out, Russ?*

No, I like it.

Yeah, I like it too. It's sort of the high point of my day.

I asked, *What about Jameson? Do you ever visit him?*

That tool? Are you kidding? Although...

What?

In my mind I heard her giggle. *One time I projected into his house. He didn't know I was there and he was in front of the mirror...*

Yes?

Totally flexing his biceps and admiring himself.

That didn't sound too bad. I said, *I was expecting you to say something far worse than that.*

Like what?

Oh no, I'm not going there. Some things a guy doesn't say to a girl.

Awww, you are a true gentleman, Russ Becker.

I try.

You know what's kind of weird? Nadia asked.

What?

Not everyone can see me when I astral project. It's like I can make myself known to some people, but if I don't want to be seen it's like I'm invisible.

How does that work?

I couldn't tell you. It just is.

We talked for a while longer, and then I could feel myself starting to doze. I yawned. *I hate to kick you out, Nadia, but I have to get up early tomorrow.*

Yeah, me too. Good night, Russ.

Good night.

But Nadia didn't leave. I still felt her energy hovering above me as I drifted off. An immense wave of peace washed over me and I slept more deeply than I had in a long time.

The next day in school, I still carried the relief of being home free. After nearly two weeks of stress, life was back to normal. Mallory and I were on friendly speaking terms, but our relationship had never ignited the way I'd hoped. Before the school day was over, I planned to ask if she had plans for the weekend. Maybe we could go out for those wings after all. And without Jameson this time. I didn't care if he was a genius who could move things with his mind. Nadia was right—he was a complete tool.

In Mr. Specter's class that day the topic was physics, and he had us doing an experiment involving Slinkys. Having toys in class made every guy in the room regress to about age six, and the metallic shush-shush noise of Slinkys filled the air.

Mr. Specter sorted us into groups of four, with every group getting a sheet of instructions. I'd zoned out during the

explanation portion of the class, but with three others in my group, one of them Mallory, I would be fine.

Mallory said, "Okay, Russ, you read the directions. Brad can do the drop, and Crystal and I will take care of measuring and recording."

Yeah, Mallory's a little bossy, but no one else was taking charge and she gave me the easiest chore, so I was okay with it. I started reading off the sheet when the intercom in the room made the high-pitched squeal that precedes messages from the office. The disembodied voice of an office lady boomed out. "Mr. Specter?"

"Yes?" he said.

We all looked up at the speaker as if there would be something to see. "Could you send Russ Becker down to the office? Tell him to bring all his things. He's leaving for the day."

Mr. Specter gave me a look and raised one eyebrow. "Is this a disciplinary issue?"

"No."

He tried again. "I'd hate to have him leave in the middle of class. Can't it wait?"

The speaker clicked back on. "His sister is here. There's a family emergency and he needs to go home."

"Very well then," Mr. Specter said. "He'll be down in a minute."

I shoved my notebook into my backpack and slung it over my shoulder. A family emergency? I wondered if something was wrong with one of my parents. A car accident? A heart attack? I couldn't even imagine. I'd seen both of them at breakfast and everything was fine.

Mallory said, "I hope everything's okay."

"Me too."

Mr. Specter said, "Everyone carry on. I'll be back in a minute." Then he followed me out into the hallway, where he rested a hand on my shoulder. "Russ, do you know what this is about? Why your sister is here?"

"No," I said. "Everything was okay when I left home this morning."

He leaned in so close I could smell his coffee breath. "It might not be anything, but if it's related to what we've discussed before, you need to let me know immediately."

I bristled. He might be my science teacher, but I didn't have to report to him about my personal life. "I know what to do," I said. I meant it one way, but it was taken another.

"I knew I could count on you." Mr. Specter released his hold on me, and I headed down the hall to where Carly waited in the office.

CHAPTER THIRTY-THREE

———— ○ ————

I spotted Carly through the double glass doors while I was still out in the hall. Wearing designer jeans with the bedazzled back pockets, she almost looked like a student, one of those girls who spend a lot of money on clothes trying to get noticed. She paced in front of the reception counter, one hand up to her forehead like she had a headache. When I walked in, she lowered her hand and I saw the strained look on her face, like she was just barely managing to hold it together. I rushed up to her. "Carly, what happened?"

"I signed you out, let's get going," she said, her car keys hanging off the crook of her finger.

From behind her computer, Mrs. Bomberg, the lady who handled attendance, called out, "I'm sorry to hear about your aunt, Russ. I'll be praying for her."

"Thank you," Carly said, steering me toward the door.

"What is she talking about?" We were in the hallway now, heading for the door that led to the parking lot. I thought I was keeping my voice down, but it echoed in the open area. "Which aunt?"

"Keep going, just keep going," she said, propelling me out the door. Once we were on the front sidewalk she stopped and burst into tears. She buried her face in her hands and sobbed, scaring the hell out of me. I'd seen my sister put on displays of drama before, but I'd never seen her like this.

"Carly, what is it?" I asked frantically, wanting to know but also dreading finding out. All I could think was that someone was dead.

She gulped and when she answered, the words took effort. "It's Frank," she said. "They've got Frank." She hugged me and buried her face in my shoulder. "Oh, Russ."

"Who has Frank?"

"The Associates. They took him and they won't give him back unless you go and meet with them."

"So there's no sick aunt?"

"No, no, no. I just made that up to get you out of there." Carly pulled back to rummage through her purse for a tissue. "Russ, what are we going to do?" She wiped her eyes and blew her nose.

"I don't know." I put my arm around her shoulder and glanced back at the row of windows which fronted the building. We were visible from any number of classrooms. "Let's talk in the car."

She led me through the parking lot, babbling as she went. "I've been completely freaking out. They left this horrible voice mail and I knew right away it was the Associates. I'll let you listen to it."

"Okay."

"They said if we go to the police they'll kill him." She paused before the word "kill" like it was too awful to even say.

"That's not going to happen. We'll handle this. I'll meet with them and we'll get him back. Everything is going to be fine." I

had no idea where I'd gotten this smooth confidence. I wasn't just saying the words, I meant them. It seemed that along with acquiring electricity I'd gotten a boost of certainty in myself.

My reassurances calmed her. By the time we got to the car, her sobbing had subsided somewhat. I was a true sister whisperer.

When we settled into the car, Carly put on her seat belt and locked the doors right away, as if that would make us safe. Then she stuck the key in the ignition and got her phone out of her purse. "I've listened to the message six times already," she said. "It makes me sick. Do you know how scared Frank must be? He doesn't even sleep unless I leave the hall light on."

I knew this was true from his overnights at my house. He said he kept the nightlight on in case he had to get up in the middle of the night to go to the bathroom, but we all knew he didn't like the dark. Although, to cut the kid a break, our house did make weird noises sometimes, especially when it was windy out. When I was his age, it freaked me out too.

She wiped her eyes and pressed some buttons to retrieve the message, then held it out so we could both hear it. The man who left the message used a voice changer: the words came out thick and deep. "We have your son, Frank Shrapnel Becker. To get him back, send Russ Becker to the downtown Greyhound bus station in Milwaukee today by five thirty. There will be instructions at the ticket counter. Do not contact the police. Do not tell anyone. Your son's life depends on it." And then Frank's voice, sounding amazingly calm, "Hi, Mom. Can you send Russ to come get me so I can come home?" A click, and it was over.

They didn't specifically say they wanted to meet with me, or that they'd kill Frank, but I guess both things were implied. "Are you sure this isn't faked?" I said. "Frank's not at school or a friend's house?"

She sniffed. "Do you think I'm an idiot? Frank stayed home from school today. I called in sick to stay home with him, and I ran to Walgreens for cough syrup—I swear I was there and back in like fifteen minutes, okay a half hour at the very most—and when I returned he was gone. Just gone. I couldn't believe it. There was a note on the counter saying to check my phone messages. That's when I heard this." She still had the phone in her hand. "I knew it was the Associates who took him. I couldn't call the police, so I came right over to pick you up. Oh, Russ, what are we going to do?"

"We're going to the Greyhound station in Milwaukee," I said, looking at the time on her phone and doing a mental calculation. "And we better hurry. We'll be cutting it close."

She started up the car and gestured toward the glove compartment. "Get out the GPS. I can get us to Milwaukee, but I'm not sure which exit we need to use."

I got the address off my phone and programmed it into her GPS, wondering all the while if the Associates had tapped into my phone and were following our movement even now. I imagined some guy in an office whose job was viewing my life as it played out on a computer screen: monitoring all the stupid texts I got from friends, knowing what I looked up on Wikipedia, seeing my grades when I checked my student page on the school's online site. I knew it was possible for them to do that and so much more. If they got into Carly's apartment and took Frank without the neighbors hearing and calling the police, what else could they do? Maybe my bedroom or even my whole house was bugged and they knew everything I ever said and did in the privacy of my home. But, I thought with some satisfaction, they didn't know what I talked about with Nadia during her night-time visits. No one could get inside our heads.

After we'd been driving on the interstate for half an hour or so, Carly said, "I just had a thought. You're going to be expected at home. What are we going to tell Mom and Dad?"

"We'll tell them I'm staying overnight at your house to help Frank with homework."

"But there's no school tomorrow. It's Good Friday—the beginning of spring break. How's that going to work?"

I thought for a minute. "I think I got something," I said, pulling out my cell and dialing home. After the beep, I said, "Hi, Mom, this is Russ. I'm with Carly. Frank had a big science project for school that he didn't do. His teacher said if he dropped it off at her house tomorrow he could still get full credit for it. The kid is having a breakdown, so I said I'd help out. We're going to be working on it until late, so I'm just going to stay overnight at their place. Carly said she'd drive me home tomorrow."

I held the phone under Carly's chin. Quick as always, she improvised. "Frank is practically having a breakdown over this. Thanks for letting Russ help out. He's a real lifesaver. Right after we drop off Frank's project tomorrow morning I'll bring Russ home. Love you!" After I ended the call, she glanced my way. "Aren't you the sly little liar? I didn't know you had it in you." I wasn't sure if she was being disapproving or admiring. A little of both, I guess.

"I don't normally lie to them," I said, defending myself. "But in an emergency…"

"Yeah, I know," Carly said. "Russ, can you do me a favor and get me a piece of gum? There's some in the glove compartment."

Since she quit smoking a few years earlier, Carly had become gum dependent whenever she was stressed. At first she used the kind with nicotine; eventually she worked her way to regular sugarless. I dug around until among the fast food napkins and broken sunglasses until I found a pack, then handed it to her.

Carly popped a piece into her mouth and then held it out to me. "Want a piece?"

"No thanks. I'm trying to cut back."

She shrugged. "Suit yourself."

CHAPTER THIRTY-FOUR

——— ○ ———

The Greyhound station wasn't what I expected at all. In books, bus station buildings are short, nondescript cubes with seedy interiors consisting of hard plastic chairs, dirty restrooms, and scuffed linoleum. The Milwaukee Intermodal Station was a shining glass structure—the front of the building was made up almost entirely of windows divided by narrow metal strips. It was beautiful, in a way. I said, "This isn't what I expected at all."

"It's pretty new," Carly said. "A bus and train station combined."

Across the street was a parking lot with a sign that said "$6 All Day." After we pulled into a space and I paid the attendant, we made our way across the intersection to the building. Carly walked purposefully and fast, as if that would get Frank back to us more quickly, like maybe we'd get to the station and find him inside waiting for us at the ticket counter, and we'd all go home and everything would be okay again.

Inside it was airy and open. Full-sized trees in planters divided up rows of seats. We'd entered the Amtrak end of the building. The place was crowded with people coming and going

and waiting. Mothers with small children, businessmen and women, people with suitcases like they were on a leg of a long-distance trip. A man pushing a cleaning cart came by, and Carly grabbed his sleeve. "We need to be at the Greyhound counter." The urgency in her voice suggested we were late, but in fact, we were well ahead of our five thirty deadline.

The man looked startled, but he had a kindly face. "Pardon?" he asked.

She softened her question. "We're looking for the Greyhound counter. Can you direct us, sir?"

He pushed back his baseball cap and pointed down to the other end. "The Greyhound ticket office is at the west end of the building. Just keep going. Can't miss it."

Carly took off running, and I went after her, turning back for just an instant to yell, "Thanks," to the maintenance man. "Carly, wait!" I called out. I had longer legs than she did, but she was still quick, past the All Aboard Café, darting around individuals, pushing through clusters of people, passing rows of seated customers who looked up as we went by.

When we got to the counter there was a short line. Carly skidded to a halt and leaned over to catch her breath. She had her hands on her knees and was bent at the waist.

Clearly her office job had not prepared her for this.

"Are you okay?" I asked. A clock on the far wall indicated we had plenty of time.

She straightened up. "No, I'm not okay, Russ. I'm going out of my mind here. They have Frank. They have my baby and I—"

I shushed her; people were looking. I spoke under my breath. "It's okay, Carly. I told you, we'll get him back."

She took in a big gulp of air and lowered her voice. "I keep thinking about how scared he must be."

"I know, but we have to be on top of this. Falling apart isn't going to help Frank." The words coming out of my mouth sounded like something a character in a movie would say, but they had a calming effect on Carly.

"Okay, okay. We'll get through this." She said it like she was trying to convince herself.

"We're already getting through this," I said.

When I got to the front of the line, I told the older gentleman behind the counter, "I'm Russ Becker."

I was about to explain when he said, "Oh yes, Mr. Becker, we've been expecting you." When he looked down to open a drawer, I got a view of the thin strands of hair artfully arranged over the top of his head. While he was hunting through the drawer, Carly took her sugarless gum out of her mouth and purposely stuck it to the underside of the counter. Her small way of showing her contempt for this whole situation. The pink gob marred the perfect white underside of the counter, but luckily no one else noticed it. A microsecond later the clerk pulled out a sealed envelope, which he handed over the counter to me. "I see you're one of our VIP passengers," he said. "Please let the staff know if you require anything at all during your trip. Your happiness is a priority for us."

"Thank you," I said, stepping away from the counter.

"What the hell was that about?" Carly hissed when we'd moved out of earshot. "You're a VIP passenger? Your happiness is a priority for us? It's a Greyhound bus. They're mocking us, Russ."

"Maybe so," I said, tearing into the envelope. "But we can't get distracted by any of that." I pulled out a ticket; it looked a lot like a concert ticket, scan code and all. I read the destination aloud. "Apparently, I'm going to Chicago. Leaving at six fifteen."

I peered inside the open envelope. It was empty. "No note or anything."

"Why don't you ask Baldy what's going on?" Carly said, looking back at the service counter. "Maybe he knows where Frank is." From the look on her face I could tell she was going to start something.

I grabbed her arm. For the first time I wished I had Mallory's gift of mind control. I'd have loved to be able to force her to release her anger. "Don't. Make. A. Scene." I said it in a low key-way, but I think I made the point. Miraculously, she calmed down, which was a good thing. I had the feeling we had to play by their rules. They'd said no police. Screaming at the clerk at the Greyhound station wasn't quite the same thing as calling the authorities, but it still wasn't good. "I'm going to get on the bus and go where they want me to go, and I'm going to get Frank and bring him home. Be cool."

She started crying again, but at least this time she did it silently. She sniffed and said, "I have a very bad feeling about this. You're going to get on that bus and I'll never see either of you again."

"That's not going to happen." In fact, I knew it could happen, but one of us had to be rational and calm here and it was turning out to be me. "You've seen what I can do. I can take care of myself."

"Oh, Russ, you have no idea." She wiped her eyes. "They can do things you can't even imagine."

"Hey, I once got shot and pulled the bullet out of my neck and was completely healed half an hour later. Don't worry, I'm fairly indestructible."

"That's what David thought. And he's gone. And now they have Frank."

Across the way, a businessman holding a briefcase stared in our direction. When I made eye contact, he shifted his attention to his phone. Behind him, a short chubby woman wearing a Green Bay Packers jersey leaned against a wall and chewed on a granola bar. She too seemed to be watching us. All around us people swirled and moved and talked on phones and glanced our way. Any one of them could be with the Associates. They couldn't all be wearing dark suits. That would be way too obvious. "Try to keep it together," I said. "I know it's hard, but we can't lose our cool. If they're watching, we want them to think this doesn't faze us. We don't want to show our hand."

She sniffed. "When did you get so old and wise?"

"About two weeks ago," I said. "I was out walking late at night and I saw these lights up in the sky..."

"Say no more," Carly said, giving me a slight smile, even though her eyes still glinted with tears. "I think I've heard this story before."

"Here's the plan," I said. "I'll get on the bus just like I'm supposed to, and you head for home and wait for me to call."

"Go home? I don't think so."

"Carly, someone has to be at your place. What if Mom and Dad stop over and no one's there?"

"And what if they do stop over and you and Frank aren't there? What am I supposed to say?"

"Make some excuse. You could tell them we went out to buy supplies for the project. You'll think of something. You're good like that."

Carly hesitated; I could tell she was thinking it over. She shook her head. "I don't think I can just sit on the couch and not know—"

"And what if we piss these people off by having you come along? They only want me." I held up the envelope. "There's only

one ticket. Mine. I *promise* I'll call you every step of the way."
I was making some good arguments, but I had to keep talking
for a few more minutes until I saw her opening up to the idea.
Even so, she only agreed after I suggested Frank might already be
home. "Who knows," I said, "this whole thing might be a decoy.
Maybe he's already back at your place."

"He'd call my phone," Carly said. "He knows to call me, no
matter what. He'd call. I know he would," she added firmly.

"Unless he's sick or exhausted or scared or they told him not
to. I know it's a long shot, but I really think one of us needs to be
at your apartment, in case he shows up. And it can't be me." My
logic was convoluted, but it worked. She caved in.

"You'll call and keep me updated?"

"I said I would, didn't I? Just ask Mom and Dad. They'll tell
you I'm reliable." I noted the time on my phone. "I hate to be this
way, but I have a bus to catch. Go home, and try not to worry."

"Like that's going to happen." She threw her arms around me
and squeezed so tightly I could have walked away with her still
hanging off my front.

I knew what she was thinking. "Jeez, Carly, it's not like you'll
never see me again."

"David said the same thing. I never did see him again."

"It'll be okay." I patted the top of her head.

She let go and looked me square in the eye. "They want you to
join them, you know. That's what this is all about. They're going
to recruit you and if you refuse..."

The sentence hung there, unfinished. "Let's not worry about
that just yet," I said. "Let's get Frank back first."

After we said our good-byes, I watched as she walked back
through the terminal. Her head was down and her shoulders
hunched, which gave her a defeated look. Not like Carly at all.

My sister had always seemed larger than life to me, not only because she'd always been my big sister, but also because she was what my father called "a presence." She laughed a little too loudly and had opinions about everything. Unlike me, who hated conflict, Carly had no trouble telling people what she thought, especially when she thought they were wrong. She once picked Frank up from a weekend at our house with a black eye—some girl at a bar thought Carly had been flirting with her boyfriend. True to form, Carly hadn't backed down and she had the shiner to prove it.

I had underestimated her though. She cared about Frank more than I'd realized, and she had helped Gordon Hofstetter. I tried to imagine her driving him to doctor's appointments in her dirty car, the empty soda bottles skittering from side to side when she made her drastic sudden turns. She was kinder than I'd thought, but she was still a mess, and not the greatest driver either.

CHAPTER THIRTY-FIVE

———— o ————

O ne of the disadvantages of being one of the first ones on the bus and sitting by a window seat is that you have no control over who sits next to you. I found this out the hard way when a woman my mother's age hoisted her abundant mass into the seat right next to mine. There were clear divisions between the seats, not that it made a difference. Her body spilled over into my half. I pulled my arm over, but it didn't help.

The woman settled in like she was there for the long haul. She pulled a Kit Kat bar out of her purse, broke off a section, and offered it to me. When I said no thanks, she responded, rather offended, "My hands are clean, if that's the problem."

I wanted to tell her that my mind was consumed with getting to my kidnapped nephew and wondering if I'd live to see tomorrow. The germs on her hands didn't scare me. But all I could come up with was a little white lie. "Sorry, chocolate allergy."

"Oh, you poor thing. I don't know what I'd do if I couldn't eat chocolate." She prattled on about candy and sweets and her daily diet. She only stopped talking when the driver spoke over the loudspeaker, welcoming us and giving us a rundown on all the

stops between Milwaukee and Chicago. After he finished speaking, my seatmate started up again with her annoying chatter. I looked out the window, hoping she'd get the hint.

The driver honked before backing up, then eased forward out of the lot. As it turned onto St. Paul Avenue I caught sight of a figure running breathlessly alongside the bus. Carly. She held a ticket in the air with one hand and banged on the side of the bus with the other as she went. She was so close I was afraid she'd get caught under the wheels and be killed. "Wait!" I yelled, standing in place. I pushed my way out to the aisle. "Stop the bus!"

Other passengers saw Carly now too, and they called out to the driver.

"Hey! There's another passenger."

"Stop the bus!"

"Let her on!"

The bus jolted to a stop and the door swung open with a whoosh. After Carly climbed the steps and handed her ticket to the driver, he said, "That was a close one. You almost didn't make it, little lady."

"I know. Thanks for stopping," she said. A smattering of applause came from the other passengers, but she didn't smile.

As she walked toward me, I said, "Oh, Carly, what have you done?"

"I got in the car to drive home, but I just couldn't do it, Russ. I'm sorry."

The bus was moving now. There was no turning back. I jabbed a thumb toward the back. "Let's sit down."

Toward the back we found two aisle seats, one in front of the other. Before I could say anything, Carly handed a sheet of paper back to me. I unfolded it and saw, in her scribbled handwriting: *Don't say anything. I think there might be some of them on the*

bus. She must have written this ahead of time. Maybe when she was in line at the ticket counter? How did her mind work? It was a mystery to me.

And so, because we didn't know who might be listening, we traveled in silence, the thrumming of the bus providing a soothing backdrop for the passengers who buried themselves in their own world—reading, listening to iPods, staring out the window. Only a few people talked, thankfully, and none of them to us. I looked around, but if there were any Associates on board, I couldn't pick them out. Carly coming along was a big mistake. I knew that and yet I understood. I couldn't have gone home either. The not knowing would have killed me, and it had to be even worse for her. Frank was my slightly annoying, sometimes endearing nephew. For Carly, Frank was her one and only child.

We were heading south, about an hour into the drive, when a plume of dark smoke on the road ahead got everyone's attention. The bus slowed to a crawl before coming to a complete stop. Around us, every lane of the expressway was stopped, making the interstate look like a long, narrow parking lot. Passengers unbuckled their seat belts to get a better view. Those riding closest to the front yelled commentary to those of us in back. "There's an overturned semi," one guy called out. "And it's smoking up a storm."

Worried voices began speculating. Why would it be smoking? "I hope it doesn't explode," said the lady with the Kit Kat bar. "If that happens we're all goners."

The bus driver got on the PA system to tell everyone to stay calm. He was going to be in touch with his superiors at Greyhound and we'd be back on course in no time.

As Carly and I exchanged worried looks, my phone went off. The number on the display read "Private." I showed it to Carly, who said, "Answer it."

"Hello?"

The voice, thick, deep, and distorted, was the same as the message on Carly's cell. "Get off the bus. Walk to the top of the exit ramp and wait." Almost a growl. I started to ask for more information, but a sharp click indicated the call was over. I motioned to Carly. "This is our stop. We're getting off." Unquestioningly, she followed me down the aisle.

When we got to the front, I told the driver, "We need to get off here."

He regarded me with wide eyes. "Really?"

"Yeah, we need to get out."

He threw his arms up like *I can't believe this guy*, and chuckled. "That's rich. Sorry, son. Not going to happen."

"I'm serious," I said. "We really need to get off the bus. It's an emergency."

He wiped his forehead with the back of his hand. "I don't think you're getting it. I would never let a passenger out in the middle of the expressway. Company policy. There are liability issues."

Carly pushed ahead of me. "I need to go outside. I feel sick. I think I'm going to throw up." She leaned over him and made a face like she was going to yak right on him.

Reflexively, he shoved her aside with an outstretched arm. "Lady, there's a bathroom in back. Throw up there."

"Get your hands off me!" Carly said.

"You need to take your seat." His face was turning red. And then, under his breath, "I really don't need this right now."

She turned to me and, through clenched teeth, said, "Zap him, Russ."

Earlier she'd told me never to use my powers in front of other people. Now she wanted me to shoot electricity in front of

a busload of people. That was Carly for you. Impulsive, my mom always said. Carly just didn't always think things through.

I shook my head. I had a better idea. I put my hand on the bus driver's shoulder, and just like I'd infused healing energy on previous occasions, I now tried to use mind control. I'd never done this before, but something told me I could. "Sir, you need to open the door right now."

He didn't respond for a moment, but his body relaxed. I felt his shoulder loosen, and I knew something was happening.

I said, "Listen carefully. I'm telling you that you need to open the door for us."

His eyes became vacant as my thoughts became his thoughts. "I need to open the door right now?" he asked.

"Yes, please. And then, after we're through, close the door behind us and resume doing whatever it is you'd usually do under the circumstances."

And just like that, he reached for the button and the door swung opened. "Thank you for riding with Greyhound. Have a pleasant day," he said, nearly robotically.

Carly and I rushed down the stairs. Behind us on the bus I heard a woman yell, "Hey, how come they get to go?" Then the door swung shut and we were out in the middle of the interstate.

"We really didn't need the theatrics, Carly," I said, pulling her sleeve.

"Where are we going now?"

I gestured beyond the accident scene. "To the top of the exit ramp, just like the man said."

The entire roadway was at a standstill. We wove our way around idling vehicles, inhaling exhaust and getting stares from the occupants of the stopped cars. When we approached the overturned semi, we veered to the far right shoulder. I didn't see

a fire or any human beings, but smoke surrounded us and I could feel the heat. "Is this a real accident, do you think?" Carly asked. "Or was it staged for us?"

"I don't know." We plunged through the smoke and came out the other side, coughing and choking. "It's real smoke, anyway," I said.

Carly pulled a water bottle out of her purse and took a swig. When she handed the bottle to me, I took a swallow as well and then splashed a handful on my face to ease my stinging eyes. We continued on to the exit ramp, one hundred yards past the accident site. Climbing the hill alongside the ramp, we made our way up. At the top was a quiet two-lane country highway. And parked by the other side of the highway was a white cargo van.

"I think that's our ride," I said.

CHAPTER THIRTY-SIX

———————— o ————————

Iexpected two men in suits to leap out and toss us bodily into the back of the van, but that didn't happen.

When we approached, two women wearing jeans, T-shirts, and sunglasses ambled out of the van and greeted us with smiles. They were Associates, I assumed. Both had dark hair, were slim, and were, I'd even say, on the attractive side, although too old for me. They could have been friends of Carly's, which I think, in retrospect, was the point. They were trying not to intimidate me. "Russ Becker?" one said, but I think the question was only a formality. I definitely got the impression they recognized me.

We crossed the highway. "That's me. I'm Russ Becker."

"You were supposed to come alone," the second one said, lowering her shades to give Carly a long stare. She sounded disapproving, but not angry.

"Actually, the message didn't specifically say to come alone," I said. "We can play it back for you if you want."

Carly said, "You have my son. Where is he?" Her voice had a harsh, ragged edge to it, and even though I understood what she

was going through I winced, afraid she was going to screw this thing up and we'd never ever get to Frank.

"Frank is fine. He's not upset at all. He's waiting for you." This from the first one. With their sunglasses on they looked unnervingly alike, but I now thought of this one as the "nice" one. Whether or not either of them was nice remained to be seen. Probably not, since they were part of an organization which kidnapped little boys and killed teenagers.

"You're going to take us to him?" I asked, and when the first one nodded, I added, "Well, then let's go."

One of the women got in to drive, while the other motioned for us to follow her around to the back of the van. She opened the door to reveal an area with two bucket seats. There was a wall at the far end, making this space completely separate from the driver and passenger compartment up front. "It's a short drive," she said. "I hope you'll find it comfortable."

Carly glared at her before climbing in; I followed her in. "How long will it take?" I asked, but she slammed the doors shut and didn't answer.

I noticed the lack of windows in the back and the fact that the door we'd just entered couldn't be opened from the inside. Track lighting on the floor gave us enough illumination to see each other. The rest of the space around us was bare, as far as I could tell.

"They didn't pat us down for weapons," I said. "That's good."

"You're the weapon," she said, running her fingers through her hair. "They can't take that away."

"And they didn't make a big deal out of you coming along." I was trying to look on the bright side.

"No," she said, thoughtfully. "It was like they sort of expected it. They put up the pretense of being irritated that you didn't

come alone, and then you pointed out that the message didn't specifically say that, and they let it drop."

"Do you think we're being watched and listened to right now?"

"Yes," Carly said. "I think they know everything. Everything we say and do. There's no getting around it." She spoke to the emptiness of the van. "Frank is a good boy. If you've hurt him, I hope you all rot in hell." She got a Kleenex out of her purse and dabbed at her eyes.

When the van started moving, we put on our seat belts, riding in silence for the next few minutes. Carly looked grim and exhausted. I wasn't sure if it was the ordeal or the lighting, but she'd never looked worse. "What if they don't take us to Frank?" she said, in a low voice. "What if he's not even…"

Her voice cracked with emotion. She couldn't finish the sentence, so I did. "He's not dead, Carly. We're going to get him and take him home. He'll be sleeping in his own bed tonight."

"What if they want you to stay? Like, as a trade for Frank?"

"Then I'll stay."

"No, Russ, you can't do that." The expression on her face was one of horror. "You have no idea what you're saying. You don't know what they're capable of."

"I'm starting to get a clue."

She buried her head in her hands. "I can't even imagine a way this can end well."

I said, "Carly, don't borrow trouble. There's no point in worrying about anything just yet."

The van went over a bump and made a turn, then started accelerating. If I had to guess, I'd say we were back on the expressway now. The quiet was unnerving. I never realized how much I relied on music to fill the driving void until I didn't have it.

"How is it you were you able to do that to the bus driver?" Carly asked. "Getting him to change his mind like that."

I took a deep breath. "I'm not sure. I mean, I just suddenly felt like I could get inside his brain and get him to do what I wanted. I was pretty sure I could do it, actually. It felt like—you know how it is when you get a growth spurt and without even trying you suddenly realize you can now reach the top shelf in the pantry closet, the one where Dad keeps the candy bars?"

"Yeah. I mean no. I never got that tall; I still can't reach that shelf."

I grinned. "Okay, bad comparison."

"I understand what you're saying. But why are you suddenly getting all these extra abilities? I thought each person just got one."

"I don't know. I'm not sure there are actual rules that come with this."

We were quiet for a time, staring at the place where there would be windows, if there were any. Like being in a paddy wagon, I thought. Not that I'd ever been in one, I just knew about it from the movies.

Carly said, "So Dad keeps candy bars on the top shelf?"

I nodded. "Yeah. He's got a stash. I found it in seventh grade."

She twisted her hands in worry. "I wonder what Mom and Dad are doing right now."

I didn't know for sure, but I could imagine them finishing up dinner, then rinsing the dishes and putting them in the dishwasher, exchanging small talk about the weather and the annoyances of their work day. My mom would be saying how nice it was that I was staying at Carly's to help Frank with his project for school. For years she'd yearned for Carly and I to become closer. How ironic that this is what it took.

My phone went off, startling me. I'd felt cut off from the world, completely forgetting both of us still had our phones. Carly's eyebrows rose questioningly as I answered. "Hello?"

"Russ?" I hadn't recognized the number, but I knew the voice even though it was slightly different from the version I heard inside my mind during our evening talks.

"Nadia!" Despite the fact that we were in the middle of the most depressing drive of my life, I couldn't help myself—I was happy to hear from her. It was like unexpectedly running into a friend while visiting another country.

She got right to the point. "Mallory told me you left school early. Is everything okay?"

I hesitated, remembering Carly's opinion that we were being watched. "Just a minute." I made a pretense of covering the phone and said to Carly, "Hey, Carly, it's my friend Nadia." I went back to the phone. "Yep, everything's fine. I'm just hanging out with my sister."

Nadia was perceptive. She knew I didn't normally hang out with Carly, and she understood that I couldn't tell her what was actually going on. "Oh great," she said, playing along. "I was a little concerned, but it sounds like everything's fine."

"Yep, all good."

Nadia said, "Okay, well I hate to cut this short, but I have a ton of homework to do. Talk to you later."

"Take it easy," I said, signing off. And then to Carly, "She had homework to do."

To Carly's credit, she didn't question the phone call any further, although she did look puzzled. "Maybe I should call Mom and Dad," she said.

"No, you'll just make them suspicious. If they haven't called us, everything's okay. Let it go."

A minute or so later, Nadia was in my head. I heard her say: *What in the hell is happening to you?* I felt her energy all around us, but Carly didn't seem to notice it. I got the impression Nadia was a radio frequency only I could hear.

How did you find me? I asked, incredulous. It was all the more amazing considering we were on the move in an unmarked van, and I didn't even know where we were.

Nadia sounded gleeful. *I used my Russ tracker!*

Seriously?

Seriously, no. I have no idea how I found you. I just thought about you and here I am. What's going on?

I filled her in on everything that had happened from the time I left Mr. Specter's class until now. It had only been a few hours, but it felt like a lifetime.

When I finished, Nadia said, *What do you think they want?*

I don't know. We'll find out, I guess.

Do you want me to stick around?

She had to ask? Just having her around made everything better. I would have wrapped myself in her energy if I could have. Smiling, I said, *Yes, if you can.*

You're in luck. I'm grounded until I'm eighteen, so it turns out I've got plenty of time and nowhere else to go. Count me in. I'm along for the ride.

CHAPTER THIRTY-SEVEN

———— o ————

I could tell when the van had left the expressway and switched to side streets, and from there I noted a slowdown that meant we were approaching our final destination. I'd heard of people trapped in trunks of cars who figured out where they were going based on the sound of the road and by keeping track of turns, but I hadn't really been paying attention. Frankly, I had no idea where we were or how far we'd come. Neither Carly nor I had thought to look at the time when we left the bus, so I couldn't use that as a guide either. Eight hundred hours of watching crime shows on TV and I still came up with nothing. Worst hostage ever.

When the van jolted to a stop, Carly's eyes got wide. "We're here," she said.

I knew it was either the end of everything or just the beginning.

Through it all, I sensed Nadia's reassuring presence. At least, if they killed us, I thought, she could bear witness.

Muffled voices came from outside the van, and I sensed that our lady drivers were joined by others—men from the sound

of it. The back doors to the van swung open, and both Carly and I blinked from the sudden light. The van was inside what looked like a big warehouse. Again, shades of the movies. These guys might be menacing, but they weren't all that original. A half dozen people clustered around the opened doors: the two women who drove us, and four men dressed more formally in button-down shirts and dark pants, not a tie in the bunch, but they still resembled the men in the suits we'd encountered driving Mallory home. All six looked to be about Carly's age. And all of them stared at me like I was the most interesting specimen in the zoo.

"Mr. Becker?" one of the men said.

"Yes?" I said.

"I think we've covered this," Carly snapped. "He's Russ Becker. I'm Carly Becker. You're the Associates, and you have my son Frank. We want him back." As always, Carly was not about to pave the way with diplomacy. She was never one to do things the easy way.

"Thank you for coming," the same guy said, completely ignoring my sister's angry outburst. "We appreciate it."

Carly started to say something else, but I held up my hand to quiet her. "We did what you asked," I said. "And now I hope you'll live up to your end of the deal and release my nephew. He's just a kid, and it was morally reprehensible to involve him in any of this." I had no idea where the phrase "morally reprehensible" came from but it fit. "Let's get this over with," I said, unbuckling my seat belt and climbing out of the van. None of them tried to stop me, in fact, they moved back to give me space. When Carly climbed down, one of the men offered her his hand, but she angrily shook it off. My sister was nothing if not consistent.

"Right this way," one of the men said, leading us toward the far end of the warehouse and leaving the rest of the group behind. "I'm Tom, by the way," he said, as if we were on a tour and he was the guide.

Carly and I followed, barely keeping up with his quick steps. "Where are you taking us?" she asked, but he didn't answer her question. Instead, Tom turned to me. "Just between us, we were all very excited to hear you were coming today. Everyone wants to meet you, or at least get a look at you."

"Why?" I asked.

"Because you're Russ Becker," Tom said. "A second gen. Someone like you only comes along every hundred years or so."

"What do you mean—a second gen?" Carly asked, but again, he didn't answer. It was like she wasn't even there. I knew it had to be pissing her off, but to her credit, she kept her cool.

In the back far wall, near the corner, were several doors. Tom opened one and ushered us into a large room that looked like a doctor's waiting room, complete with upholstered chairs, magazines, and a receptionist's desk occupied by a dark-haired older woman. Judging by the photos on the shelf behind her chair, she had several children and grandchildren, many of whom played soccer. To the right of her desk was another closed door. "Welcome," she said, all smiles. She waved a manicured hand in our direction.

"I'm surprised to see you here, Shirley," Tom said. "Don't you usually leave by five?"

"Usually," she said, "But I stuck around tonight to meet Russ Becker." She got up from her seat and approached me, hand extended. "It's a pleasure, sir."

"Suck-up," Tom said, teasing.

I shook her hand and shot a glance at Carly. What was going on? "I came to get my nephew, Frank," I said.

"Of course," she said, returning to her desk. "Miss Becker, can I get you something to drink? You'll be waiting here."

"And Mr. Becker, you'll be coming with me, please," Tom said to me, gesturing with his chin. "Can you buzz us through, Shirley?"

"Wait a minute," Carly said. "We came together and we're staying together. We're not splitting up." She took a step closer to me, to show unity, I guess.

Tom and Shirley exchanged the kind of look parents use when toddlers are being unreasonable. "I'm afraid this isn't negotiable," he said.

"I know what you people are capable of," Carly said. "And I know we have a better chance of leaving here in one piece if we stay together."

"Oh, honey," Shirley said, and her voice had the same tone my mother's had when she'd learned I was being picked on in grade school.

But Carly was not going to be placated. "How do I even know my son is alive? Except for one voice mail hours ago, I haven't heard a thing."

"Your son is fine," Shirley said, but her words didn't help. Carly started demanding they bring Frank out, *right this minute* or she was going to expose all of them for the murderers they were. Shirley tried to calm her, while Tom went off in the corner of the room to make a phone call. I stood frozen, not knowing what to do. I watched my sister having a meltdown and Shirley acting like a kindly den mother, all the while feeling like I should be taking some action.

And then I heard Nadia's voice coming through clearly and calmly. With all the commotion, I hadn't even noticed the absence of her energy. *It's all right, Russ. I've seen Frank. He's fine.*

I came to attention. *Are you sure?*

They've got him in back watching cartoons. He looks a little bored, but he's fine.

How do you know for sure that it's Frank? I wanted to believe her, but it occurred to me that it could be someone else's kid.

He answered to that name when they gave him the root beer, and besides, he kind of looks like you. Who else could it be?

I took charge of the situation, interrupting Carly's ranting by waving a hand in front of her mouth. She stopped carrying on to glare at me, but at least she stopped. I took my hand away. "Carly, really, it's okay. Just wait here for me."

CHAPTER THIRTY-EIGHT

———— o ————

Tom led me into an adjoining room, which was suspiciously empty except for a metal folding chair positioned under a ceiling light fixture. The floor was bare concrete and the walls and ceiling were painted a stark white. He watched my face to get a reaction. "So what do you think?"

"No windows, two doors," I said, more of an observation than anything else. The second door was opposite the one we'd entered. "Are you going to be bringing Frank in?"

"I wish it were that easy," he said, sounding sincere. "But it's not up to me."

"Who is it up to?"

"My orders came from the top. The commander has specified that you're to take a series of tests. Once you've completed all the tests, you and your nephew will be reunited, and after a brief interview, you'll be allowed to go home."

I didn't like this at all. "What kind of tests are we talking about?"

"Different sorts of tests. We'll be assessing your abilities, which we know are considerable. This is how it will work," he

said, gesturing enthusiastically with his hands. "This particular room is the first in a series of rooms. Each room you enter after this one will have three doors. Your job is to get through the rooms using the correct doors in a timely manner. In fact," he said, pulling a device out of his pocket, "you will be timed." He leaned in conspiratorially. "They're giving you an hour to complete the course, but I don't think it'll take you that long. In the office pool I put in for thirty-two minutes."

"Wait a minute—people are betting on me?" I said, practically sputtering.

"Just a few of us." He waved a hand like this was inconsequential. "And we're all really pulling for you. So do you understand?"

"No, I don't understand at all." I felt panic rise in my throat. Dr. Anton said my test scores indicated I was highly intelligent, but I wasn't grasping what this was all about. "Tell me again."

"Okay." He took a deep breath and gave instructions like a quarterback in the huddle spelling out a play. "Series of rooms. Each room after this one will have three doors. You need to get past the obstacles in each room and pick the right door to move on to the next. The door will be locked until you've taken care of the obstacles. Think of it as a maze with challenges. If you get past the obstacles and choose the correct doors all along, when you've reached the last room, the tests will be over, and you'll be reunited with Frank."

"What if I pick the wrong door, or can't get past the obstacles?"

"Oh, that would be very bad," Tim said. "*Really* bad for you and your loved ones." He clapped me on the shoulder. "But let's not think like that. Positive thoughts. Okay?"

"What if I refuse to play this sick game of yours?"

Tim's face dropped. "That's not an option. If you want to go home you have to take the tests."

We'd reached an impasse that only I could break. I thought about my options and I came up with this: I could participate in their tests, or (the inference was) Carly, Frank, and I would die.

Finally I said, "Okay. When do I start?"

"Oh it's already started in a way. I'm going to be leaving the room. Once you hear the door click shut, it will officially begin. I wish you the very best of luck." He extended a hand. When I started to reach for it, I heard Nadia's voice: *No! Don't touch his hand, or you'll get electrocuted. This is the first test.*

I jerked back. "No thanks." How ingrained are the social niceties that I felt compelled to thank someone about to shoot voltage into my body? "I have enough electricity in me right now. I'll take a pass."

"Very good!" Tim said approvingly. He pointed to the door we'd entered. "You may proceed."

"I don't think so," I shot back. "I'll be going through the other door."

He laughed. "I didn't think you'd fall for that, but I had to try."

After Tim retreated to the reception area, I was able to touch base with my new guardian angel, Nadia. *Thank you.*

No problem. I've got your back, Russ.

When Carly used that expression it made me cringe, but Nadia's use of it was reassuring. It meant I wasn't alone. I said, *I know. I appreciate it.*

They're watching you. They have cameras built into the light fixtures and the woodwork around the doors.

Do they know you're here with me?

I'm not technically there, Russ. In reality, I'm lying on my bed at home.

You know what I mean.

No, no one knows I'm talking to you. It's just between us.

I turned to the door and waved to show I knew I was being observed. I pictured a bunch of Associates huddled around a TV screen, watching like I was part of a reality show. What kind of sick losers got off on watching this kind of thing? I headed to the door on the opposite wall, tentatively touching the knob.

Take the chair with you.

Without hesitation, I went back and collected the chair. Folded, it fit nicely under my arm. I opened the door and walked through it into another room very much like the first. Empty, lit only by an overhead light fixture.

I shut the door behind me and the light suddenly went out, putting me in complete darkness. The dark had depths of darkness; my lack of spatial awareness made me dizzy and I felt the room spin around me like the time I was eight and I snuck a wine cooler. I stood there for seconds or maybe minutes, losing my sense of time while trying to get my bearings. The nothing that was happening made me nervous that I'd be caught off guard when something finally did happen. *Nadia?*

I'm here, Russ.

Do you have any idea what's happening next?

Listen carefully. They're going to let several large attack dogs into the room in a few minutes. They're vicious and snarling and ready to bite.

Ready to bite me?

Of course, who else? Here's what you need to do. Take off your shirt.

Take off my shirt? Why?

When that guy touched you he put some kind of meat odor on your shirt to attract the dogs. Take it off and drape it over the chair.

I don't smell anything on me.

You're not a dog.

I opened the chair and pulled my T-shirt over my head, then laid it across the chair back. *Now what?*

Run like hell!

You're very funny, Nadia.

Okay, you'll need to stand next to the door.

I fumbled my way across the room until I found two doors on the opposite wall. *Man, it's dark.*

If only there was some way for you to produce light... Even in my head, her sarcastic tone came through.

Oh yeah. I concentrated on the space between my hands until I generated sparks that flew back and forth between them. Now I could see well enough to get an awareness of the room. I looked up at the light fixture and said, "Let there be light." I was juggling the equivalent of a small fireball back and forth between my hands. Looking straight at it was blinding, so I kept my eyes above the glow. I was standing between the two doors.

I could hear the pack of dogs on the other side, and they were, as Nadia warned, snarling and growling. I've always avoided angry canines with sharp teeth, mostly by not breaking into junkyards at night, but there was no avoiding them this time. The dogs lunged at the other side of the door. I heard the scratch of their nails against the wood and the sound of the door banging in its frame. When they were released into the room it would be the hounds of hell against Russ Becker, high school sophomore. I wasn't sure my electricity would help this time around. I could shoot straight, when I had one target at a time and the target wasn't moving. What were the chances that would happen?

Even though I'd been expecting it, when the door flew open and the dogs burst in, it startled me. I dropped the fireball of

sparks, which fizzled to nothingness and left me back in the dark. I'd seen enough though. The dogs were big, with boxy snouts and strong flanks, and there were three of them, identical like triplets. They lunged into the room, past where I stood and right for the shirt draped over the top of the metal folding chair. The impact to the chair sent it careening across the room and it clattered as it hit the opposite wall.

Seizing the opportunity to get away, I grabbed the knob of the other door, the one that hadn't contained the dogs, thinking it was the obvious choice. I couldn't turn the knob, and when I pulled, it didn't budge. Frantic, I tried the other door, but that one too was locked. Why?

I yelled, "I overcame the obstacle. Open the door!"

The overhead lights came on and the dogs took a sudden interest in me. Their ears raised, they turned toward me, teeth bared and growling. I'd gone through a morbid period in middle school during which I'd pictured my death a million different ways. But getting eaten by dogs hadn't been one of them.

"Nice doggies," I said, backing into the corner. The triplets had slowed and were approaching me slowly, like they'd been trained to take their time. I looked around the room, but there was nowhere to run to, no place to hide, nothing I could use as a weapon. Panic crept up like bile in my throat.

And then I remembered what Carly had said when we were being transported in the van. *You're the weapon.*

True that.

I recovered from my fear, and I held my hands out over their heads, palms down, and directed energy toward them. I spoke authoritatively. "Sit." The dogs stopped moving and growling, but didn't follow my command. One tilted his head to the side as if considering it, which I took as a promising sign.

I tried again. "Sit." And amazingly they all lowered their haunches and sat. I tried to remember common dog commands and came up with: "Stay," and then, "Down." The three dogs lowered their bodies to a resting position. "Good dogs!" I noticed then that one of them had my T-shirt in his mouth. I went over and rested a hand on his head. "Drop it."

When he released the shirt, I took it and put my arms through the sleeves, which caused a comment from Nadia: *Gross*.

Girls got grossed out so easily, I thought as I pulled it over my head. Dog drool didn't bother me. I couldn't even dwell on something that insignificant. I needed to focus on the next challenge.

I chose a door, opened it, and walked through.

CHAPTER THIRTY-NINE

———— o ————

On the other side was a slightly larger room with one major improvement—actual windows looking out to a parking lot and a highway beyond. Music blared from speakers I couldn't see. I didn't recognize the song, but it was peppy, happy music, a contrast to the inner turmoil swirling around in my stomach.

Two beefy-looking guys about my age stood on the opposite side of the room, each of them in front of a door. The first thing I noticed about them was that they were built like football players. The second thing—they wore track suits. Not even kidding. Besides the presence of these two actual human beings, the place was empty. I was guessing these two guys were my obstacles.

"Hey, fellas," I said. "I'm kind of working my way through here. Can you direct me to my next destination?"

No sense of humor, these guys. They didn't say a word, and their faces didn't give anything away, but they crossed their arms in front of them.

A little help here, Nadia? I didn't sense her presence anymore. For whatever reason, she was gone, and I was on my own.

I looked at the guys' faces. One looked a little younger than the other. He had bad skin, but a good head of wavy hair. The other teenager, the one guarding the door on the left, had a tattoo on his neck. A wicked-looking snake. The kind of tattoo you see on guys being released from prison (or on their way in). Both of these guys outweighed me by at least fifty pounds, and each of them had a look on their face like they couldn't wait to pound me into ground beef.

When Snake Boy finally said something, it wasn't to me. "So this is the guy who's supposed to be *the one*? I'm not seeing it."

His friend smirked. "We could use him to power a flashlight, maybe." He pronounced the word like "meb-be," making him sound like a hick.

Clearly these Neanderthals were eager for a fight to break out. I knew that once I made a move to get past them I'd be starting something, so I had to choose my door ahead of time. I took a half-step toward Snake Boy's door and neither one of the guys flinched. I stepped back and did the same for the other door, the one guarded by the younger looking kid. Both of them tensed, as if getting ready to stop me. It was a very slight, involuntary twitch, but it was there, clear as day. They really didn't want me anywhere near the door on the right.

I made a mental X on that door. In my mind it became *mine* and these guys were keeping it from me. I took a deep breath and stood up as straight as I could. "Hey, caveman," I said, gesturing to Wavy Hair. "Move aside."

And then he said, and I would swear to this in court, "Make me."

I think I mentioned before that I was never one for fighting. I avoided conflict and kept out of trouble, if I could. In middle school, my usual response to someone blocking my way into

a room and saying "Make me," was to walk away and use the bathroom on the other end of the building. I didn't think I was a fighter, but I was finding out that when life was on the line I could bring it.

I shot a bolt of electricity at his feet, making him jump back against the door. He looked startled, but his friend, Snake Boy, whooped and yelled, "We got ourselves a live one!"

A wisp of smoke came off of Wavy Hair's left foot. My zap had come a little too close for comfort. He frantically pulled off his shoe and threw it at me. "Those were new," he said, irate.

"Sorry," I said, and charged right toward them. They hadn't made a move yet, and I had the idea that I could throw a few more zaps their way and be through the door in no time. If I hurried, Tim might win the pool yet.

Here's something to keep in mind for future reference: don't underestimate people just because they talk like hicks or have questionable tattoos. These guys had more going on than I gave them credit for. They tag-teamed me by rushing forward and knocking me to the concrete floor, then jumping on top of me like they were television wrestlers. Wavy Hair pinned me down and struck me in the face with the side of his fist over and over again until I felt the crack of my nose breaking and a resulting river of blood gush out of my nose. Some of the blood trickled down the back of my throat and I could taste it, making me want to puke. These two goons didn't have the electrical power or range that I had, but for their strategy they didn't need them. Once they had me trapped beneath them, Snake Boy shocked me repeatedly at close range. I was too busy trying to defend myself to utilize my offensive skills. They weren't as powerful, but there were two of them and they were beating me up old school.

"Hey!" I struggled to get up, but they kept pushing me back. I wondered at the venom in their eyes. They didn't even know me. Why would they hate me?

Snake Boy's hands were on my chest thrusting electrical charges repeatedly into my torso; his buddy was squeezing my head so hard my eyes hurt. "Admit defeat," said Wavy Hair, in the same tone he'd used when he'd said, "Make me." This was war, grade-school style. "Say it. Say we've won."

I choked out one word: "Never."

Every time I managed to get myself up on one elbow, I got pushed down again. It looked like I couldn't win at this game. I stretched my arm toward the door, longing to be there. Voices swirled around me—memories of everything I'd heard that day.

Carly saying: *You're the weapon.*

Tim, our tour guide, leading us like an overeager puppy, saying: *You're Russ Becker. A second gen. Someone like you only comes along every hundred years or so.*

Shirley, at the reception desk who said: *I stuck around tonight to meet Russ Becker.* And shaking my hand like it was an honor. Like I was somebody special.

And finally I remembered Frank's message on Carly's phone: *Can you send Russ to come get me so I can come home?*

Frank was waiting to go home. What I was currently doing, getting the crap beaten out of me, clearly wasn't working. I needed a new strategy.

I sucked in my breath, stopped using my muscles to resist, and thought about the electricity instead. I'd been carrying around my own share, and they were giving me more. Just like when the Associates were trying to abduct Mallory, I summoned all of the electricity together, and like a surge of adrenaline, it gave me a boost of superhuman energy.

I don't remember getting up. It happened fast. One second I was pinned to the floor by Snake Boy, the next I was on my feet, a force to be reckoned with. The abrupt movement knocked Snake Boy and Wavy Hair off balance.

As soon as I reached the door, they were on their feet and after me. I turned the knob and was almost through, with both of them on my heels. Using his full weight, Wavy Hair slammed the door against me, holding me pinned halfway through. His buddy came up and zapped my shoulder, making me wince only slightly. I was so close, so close. I was two-thirds of the way into the next room, but that didn't matter. If I couldn't get away from these guys, I'd never reach the next challenge.

I heard Snake Boy's voice taunting me. "What you gonna do now?" The door pressed against my chest, holding me in a vise grip. Someone was now yanking on my arm, and it felt like it was just about to come out of its socket.

I didn't hold back, but shot a violent shaft of electricity out of the arm being yanked. I'd never released so much electricity before: it created a deafening boom and a blinding flash of light. The bolt lacked direction, but I knew it made contact because both of the guys let go and the door swung open. I heard an ear-shattering scream of pain coming from one of the guys, and when I looked back into the room, I saw Wavy Hair on the floor, legs thrashing, his head shaking like he was having a seizure.

Snake Boy, who stood over him, gave me a horrified look. He opened his mouth as if to speak, but nothing came out.

I shut the door behind me.

CHAPTER FORTY

───── o ─────

I found myself in a doctor's office waiting room, complete with a scattering of people sitting and reading magazines and a motherly-looking receptionist behind the counter. One woman sighed and glanced at the time on her phone, while a young mother jostled a crying baby on her lap. An elderly man was checking in at the front; the receptionist handed him a clipboard and was giving him instructions on how to fill out the forms.

Call me puzzled. I had no idea what to do. My body was on high alert watching for ninjas or sharpshooters, but none jumped out. In fact, no one even looked up when I walked into the room. I wondered if being in a doctor's office had something to do with the fact that I was injured. Even without a mirror, I knew I was a mess. Blood stained the front of my T-shirt, the side of my face felt swollen, and I could have sworn I'd broken a few ribs. Every breath brought stabbing pain.

I walked up to the front, past the old man who had just walked away with the clipboard. I stood nervously at the counter. The receptionist looked up and said, "Yes? Do you have an appointment?"

An appointment? She had to be kidding. I played along. "I'm not sure," I said. "My name is Russ Becker."

Her face lit up. "Oh yes, Mr. Becker. The doctor is expecting you. Please take a seat. We'll be calling you shortly."

I sat down next to the woman with the baby, which seemed like a fairly safe decision. The baby screamed, his face bright read and his eyes filled with tears. His mother, talking over his crying, said, "He's usually such a good boy, but he's teething and he's in a lot of pain."

"Poor thing," I said, letting my guard down a little bit. I was fairly sure no one was going to try to kill me when I was next to a baby. The next thing I did, completely on instinct, was to hold out a finger. The baby looked at it with wide eyes and grabbed hold. "He's got a good grip." I made a funny face at him and he stopped crying to regard me curiously.

"He likes you," she said.

The baby appeared fascinated by me. He seemed to have forgotten that he'd been busy crying, and stared, unblinking, directly at my face.

"What's his name?" I asked.

"Terry," she said. And then she turned her attention back to the baby and spoke in the way people do to small children and animals. "He's a good little man. Yes, he is."

"Hi, Terry." I felt my finger getting warmer and the connection between the baby and me growing. His mother was right, his gums were hurting badly. Those molars were killer. But the longer he held my finger, the more the pain subsided, and within a minute or so he felt fine. I sensed the shift in his mood from crabby to happy. And when he got all the way to happy, he was really happy—Disneyland style. "Poor little guy," I said to his mother. "It's no fun being in pain."

"Mr. Becker?" the receptionist called out.

I pulled my finger from little Terry's grasp and went up to the front.

"The doctor will see you now."

A petite woman in a white jacket, a stethoscope around her neck, came out into the waiting area to greet me. She was young, early thirties at the most, and had dark hair and straight white teeth. The embroidery above her pocket identified her as Dr. Poore. "It's a pleasure to meet you," she said, extending her hand.

Oh, Nadia, where are you? I got nothing in response. Since Dr. Poore didn't look too menacing, I took a chance and shook her hand.

"I won't keep you long," she said, "because I know you're trying to get through the challenges, but I do have a patient I'd like you to see." She beckoned with one finger and led me down a hallway.

"You know about the challenges?" I was talking to the back of her head, while also trying to stay aware of my surroundings. I still wasn't entirely convinced that I wasn't going to be ambushed.

"Well, of course."

"So is this an actual doctor's office?"

"For now."

"But will it be one tomorrow and next week?"

She stopped before a doorway and said, "Well, no, just for today as a scene setting for part of the test."

"So you're not a doctor then?"

"No, I'm a doctor, an MD. I work for the organization that's testing you."

"The Associates."

Her lips pressed firmly together. "I can't divulge the particulars. My role in this is to see you through this particular

challenge." She put a hand on her hip like, *Do you want to continue or not?*

"Go ahead," I said. "I'm with you."

She continued down the hall and turned into what proved to be an exam room. A red-haired teenage girl in a hospital gown sat on the exam table, her legs dangling down over the edge. "Oh, I'm sorry," I said, backing out of the room.

"Don't be silly," Dr. Poore said, pulling me back in by the front of my stained shirt. "Clarice is why you're here."

"What happened to you?" Clarice asked, forehead furrowed. "I've got cancer and I look better than you do."

"I had a disagreement with some friends."

"Looks like they won."

"Actually—"

Dr. Poore interrupted. "We want you to try your healing powers on Clarice."

So they knew about the healing powers. Carly was right. I shrugged. "Okay, I'll give it a go."

"She has been diagnosed recently with stage—"

"Don't." Now it was my turn to interrupt. I raised my palm and explained. "I don't need to know." Part of me didn't want to hear this cute girl's sad story, and part of me knew I could figure it out on my own. Clarice still had a head of thick red hair and she didn't look sick. But I knew that looks could be deceiving.

I held out my hands and Clarice rested her hands in mine.

"You don't need to touch the affected areas?" Dr. Poore hovered to one side and craned her neck to watch.

"No." Remembering what Nadia had said, I looked toward the door. "Are all of you getting this?"

Clarice smirked.

Feeling my hands get warmer, I knew something was happening. I concentrated, trying to send energy where it was needed most. I knew what it felt like when I'd healed my own bullet wound, and when I'd healed Mallory's cut finger and when I'd infused healing currents in the two Associates who'd tried to abduct her. In each case, I'd instinctively felt where the damage had been, and my energy had been pulled right to that area. With Clarice the energy was searching, but not finding anything.

After a few minutes, I shook my head. "I'm sorry. I can't figure it out."

"What can't you figure out?" Clarice asked. "I have cancer. Cure it."

I said, "I'm sorry. I don't feel like anything is wrong with you." I pulled my hands away and a knot in my stomach twisted. I'd gotten through three challenges, only to fail this one. "Maybe I could try with another patient?"

"No, thanks for trying. I think we'll just pass you on to the next level," Dr. Poore said, pressing her hand against my back to guide me out of the room.

As we walked back, I turned to Clarice and said, "I'm sorry I couldn't help."

"S'okay," she said, sounding bored. "Don't worry about it."

Dr. Poore walked me down the hall, away from the reception area. At the end of the hallway was a closed door, and adjacent to that, on my right, was another. "One of these will take you out of this office and on to your next and final challenge," she said.

I looked at the closed doors and hesitated. They looked identical and yet one would lead me to doom while the other meant life and liberation. *Nadia, are you there?*

No reply.

Dr. Poore leaned in sympathetically and said, "Sometimes, when I'm lost, it helps me to think about where I've been."

Good for you, I wanted to say, and then I realized she'd given me a hint. Where I'd been. Think, Russ, think. I looked back down the hallway and realized it ran parallel to the waiting room. If I took the door on the right, it would lead me back behind the receptionist's desk, clearly not where I needed to be. The door at the end of the hall, that would be the right one.

I turned to shake Dr. Poore's hand. "It was a pleasure meeting you," I said, and I really meant it. Besides the baby, Terry, she was the only one in the place who seemed like a real human being.

CHAPTER FORTY-ONE

———— o ————

Talk about a shock. As confusing as it had been to walk into a doctor's waiting room, this was even more mind-boggling. I opened the door to find myself in what looked like a public place, a large, open sunny area filled with people coming and going. It took a second to get my bearings, but then I realized I knew this place. It was the Milwaukee Intermodal Station, where Carly and I had purchased the ticket to get on the bus.

Had the van circled back on the expressway and returned to Milwaukee without us realizing it? That's what must have happened, and yet I was sure there wouldn't have been enough time for them to do that. Of course, Carly and I had completely lost our sense of time and distance being in the dark in the back of the van.

I stood against a wall, unsure how to proceed from here. If I went out to the parking lot, would Carly and Frank be waiting in the car? Was I supposed to be doing something, and if so, what exactly? A voice over a loudspeaker announced a departure, and people came and went. It was a little busier than I remembered it being before.

Déjà vu all over again, as the saying goes. And yet.

Something wasn't right. I looked at the slant of light coming through the window and remembered it coming in at the same angle when I'd picked up my tickets. Time had passed. Why hadn't the sun moved?

I made my way through the crowd to the one place I was familiar with—the Greyhound ticket counter. The same bald-headed man was working. I went up and rested my elbows on the counter. When he looked up, I sensed recognition on his part. He smiled. "Mr. Becker! How nice to see you again. Did you enjoy your ride with us yesterday?"

"Yesterday? No, I saw you just a few hours ago."

"I hate to correct you, sir, but I last saw you yesterday." He sounded assured, but I sensed something underneath that confident tone. A quiver of deceit. He was lying.

I said, "I didn't see you yesterday. That was earlier today. And it wasn't here, but at the Milwaukee Intermodal Station."

"Sir, this is the Milwaukee Intermodal Station."

I said, "No, it looks a lot like it, I'll give you that, but it's not. It can't be."

He turned to his coworker. "Gary, what's the name of this building?"

Gary, who was handing change over the counter to a customer, looked confused. "The Milwaukee Intermodal Station? Sometimes people just call it the Amtrak station or the bus station."

"You see?" Baldy said, as if Gary's testimony proved his point.

"The clocks are wrong too," I said. "I left here at six fifteen, and at least two hours have passed since then."

"I'm sorry, sir," he said, "but you're mistaken. The six fifteen bus hasn't even left yet today."

"You're the one who's mistaken." Because, I realized as I looked around, I couldn't be in the Milwaukee Intermodal Station. And I wasn't back in Milwaukee. They'd recreated it somehow. What they'd done here was close, but not close enough. I looked around, wondering what it would have taken to recreate a massive glass structure like this. A lot. Was it all for me? And why? "I know what time it really is and that I'm nowhere near the Intermodal Station. It's a nice recreation, though." I looked around. "You've gotten most of the details right. But not all of them. That tree for instance," I said, pointing to one of the potted trees in the center, "is shaped slightly different than it was before."

Baldy shook his head. "I don't want to upset you because I can tell you're confused. But I last saw you yesterday when I gave you the envelope with the ticket for the six fifteen bus. I went home last night, had a good night's sleep, and now I'm back here at my place at the counter today."

"And I don't want to upset you," I said, hitting the ball back over the net, "but I saw you at the Milwaukee Intermodal Station a few hours ago, and now we're here at this place that's supposed to look just like it."

"Say that's true," he said slowly. "Say you left just a few hours ago and your bus ride took you to a place just like this but located somewhere else. How would I have gotten there? I mean, you left, didn't you? And I was still working. I wouldn't have had time to leave there and arrive somewhere else already."

I hesitated. It was all getting muddled in my brain. How would he have gotten ahead of the bus and van? Maybe if he'd driven really fast... But so much would have had to work perfectly for that to happen.

"They rotate the trees periodically," he said. "To make sure they all get the same amount of light."

That almost made sense.

"Have you had a head injury recently?" he asked kindly. "People have been known to lose track of time due to brain trauma."

I'd been so sure that I wasn't back at the station, but maybe I'd been knocked unconscious, and they'd transported me back to Milwaukee without my knowledge. I guessed it was possible.

"You look like you've been through a horrible ordeal," Baldy said, gesturing toward my blood-splattered shirt. "Why don't you sit down over there and I'll have someone bring you a cup of water. We can arrange a ride home for you, if you want." His voice had a lulling effect on me and I found myself, against my better judgment, wanting to sit down and have someone take care of me. And really, all I wanted to do was go home and have everything back the way it was.

I glanced at the place he pointed to and imagined sinking into the seat and having someone bring me a cold drink of water. Maybe they could direct me to the restroom, where I could splash some water on my face before my trip home. For just a few minutes it would be nice to put my head back and rest my eyes. I braced myself against the counter, vacillating. I wanted this to be over in the worst way. It would have been easy to give in, but then I remembered something: Carly's gum. In an act of defiance she'd stuck it under the counter when I'd picked up the ticket.

I took a step back to look underneath. I clearly remembered seeing her two fingers press a pink glob of gum to the white underside of the counter. But it wasn't there now. No gum, and no sign there ever had been. Not only that, but the underside of the counter was dark gray, not white. This place came close, but it wasn't exactly the same. I was sure of it now. I straightened up and looked him square in the eye.

"Look," I said. "If the challenge was for me to see through this charade, it's over. I don't, for one instant, believe I'm in the Milwaukee Intermodal Station. Earlier today, I saw you, or a man who looked exactly like you, in the station in Milwaukee, but that's not where we are now. That tree is different," I said and pointed, "and this counter is different." I knocked on it for emphasis. "And the sun should be lower in the sky by now. You can make any changes you want and say what you want, but I know what I know. I'm not in the Milwaukee Intermodal Station. You can't mess with my head this way."

He stared at me unblinking. "Is that your final answer?"

"Damn straight it is."

"Well done, Mr. Becker," he said, nodding approvingly.

Over the loudspeaker, a loud tone chimed. As if on cue, everyone in the terminal stopped what they were doing. The maintenance man set down his mop, the people sitting in chairs closed their magazines and laptops, and the people walking through stopped in their tracks.

And then, spontaneously, every person in the terminal began clapping. A slow clap. Each and every one of them clapping and walking toward me. The employees and the travelers, along with a crowd of others who materialized seemingly out of nowhere. They gravitated in my direction, all the while cheering like they'd witnessed a winning touchdown at Lambeau Field. And all of the attention was aimed at me.

Tim appeared at my side and pulled my arm up in the air. Around me people were high-fiving and talking excitedly. When the crowd finally settled down, Tim released my arm to announce, "Forty-eight minutes and fifty-three seconds," which set them off again. I caught bits and pieces:

"Unbelievable!"

"Can you even imagine everything we'll be able to do now that we have this guy?"

"So that's what a second gen is like!"

Tim turned to me. "Your powers are most impressive. Is there anything I can get for you—something to drink, some fresh clothes?"

I said, "I want my nephew."

CHAPTER FORTY-TWO

———— o ————

Frank Shrapnel sat on a couch in front of a TV, barely looking up when I walked through the door. The room consisted solely of a couch, a television, and a side table covered by an assortment of salty snacks and a half mug of root beer with a bendy straw in it. "Hey, buddy," I said, something that normally would have made him light up with happiness, but this time the only reaction was the brief flick of his eyes darting my way.

I knelt down in front of him. "Are you ready to go home?"

"Okay," he said noncommittally. There was no expression on his face, no smile of recognition. All of his usual energy was gone, just a shell of a boy left behind.

I choked back my outrage to confront Tim. "What have you done to him?"

"What do you mean?" Tim said, innocently. "He's right there in front of you, fine and happy. Look him over. You won't find a mark on him. And I think if you'll ask him, he'll tell you he had a good time visiting us here at the testing center. Isn't that right, Frank?"

"I had a good time at the testing center with Russ," he said, his eyes still on the screen.

"You used mind control on him?" I said, incredulous.

"Would you have preferred he be frightened and hysterical?"

I got right in Tim's face. "I would have *preferred* that he be safe at home where he belongs."

"Please calm down."

"Calm down? I don't think so. You people are monsters. First you abduct Frank and then you mess with his mind. He's just a kid." I wished I could scoop Frank up and carry him out, the way I used to when he was little.

"No need to overreact," Tim said. "He's fine. He'll go home and have happy memories of his visit at the video game testing station with Uncle Russ."

"He thinks he's at a video game testing station?"

Tim nodded. "He's sure of it. In his mind the two of you have been testing video games for a big company. He won't be sure of the name of the company. We left that ambiguous, but he'll certainly remember the fun he had and how special it made him feel to spend an evening with Uncle Russ."

"You've got to be kidding."

"Not kidding at all. Years from now, he'll still be talking about it, and what's wrong with that?"

"What's wrong with that is that it's not *real*," I said. "It never *happened*."

"As far as he'll be concerned it happened. Really, how do you know that all of *your* memories are factual? We create the reality we want to believe. One child thinks they have the meanest parents in the world. His brother thinks they're strict but fair. Which one is right? Is the second one downplaying it or is the first one a whiner? So much of life depends on your perspective."

"It has nothing to do with perspective," I pointed out. "What we're talking about is—"

At that very moment, Carly rushed into the room, interrupting the debate. "Frank!" she cried, joining him on the couch and crushing him into a hug. Normally he would have wriggled out of her grasp, but now, docile as a teddy bear, he accepted it. Like me, she soon realized this was not the Frank we knew. She looked up, outraged. "What's wrong with him?" she demanded.

"They used mind control on him," I said bitterly. "They implanted false memories. He's going to think he and I spent the evening at a video game testing station."

Frank gave Carly a blank look. "Russ and I have been testing new games. It was really cool." His voice had a prerecorded quality to it.

Carly said, "Snap out of it, Frank. Look at me, look at me right now." She took him by the shoulders and gave a little shake. Even though he stared straight at her, nothing registered. His enlarged pupils gave him the odd look of one who was hypnotized.

"There's no point in doing that," Tim said. "It will wear off soon enough, probably by the time you get home, in fact."

But Carly wasn't listening. She snapped her fingers in front of his face. "Frank, answer me. Do you know where you are?"

"At the video game testing station," Frank said, each word as monotone as the next. "Russ and I played some really cool new games. I can't wait until they're available for preorder."

"Oh, Frank." Her eyes filled up with tears. She turned to me. "Do something, Russ."

Tim said, "He's fine, just fine."

"He's under some kind of spell. Where are you, Frank?" she asked, tracing the side of his face with her fingertips. "I never should have left you alone. I'm sorry."

"It's okay, Mom," Frank said, his gaze back now on the TV screen. "Russ and I had fun."

Carly took his hand between hers and curved her body protectively around Frank. "I want to go home," she said, her voice sounding much younger, as if she were a child instead of an adult woman.

I wanted to go home, too, but going now would mean leaving things unfinished. I didn't want to live my life looking over my shoulder, wondering when the Associates would be coming for me. Because they would be coming for me. Getting through these challenges wasn't the end of it, I knew. It was just the beginning, and I needed to know more. "Just hang in there, Carly," I said, and to Tim: "I don't want to go until I talk to whoever's in charge."

"You're in luck," Tim said. "He wants to talk to you too."

CHAPTER FORTY-THREE

———— o ————

W e encountered locked doors along the way. Tim leaned over and had his eyeball scanned, which gave us access to the corridor leading to our destination. The actual room required a punch code and a reading of his handprint before we were allowed entry. A woman's voice said, "Access is granted," and then double doors slid open to each side, revealing what looked like a war room. Or at least what I knew of war rooms from the movies. Several people worked behind computers set up on a boomerang-shaped counter. One man stood off to the side, his arms folded. All of them wore business-type clothing—dress shirts and dark pants.

They didn't notice us entering the room because their attention was on a large screen covering the far wall. On either side of the main screen were two smaller screens. The configuration reminded me of mirrors in the changing rooms at Kohl's department stores. I hated trying on clothes in stores, but if my mother was with me she always insisted. The worst thing about it was coming out to stand for inspection while she assessed shoulder fit and took a mortifyingly long time determining whether or

not there was enough extra growing length in the pants. Not my favorite form of humiliation. This view was equally embarrassing because the images on the screen were of me battling Snake Boy and Wavy Hair. Or maybe battling wasn't quite accurate. In this particular clip, Snake Boy and Wavy Hair were giving me a pounding like I was meat that needed tenderizing.

Standing at the back of the room, I winced with each blow, remembering how it felt at the time. Since then, I'd healed considerably, which was good. By the time I got home there would be nothing I'd have to explain to my parents.

During the incident with the two thugs, Snake Boy and Wavy Hair, there was a moment when I'd realized I could summon my strength using the electrical energy inside of me, and that exact moment was visible on the video. My face changed expression, and I leaped off the ground in an almost superhuman way. The Associates in the room made approving noises at this part, and the man standing off to one side said, "Go back about five seconds and replay that frame by frame." And frame by frame, they studied and discussed the angle of my body from prone to upright and the speed at which I'd jumped.

I'd known of course, that I had been watched, but seeing this footage and knowing it was being analyzed was another thing entirely. These people had no boundaries. I was a monkey in the zoo being put through an obstacle course to get a banana, the banana being Frank.

The next scene they viewed and discussed involved the two goons attempting to abduct Mallory the night we'd driven home from Mr. Specter's house. One of the two men apparently had a hidden camera on his person because they had a record of all of it: me hitting them with lightning bolts, and then healing them, and Mallory using mind control to persuade them that the kids

in Edgewood hadn't been affected by the light particles. So much for that. And I'd thought it was such a good idea at the time.

I glanced over at Tim to see if he'd interrupt and let them know we were there, but he stood quietly and shook his head when I made a gesture asking if we should step forward.

Finally, I'd had enough. "Excuse me," I called out. "Who's in charge here?" Tim looked horrified that I'd interrupted, but I didn't care. I figured that if they were going to kill me, they'd have done it already.

* * *

Five minutes later, the room had been cleared; the only ones left were me and the man in charge, the one who'd been standing with his arms folded. I'd been granted a private interview.

"So, we finally meet," he said with a warm smile as if we'd been introduced at a social function. He could have been any one of the men Carly dated and brought to the house to meet the family. He had the pleasantries down, anyway. His appearance, though, was better than most of her boyfriends. He was clean cut, with good teeth, a wrinkle-free shirt, and pressed pants. A young executive, probably an overachiever in his school days. I'd seen his type before. He was much older than me, but I wasn't intimidated.

"Yeah, I'm thinking we haven't officially met since I don't know your name," I said. He sat in a chair and indicated I should do the same, but instead I leaned my butt back against the countertop holding the computers. My psychology teacher told us that towering above someone establishes dominancy. The whole alpha male thing. I wasn't sure about that, but at least I didn't look afraid, which is what I was going for. She also said that the

correct thing to say when you don't know what to say is, "Really." The things you learn in school.

"Oh, sorry about that," he said, standing to clasp my hand. "The name's Miller."

"Are you the commander I keep hearing about?"

"Me, the commander?" He chuckled. "No, I'm the division leader. No one gets to just meet the commander. He wouldn't be here today for something like this." He sat back in his chair, clearly amused.

"So the commander is the Wizard of Oz of your organization?"

"Excuse me?"

"You know—'nobody sees the wizard, pay no attention to the man behind the curtain,' that kind of thing?" He didn't seem to get the reference, so I let it go and went on. "Never mind. I have a few questions for you."

"Certainly. Ask away."

"Why me?"

"Why not you?" he asked.

Okay, this was seriously frustrating. I said, "Look, I don't want to play games. I just want answers. Why was I put through these challenges? Clearly you know that I'm not the only one who was exposed to the light particles."

Miller said, "No, you're not the only one who was exposed. Let me show you something." He sat at a computer terminal and clicked on a few things on the keyboard. On the large screen in the front of the room popped up a still photo of Jameson along with a list of stats—his name, age, address, and at the top: Power: Telekinesis, Low. "You know him?" he said, pointing.

A rhetorical question, but I answered it anyway. "Yes."

"But you don't like him." A statement.

"He's okay," I said.

"Here's one you know, and you like her a whole lot better than the first guy." Miller clicked and up came a screenshot of Mallory alongside a listing of her information. "Mallory Nassif, a very talented young lady. Not as talented as you, but then, nobody is." He glanced to get my reaction, but when I didn't comment, he continued. "And finally, the fourth Edgewood teen." The screen image showed Nadia in her usual dark jeans, her upper half embedded in her hoodie. Only her small hands and the tip of her nose were visible in the photo. Her stats were also listed along with her power. "All three have what we call low to medium powers. Jameson is the least impressive of the bunch. I can't tell you the number of people on the planet who can do what he does. Most of them work as magicians until their powers start to fail them in their thirties. Yes, your friends' abilities are marginal. You, on the other hand, have something very unusual."

"Really."

"Yes."

"So if you already know so much about me, why bring me here? Why the big subterfuge with kidnapping my nephew and sending messages with a voice changer? What was the point of putting us through this whole ordeal?"

"To see how you'd react under pressure," he said. "To test how you conduct yourself. You're very brave and you think quickly. Those are things we didn't know until we put you through the obstacles. You've exceeded our expectations every step of the way."

"But I didn't cure Clarice's cancer."

"Clarice didn't have cancer. That was the test. The baby, on the other hand, had been screaming nonstop for three days. Damn molars." Miller shook his head and sort of tsked-tsked.

"The baby was the only one in the room in pain. You gravitated right to him and immediately fixed the problem."

"Really."

There was a long silence; Miller broke it. "You, Mr. Becker, not only have powers in the high range, but you have multiple abilities and you seem to be accruing more and more as time goes on."

"And that's because I'm a second gen?"

"Yes!" he said. "That's been our theory. Can you confirm that?"

"I have no idea what that means. I've just been hearing it all day."

"Oh." Miller's face fell in disappointment. "Well, that means that you'd be the second generation to acquire these powers. We have a theory, not yet proven, that DNA can store, if not the actual abilities, the memory of the abilities. And the resulting offspring, if exposed to the particles, builds from there. It would certainly account for you."

"Are you saying that one of my parents had powers? Because I hate to contradict you, but I'm pretty sure you're wrong." I thought of my dad snoozing in his recliner and my mom, bone-weary after a day at work. If they'd ever gone through a period where their life had been exceptional, you couldn't tell it by me.

"It's a theory," Miller said firmly. "And if anyone has the answer it would be Carly."

"Carly? My sister, Carly?"

He nodded. "Our information doesn't go back far enough, but we know she knows. You'd need to ask her."

"Why don't you ask her yourself?"

"Believe me, we've tried. She won't talk to us."

A sick feeling came over me, and all at once things made sense. Carly had been dealing with this for the past sixteen

years and my parents and I never knew. All the times she'd been incommunicado or flaked out on us and missed family gatherings, she'd probably had a good reason. Maybe she'd been protecting us by not saying anything. It was like the planet shifted and revealed itself to me. I'd been thinking trash about my sister, when really she was a hero.

"You might be thinking, Russ, that our tactics are extreme," Miller said. "And I would agree that on the surface, it looks that way. But if you knew more about our organization, I think you'd understand." He turned back to the computer and started an actual PowerPoint slideshow. Despite myself, I listened and watched. The first screenshot was a map of the world covered in dots. "We're international and have headquarters in all the major cities. The official group name is the Associates, although you won't find us listed that way anywhere. Instead, our members are present in government and business, anywhere structure and stability are needed."

He clicked to the next image—an old painting of a serious man, the kind you see in museums. "We've been around for centuries. Our founder, Matthew Bradford, was one of the first to be exposed to the light particles, as you call them. He recruited others with powers with the idea that collectively they could make a difference. And they did."

"Eventually," Miller said, clicking to an image of the light particles on a field, not my field though, "the group figured out that these fragments fell periodically in various spots around the country. They also realized that the people coming into contact with them were teenagers, all of whom had insomnia and felt compelled to walk outdoors prior to and on the night of the event." He turned to me. "What was it like, Russ? Was it as incredible as they say?" His voice had a wistful tone.

"Incredible, yes," I said. "There's really no way to describe it. And nothing in the world comes close, at least not that I know of."

He sighed. "That's what I hear." We both stared at the photo of the light particles configured in a perfect spiral on the field. The photo had captured the shape and glow, but it lacked the glittering magic of the real thing. A picture couldn't possibly convey the feeling the lights gave off—like the first day of summer vacation times a thousand. Miller moved forward in the PowerPoint, and we found ourselves looking at a timeline. "Although some of the initial groups were found out and condemned, the Salem witch trials being an example, those in our organization became good at covering their tracks. Using our talents, we've made improvements in the quality of life for Americans and others around the planet."

"What kinds of improvements?"

"Thousands of improvements, mostly of the preventative kind. How do you think the United States became a supreme power with so much material wealth? Just between us, there have been Hitler types who have tried to seize power and who *would* have taken over, if not for us. While the citizens of our country sleep, we're quietly working behind the scenes to do everything we can to keep the economy from collapsing and to keep order in our cities."

It was a hyped-up sales pitch, but I didn't challenge him. Instead I asked, "So not everyone in the Associates has powers?"

"That's right. In fact, most of us don't," he said. "Some of us are scientists or politicians or handle the day-to-day operations. The ones with the powers, they're sort of the James Bonds of our group. Well regarded and vital to our cause."

"You send people on missions."

"That and more. The Associates with powers are well provided for. When you join our organization, you'll never have to worry about anything again. We can arrange anything for a young guy such as yourself. We make things happen."

"What kind of things?"

"Anything you want. You want to graduate from high school early? We can arrange that. You want to own a certain car, maybe something sporty that will get the right kind of attention from girls? Amazingly, you'll win one in a contest you don't even remember entering. You want to go to Harvard? We can arrange a full scholarship and make sure you're on the honor roll every semester until graduation. And the best part, my friend? You don't have to do any of the course work if you don't want to. In the meantime, of course, you'll be working for us, here and there as time allows, and when you graduate, we'll offer you a lucrative position working for any company in any city you're interested in."

"But I won't really be working for them because it will be a cover. I'll actually be working for you."

"Bingo," he said, pleased I was getting it. "You'll be paid well, of course. Very well. And the benefits are endless. Best of all, my friend, you'll know you're making the world a better place. We would love to have someone with your talents on board. So," he said, standing up, so that now he towered over me, "what would you say to that?"

"I'd say I'm not your friend." I hadn't planned on blurting it out in such a mean voice, it just came out that way.

A thin smile spread across his face, like he'd been expecting this reaction. "Fair enough." He shrugged. "We'll check back with you later this summer. I have a feeling you'll be changing your mind."

CHAPTER FORTY-FOUR

———————— o ————————

By the time they returned us to the parking lot across the
street from the real Milwaukee Intermodal Station, Carly,
Frank, and I were exhausted. Frank, in fact, fell asleep in the
van during the drive back. We were in a different van this time
around, but again, we were in a windowless back area. Our driver
seemed to loop around endlessly, but there was no way to know
if he did that on purpose or if we were on a direct route that just
happened to be circuitous. You could have paid me a million dollars and I couldn't have retraced our drive back to the building
where I'd gone through the obstacle course.

Carly and I didn't talk in the van. Both of us were emotion-
ally spent, and we also knew the Associates were watching and
listening. I'd gotten past it being creepy. It just was the way things
were.

When we arrived at the lot in Milwaukee, the back doors
of the van popped open. We climbed out disoriented, me half-
carrying Frank, who moved sluggishly as if drugged. Carly got
her spark back and angrily slammed the van doors to make a
statement, but I don't think it made an impression. The driver of

the van didn't get out or speak to us, just waited until we were in Carly's car and then sped off, tires squealing.

After I got Frank situated in the back seat, Carly arranged his feet and buckled him in like he was a small child. With his eyes closed and his hair in his face, he looked young and innocent. I was glad he wouldn't remember getting forcibly kidnapped from his home, but there was no erasing the fact that he'd been a victim.

Once we'd returned to their apartment and Frank had been settled into bed, Carly opened a bottle of red wine and poured herself a glass. "I'd offer you one, but I feel badly enough that I've exposed you to all of this. I'm not going to be the one to start you drinking too," she said, sinking into a chair and setting the bottle on the end table. She had both hands around the glass like it was a lifeline. "Help yourself to a Coke. They're in the fridge."

"No thanks." I was on the couch, appropriate since it was going to be my bed soon if we were going to perpetuate the lie I had told my parents—that I was sleeping overnight because I was staying to help Frank with a science project. Carly had discovered that Mom had left voice mail saying it was fine that I'd be at her place for the night. In fact, my parents were taking advantage of my absence by driving up to Door County for an impromptu overnight at their favorite bed-and-breakfast. So much for them being worried about me. I said, "I don't know why you'd say you exposed me to this. I was the one who went out walking and saw the lights. You had nothing to do with it."

"I should have paid attention," she said. "If I had known Mom and Dad were taking you to Dr. Anton for sleep problems, I could have prevented everything."

"But you didn't know. No point in beating yourself up over it."

"Easy to say. I still feel guilty." She took a big sip, polishing off the glass, and then poured herself some more.

"So you've known about the Associates for sixteen years and managed to keep it a secret?"

"Yeah. I'd like to forget and just live my life like a normal person, but I can't. They're always keeping an eye on me. I don't know enough that they want me dead, but I still make them nervous. They don't like loose ends." She looked into the red liquid and swirled the glass. "And now I have to get another cell phone. That sucks."

A realization dawned on me. "Is that why you keep getting new phones and different numbers?" My parents could never get over how often Carly changed numbers. She always had an excuse—a problem with the phone carrier, a stalker boyfriend, a better phone plan. None of her reasons were convincing.

"Duh. Why else would I switch phone numbers all the time?"

"I don't know."

She sighed. "I used to move all the time too, until I got tired of it. Now I just do periodic sweeps of the apartment looking for bugs. I'm sure I miss some, but it sure feels like a victory when I find one. Then I squash it like a real bug and flush it down the toilet."

"And all your boyfriends...?"

"The best of them have turned out to be undercover Associates," Carly said. "Believe me, that's a definite deal-breaker. I don't trust men anymore." She paused and added, "Except Dad."

The time seemed right for me to ask her something I'd wondered for hours. "Carly, what's a 'second gen'? The Associates kept calling me that."

"Oh that," she said. "They think you're the second generation to have these powers and that's why you're so good."

"But I'm not, am I? I mean, Mom and Dad never had this happen, did they?"

"I think it's safe to say Mom and Dad never had superpowers. They don't know anything about this, and I hope they never do."

"You never were tempted to go to the police?" I asked. "Ever?"

Carly scoffed. "And tell them what? That my high school boyfriend was exposed to a bunch of falling stars and could shoot lightning bolts out of his hands, but then was murdered by a powerful secret organization because he turned down the opportunity to join them? They'd think I was crazy."

"I could show them what I can do, and then they'd have to believe."

"Yeah, go ahead and do that. Then we'd all be dead."

"Seriously. We'd all be dead? Everyone?"

"Everyone involved. Anyone who witnessed anything."

Carly could be so dramatic at times. I tried again. "I can't believe they'd kill a whole police station. What if we call a press conference and there are hundreds of people there to witness it?"

"Oh, Russ." She shook her head sadly. "Have you ever read in the news where a whole community is killed in a flash flood or a tornado or a wildfire?" She met my eyes. "And then you think, 'Oh those poor people. What a terrible random thing to happen. Mother Nature can be so cruel.'"

"Those things aren't random?"

She exhaled loudly. "Those are the kind of things the Associates do on a regular basis. You have no idea how much power we're talking about."

"So now what?"

"One day at a time. That's all we can do is live life one day at a time. If there's a better way of dealing with this, I haven't figured it out."

"What if I talk to Mr. Specter—"

"No!" She sat up suddenly, the wine in her glass lurching from side to side. "Leave it be, Russ. Just let it go."

"But I can't let it go. That Miller guy said they'd be checking in with me later in the summer."

"And they will. Put them off as long as you can, would be my advice. Try to get through high school and college at least. And when you join them, see if you can work in some capacity where you don't have to kill people."

"So you're telling me to just give up?"

"Don't think of it as giving up. Think of it as surviving. If you don't let this go, you'll wind up like poor Gordon Hofstetter with an apartment filled with maps and lined notebooks full of illegible scribbles. He made himself crazy over this and wound up electrocuted."

"How do you know what he had in his apartment?"

"I stopped over when David's parents were cleaning it out," she said. "They gave me some photos of David and some other things. And when they weren't looking, I found this and I just took it." She had a gleam in her eyes as she pulled a chain out from under her T-shirt. An old key dangled off the end of it. "You know what this is for?"

"Haven't a clue."

"It opens the door to the old train station building. David had the key, and we used to meet there. It was like our own clubhouse. We used to go there to make out. Among other things." Now she had a grin on her face and the old Carly was back.

I knew it had been boarded up for decades. I could only imagine what it looked like inside. "Weren't there like mice and bugs and stuff?"

"Not that I noticed," she said cheerfully. "We had a blanket. And of course, I had other things on my mind at the time."

"How did David get the key in the first place?"

"His great-grandfather, Gordon's father, was the train station master a million years ago. The key stayed in the family."

"What are you going to do with it?"

"Nothing." She slipped it back inside her shirt. "I just like having it."

After polishing off her glass of wine, Carly got me a pillow, some blankets, and a spare toothbrush and left me to work it out. Sleeping on a couch is not the same as a mattress, but hers, at least, was fairly long, and I was dead tired. I knew I wouldn't be awake much longer.

I sank into the pillow and pulled the covers up to my chin. It was then I was aware of Nadia's presence in the room. Her voice cut through the silence in the room. Even in my head it seemed loud.

Oh, Russ, thank God you're okay.

I could feel her relief. Until a second ago, I sensed, she wasn't sure if I was alive or dead. I played it cool. *Of course I'm okay. You know me, I'm indestructible.*

I've been worried sick.

Where'd you go, Nadia? You were with me and then you were gone.

I know, I know. I'm sorry. My mom thought I was napping and she shook me until I was pulled back. I wasn't able to be alone until just now.

I got a flash of her mother, an image in my mind. I saw her angry face, her hands like claws coming after her daughter. And I felt Nadia's fear. I said, *I'm sorry she treats you like that.*

She didn't question what I said. I guess both of us were getting used to being inside each other's head. Instead she just told me: *Some days I think I won't be able to stand another minute in this house.*

Hang in there.

I'm trying.

Nadia, I'm sorry, but I'm seriously falling asleep right now. I had a really tiring day.

Go to sleep. I'll watch over you.

CHAPTER FORTY-FIVE

——— o ———

I'd thought I was through with sneaking out of the house, but just after midnight on the following night I found myself creeping down the stairs, putting on my shoes, and slipping out the back door. It felt good to be out on my own in the dark. The night air was fresh and the slight breeze felt good against my skin. All familiar, but I wasn't going to be following my usual route tonight. Instead, I headed straight to Mr. Specter's house.

He wasn't expecting me, but when I got there, the lights were on in his living room and over his front porch, which made me feel better about my late-night visit. He did say to come over *any* time of the day or night, but still. I rang the doorbell and stepped back so I could easily be seen through the peep hole. After a slight pause, I heard fumbling on the other side of the door: a deadbolt being released, the clinking of a chain fastener sliding to one side, and finally, the turn of the knob.

Even though it was twelve thirty at night, a big smile crossed his face as he stood in the open doorway. "Mr. Becker. What a nice surprise." He held the door open for me, and as I walked through he said, "So to what do I owe the pleasure of this visit?"

"I need your help," I said.

He nodded thoughtfully. "I think it's best if we talk downstairs," Mr. Specter said, leading me through the house to the basement door. When he saw me hesitate, he said, "Don't worry, I'm not going to ambush you. I'm home alone, and I'm quite sure you could overpower an old man like me if you wanted to."

He was right about that. I followed him down, and when we got to the U-shaped couch I saw that it was true—we were alone. He turned on the overhead lights and switched on a floor lamp that stood behind the couch, giving us some more light. "I wanted to talk down here," he said, "because this room is secure. I've spent a lot of time and money making sure it's impervious to any electronic listening devices or any of that other spy nonsense the Associates use."

"I could use a room like this in my house," I said.

"We could use a world like this," Mr. Specter said, taking off his glasses and polishing them on the front of his shirt.

"Were you expecting me?" I asked.

"No."

"But you're awake and dressed," I pointed out. "And you didn't seem shocked to see me here so late."

He put his glasses back on. "I'm a night owl by nature and an insomniac on occasion. You'll often find me awake at this hour, alone in my thoughts. I also like to read late at night. The world doesn't intrude like it does during the day."

I nodded, knowing what he meant.

"Am I right in guessing that you've had something significant happen lately?" he said, gesturing for me to take a seat.

I sat on the opposite end of the horseshoe couch—close enough to see him, but not close enough to be awkward. Before I got here, I wondered how much I was going to tell him, but as

it turned out, there was no way to tell the story unless I revealed everything. "The Associates abducted my nephew Frank," I began, and then it all came spilling out. I told him about Carly's cell phone message and how we rushed to the Greyhound counter. How the bus was stopped by an overturned semi, and Carly and I received instructions to get out, and how we wound up getting picked up by a cargo van and taken to a mystery location. "And once I got there, Carly had to stay in a waiting room with a secretary, and they sent me through these obstacles. They said I had to do it if we wanted Frank back."

Mr. Specter leaned forward, his elbows on his knees. "What kind of obstacles?"

I told him about Tim wanting to shake my hand, and how I refused, and then I detailed all the tests: the dogs, the two thugs who tried to beat me up, the doctor's office, and the mock Milwaukee Intermodal Station. The only thing I neglected to tell him was how Nadia was along for part of it. "The Associates timed me during this whole thing, if you can believe it."

"Oh, I believe it," he said gravely. "How'd you do?"

"Forty-eight minutes and fifty-three seconds."

"Impressive."

"They thought so. They practically had a parade."

"Hmmm." He looked off to one side. "Now that they know all you can do, they'll certainly want you to join them."

"They already asked and they made me an offer."

"Which was?"

"Anything I wanted, basically."

"Most people would find that hard to turn down. What did you tell them?" He peered at me over his glasses.

"I said no thanks."

His face lit with admiration. "Good for you, Russ!"

I realized then that he'd used my first name for the first time ever. For some reason, I felt like I'd made a breakthrough. "They weren't happy about it."

"Well no, they wouldn't be."

The room became noticeably silent now that my story was over. Both of us knew that this wasn't the end of it. The Associates weren't going to take no for an answer. They'd just given me some time to come around to their way of thinking.

Mr. Specter said, "How is your nephew?"

"Just about back to normal except for a bad headache the next morning," I said. "He woke me up by jumping on top of me."

"It sounds he won't have any long-term damage."

"He really thinks we spent hours testing video games. He remembers specific things I said to him, and he can describe the games. They really got into his head."

"That's a shame." Mr. Specter spoke in a sympathetic tone. And then, he abruptly switched the subject: "You said you needed my help?"

"Oh yes!" I practically smacked my forehead with the realization of the real reason I'd come here tonight. "It's about Gordy—I mean Mr. Hofstetter."

"What about him?"

I stood up and reached into my pocket, pulled out the folded piece of paper, and spread it out on the coffee table in front of me. "Before he died, he gave me this." I smoothed out the edges so it would lie flat. "He said his grandson was imprisoned and I needed to find him."

Mr. Specter got up and sat next to me to get a closer look. "Have you shown this to anyone else?"

"No, I haven't shown it to anyone else." True that. I hadn't shown it to anyone, but I'd told Nadia about it during our nighttime visits.

He stared intently at the page. "Would you mind if I made a copy of it?"

"No."

Holding the paper between two fingers, he got up from the couch and disappeared through a door into the other part of the basement. A minute later, I heard the whirring of a copy machine. When he emerged from the room he had a stack of papers in one hand and a pencil and magnifying glass in the other. Taking his place, he said, "I made a few extra copies so we can write on them."

I twisted around to look at the open doorway. "That's not your laundry room?"

"No, my laundry room is upstairs. That room is my top secret home office," he said, amused. "I keep it locked up when I'm not home so it's Associate proof."

"Good thinking," I said.

He shrugged. "Better safe than sorry. I had a cleaning lady once who seemed a little fishy. You never know." He set the papers down, the copies next to the original, then picked up a pencil and began going over the faint lines with sure, even strokes. Interlocking geometric shapes took form. Once done, he concentrated on the number combinations I'd been unable to decipher. After he'd darkened them, they had a familiar look. "These numbers, you know what they are?"

"Some kind of code was my guess." I was a little embarrassed. Here I was supposed to be exceptionally smart and yet I wasn't coming up with much of anything at all.

"In a way," he said. "I believe each set indicates a specific geographic coordinate."

"Latitude and longitude," I said, finally realizing the truth.

"Very good." He tapped the geometric shapes with the end of the pencil. "And my guess is that this is a map and that once we go to the specific coordinates, we'll know more. Tell me, Mr. Becker, what are your plans for this summer?"

"I'm going to take my driver's test and look for a job," I said. The driving and the job went hand in hand. I'd need money for gas and all the things I could do once I'd be driving. Dating for one.

"Do you think your parents would allow you to take an all-expense-paid class trip to Peru?"

"Peru? Oh, I don't know…"

"I think it would be best," he mused, "to take some other students along as well, so it doesn't look too suspicious. Miss Nassif, for sure. What about those other two? Do you think they'd be on board?"

"Wait a minute!" I said. "I'm not getting this. Why do you want to go to Peru?"

"To save Mr. Hofstetter's grandson, of course."

"But he died in a car accident."

"Or so we've been led to believe," Mr. Specter said.

CHAPTER FORTY-SIX

⸻ o ⸻

On the walk home I mulled over everything Mr. Specter had said. His group, the Praetorian Guard, had long believed, for reasons he didn't want to get into, that the Associates maintained a significant headquarters in Peru. They'd never been able to prove it, or even find the precise location for that matter, but he thought the map and the various latitude and longitude coordinates would point us in the right direction.

"Okay," I said, "I get that. But why do you need to bring some high school kids along? Wouldn't it be easier just to have some people from the Praetorian Guard go investigate for themselves? It seems like we'd make the trip more complicated."

"You're thinking of yourself as a high school student," Mr. Specter said, "when you should be thinking of yourself as someone with superpowers. I could bring a hundred people along and we couldn't match what the four of you can do. Not only that, but because you're young, people tend to discount you. Traveling as a school group, we can fly under the radar, so to speak."

What he said made sense. I told him I'd think about it, reclaimed Mr. Hofstetter's original paper, and said I had to

get going or my parents might notice I was gone, which wasn't entirely true. Things were getting so messed up I really just wanted to go home and wrap my brain around everything that had happened. And I wanted to do that in the privacy of my own room. I realized on the walk home that not only hadn't I told him about Nadia's astral projection, but I'd also neglected to tell him about the medallion Gordy had given to me. I still had it in my wallet and took it out from time to time. I liked the weight of it in my hand and the way the light came through the clear disc in the center. I felt like Indiana Jones examining an ancient artifact. Something about the medallion made me want to keep it to myself.

By the time I arrived in my neighborhood, the air had changed from dry to moist and the slight breeze had kicked into high gear. I'd heard the forecast for thunderstorms, but thought it would be happening later. It would be good to be inside when the rain came.

With relief, I reached my yard. The crabapple tree along the rear lot line had long since shed its blossoms. They'd fallen like snow around the base of the tree and then disappeared, but I thought I got a whiff of their floral scent as I worked my way to the back door. I was almost to the porch when I noticed a shadowy figure lurking along the dark edges of the lot. My breath caught in my chest, and I was just about to shoot electricity in that direction, when I heard, "Russ?"

It was Nadia. She stepped out from the shadows, and I could see quite clearly she was alone. As usual, she wore blue jeans and a dark hoodie that obscured most of her face.

"Nadia!" I rushed to give her a hug. A few days ago that would have been weird, but it wasn't now, not after what we'd been through. "What are you doing here?"

She pointed up to the second floor of the house. "You weren't in your room when I tried to see you, and I thought something terrible must have happened."

I heard terror in her voice. I imagined her projecting into my room and seeing the empty room, and her thinking I'd been taken by the Associates, maybe for good this time. "Oh no, I'm fine. Everything's fine." I stepped back and put my hands on either side of her head, and she buried her face in my chest. Her little body silently heaved, and I realized she was crying. "Honestly, I'm okay. I just went to have a talk with Mr. Specter. I told you about him, right? Really, I'm fine."

"I know." Her voice was muffled. "I'm just so relieved."

Waves of anguish and relief and love rolled off of her, an odd, poignant mixture of emotion. I didn't have much experience consoling girls, but I took a stab at it, making the soothing noise people made in movies. "Everything's going to be all right."

She pulled away and wiped at her eyes with her fingertips, a little embarrassed. "I know I'm overreacting."

"Don't worry about it. It's nice to know someone would care if I disappeared."

The wind whipped up, making the branches in the trees sway and sigh. In the sky behind Nadia's head a bolt of lightning cut the sky in half; for a second the entire yard was lit as brightly as if it were the middle of the day. "Whoa," she said, turning to see. "Impressive."

When she looked back at me, her hood had slipped slightly. On a whim I reached over and lowered it to her shoulders. I'd only seen her spiky bangs, so I didn't realize her dark brown hair was shoulder length. Without the hood, it was easier to see all of her face, including the part that had been damaged, but her scars didn't bother me. I only saw Nadia, my friend. I searched her

face and saw her eyes still fresh with tears, her lips quivering. She made a move to put the hood back up. "Don't," I said, stopping her hand. "I like seeing you."

"I hate it," she said. "I hate looking so ugly."

"But you're *not* ugly." I put my hands on either side of her face and looked deep into her eyes. I felt the connection between us, the warmth of her skin and the pulsing of energy, drawing us closer. "I think you're beautiful."

Nadia shook her head. "Not beautiful." She trembled and looked up at me with complete trust, her fate in my hands.

I said, "You are. You just don't know it yet." I leaned over so that our noses touched and said, "What are you doing this summer?"

END OF BOOK ONE

LOOK FOR
Book 2 of the
EDGEWOOD Series

WANDERLUST

———— o ————

Russ ran a finger from my forehead down my nose and tapped my chin. "How would you like to go to Peru?"

"I'd love that," I said. "Sure, sign me up. But could we stop in Paris on the way?"

"No, I'm completely serious." He grinned. "Remember me telling you about the paper Gordon Hofstetter gave me the night he died? How he said his grandson was being held prisoner and I needed to go find him? Well, Mr. Specter thinks the markings are a map and the numbers are latitude and longitude. And guess where they lead to?"

"Peru?"

"Exactly." His grin got wider. "Mr. Specter said he can arrange a trip to South America, call it an all-expenses-paid class trip and the four of us can go and check it out."

"Except I'm not in your class. I don't even go to your school," I pointed out. "And I'm not allowed to leave my house without a chaperone."

"Eh, details." Russ waved a hand to indicate it was nothing. He'd never dealt with my mother, that much was clear. "This is

still in the planning stage, but we'll get it all sorted out. When I know more, I'll fill you in."

It didn't matter what he found out, I knew I wouldn't be going on any trip, especially out of the country. And even if my mother allowed it, how could I go looking the way I did? I had a face that would traumatize small children on two different continents. Wouldn't that be great?

As we stood together, I picked up on what was going through Russ's mind. As much as he valued our friendship, it was the idea of traveling with Mallory that thrilled him. Knowing this crushed me, even though she was the obvious choice, of course, with her pretty face and flirty ways. A deformed girl could never compete. The fourth one in our little group, Jameson, barely registered on his meter. The two of them had some kind of pissing match going on, but now that Russ could shoot bolts of electricity out of his palms, heal people, and exert mind control, the fact that Jameson could move objects with his mind didn't seem all that impressive and Russ felt like he came out on top.

Personally, I wouldn't be that quick to discount Jameson. Yes, he looked like a nerdy kid with glasses. And he definitely lacked people skills. It would be easy to dismiss him, to think he wasn't a threat, but I'd used my powers to do a read on his character more than once and there was something intense underneath the surface, something dark and brooding I couldn't quite get a handle on. It would be a mistake to underestimate him.

"So you and Mallory and Jameson would go to Peru this summer with your science teacher?" I tried to make it sound like regular conversation, but it was hard to keep the disappointment out of my voice.

"It's not for sure yet," Russ said. I could tell he was dialing it down for my benefit. "And if your mom won't let you go, you can always astral project to me at night. It will be like you're there."

Suddenly our nighttime visits seemed like a consolation prize. If they all went to Peru without me, Mallory would be with Russ on the plane and at the hotel and everywhere else. Anything could happen. The experience would bring them closer, because really, how could it not? Meanwhile, I'd be stuck in my house writing papers and doing homework online, relegated to getting quick updates in the evenings. As cool as it was to have the freedom to travel anywhere in a moment's time, astral projecting had its limits, namely that it lacked the sensory experiences of touch, smell, and taste. I'd be a ghost, while Mallory, with her infectious laugh and flawless skin, would be right there.

But still, Russ had said I was beautiful and I could tell he meant it. And I don't think he'd ever said that to Mallory.

I think you're beautiful. And when I protested, he'd said, *You are. You just don't know it.* I could still feel the touch of his nose against mine. Not as intimate as, say, kissing, but still very personal. I mean, how many people would you do that to in a lifetime? I knew that in the upcoming weeks and months I'd replay his words and that moment in my mind over and over again, an infinite loop. Those words and that brief touch seemed like more than I deserved, even as I wanted more.

Down the block, we heard a screen door open and the scrabbling sounds of a dog being let out into a neighboring yard. It was still dark, but the interruption reminded us we weren't where we were supposed to be. Russ glanced in that direction and said, "I better get inside before my parents wake up. Will you be okay going home? Or do you want me to walk you?"

Every bit of me wanted him to walk me home, but I sensed he only asked to be polite. I said, "No, I'm good."

"You sure?" Russ sounded relieved.

I nodded. "It's not too far. I'll be there in no time."

"Astral project to me when you get home," he said. "So I don't worry."

"I will."

When I got home, I crept up the stairs. I was relieved to hear my parents snoring behind their closed door. Further down the hall, the blinds in the guest bedroom were open, allowing me to see the sleeping form of my mother's cat, Barry, from the open doorway. Barry was a gray tabby. He was also a mean, fat cat, the kind that hissed when you tried to pick him up. My mother was the only person he cared about in the world. He adored her and she fussed over him like he was an only child.

Curled up at the foot of the bed, Barry lifted his head as I snuck past the open doorway, but he didn't move or make a noise. I'd shown myself to him while I was astral projecting once and it had seriously freaked him out. Ever since then he'd regarded me warily.

After I climbed into bed, I settled back and closed my eyes and willed myself to go to Russ. No matter how many times I did it, it still seemed like magic, the way my essence knew to rise out of my body and travel to his side. I was aware of the distance—the houses, the trees, the roads—but time didn't work the way it normally did. One moment I was home, and the next I was there. The in-between part was of no consequence. I fast-forwarded over all of it.

When I arrived in Russ's bedroom, he wasn't up worrying about me after all. Actually, he was already asleep. That was fine though. I liked watching him sleep. Even with the light off

I could see him perfectly, right down to the way his lips moved slightly when he exhaled. The covers were pulled up to his chin, and he looked content. If I were actually in his room I'd have been tempted to sit on the edge of the bed and stroke his hair, so it was good that I wasn't actually there. That might have seriously creeped him out if he woke up in the meantime. *Russ?* I tried to reach him. *Russ, can you hear me?* He shifted slightly, making me think that, on some level, he heard. *I got home safely. I'll talk to you tomorrow, okay?* He muttered something in his sleep. I thought I heard my name, but maybe not. Hard to tell. It would have to do, though. It was getting late and I needed to get back. *Good night,* I said, and in a moment I was back underneath the covers of my own bed.

In the morning, I was back to my usual routine. Without a traditional school schedule all my days ran together, but on the weekends, my mother permitted me to sleep in for an extra hour and a half; since today was Saturday, I'd set my alarm allowing for the difference. When it went off, I struggled out of sleep and went right for the shower. For a teenage girl, my morning routine was relatively quick; no makeup to apply, and since no one besides my parents ever saw my hair, I didn't do too much to it. I tried to dry off and comb my hair without looking in the mirror because seeing my scars still upset me, even now. My one eyelid wasn't quite right, and the whole left side of my face was ugly. Sometimes I turned out the bathroom light and covered the worst of it with my hands and peered cautiously at my reflection, trying to imagine how I'd have looked if I hadn't been burned that day on the bus. I know this sounds conceited, but I think I might have turned out to be pretty.

After getting dressed, I joined my father at the breakfast table. He took thin sips of coffee while he read the news on his

tablet. Behind him, my mother stood at the stove cooking eggs and bacon. "Morning, Nadia," my father said, giving me a small smile. In our house, we were silent partners.

"You slept well?" Mom asked.

For a moment, I thought maybe she'd noticed I'd snuck out of the house. It was hard to tell because almost everything she said sounded accusatory to me. "Yes, I did. Thank you." I went to the stove, and she lifted an egg and two pieces of bacon out of the pan and plopped them onto a plate, then handed it to me.

"Very good," she said, nodding approvingly as if I'd done well on a test.

Within a few minutes all three of us were at the table, eating our usual Saturday morning meal, me with my orange juice and them with their strong coffee. I added Tabasco sauce to my eggs, a habit I'd acquired after getting burned. The cat slinked in and lapped at his water dish, then jumped into Mom's lap for a neck massage.

Everything was as usual, until my mother said, "What happened to your face?"

I looked up from my plate to see she was talking to me. Call me confused. Did she somehow forget the events of the past four years? I looked to my dad, who appeared to be just as puzzled. "I got burned from battery acid?"

"I know that," she said sharply. "But something is different." She lifted her hand from the cat and pointed. "Your scars have changed."

My hand flew to my cheek. It felt the same. "Changed how?"

"They look better." She squinted and turned her head to one side.

My father smiled. "Have you been using that ointment I gave you?"

Such a sweet man. He'd given me a tube of some cream that was so thick and stinky that I'd only applied it once. I knew it wouldn't help, so I didn't bother with it after that, but I didn't say anything because I didn't want to hurt his feelings. "Here and there," I said.

"Well, keep using it," he said. "It's definitely helping."

"See, I told you plastic surgery wasn't necessary," Mom said.

After I finished eating and loaded the dishwasher, I went to the bathroom and cautiously looked in the mirror. My forehead still had the dark splotches and the one protruding ridge above my eye, and the lid was still messed up, but my cheek *was* different. In places the skin had smoothed and the skin tone had evened out. Like it was healing. But that wasn't possible. I put a hand up to feel and realized that the improved part matched up with my fingers. And then I knew. Not my fingers. Russ's fingers. He'd placed his hands on either side of my face and said I was beautiful. And something from inside of him had transferred to me and made my scars soften and fade.

A REQUEST FROM
THE AUTHOR

○

If you enjoyed reading this book, please tell your friends, give a shout-out on Facebook, and post a review on Amazon or Goodreads. Nothing makes an author happier than seeing readers spread the word. If you could help out, that would be awesome.

And if you didn't like *Edgewood*, just put the story out of your mind. We shall speak of it no more.

Made in the USA
Middletown, DE
16 August 2016